D1293766

The Impact
of Attachment

The Norton Series on Interpersonal Neurobiology

Allan N. Schore, PhD, Series Editor
Daniel J. Siegel, MD, Founding Editor

The field of mental health is in a tremendously exciting period of growth and conceptual reorganization. Independent findings from a variety of scientific endeavors are converging in an interdisciplinary view of the mind and mental well-being. An interpersonal neurobiology of human development enables us to understand that the structure and function of the mind and brain are shaped by experiences, especially those involving emotional relationships.

The Norton Series on Interpersonal Neurobiology will provide cutting-edge, multidisciplinary views that further our understanding of the complex neurobiology of the human mind. By drawing on a wide range of traditionally independent fields of research—such as neurobiology, genetics, memory, attachment, complex systems, anthropology, and evolutionary psychology—these texts will offer mental health professionals a review and synthesis of scientific findings often inaccessible to clinicians. These books aim to advance our understanding of human experience by finding the unity of knowledge, or consilience, that emerges with the translation of findings from numerous domains of study into a common language and conceptual framework. The series will integrate the best of modern science with the healing art of psychotherapy.

A NORTON PROFESSIONAL BOOK

The IMPACT
of ATTACHMENT

Developmental Neuroaffective
Psychology

SUSAN HART

W. W. Norton & Company
New York • London

UNION COUNTY COLLEGE

3 9354 00198795 3

Copyright © Forfatteren og Hans Reitzels Forlag 2006
English translation copyright © 2011 by W. W. Norton & Company, Inc.

Originally published in Danish as Betydningen af samhørighed:
Om neuroaffektiv udviklingspsykologi

All rights reserved
Printed in the United States of America

For information about permission to reproduce selections from this book,
write to Permissions, W. W. Norton & Company, Inc., 500 Fifth Avenue,
New York, NY 10110

For information about special discounts for bulk purchases,
please contact W. W. Norton
Special Sales at specialsales@wwnorton.com or 800-233-4830

Manufacturing by R. R. Donnelley, Harrisonburg
Production manager: Leeann Graham

Library of Congress Cataloging-in-Publication Data

Hart, Susan, psychologist.
  [Betydningen af samh?righed. English]
    The impact of attachment : developmental neuroaffective psychology / Susan
Hart.
      p.   cm. — (The Norton series on interpersonal neurobiology)
  "A Norton Professional Book."
  "Originally published in Danish as Betydningen af samh?righed: Om
neuroaffektiv udviklingspsykologi."
  Includes bibliographical references and index.
  ISBN 978-0-393-70662-8 (hbk.)
  1. Attachment behavior in infants. 2. Attachment behavior. 3. Parent and
infant. 4. Affective neuroscience. 5. Neuropsychology. I. Title.
  BF720.A83H37 2011
  155.4'18—dc22   2010013144

ISBN: 978-0-393-70662-8

W. W. Norton & Company, Inc., 500 Fifth Avenue, New York, N.Y. 10110
www.wwnorton.com
W. W. Norton & Company Ltd., Castle House, 75/76 Wells Street,
London W1T 3QT

1 2 3 4 5 6 7 8 9 0

For my children
Mick and Liv

CHILDHOOD STREET

I am the street of your childhood,
I am the root of your being,
I am the pounding rhythm
in all that you're yearning for.

I am your mother's grey hands
and your father's worried mind,
and I am the light, wispy web
of your earliest dreams.

I gave you my somber gravity
one day marked by wild despair,
and I sprinkled sadness in your heart
one night of pouring rain.

One time I struck you down
to properly harden your heart,
but I also tenderly raised you up
and wiped away your tears.

It was I who taught you to hate,
and I taught you meanness and scorn,
I gave you the strongest of weapons,
be sure to use them well.

I gave you those watchful eyes
that will always mark who you are,
and if you meet someone with the same gaze,
you should know that he is your friend.

And should you hear purer notes
that strike a fairer song,
you shall long in your heart
for the broken and halting sound of my voice.

Though you wandered so far and wide,
though you may have lost sight of your friend
—I am the street of your childhood,
I shall always know you again.

(Tove Ditlevsen, from "Lille verden," 1942;
translated for this edition)
Reprinted with permission.

CONTENTS

ACKNOWLEDGMENTS

I want to thank Chief Psychologist Rikke Schwartz, whom I first met through my job at the children's psychiatric ward at Gentofte County Hospital in Copenhagen, and body therapist Marianne Bentzen, who originally introduced me to the recent advances in brain research. They have both remained loyal and inspiring discussion partners throughout the writing process. My secretary, Hanne Mølgaard was a great help throughout, including the final stage of typing the manuscript. The two editors for the Danish publisher Hans Reitzels Forlag, Anne Matthiesen and Henriette Thiesen, provided invaluable assistance in connection with the final revisions to enhance the readability and accessibility of the book. I thank them both for very pleasant and inspiring hours of collaboration. Last, but not least, I thank my son for his help in translating challenging texts from English and my daughter and her father for all their patience and the long excursions they took without Mommy, all to facilitate the writing process. More than once, when my daughter felt that the working process seemed overwhelming and never-ending, she suggested that I simply scrap the entire manuscript. I chose not to take her advice, and I hope that the book may contribute to the ongoing development of the neuroaffective field for the years to come.

FOREWORD

The unchallenged maintenance of a bond is experienced as a source of security and the renewal of a bond as a source of joy. Because such emotions are usually a reflection of the state of a person's affectional bonds, the psychology and psychopathology of emotion is found to be, in large part, the psychology and psychopathology of affectional bonds. . . . In the fields of etiology and psychopathology it can be used to frame specific hypotheses which relate different family experiences to different forms of psychiatric disorder and also, possibly, to the neurophysiological changes that accompany them.

John Bowlby (1978, pp. 7, 29)

In my work as a clinical psychologist it has become increasingly clear to me that even though personality patterns may be based in genetic or innate conditions, they are shaped, to an equal degree, by our personal life and experiences, with childhood and early experiences as particularly crucial sources of influence. Thanks to the tremendous plasticity of the human brain, we are prepared to interact with the environment we are born into, and our mental functions are shaped by our interactions and transactions with our social environment.

A dichotomy of brain/mind, biology/experience, nature/nurture is not very productive, chiefly because it hampers the development of a theory that is capable of fully embracing the complexity that characterizes human psychological development. The duality between, for example, neuropsychology and developmental psychology has caused an unfortunate divide and has reduced our ability to integrate information about human psychological development and disorders. Donald Hebb said in 1949 that psychologists and neuropsychologists "chart the same bay—working perhaps from opposite shores, sometimes overlapping and duplicating one another, but . . . continually with the opportunity of contributing to each other's results" (p. xiv). Understanding human behavior requires an understanding of the nervous system in its entirety (Dawson & Fischer, 1994). Currently, there is no integrated theory about the human mind, and it will probably take a great deal of additional interdisciplinary bridge building to arrive at a theory that enables us to understand both subjective and objective reality. Although it is risky to draw parallels between concepts that have evolved independently of one another within different disciplines, it is my hope that a scientifically based overview might help overcome these disciplinary divisions in favor of new ways of viewing children's and adults' psychological potential and challenges. This might help develop a common basis for helping the children, adults, and families who require support and therapy. It is my assumption that both biology and interpersonal relations are involved in shaping the human nervous system and thus personality, and that we need to develop a theory about the workings of this interactive development process. The purpose of this book is to explore this issue by bringing theories from developmental psychology into dialogue with recent developments in neuroscience. This integration marks an attempt to combine theories that have proved capable of forming the basis for hypotheses concerning personality development and psychopathology.

Psychology as an independent discipline has a brief history, and Sigmund Freud was a pioneer in terms of grasping the complexity of the human mind. Freud was a neuroscientist, and he was aware that the theories that he formed on the basis of his clinical experience had to match neuroscientific data. He was convinced that the future would offer possibilities for this integration effort (Solms, 2005, p. 21). Freud's theory on drives was a revolution in the history of psychology, and over time his theories have undergone considerable elaboration and branched out in many different directions. His theory on drives formed the basis for many subsequent psychodynamic schools, including developmental psychology, a relatively young science that grew out of and away from the British school of psychoanalysis headed by John Bowlby, among others. Bowlby viewed man as a relational being rather than an isolated energy system. He developed his theories on the basis of mammalian attachment behavior and pointed out, among other things, that maternal care and security are the foundation for healthy psychological development. Because man shares many anatomical and physiological features with other species, he believed it was fair to assume a considerable number of similarities between animals and humans (Smith, 2003). Neither Freud nor Bowlby had the opportunity to integrate their theories with sophisticated data about the brain. Bowlby was aware that a deeper understanding of the complexity of normal development versus psychopathology could only be achieved through an integration of developmental psychology, psychoanalysis, biology, and neuroscience (Schore, 2000).

Today, neuroscience has a great deal to offer developmental psychology through a better understanding of affects, emotions, and personality. New technological developments have led to imaging techniques such as MEG, PET, MRI, and fMRI that allow us to measure activity in the living, active brain, thus enabling us to shed light on the subcortical neural circuits that control our basic psychological processes. To develop a basic model for developmental psychology, we need to identify the part of the nervous system that forms the basis for attachment and personality development. Psychiatrist Eric Kandel, Nobel laureate in physiology or medicine, notes five fundamental principles in his understanding of the integration of psychiatry and biology: All mental processes are neural; genes and their protein products determine neural connections; experience alters gene expression; learning changes neural connections; and psychotherapy changes gene expression (Kandel, 2005).

The brain is sculpted, neuron by neuron, in a close interaction between genetic conditions and environmental stimulation. The nervous system matures on the basis of "user-dependent" development; it is shaped by experience and is capable of reorganization. Studies of the nervous system in infancy suggest that development is experience dependent and contains critical periods, and especially in the early caregiver-child interaction the caregiver senses and modulates the infant's physiological and psychobiological states. It appears that the caregiver's regulating functions not only modulate the infant's internal states but also shape the infant's capacity for self-organization. The development and maturation of the nervous system relies on extensive neural development processes that occur at very specific times in the child's development. Developmental progress follows a highly complex choreography that integrates and coordinates the neuroanatomic and neurobiological development with the infant's experiences through close interpersonal relationships. This dialectic between nature and nurture is the source of personality formation, and it is through this process that the child's emotional genotype is transformed and shaped into a phenotype. The child's personality emerges on the basis of the child's structured experiences of his own self in interaction with others, and the child's main task in relation to personality development is to engage in ever broader and closer attachment bonds with other humans. Our behavior, inner world, and relationships are shaped through these attachment bonds.

Since Bowlby developed his theories on attachment, the link between insecure attachment patterns and psychopathology has been the object of research. Bowlby (1978) described how attachment behavior continues to be a crucial part of our personal capacity, reflecting the psychology and psychopathology of attachment bonds. He noted that what is often described as a symptom is in fact a response that has become severed from the situation where it emerged, which is why the symptom does not appear to make sense at first glance. According to Bowlby, psychological disorders are related to experiences in the family, which are undoubtedly linked to the neurophysiological changes associated with the disorder. Mental health and psychiatric disorders reflect a wide variety of interacting processes, some of which will be easier to uncover than others. A considerable body of research now indicates that early life experiences affect the organization of the nervous system to a disproportionate degree; although later experiences may alter the mature brain, the child's early experiences are involved in organizing the nervous system. Thus, if the child experiences daily and frequent stressful states that he is incapable of regulating independently, or if the child suffers neglect, the result is not only an insecure attachment pattern but also chaotic disorders of the nervous system. Psychological disorders can be associated with an inability to regulate the physiological basis for appropriate attention and social behavior (Perry, 2001; Porges, 1996; van der Kolk & McFarlane, 1996). Additionally, Fonagy (1991, 1998a) emphasized that secure attachment is a crucial condition for developing a mentalization capacity, and that poor access to one's own and others' emotions and emotional reactions leads to a very high risk of psychological disorders.

It is my hope that by integrating psychological and biological knowledge we can begin to develop a complex biopsychosocial model that offers improved therapeutic options and is thus able to change the generational transfer of psychological disorders and violent and insensitive behavior. If, for example, we become able to pinpoint the link between psychological disorders and dysfunctions of the nervous system, we will be able to offer better inventions and target psychotherapy directly at the neurological basis of the disorder. Similarly, effect studies of psychotherapy have shown repeatedly that the therapeutic alliance that is established between the therapist and the client plays a greater role in predicting a positive outcome than the choice of therapeutic method. All psychological disorders involve inadequate affect regulation, and all types of psychotherapy aim to support the client's affect regulation. It appears to be the relationship between therapist and client that creates an environment that is capable of promoting neural development, and that it is the therapist-client relationship that has the capacity to support the client's nervous system in developing more complex mental levels. It is therefore necessary to develop a theory that incorporates both the attachment aspect and the neural basis of psychological disorders in the development of psychiatric and psychological intervention methods.

As neuroscience is still an emergent discipline, offering only glimpses of the complexity we are seeking to understand, it will be a while yet before we can move from general hypotheses to an exact, validated theory on the relationship between brain functions, behavior, and personality. For now, the integrative dialogue offered here revolves around a set of working hypotheses that require ongoing adjustment and refinement.

When I first embarked on the writing process, I was unaware of the full scope of the topic or the number of issues that would arise along the way. When the first part of the process was concluded, the book had come to encompass two separate but closely related themes. Since I could not assume that readers would be familiar with the latest neuroscientific developments concerning emotional structures, I saw that I would have to introduce the topic of neuroaffective development with a focus on neuropsychology. Eventually, this developed into a separate publication, which was published in Danish in January 2006, and in English in 2008, titled *Brain, Attachment, Personality: An Introduction to Neuroaffective Development*. The present book is an extension of this introductory volume; it has a much stronger emphasis on developmental psychology but is anchored in affective neuropsychology. The two books can be read independently of one another; thus, the present book does not presuppose prior knowledge of the introductory volume.

This book offers an amalgamation of theories that are not commonly combined into a structured psychodynamic context. It operates on three different levels: a neurobiological level, an intrapsychic level, and an interpersonal level. It has been a challenge throughout to find a uniform set of concepts, both due to the amalgamation of theories and because certain concepts as yet remain somewhat vague. For example, there is no clear-cut conceptual distinction between sensations, affects, emotions, feelings, and mood. In this context, affects are viewed as the basic neurological foundation for the formation of feelings or emotions (in this volume, the two terms are used synonymously). Experiences consist of mental representations, a term that has been understood and characterized in countless different ways. Bowlby used the term internal working models, while later scientists, including Daniel Stern, use the term internal representations, a term that I have also chosen to use. Intrapsychic conflicts broadly refer to imbalances of the nervous system; they may be described as various forms of relational disorders or as psychological, emotional, or personality disorders. In Chapters 4, 5, 6, 8, and 9, I review anonymous case stories from my own clinical practice. In most cases, I simply relate the case stories without comment, leaving it up to the reader to interpret the examples in relation to the issues explored in the text.

Each chapter intends to demonstrate and explore key aspects of the importance of attachment. The book is divided into three parts, each with three chapters. Part I looks at children's normal development: the interaction between brain maturation within the close caregiver-infant relationship and the development of the various levels of mental organization in infants. Chapter 1 looks at the infant's interactions with significant primary caregivers, which take place in dyadic interactions in small microregulated behavior patterns. In Chapter 2, the focus is on the importance of this interaction for the child's neuroaffective development, including the formation of internal representations and mentalization capacity. Chapter 3 presents a model for levels of mental organization, that is, developmental stages when the nervous system undergoes qualitative changes with regard to personality development. Part II looks at attachment and relational disorders and offers a new preliminary understanding of psychopathology based on a neuroaffective and developmental perspective. Chapter 4 describes dysregulation patterns and misattuned communication; Chapter 5 discusses the impact of early dysregulation patterns within the nervous system; and Chapter 6 describes psychological disorders within the framework of a neuroaffective developmental model. Part III aims to integrate existing therapeutic approaches within a neuroaffective framework and contribute to a higher degree of precision in the methods of intervention related to symptom formation and therapy aimed at children and adolescents. Chapter 7 summarizes considerations concerning emotional attunement and its impact on the therapist-client relationship, and Chapter 8 discusses a complex approach to therapeutic intervention based on a neuroaffective model. Chapter 9 looks at aspects of family and environmental therapy, integrating these forms of intervention with a systemic theory approach.

The writing process has been a long and integrative journey. It was a major challenge to bring two separate disciplines into dialogue, and it was an integrative task to bring together my years of observations and theoretical reflections from my clinical work with countless psychological assessments of children, family interventions, individual therapy processes, and professional supervision assignments.

*The Impact
of Attachment*

PART ONE

—ᴍ—

*The Interaction
Between Brain Maturation
and the Close Bond
Between Caregiver
and Infant*

CHAPTER ONE

The Dynamic Interaction Between Caregiver and Infant

The infant's first exposure to the human world consists simply of whatever his mother actually does with her face, voice, body, hands. The ongoing flow of her acts provides for the infant his emerging experience with the stuff of human communication and relatedness. The choreography of maternal behaviors is the raw material from the outside world with which the infant begins to construct his knowledge and experience of all things human.

Daniel Stern (1977, p. 23)

John Bowlby emphasized that childhood development takes place in a dynamic interaction between genetic predispositions and the environment, which shape each other in a reciprocal process reaching all the way back to conception. Many subsequent studies have shown that the environment determines the extent to which a person's genetic potential is realized (Cicchetti & Tucker, 1994), and Fonagy and Target (1997), among others, have pointed out that the most important evolutionary function of the human attachment system is to generate a self-regulating control system within the child. In the attachment relationship, the child learns to regulate emotions through interactive affect regulation, which helps differentiate the neural patterns. The goal is to increase the capacity for self-regulation, which enables the child to simultaneously be himself or herself and to be in touch with the other in a relationship. Genes continually express themselves and thus create capacities that enable us to change, but without an appropriate environment to shape, support, and promote these changes, they will either fail to take place or will take a maladaptive course (Stern, 1998b).

In this opening chapter, I describe what stimuli are required for the human nervous system to engage in personality development. First, I look at some of the essential conditions for the caregivers' parenting behavior; then I attempt to disambiguate some key concepts, as there is currently some degree of confusion in the psychological profession about certain terms, including attachment, attachment behavior, interaction, intersubjectivity, and relationship. Next, I discuss the infant's innate predispositions in relation to communication and temperament before I move on to the main theme of the chapter: interaction or intersubjectivity in the early caregiver-infant relationship. In relation to the infant's possibilities for self-development, three crucial features stand out, which may be illustrated as follows.

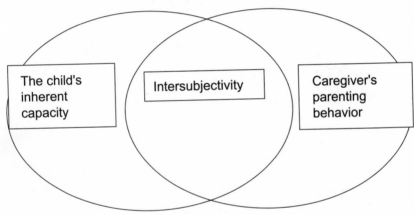

Figure 1.1. Basis for personality formation

Conditions for the Caregiver's Parenting Behavior

Harry Harlow is known for his studies of the effects on maternal deprivation on baby rhesus monkeys. He demonstrated how the mother treats the infant with complete acceptance, whatever it does. She displays sensitivity and love, and if she thinks the young monkey is misbehaving, she corrects it with extreme gentleness. She provides for the baby monkey's physical needs, gives it psychological contact, and protects it from outside threats (Harlow & Harlow, 1966). As in primates, the human motivation to enter into emotional attachment and to communicate stems from an innate readiness to take part in mutual transactions; however, communication abilities can only be acquired through interactions with others. Throughout evolution, man has gradually developed the capacity for engaging in interactions with other humans, using language, making sense, and forming attachments.

Recent brain scanning studies by Bartels and Zeki (2004) have partially established the neurobiological basis of maternal affection. Among other things, we now know that the hormones vasopressin and oxytocin are involved in the formation and preservation of attachment among mammals, and that there is a close link between attachment processes and the brain's reward system, that is, the activation of the neurotransmitter dopamine. Attachment between mother and child involves the same hormones as attachments between adults, for example, romantic love. Both forms of attachment suppress activity in brain regions associated with negative emotions, critical thinking, and social assessment, partly because the brain's center for fear and aggression, the amygdala, is deactivated. But even though romantic and maternal affection activate many of the same brain regions, there are also differences. In particular, an area deep inside the brain stem called PAG (periaqueductal gray matter) seems to be involved in maternal behavior. This area has close links to the brain's limbic areas and contains a large number of vasopressin and oxytocin receptors. This area is also known for suppressing pain in connection with intense emotional experiences such as childbirth. There are also many oxytocin and vasopressin receptors in an area located just above the limbic system: the front section of the cingulate gyrus, which is involved in various aspects of social and emotional processing. This brain region is involved in the mother's feelings of empathy and her desire to care for her baby. PAG is also associated with the orbitofrontal cortex, a region in the frontal lobes, whose function is reduced in the infatuation phase of romantic love. Among other functions, the orbitofrontal cortex is involved in the assessment of social reliability, the assessment of facial expressions, and the awareness of one's own emotions. The neural "machinery" activates specific areas of the reward system, suppresses activity associated with critical social assessments of other people and feelings of sadness and anger, and helps ensure parenting behavior and healthy social interactions. Bartels and Zeki conclude that this may be essential for understanding the severe psychological consequences of disturbances in this circuit due to genetic factors, brain injuries, or childhood experiences.

Attachment, Relationship, and Intersubjectivity

Before I turn to the child's innate capacity for engaging in interactions and the unfolding of these interactions in close relationships, we need to clarify the terms attachment behavior, attachment patterns, intersubjectivity, and relationship.

John Bowlby's attachment theory focused on early attachment in infancy. In the 1970s, video equipment began to make it possible to study caregiver-infant interactions on a micro level. At this time, researchers began to focus on very early interactions between parents and infants, among them researchers of infancy such as Colwyn Trevarthen, Edward Tronick, and Daniel Stern. They would videotape the mother-infant dyad and play it back in slow motion, examining it bit by bit. They discovered that the mother-infant dyad consists of synchronized behavior patterns, something that no one had previously been aware of. This dyad plays out with variations in a carefully planned choreography and creative interactions, and the mother's communication with the infant helps the child define himself or herself through the structure of the relationship. Stern found that these attunements are so subtle that they often go unnoticed.

Since Bowlby's time, developmental psychology has progressed from being mainly about attachment patterns to being a theory about intersubjectivity, and this shift can make it difficult to distinguish between the various concepts as they are applied. For example, the terms attachment behavior, attachment pattern, interaction, intersubjectivity, and relationship can be difficult to distinguish, and they are often confused. Stern (2004) distinguished between attachment and the ability to enter into an intersubjective field and pointed out that people can be attached without sharing intersubjective intimacy, or they may be in intersubjective contact without being attached. An autistic child, for example, is often securely attached to the caregiver but unable to engage in an attuned interaction and will therefore have a very limited repertoire of relational strategies. A severely deprived child, by contrast, only forms sporadic attachments and is capable of engaging in imitative interactions but incapable of maintaining a relationship over time.

Right from birth, infants engage in closely regulated interactions with their caregivers through countless interaction sequences. The mutual regulation that takes place, however, is not characterized by symmetry;

the relationship is asymmetrical, and in the vast majority of cases the caregiver puts in the larger effort (Stern et al., 1998). Through these interaction sequences the child develops relational strategies or patterns that become a sort of prototype for handling future interactions with others. The interaction consists of the observable behavior, while the relationship is a construction consisting of a series of interactions that take place over time. Thus, the relationship is not available to direct observation. In the field between interaction and relationship, it is necessary to distinguish between observable behavior, which is specific to an individual interaction, and aspects of the interaction, which are repeated over many subsequent interactions. A relational pattern is formed through many mutual interaction acts, and it gradually comes to reflect both the caregiver's and the child's expectations, based on previous interactions. Stability over time and the pattern of the relationship gradually develop into a relational or attachment pattern (Smith, 2003). Thus, the terms attachment pattern and relational pattern are often used synonymously. Attachment behavior, however, refers to an observable behavior as the infant seeks reassurance, care, and comfort. This behavior is activated when the infant is separated from the caregiver. Attachment behavior is based on attachment relationships and physical closeness, while attachment patterns develop through a process where the infant forms attachment bonds with his primary caregivers.

Intersubjectivity and Internal Representations

Joint attention is a basic component of human communication, and the ability to direct someone else's attention to something and to allow one's own attention to be directed by someone else is a prerequisite for empathy. Joint attention is a form of intersubjectivity, but intersubjectivity goes beyond that. In addition to the caregiver's ability to focus her attention on the infant, the caregiver's psychological accessibility and actions also help to stimulate the child's development (Emde, 1988; Schibbye, 2005). Different researchers treat the concept of intersubjectivity somewhat differently, which tends to render the term a little ambiguous, but the desire to be in an intersubjective field with someone else is essential for the formation of a relationship, and the capacity for intersubjectivity is probably part of an innate motivation system (Stern, 2004). The caregiver addresses the infant as a person with intentions, feelings, and thoughts, and at a very early stage the infant develops the ability to identify emotional facial expressions and body language and to expect certain interactions.

Stern (1985) perceives intersubjectivity as an innate ability as well as a way of relating between caregiver and infant, which he divides into joint intention, joint attention, and joint affect. Trevarthen (1979) describes intersubjectivity as the infant's deliberate effort to share events and objects, a process that begins before the infant is able to perceive the caregiver as a subjective person. Fonagy (2005) describes intersubjectivity as joint attention aimed at the external reality and argues that as humans we construct our external reality based on shared emotions, intentions, and plans. In the present book, the term intersubjectivity is used to refer to attuned microinteractions that emerge between caregiver and infant, gradually giving rise the infant's internal representations.

Intersubjectivity is formed on the basis of synchronized biorhythms (Hart, 2008; Stern, 2004). Moments of intersubjective sharing help the infant develop and maintain emotional bonds with the caregiver and also develop the child's capacity for self-regulation. Infants achieve emotional regulation by affecting and regulating the mother's behavior; for example, if the infant cries, the mother responds by soothing, comforting, and calming the child, and the child's tension is reduced (Schibbye, 2005). Intersubjectivity and external interactions shape the infant's nervous system and gradually lead to the development of internal representations of the relationship. The infant forms internal representations of tangible objects by manipulating them or putting the objects in his mouth; the infant forms attachment patterns and internal representations of people by imitating and attuning with them. Around the age of 9 months, the infant is able to form internal representations and imagine the caregiver even when she is absent. The 9-month-old child is able to recall interactions with other people; at this age the child has internalized the representation of the parents and has come to expect a certain form of behavior (Aitken & Trevarthen, 1997). Once the child has formed internal representations of generalized interactions, the attachment pattern develops that the child will draw on in future interactions with other people.

Trevarthen (1979, 1998) distinguished between primary and secondary intersubjectivity. He explained that primary intersubjectivity develops at the age of 2–3 months when the infant has developed a sense of the caregiver's attention and about his effect on the caregiver. Primary intersubjectivity can be observed in very young infants, evident through the timing of movements, mutual facial coordination, and expectations of mutual behavior. The child incorporates part of the caregiver through acts of imitation; this bolsters the child's sense that the caregiver is "like me," and "I am like her." The basis of primary intersubjectivity is innate and facilitates emotional communication. The perceived closeness in the interaction with the caregiver leads to basic sensations and affects, which in turn form the basis for more complex emotions. In the primary intersubjective process, the caregiver attunes with the infant's emotions while attempting to match the emotion that the child expresses. This match should be achieved in terms of both timing and intensity, and its form should correspond to the infant's contributions. When the experience is matched and clearly communicated back to the infant, we speak of intersubjective sharing.

Secondary intersubjectivity does not develop until the child is able to attune emotionally with the caregiver's feelings as well as her actions. According to Trevarthen, secondary intersubjectivity develops at the age of 7–9 months; its characteristics are that the caregiver and child have joint attention on something outside themselves, and that each is aware of the other's attention. Secondary intersubjectivity develops once the child is able to share experiences and achieve psychological closeness in the same way as he achieves physical closeness.

Innate Communication Systems

One purpose of the child's innate signals is to facilitate attachments with adults and trigger caregiving behavior. All the infant's communication systems are open to beings that resemble humans and to events that resemble human behavior. Immediately after birth, babies explore their environment and attempt to make sense of what they are seeing, hearing, and feeling. The ability to reach out, respond to, and organize in relation to the environment is strong from the first moments of life; initially in the form of primitive reflexive behavior but gradually in more sophisticated forms. Babies also have an innate capacity for initiating, maintaining, and terminating social contact with others. Some of these abilities are present from birth, including the ability for gaze contact and for being calmed by soothing, caresses, and rocking. The infant's open communication systems enable the child to establish and engage in interpersonal relationships that later develop into attachment relationships. From birth, the infant actively and competently seeks contact with the caregiver, and the innate reflex system helps the child attach his immature nervous system to the caregiver's more mature nervous system in order to organize and develop his own mental and affective processes (Brazelton, 1984; Emde, 1989).

The infant relies on a wide range of affective expressions in the form of movements, including facial mimicry, motor expressions, and vocalization, and there seems to be an innate structure in the central nervous system for imitating behavior. The capacity for imitation appears to rely on a particular category of neurons called mirror neurons. Man is the most imitative species of all, and imitation enables us to empathize with others and engage in sophisticated interactions. The infant's expressions are triggered by the caregiver's actions, for example, her mimicry. That helps make the caregiver comprehensible to the child while also enabling the caregiver to interpret the infant's expressions as communicative. The capacity for imitation, mimicry, and gestures is innate, but in order for the infant's full communicative potential to unfold the caregiver must be emotionally open and available to the infant's subtle signals, and she must help the infant regulate his varying states. Furthermore, the caregiver's parenting repertoire includes an eagerness to attribute meaning to the child's actions. This overinterpretation has a positive influence on the child's communicative development, as the child learns what sort of responses his expressions elicit (Brodén, 1991; Hart 2008, 2006; Smith, 2001; Sroufe, 1989a).

Innate emotional expressions play a key role for the infant's adaptation, but it takes a few months before the emotions take on direction and meaning, and infants begin to expect certain responses from their environment. Children will draw attention to their needs right from birth, initially through crying. Crying helps most infants at the moment of birth, as they transition from life in the womb to an independent existence; among other functions, crying promotes the ability to breathe. During the first few weeks of life, crying is mainly associated with physiological activation and homeostasis, but gradually the pattern of crying becomes more varied, which lets the caregiver attribute different meanings to the crying. Most infants display the same pattern of crying, but the crying does contain unique features that set children apart.

Arbitrary facial expressions and crying also trigger a response from the caregiver because she attributes specific meaning to them, and her interpretation affects internal distinctions in the infant. Parents are often unsure about the cause of their baby's crying, and as they try to determine the cause they draw on their knowledge about the child and recent or current events, for example, whether the child has eaten, is tired, and so on. Sounds that are not perceived as crying do not develop until the age of 2–3 months (Emde, 1992; Sroufe, 1996).

The first social smiles play an important role for the caregivers' sense of connecting with the infant. The smile of recognition is important in relation to social interactions and helps motivate the caregiver to engage in interactions. The infant smiles much more frequently at familiar persons than at familiar objects and smiles even more when the caregiver responds to his contributions. From an early age, the human face and human voices are the environmental features that attract an infant most, and which form the most essential beacons for the infant's perception of a situation. Infants have a limited repertoire for regulating their own state and often withdraw from situations that are perceived as too stimulating. During a positive interaction, infants often withdraw in order to curb their emotional excitement and then resume the interaction. Children also seek comfort by sucking on their thumb or a pacifier in an early attempt at emotional regulation. Crying, vocalization, and smiles help a baby come across as a social individual, capable of engaging in social interactions and with emotional responses to events. The parent's gaze contact with the child is an important indicator that helps the infant determine which aspect or aspects of an event are pertinent in relation to the adult's communication (Emde, 1992; Sroufe, 1996; Tetzchner, 2002).

The Infant's Inherent Temperament and Its Influence on the Interaction

Right from birth an infant has his own way of engaging with the world, an inclination that is usually referred to as temperament. Temperament includes the infant's degree of emotionality, irritability, activity level, attention capacity, and self-regulation as well as the infant's responses to and ability to cope with emotional situations and changes. The environment and the infant's inherent temperament interact and modify each another. The child's temperament affects the caregivers and causes them to engage in particular interactions with this particular child. The caregivers also bring their temperament and their particular response to the child's temperament into the interaction, which in turn also shapes the child's temperament. Caregivers treat different children differently, and even if the caregivers treated their children the same, the children's individual temperaments would still produce different perceptions and experiences. Some children will act needy and put pressure on the mother, and features in the child's personality, for example being hard to satisfy, influence the child's perceptions of the environment (Chess, Thomas, & Birch, 1965; Karen, 1998; Tetzchner, 2002).

The caregivers can help the infant regulate and adapt to difficult situations; for example, an infant with a tendency to be low-spirited can become more positive if the interaction takes place in a positive atmosphere. If an infant who adapts easily is repeatedly confronted with impossible demands, he will become increasingly less adaptive over time. A newborn child with a nervous system that is easily calmed will help an insecure mother develop a good caring pattern, while conversely, an unpredictable and difficult infant may tip the balance in the opposite direction. A sensitive mother's capacity to handle an unpredictable infant who is difficult to regulate will help the child develop appropriately. Confident mothers can handle both easy and difficult children without feeling insecure, while insecure mothers may become competent when they feel that they master the situation, for example, when they are able to soothe their child, but insecure when the child is difficult to regulate. Any caregiver-infant relationship fosters its own unique regulating acts that help the infant become aware of his own states, produce internal experiences, and organize self-regulating behavior (Bowlby, 1969; Karen, 1998; Sander, 1985; Tetzchner, 2002).

A temperament is neither good nor bad in itself, but the caregiver's and the infant's temperaments may constitute a good or a bad match. Therefore it only makes sense to talk about the infant's temperament in interaction with the caregiver. Once the infant is involved in an attachment relationship, the infant's innate dispositions both are reshaped and become subject to the relationship. Thus, an innate temperament does not exist as a separate entity (Sroufe & Fleeson, 1986).

Dyadic Transactions and Microinteractions

I now turn to the main topic of this chapter. In this section I offer a general description of the content of intersubjectivity: the dyadic microinteractions between caregiver and infant. Sander (1988), who studied interactive regulation between caregiver and infant, distinguishes between physiobiological and psychobiological regulation as the biological basis for the development of intersubjectivity, a point that is explored below. This regulation develops the child's innate capacity for imitation, and intersubjectivity lets the infant refine imitation into protoconversations and affective attunement in successive leaps.

Winnicott (1958, 1960, 1970, 1987), a British psychoanalyst who practiced as a pediatrician and studied personality development, pointed out that it is the caregiver's ability to empathize with the infant's needs that form the basis for the child's psychological development. The caregiver-infant interaction is asymmetrical; the caregiver brings her past history into the interaction with the infant, while the infant's development takes place within the relationship (Tronick et al., 1998). For example, parents who have difficulties of their own with regard to emotional regulation and who are overwhelmed by the infant's negative affects will be less able to achieve an appropriate dyadic transaction. The caregiver's modification of the feelings transferred to her by the infant enables the infant to handle his own emotions and to develop psychologically. The infant relies on the caregiver's regulation in organizing and regulating his own internal states. When the parents leave the infant to his own regulation, unable to engage in the emotional attunement that is needed to calm the infant down, the infant will fail to develop adequate self-regulation, self-perception, and a boundary between self and caregiver. It is through the experience of being seen that the infant feels his own existence and learns to relate to others. Those aspects of the child that are never affirmed will fail to develop (Fonagy, Gergely, Jurist, & Target, 2002).

The caregiver's sensitivity to the infant's communicative signals forms the core of secure attachment, and it is through the caregiver's sensitive regulation that the infant's nervous system develops. As the nervous system develops, the infant learns to attune with other people's states and develop self-regulating capacities. Attunement enables the caregiver's and the child's nervous systems to synchronize, and a neural field of resonance emerges where each affects the other's nervous system. Here,

resonance means that the infant's nervous system encounters a frequency that is close to his natural or innate frequency. When the frequency of
an external sensory stimulation matches the genetically encoded endogenous rhythms of the organism, the state is intensified. Thus, emotional
information is intensified in contexts that lead to mutual resonance. The
mutually attuned patterns of communication support the child's affect
modulation and affect his perception of what seems personally relevant.
The caregiver's actions give the infant a sense of what it means to communicate and to be connected. The relationship stretches beyond the
early dyad; it develops throughout childhood and comes to apply to
peers as well as other caregivers (Schore, 2002b; Stern, 1985).

As Stern (1985) mentioned, there are gazes or gaze aversion, there
are vocalizations or silences, body orientations, physical distances, gestures, ways of being held, rhythms, timing and durations of acts and activities, and so on, and there is substantial evidence to suggest that we
have an innate, biologically founded ability to feel other people's actions
that can take on a variety of culturally determined forms. In order for
this multitude of interactions to develop into internal representations,
the infant must have the experience of being with a primary caregiver
who regulates his self-perception. Caregiver and infant combine their
activities, and what happens between them only happens when these
two particular individuals combine their behavior patterns. As Stern
pointed out, "self-experiences . . . can never occur without being elicited
or maintained by the action or presence of an other" (1985, p. 102). The
attachment bond between caregiver and infant develops when the caregiver is sensitive, responds to the infant's input, and is emotionally available. The infant needs to be vitalized, and the vibrant energy or vitality
that this requires arises through the interaction or dialogue that caregiver and infant create together. Emotional attunement and rhythm form
the basis of communication within the relationship and make the relationship reciprocal. "We know ourselves through the other's response.
Attunement lifts, activates and reveals one's own state" (Øvreeide, 2002,
p. 48; translated for this edition). Tiny microregulating affective processes lead to the development of the reciprocity or bond that the infant
needs to be able to connect his nervous system to the caregiver's, and
which enables the development of the infant's brain organization (Tronick et al., 1998). The reciprocity and sensitivity between infant and caregiver lay the foundation for future social interactions, which will continue

to play out throughout the life span. The child's way of relating to others is developed within subtle interactions through tiny behavioral exchanges between caregiver and child, which over time develop into acquired expectations. Without the subtle, attuned interactions, there is no dyad for relationships to develop within; this occurs, for example, if a mother's understanding of her baby's needs is so far from the child's physiological and psychological needs that the two are unable to meet in a joint interaction (Karr-Morse & Wiley, 1997).

The importance of shared and attuned experiences can be illustrated with Tronick, Als, Adamson, Wise, and Brazelton's (1978) famous "still face" experiment. In this experiment initially, infants interact with their mothers. After some time the mothers are asked to avoid responding to the infants' input, and the mothers render their faces expressionless in the middle of an interaction. A typical 3-month-old will be distressed when encountering the mother's expressionless face. At first, the child tries to elicit a normal interaction, attempting to get her attention by smiling. When the mother continues not to respond, the baby repeats the sequence by looking at the mother with a lively and expressive face and then begins to look away. After many repetitions the baby withdraws and turns his head and body away from the mother, often with a slumped posture, appearing defeated. For several minutes after the mother has resumed normal interactions, the infant continues to be affected by the experiment, appearing to be in a bad mood and avoiding looking at the mother. Tronick (1989) concluded that 3-month-old infants are not only subject to the immediate stimulus situation; events in fact have a longer-lasting influence and are represented internally. Cohn, Campbell, and Ross (1991) found that the interaction style applied by 6-month-old infants in the still-face situation form a characteristic pattern that predicts the children's attachment pattern at the age of 1 year.

Tronick et al.'s experiment shows that when an infant is unable to establish an interaction with the mother, the child often loses posture control, withdraws, and attempts to soothe and stimulate himself. When infants realize that communication is impossible, they direct attention at their own bodily functions, maybe staring at their hands or becoming expressionless while touching their clothes or face. At an early age, an infant begins to form emotional and communicative expectations of others. The experiment illustrates how the infant will take the initiative to attempt to vitalize the mother, searching for strategies that will bring her out of her expressionless state. It illustrates the severity of the infant's response when the mother remains expressionless despite the child's efforts. Reciprocity is crucial for children, and an infant who stops attempting to make the mother interact displays withdrawal behavior and a depressive stance resembling the one observed in the isolated and maternally deprived rhesus monkeys in Harlow's experiments or Bowlby's descriptions from the mid-1950s of hospitalized children who had been separated from their parents. Bowlby's study eventually made it possible for parents to be hospitalized along with their children. Even though the mothers in Tronick et al.'s experiment only remained expressionless for 3 minutes, the infants found the temporary abuse extraordinarily disturbing.

Children's expectations of regulation are based partly on their ability to discover and predict what is repeated and what is to be expected. Children base much of their organization on predictable relations between their own behavior and environmental responses. Trevarthen carried out experiments where he showed an infant video recordings of the mother from earlier incidents of communication between her and the child. Initially, the child would try to interact with the mother on the tape, but the child soon grew distressed and seemed scared. It is the precision in the interaction and the living interactive contact that maintains joy-filled involvement. To achieve communication, the mother must offer an affective response to the infant's signals (Trevarthen, 1993a, 1993b).

Physiobiological and Psychobiological Regulation

The child's identity development requires an emotional bond with the caregiver. The better she is at identifying with the child's individuality, the more unique the child will be to her, and the stronger their mutual bond (Brodén, 1991). The biological foundation of the development of mutual behavior and the ability to understand each other's actions depends in part on the child's capacity for physiobiological and psychobiological regulation, which develops gradually through early interactions.

All living organisms organize themselves around rhythms such as the circadian rhythm, sensorimotor rhythms, and so on. We also establish rhythms and synchronize with each other's nervous systems (for a more detailed description, see Hart, 2008). The human capacity to connect with others' nervous systems through interactions is not exclusively instinctive. The organization of rhythms occurs through repetitive events, and for these events to unfold they must be regulated within a time frame. Rhythms and synchronization between nervous systems develop through the mutual establishment of a joint rhythmic structure that first emerges within the framework of the caregiver-infant relationship. Sander pointed out that the fundamental ability of the nervous system to develop rhythms and synchronization springs from the child's innate physiobiological rhythms, which gradually unfold within the early caregiver-infant interaction. The interaction of the nervous system with an optimal environment leads to the development of systems for self-regulation (Damasio, 1998; Sander, 1988; Schore, 2003b; Stern, 2004).

A newborn baby often moves in bursts interrupted by breaks (e.g., the sucking pattern), and the mother adjusts her activities to match the child's rhythms. From the first days of life the child's internal experience is organized through close interactions with the caregiver. The internal experience begins with sequences of arousal, sleep/wake, and hunger/satiety cycles. At a very early stage the infant begins to adapt to the caregiver's behavior, because she tends to act in predictable ways. Already within the first 10 days of life, the sleep cycle of newborn babies begins to be affected by certain care routines. The caregiver's repetitive rhythmic movements match a fundamental motivation for human contact. The human voice helps regulate the behavioral state. Neisser (1993) has described how the face of a happy mother talking to her baby will be exaggerated, kind, and loving. Her voice will be gentle and relaxed with a breathy quality, often in a certain frequency: 300 Hz. When the mother speaks, she modulates her voice; speaking to the baby in a soothing and modulated voice helps keep the baby physically calm and attentive. The caregiver's activity helps determine the infant's attention, and the infant's heart rate increases until the child becomes agitated and turns his head away (Sander, 1969, 1977, 1983, 1985; Smith, 2001). These forms of coordinated or synchronized movements, which are regulated by the mechanism required to optimize the caregiver's communication with her infant, are characterized as physiobiological attunement.

Psychobiological attunement develops on the basis of physiobiological attunement. The caregiver's contact with her infant child is a theme with variations, like all social interactions. The caregiver alters the tim-

ing and intensity of her sounds and movements, and each smile is slightly different from the previous one but still represents the same basic
facial expression. This psychobiological attunement gradually initiates
the infant into new categories of human behavior, and the child partici-
pates more and more in variations on a theme, thus expanding his behavioral repertoire. The caregiver's regular pace provides the infant with
sequences of human behavior at regular intervals, and each incident
presents the infant with behavior that is sufficiently predictable to serve
as the basis for expectations, even if there is some variation. Already at
the age of 2 months, the infant's communication is better coordinated
and more lively and detailed when the caregiver is able to engage in appropriate affective attunement. Even babies with unpredictable and
emotionally volatile parents desperately try to find a style and a meaning
in the parents' behavior, and if they fail to do so, their behavior becomes
disorganized (Bertelsen, 1994; Katzenelson, 1994).

Psychobiological regulation may be a one-way process, where the infant attempts to alter his internal state to match the caregiver's; this is
seen, for example, in infants' contact with depressive mothers, as infants
will attempt to adjust their arousal level to match the mothers'. Sørensen
(2006) argued that a distinction between the need to receive interactive
affect regulation (following) and the need to provide interactive affect
regulation (leading) may be the key to a clear description of the relationship itself. The caregiver may also try to bring the infant into a particular
state, for example, in trying to calm the infant down. At an early stage
the infant learns how to affect the caregiver's emotions and behavior by
attuning with her gestures, behavior, and sounds. For example, if the
caregiver wants to get an excited child ready for bed, she has better
chances of succeeding if she approaches the child's state and then tries
to calm the child down than if she demands the child to calm down on
his own. This form of attunement will make the infant feel supported by
the parents in a jointly attuned process.

Around the age of 4 months, infants begin to coordinate and synchronize the duration of their vocalizations. At this time it makes no difference whether the infant interacts with the caregiver or a stranger, and
the coordination and synchronization displays a general social perceptual ability that is not reserved for the attachment figure. An infant is
able to turn the interaction on and off through gaze contact with the
mother, for example, by glancing away briefly when he is impatient and

wants to vocalize and looking away more definitively when tired or distressed (Beebe & Lachmann, 2002; Trevarthen, 1993a, 1993b).

A mother's most effective technique for maintaining the interaction is to be sensitive to the infant's capacity for attention and need for withdrawal after a period of attention. The responsive mother imitates and exaggerates the infant's social acts and withdraws briefly when the child looks away. Through this behavior the parents facilitate the infant's information processing by adapting the mode, amount, and timing of information to match the infant's current integrative capacity, which helps shape the infant's emerging identity (Brazelton & Cramer, 1990; Tronick, Ricks, & Cohn, 1982). The stimulus events that constitute the mother's behavior have to be modified almost constantly to maintain a given attention level. The mother has to be able to improvise on a theme to maintain her child's attention (Stern, 1977).

Imitation

The ability to imitate is the biological basis for our ability to understand each other's acts and for our ability to learn. Imitation refers to any situation where the child is affected by the caregiver's gestures, mimicry, or movement and responds in kind. When infants communicate, they are sharing their states with the caregiver, including affects, body sensations, and so on, and it is through this diversity of communication that we learn to "read" other people (Mead, 1934; Trevarthen, 1993a, 1993b).

Our attachment capacity is innate, but it unfolds and develops through the close relationship between caregiver and infant. Initially, the infant's use of affective signals is mainly intended to attract the caregiver's attention to make her provide care and comfort and stimulate the child's development. At an early stage the infant begins to respond to other people's emotional expressions. For example, a newborn baby begins to cry when she hears other babies cry, and a 3-week-old baby is able to imitate facial expressions. If a mother sticks out her tongue at her 3-week-old baby, the baby does the same. This imitation requires the baby to form a mental image of the caregiver's act. Thus, at this stage the baby is able to link the visual appearance of the caregiver's tongue with the felt position of his own tongue (Meltzoff & Moore, 1977; Ramachandran, 2003; Stern, 1985). Field and Fogel (1982) described how 2-day-old babies imitate certain aspects of facial expressions, for example, happy, sad, and surprised expressions.

In the early interactions, the mother uses imitative exaggeration when playing with her baby and thus acts as an amplifying echo. One of the expressions of this emotional interaction, which strengthens the bond between the 0–2-month-old baby and the caregiver, is when the caregiver compensates for the immature level of the infant's sensory apparatus by exaggerating her mimicry and movements, for example, by opening her mouth wide in slow motion or by opening her eyes wide. From the outset, the imitation is not one-to-one, as the mother and infant do not mirror each other directly but display different levels of arousal and engagement. In her imitative exaggeration, for example, the mother attunes her temporal pattern with the baby's and then varies and exaggerates her prosody. It is her control, attunement, and exaggeration that make the infant interested in the contact and eventually makes the child laugh (Beebe & Lachmann, 1988; Trevarthen, 1990).

Imitation goes beyond mirroring behavior directly, and right from birth babies are able to transfer information between sensory modalities and recognize a link or a match between different sensory phenomena such as taste, vision, touch, smell, and so on. This phenomenon is characterized both as cross-modality and amodal perception. For example, the infant's voice will be synchronized with the mother's body movements, or the infant's arm movements will be synchronized with the mother's voice. Regardless whether a stimulus is perceived visually or through touch, the activation elicits the same pattern. The human nervous system has an innate ability for holistic perception, including the ability to tie mimicry, gestures, and other bodily expressions together into a whole. We use links between sensory and emotional qualities when we direct our perception at another person's behavior. Successful attunement requires interchangeability between behavioral expressions that appear in a variety of forms and sensory modalities; for example, the infant will be able to transfer the rhythm of the parent's voice to the rhythm in his own arm movements. Attunement often involves cross-modal matching, and the baby's and the caregiver's expressive modalities will often differ, with the infant's voice, for example, matching the mother's body movements, and so on. The infant responds to the caregiver's internal state, and the match occurs between various expressions of internal states, which can take on different forms. In studies, Stern (1984) found that most attunement is cross-modal. If the infant's expression is vocal, the mother is likely to attune with the infant through mimicry or gestures. In 87% of the cases, the mother responds in a fully or partially cross-modal way; thus, in only 13% of the cases does she achieve attunement by drawing on the same modality as the infant. Infants between 4 and 12 months of age and their caregivers are able to time the beginning, the end, and the breaks in their mutual vocalizations precisely, thus achieving a rhythmic link and coordination.

Imitation and amodal or cross-modal transfer require the caregiver's response to be attuned with the infant's expression; otherwise, the infant will not be able to perceive the link between his own experience and behavior and the caregiver's response. For example, the caregiver notes the infant's distress and mirrors the feeling while also linking it to her own calm state. For example, imitation does not require the infant's and the caregiver's experiences to be identical; however, they will have a shared experience, for example, a shared experience of joy or excitement. The caregiver may not be excited in the same way as the infant, but she recognizes a similar feeling of excitement in herself and is thus able to share the child's excitement. When the infant cries, for example, the caregiver does not begin to cry along with the child, but she may look a little sad and attempt to comfort the child. She perceives the infant's distress and signals that she understands it as she comforts the child. In this way, the caregiver helps modify the child's feelings by signaling that this is not about her emotional state but the child's, which is essential for the child's ability to define a self. For example, she may mirror anger or sadness, which the infant may imitate, but that does not mean that she is necessarily angry or sad (Schibbye, 2005).

Infants under the age of 3 months are only interested in events that match their own behavior completely (Stern 1984, 1993, 2004; Trevarthen, 1993a, 1993b). Fonagy (2005) noted that newborn babies like to engage in completely imitative behavior (perfect contingency), and that they prefer acts that are part of their own behavior. For example, if a string tied around the baby's leg is attached to a mobile that coordinates with the baby's movements, the child enjoys this game. At the age of 4 months approximately 70% of children show intensified attention to any delays or deviations in movement coordination. The infant seeks stimulation that avoids directly imitative behavior. Autistic or disorganized children (see Chapter 4), on the other hand, continue to seek direct coordination. Fonagy (2003) speculated that delays or deviations in coordination offer the child a chance to distinguish himself or herself from the caregiver. He believed that the child's search for perfect contingency is an attempt at sensing internal states, but in the context of human interaction this approach will have limited effect in the long run.

Protoconversations

In the first 2 months of life, the interactions between caregiver and infant revolve around imitation. Around the age of 2 months the social smile emerges, and psychobiological contact develops as the infant begins to engage in much more dialogic interactions through nonverbal communication. These nonverbal dialogues or interactions are called protoconversations, and they are regulated with regard to timing and affective modulation.

The term protoconversation was first used by Mary Catherine Bateson in 1975, as she described how 7–15-week-old babies focused on the mother's face and voice and responded to her smile and expressions in a reciprocal way. Both imitation and protoconversations are initiated by gaze contact, vocalization, and gestures and coordinated within a focused field of attention between infant and caregiver. The caregiver invites the interaction in a questioning manner; she invites a response from the child and imitates the child's movements. The child's expressive responses are imitated as soon as there is a clear positive response, and the mother smiles and expresses her joy through vocal expressions. Around the age of 2 months, the infant has developed the ability to respond to the caregiver's invitations in other ways besides imitation; the child smiles and is encouraged to respond to her input with babbling and gestures. The mother and the infant are drawn into a rhythm, and the patterns in their engagement become synchronized. The mother helps the infant regulate the exchange; she vitalizes the child and supports his expressions (Neisser, 1993; Stern, 2004).

The caregiver must be able to read and match the infant's emotional state based on external behavior, and similarly, the infant must be able to read the parents' behavior as a response to the infant's own behavior for protoconversations to emerge. During the first 9 months of life, sequences of mutual behavior emerge within the dyad that form the basis for social dialogues. Infants under the age of 2 months practice engaging in protoconversations, for example, by opening and closing their hands or by moving and shaping their tongue as if they were about to speak while maintaining gaze contact, and eventually the infant begins to try to vocalize. Bråten (1998) described how already during the first month of life, the infant engages in contact with the parents through gaze contact, and the parent promotes the synchronization of the interaction, for example, by placing her face at an optimum angle and distance for the infant's immature vision.

Both imitation and protoconversations occur spontaneously in close interactions when neither the infant nor the caregiver is distracted, nervous, or under pressure. Infants do not engage in interactions without the caregiver's invitation, and the frequency of this sort of invitation varies with the family or cultural context. Infants under the age of 1 month cannot engage in mutual communication as quickly as slightly older infants. Infants around 2–6 months still imitate the mother's expressions and often mirror her changing moods instantly. When a mother smiles at her baby, the baby tends to smile back with far more intentionality than before, and the affect is shared. The mother might add a vocal component and an exaggerated, perhaps more vital facial expression, which pushes the infant to an even higher level of joy, or she may tone the process down to reduce the infant's activity level. The infant's affects are subtly and smoothly regulated by the mother in a well-coordinated process made up of mother-infant protoconversations (Neisser, 1993).

Affective Attunement

Stern introduced the term affective attunement to describe a more sophisticated level of imitation behavior and protoconversations. This ability is essential for our ability to understand other people's emotions and to develop empathy. Affective attunement is essential for our ability to feel other people and to feel that we are felt, which facilitates the development of attachment capacity and enables us to relate to significant others throughout our life span.

When the child has developed the ability to share an affective state through protoconversations without imitating the other's exact behavior, we speak of affective attunement. At this time the infant is able to relate to the caregiver's internal state, not just the external behavior. The main distinction between affective attunement, imitation, and protoconversation is that while imitation and protoconversation relate only to external behavior, affective attunement mediates internal states. In imitation and protoconversation the focus of attention is still on external behavior. It takes attuned behavior to switch the focus of attention to the inside: the quality of the emotion that is shared. Imitation reflects actions, and protoconversations reflect emotions through external expressions, while affective attunement makes it possible to be together through the sense of sharing inner experiences. Imitation reproduces form, while attunement reproduces emotions. Thus, affective attunement expresses the emotional quality without mimicking the exact behavioral expression of the internal state. Attunement behavior deals with the emotional quality underlying the behavior. It is our capacity for attunement that gives us the sense of being emotionally connected, and attunement behavior begins the moment that social interaction begins. During the first 2 months of life, interactions consist of imitation. When the infant is between 2 and 6 months old, protoconversations come to prevail over imitation in a gradual process, and between 6 and 9 months of age, affective attunement gradually comes to prevail over protoconversation and imitation (Stern, 1984, 2004).

After the age of 9 months, imitation, protoconversations, and attunement all remain important elements of the interaction, but they are different phenomena with different functions. Attunement behavior lets us connect with the other person's emotional state. The sense of a human community arises through attunement and plays a crucial role in shaping the infant's awareness of internal emotional states as a human experience that is not necessarily identical with other people's emotional states, but which can be shared with others. Affective attunement mostly takes place on the unconscious level, and the caregivers shape the development of the child's personality through selective attunement. The caregivers' internal representations and notions about their infant influence the infant through affective attunement, and the attunement makes it possible to express what is included in or excluded from mutual care and acceptance. Through selective attunement the parents' responses become a sort of template for intrapsychic experiences within the child. The parents' approach to the child, their hopes, fears, prohibitions, and fantasies, are communicated through affective attunement (Stern, 1984, 1985).

Attuned interactions require a caregiver to use facial and vocal expressions to show the infant the feelings that she assumes the infant has. This process of affect mirroring is essential for the child's development of a capacity for self-regulation, and later the image of the caregiver's comforting behavior will help organize the child's emotional experiences. In essence, human personality is an extension of childhood experiences with the primary caregivers, and affective attunement is embedded in their frequent and often very subtle joint behavior patterns. Affective attunement offers an impression of the quality of a relationship, that is, how the caregiver and the infant manage to engage in ongoing interactions with each other (Stern, 1985).

To feel that one is felt is the subjective experience of attunement. A lack of affective attunement leaves the child emotionally isolated, and later in life the child will have difficulty self-regulating emotions that have not been affectively attuned. The child's capacity for affect regulation develops in a gradual process, where initially the caregiver provides all the regulation in a sensitive interaction with the infant's signals; gradually the infant develops a stronger capacity for self-regulation on the basis of affective attunement. The developmental strategies around affect regulation are influenced by the caregiver's response as well as the infant's capacity to respond (Schore, 1994, 2003a; Sroufe, 1989a, 1989b).

Affective attunement often occurs implicitly and does not involve cognitive processes. Affective attunement lets the infant continue, alter, or intensify a joint affective experience. The infant's affects help the infant perceive the self and others as coherent and are thus of fundamental importance for the child's self-organization and sense of continuity. Affective attunement is the precursor of empathic understanding. It enables the expansion of consciousness that leads to empathic understanding, as both caregiver and infant sense the other's consciousness, for example, when the infant feels the mother's pain when her hair is being pulled. When the caregiver attunes affectively with the infant's emotions and signals that the infant's emotions are familiar to her, she returns the infant's emotions to him or her by matching and exchanging within an intersubjective bond. Through affective attunement the infant learns that it is possible to maintain one's own perspective while sharing the other's. If the caregiver is unable to mark and clarify the distinctions and, for example, places her own emotions inside the infant, the infant will not be able to distinguish between self and caregiver (Schibbye, 2005; Tronick et al., 1998).

The Interactive Dance and Present Moments

All communication requires joint attention on events taking place in the present. What characterizes these moments is that the infant's and the caregiver's states of consciousness are connected. The mutual feeling of a shared experience, understanding, and meaning is an essential function of intersubjectivity; it consists of several processes, which Stern (2004) characterized as moving along, now moments, moments of meeting, and open space.

Sander (1995) introduced the term moments of meeting based on the biorhythms that develop in the mother-infant interaction around the establishment of sleep/wake and feeding cycles, and which rely on the caregiver and infant engaging in joint activity. The feeling of connectedness or rapport springs from the mutual influence that caregiver and infant have on one another during the first 6 months of the child's life, and it is established through mutually synchronized regulation where the caregiver's and the infant's nervous systems form a joint field of resonance. The synchronization of the two nervous systems is achieved through moments of meeting, which play an important role for brain organization and in the regulatory processes of the central nervous system.

In the caregiver-infant interaction, the repetition of activities leads to a movement process, which Stern calls "moving along," and moving along creates a repertoire of now moments. Moving along lays the foundation for familiar libraries of expected moments in life with a specific other as the two move along together. When the now moments are linked together, they make up the process of moving along, also referred to as the process of mutual regulation. Stern (1998, 2004; Kristensen, 2006) described how the intersubjectivity process springs from tiny, ordinary moments; very brief, natural units in the interaction, each lasting 3–4 seconds. To describe ordinary now moments, he uses the metaphor of a bird flying from branch to branch: every time it lands on a branch consti-tutes a now moment. The now moments give rise to sudden moments of meeting; these moments are more emotionally charged and stand out in the interaction. The moments of meeting increase the ability of the ner-vous system to intensify and coregulate with someone else's activity, and they occur only when the infant's and caregiver's nervous systems have been able to engage in mutual adjustment and self-regulation, the condi-tion that Stern refers to as moving along.

The now moments bind the infant's and caregiver's individual states of consciousness together, resulting in a mutual recognition where they both share a sense of the other's experience: This constitutes the mo-ment of meeting. All social animals synchronize and attune their behav-ior through the process of moving along, now moments, and moments of meeting. For example, when a mother and an infant engage in protocon-versation, a certain smile from the infant, which the mother finds sur-prising or amusing, makes the mother look at the infant with a big smile, which makes them both burst out laughing. In a moment of meeting, attunement is on full power, and there is an overwhelming sense of close-ness and authenticity. These essential moments help nourish and stimu-late the development of the nervous system (Beebe, 1998; Sander, 1992; Siegel, 1999; Stern, 1977, 1998a, 2004). The transfer of emotional infor-mation is intensified through moments of meeting, and the raised level of energy produces a sense of vitality that promotes the nervous system's emerging capacity for self-regulation and attention control. The mo-ments of meeting are a dyadic expansion of the consciousness. For example, when the caregiver and infant are playing, and there is an ex-change of laughter that escalates and pushes both the caregiver and the infant to a higher level of arousal, that will expand the infant's capacity for tolerating high levels of mutually created positive excitation in future interactions. Tiny changes at the right time stimulate the nervous sys-tem to reorganize and develop (Sander, 1988; Schore, 2003a, 2003b; Sroufe 1996; Stern 1990, 1998).

Engagement and Lack of Engagement

When moments of meeting occur in a sequence of mutual regulation, at some point there is a state of relaxation. The regulation and integra-tion of all living systems involves shifts between engagement and disengagement, and the infant needs breaks to be able to self-regulate. The better the caregiver is at noticing the infant's signals, allowing the infant to withdraw when needed, and noticing and responding when the infant seeks to reengage, the higher the likelihood of moments of meeting. Normally, both parties break off the engagement following a moment of meeting. Inspired by Winnicott, Sander (1988) called this separation an open space, where the two can be together, being themselves, and where for a short while the infant can be alone in the other's presence. Thus, the infant learns to self-regulate together with the caregiver. The open space means that the effect of the moment of meeting can be assimilated, and the infant has an opportunity to find a new equilibrium in the altered intersubjective state. To preserve joy-filled interactions, an attuned caregiver will hold back and reduce the stimulation level when she notices that the infant withdraws, waiting for the infant to signal readiness to reengage. Thus, it is not only the tempo but also the engagement, the withdrawal of engagement, and the reengagement that are coordinated. Withdrawing from contact by looking away gives the infant the time and space for psychological processing and for developing the capacity for self-regulation (Lester, Hoffman, & Brazelton, 1985; Øvreeide & Hafstad, 1996; Schore, 2001).

Winnicott (1958, 1962) argued that one of the factors that promote attachment is the capacity to be alone in the company of a present and available caregiver, as this helps the infant discover that he is separate from the caregiver. The sense of self is strengthened in quiet, calm, and passive periods when the infant feels safe and secure, and when there are no demands from the environment. A mother who violates the child's boundaries because she is unable to distinguish her own needs from the child's fails to attune with the child. This makes it difficult for the child to develop separately from the mother, a situation that Winnicott described as the development of a false, compliant self. The child needs to develop a distinct identity in relation to the caregiver, and the time and space to process and integrate experiences. To develop a form of self-delimitation, the infant establishes the boundaries that are possible within the relationship, that is, boundaries that do not threaten the attachment. If the mother is too intrusive, that is, too focused on responding to the child's every expression, the child may have difficulty developing personal boundaries and will lack sufficient psychological distance and space. Generally, the child balances between intimacy and distance, which corresponds to the balance between attachment and delimitation (Schibbye, 2005).

Misattunement, Selective Attunement, and Lack of Attunement

Winnicott (1958) has pointed out that the attuned mirroring function in early mother-infant contact helps develop the child's ability to engage in gradual misattunement, which is also a key function in interpersonal interactions.

Tronick and Cohn (1989) found that when caregiver and infant engaged in unattuned contact, it took about 2 seconds before approximately 70% of the misattunements were turned into attunement. Thus, in connection with the repair of misattunement and miscoordinated states, there is a powerful tendency to reestablish the interaction as more coordinated states within just 2 seconds. Any dyadic contact consists of attunements, misattunements, and lack of attunement. Affective attunement promotes feelings of omnipotence, and as the infant develops, the contact changes from consisting exclusively of attuned imitative functions to including a growing number of misattunements (Tronick, 1989; Tronick & Gianino, 1986).

The ability to handle misattunements develops the child's capacity for distinguishing and differentiating himself from the mother. When the child enters the second year of life, the caregiver must be able to tolerate stressful socializing transactions between herself and the child. The development of psychological agility and strength springs from interactions between the caregiver and the child, from positive to negative and back to positive affect. The child learns to handle stressful situations through misattunements, and gradually learns to self-regulate out of these states with the support of the caregiver. Thus, the child learns to recover from negative affective states and develops an expectation of being relieved of pain by a predictable caregiver, which in turn promotes the child's own sense of being able to cope with negative emotions.

The child's nervous system organizes in the interaction through attunement, misattunement, the reparation of misattunement, and affective moments with high levels of arousal. Misattunements are essential in developing the capacity for differentiating and separating oneself from the mother. The caregiver is responsible for the misattunements and for repairing them. Parents are not perfect, and as long as the lack of attunement is not a dominant feature it acts as a constructive aspect that helps the child learn that close relations can develop through attunements, and that misattunements distinguish people from each other. The mutual process of repairing misattunements organizes coping experiences, for example, in relation to transforming negative emotions into positive ones, the capacity for self-regulation, and the formation of friendship bonds (Beebe & Lachmann, 2002; Stern, 1985; Tronick et al., 1978; Tronick & Cohn 1989).

The typical caregiver-infant interaction moves from coordinated to miscoordinated states and back again. Misattunements are normal occurrences, which emerge when one of the parties fails to understand the precise meaning of the other's emotional expression and hence responds inappropriately. If both the caregiver and the child are active in the regulation of the other's behavior, reparation is a jointly regulated process (Tronick et al., 1998). When the caregiver attempts to guess the child's needs, she sometimes gets it right and sometimes wrong; this gives her a sense of what works and of knowing the child's needs and being able to meet them. This physiological regulation becomes a prototype for behavioral interactions (Sroufe, 1979, 1989a).

The caregiver uses attunement and misattunement to transfer her perceptions, ideas, and so on about the child. Attunement and misattunement can be used for better or for worse. Mutual attunement enables intersubjectivity between people and creates a sense of sharing, but if certain categories of experience are not attuned with the caregiver they will fail to develop. The caregiver can play a role in keeping certain emotions from being organized and integrated into the ongoing development of the nervous system. When the infant attempts to repair a misattunement, the misattunement has successfully altered the infant's experience and behavior in the direction that the caregiver wants, which is a common occurrence in the process of socialization. If misattunements are exaggerated and are not balanced with attunements, children will doubt their own experience and assessment of their own as well as the caregiver's state. When the caregiver fails to attune with the infant and instead corrects the child through exaggerated misattunements, the child is left with a feeling of being wrong and unloved. If instead the caregiver attunes with the infant's state and establishes a joint feeling and then alters the experience, the child misses an opportunity to maintain his own experience, which undermines the possibility of establishing an independent identity (Stern, 1985).

Love and Joy

Although misattunements are important occurrences for the ability to distinguish oneself from the caregiver, joy or positive body language are important elements in a secure and safe emotional base. The child is able to initiate, maintain, and terminate social interactions with other people. This is expressed by establishing gaze contact, responding positively to other people's sounds and movements, responding when held, and the tendency to pay attention to human faces and voices. The caregiver's love is a biological prerequisite for the child's ability to live out this innate biological urge. Adaptation relies on social relations, and attachments with others are crucial for personality development (Emde & Sameroff, 1989; Karen, 1998).

Initially, the child's ability to experience positive affects is externally regulated by the caregivers' participation in the psychobiological attunement process. Their love of the child, the affirmation that the child is seen, and the sharing of joy and vitality are crucial for the infant's emotional development. The twinkle in the parents' eyes shows the child their attention, attachment, and love. The reflection that the child sees in the parents' eyes and in their actions tells the child whether he is worthy of being loved. The parents' pride is expressed through the twinkle in their eyes along with their smiles, and their "infatuation" with the child intensifies the feeling of joy. The parents' attitude toward the child shapes his self-perception and sense of self-worth (Øvreeide & Hafstad, 1996; Schore, 2003a; Sørensen, 1996).

The infant forms an attachment bond with the biologically attuned caregiver who maximizes the potential for positive affect. Her facial expressions trigger supportive, mutual-gaze transactions that intensify the child's positive affect, and the child's internal state of joy is communicated back to her. Infants seek stimulation that will activate, excite, and vitalize them, and they enjoy the high-intensity state of joy tremendously. In a good-enough parent-child contact, joy is a frequent occurrence that springs from mutual exchanges. An excited, happy baby seeks high activation levels, where one additional drop of excitement in the nervous system would cause discomfort and distress. Bringing the infant into this joy-filled state of excitement requires the careful and precise regulation of arousal, keeping it just below the point of overflowing where the situation becomes unbearable. This form of joy is vital for the development of the attachment bond (Schore, 2001a 2003b; Stern, 1990).

Joy is a product of mutual regulation in connection with social exchanges. The exchange of smiles often begins on a low level of intensity with overlapping waves of exchanges, and the baby and caregiver have the same degree of control of the buildup. The dyadic contact in the early caregiver-infant interaction is about having fun, taking an interest in each other, and enjoying spending time together. Experiences that create shared joy, interest, curiosity, excitement, peaceful moments, and so on are what build a mutual relationship based on love. Stern (1990) summed this up with a quote from the song "Suite: Judy Blue Eyes" by Crosby, Stills and Nash: "Fear is the lock and laughter the key to your heart." Parents who enjoy spending time with their child will engage in behavior initiated by the child, such as "I'm gonna come and get you" games, which make the child laugh. To the infant, this type of play is the most stimulating experience possible, and in addition to cementing the attachment bond between parents and child (Stern, 1998b) it is also important for the release of dopamine, which produces joy and curiosity and lets the nervous system practice handling increasing levels of arousal.

The Importance of Gaze Contact for Communication

In the womb, the sense of hearing and the kinesthetic sense are both well-developed, and the sense of smell is active from birth. At birth, the visuomotor system becomes active instantly, and the newborn child is not only able to see but is born with reflexes that make it possible to follow and fixate on an object. Gaze becomes increasingly important, and an infant who is about 6 weeks old has the capacity to maintain selective visual orientation and focus. It is only in the past few decades that we have begun to recognize the key role of gaze contact in relation to communication and attachment behavior. The infant has an innate focus system that makes objects at a distance of 12–16 inches stand out most clearly, and indeed, mothers tend to keep the infant at just this distance. Extended gaze contact leads to the most intense form of interpersonal communication. Gaze contact gives an impression of someone else's affective state, and the time structure of gaze contact offers a hint of the readiness to receive and process social information. Mutual gaze contact is a highly charged interpersonal event that increases the general arousal or activation state and elicits powerful emotions. Two people do not normally engage in gaze contact for more than approximately 10 seconds without speaking. The mother and the infant can easily remain in a mutual gaze contact for 30 seconds or more. In play sequences the mother looks at the child approximately 70% of the time while also speaking or making sounds. During feeding the mother will not simultaneously look at the child and speak, since this combination is a strong invitation to play and would tend to interrupt the feeding (Anders, 1989; Stern, 1977).

In social interactions, the child will withdraw from gaze contact to regulate his own arousal level; this is reflected in the child's heart rate. Five seconds before the child looks away, the heart rate increases; 5 seconds after the child has looked away, the heart rate drops back to normal, and immediately after this the infant begins to look at the caregiver again. Often, it is the infant who regulates the gaze contact, and from around the age of 2–3 months the child withdraws from gaze contact sooner than the caregiver. If the caregiver responds to the infant's signal and lowers the stimulation level, the child is able to regulate his arousal. When the child resumes looking at the caregiver, an appropriate interactive regulation will be resumed, but if the caregiver "chases" the child instead and increases the stimulus level when the child looks away, the child's self-regulation will be disturbed (Beebe & Stern, 1977; Brazelton, Koslowski, & Main, 1974; Stern, 1977).

Basic Attention Regulation

The child's development goes from mutual gaze contact to following someone else's gaze to looking at something new within a shared attentive focus. Joint attention connects two individuals. Following someone else's gaze opens a joint experiential domain, and seeing something new makes it possible to collect information for learning. Joint attention means two minds sharing one particular focus, eventually engaging in a joint attention focus on an external reality (Fonagy, 2005). In relation to the very young infant, the adult takes a physical position that enables the adult to pay close attention to the infant's mimicry while also allowing the infant to examine the caregiver's mimicry and responses. The caregiver's observation of the infant's attention supports the child, meets the child's needs, and enhances the child's vitality. Already at the age of 4–6 months the child has become used to certain ways of organizing communication, and the child shows signs of discomfort or rejection when invited into an unfamiliar context.

The caregiver's attention to the child intensifies the child's concentration on whatever is in focus and triggers the attunement process. This focus supports and satisfies the child and enhances the child's vitality. If the caregiver fails to affirm the child's expression, the child misses an opportunity to initiate affective attunement. The caregiver's behavior must be vitalizing enough to capture the child's fleeting attention. Her contact initiatives and the child's responses create a focus that enhances the child's ability to maintain concentration for extended periods of time. She must adapt to the child's rhythm before attempting to lead the child into a stimulating situation, and she must offer distinct affirmation that she is aware of the infant's focus and perception. Her selective attention helps maintain and stall the infant's attention flow, and this lets the child center and enhance concentration (Øvreeide & Hafstad, 1996).

From Dyadic Relationship to Triangulated Relationships

Initially, the focus of attention is on events within the caregiver-infant dyad. Already at the age of 3–4 months, the infant begins to take an interest in objects, such as a rattle, a mobile, and such, and gradually the focus of attention begins to shift from dyadic to triadic, that is, the caregiver and infant begin to direct their joint focus of attention to a third object.

Very early in the infant's life, the caregiver engages in attunement, where she follows the infant's attention as it is aimed at something outside the relationship, such as lights, a pattern, an object, and so on. She defines and labels what the infant sees by introducing and naming objects and later individuals that she thinks the child should know. This enhances the child's attention and concentration. Once the child understands the caregiver, the child will turn and look at her, which elicits a familiar smile and a new episode of joint attention. The caregiver helps establish the focus of attention outside the dyad by following the infant's attention; she affirms what the child sees and thus acknowledges the child along with his experience. At the same time, the child receives new information, as what is seen is verbalized. This triangulates the child's world and helps develop the child's ability to focus on objects outside the dyad, which is simultaneously embraced by the relationship. This ability develops gradually, and eventually the caregiver is able to focus her attention in a particular direction or on a particular object. The infant understands the intent and engages in a joint field of attention or what is referred to as joint attention (Bertelsen, 1994; Øvreeide, 2001a). Triangulation is important for the infant's ability to master new social relationships. Once the infant is triangulated into a new social situation, the caregiver confirms and acknowledges the relationship, and the child feels supported (Øvreeide & Hafstad, 1996; Rye, 1997).

Parents often attribute qualities to their child that have not yet developed but which are promoted by the parents' perception. Their ideas about who the child is and will become are a key psychodynamic driving force, provided these ideas are not too far removed from the infant's actual competences, a topic we will discuss in the following section.

Proximal Zone of Development and the Impact of the Parents' Internal Representations

Already from birth parents tend to have ideas about their baby, and the child is perceived as a personality with his own motives. Both the parents' ability to empathize with the child's immediate needs and their ideas about developmental potentials constitute a developmental driving force for the child (Bertelsen, 1994). Zeanah, Keener, Stewart, and Anders (1985) found that parents are overwhelmingly likely to attribute positive qualities to their unborn and newborn babies. The absence of these positive distortions is a serious prognostic indication in parents.

Stern has repeatedly pointed out how self-perception depends on other people's presence and actions, and how the child is pulled forward by the caregiver, who develops an interaction now with her future child

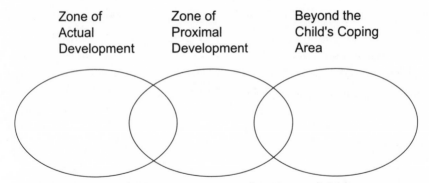

Figure 1.2. Vygotsky's theory about the zone of proximal development

(Stern, 1995, p. 51). More than 60 years ago, Vygotsky (1978) studied the basic mechanisms for the internalization of higher psychological functions and described how the normal psychological development process emerges within interaction through external regulation; only later is it incorporated into the personality in the form of self-regulation. The internalization process takes place within what he called the proximal zone of development, which he defined as the functions that have not yet developed but which are emerging. What the child is currently only capable of with help from the caregiver, he will be able to manage independently in the future. Thus, all higher functions develop as the result of social interaction. Vygotsky divided children's communication process into three zones of development (see Fig. 1.2). The first zone is what the child already masters, and the next is the child's zone of proximal development, while the third zone lies outside the child's current resources and coping capacity. The caregiver must respect the child's autonomy within his current coping capacity and promote the child's zone of proximal development by making room for experimentation.

It is the caregiver's responsibility to protect and assist the child through the zone that lies beyond his current coping capacity. She prepares both herself and her child for the next level while supporting the child on his current level. The infant's nervous system develops rapidly and constantly drives the child into new areas of experience. When the caregiver communicates with the infant, she constantly drives the child forward by staying one step ahead, yet always close enough to match the child's zone of proximal development. The child is guided in the direction of development; for example, when the child takes his first steps, he focuses on his mother's eyes and looks at her with joy and excitement. The mother shares the child's enthusiasm, offers praise, and encourages the child to take one more step. The caregiver "scaffolds" the skills that the child is moving toward but has yet to master (Øvreeide, 2002).

Summary

Mastering psychological intimacy requires an intersubjective system where caregiver and child are able to attune with one another, an aspect that receives less attention in attachment theories. Children who take part in well-regulated interactions will internalize positive expectations of their own competencies. Attachment theories address two opposite poles: intimacy and security at one end and investigative curiosity at the other. The attachment system is constructed for physical closeness and group attachment, not for actual psychological intimacy. People are able to feel strongly connected to each other without experiencing the depth that develops through psychological closeness or intimacy. Stern (2004) argued for the importance of distinguishing the attachment system from intersubjectivity, theoretically as well as clinically. The most powerful connection between people occurs when attachment, intersubjectivity, and love are combined. As Stern puts it, "Relationships are made up of interactions. Relationships are the cumulative constructed history of interactions, a history that bears on the present in the form of expectations actualized during an ongoing interaction, and on the future in the form of expectations (conscious or not) about upcoming interactions" (1989, p. 54).

In this chapter I have described the intersubjective space and the infant's innate conditions for entering into this space. The next chapter focuses on the infant's biological capacity for self-regulation, communication, and attachment formations and the importance of interactions and intersubjectivity for the infant's neuroaffective development. Among other topics, Chapter 2 discusses how innate, hidden regulators form the basis for the construction of internal representations and the mentalization capacity.

CHAPTER TWO

The Impact of
Dynamic Interaction on
Brain Development

One of the most mysterious aspects of the parent-infant (or any human) relationship is how one knows what another is experiencing subjectively. Yet this very ability underlies what we mean by empathy.

Daniel Stern (1984, p. 3)

We are born as social beings, and the infant must be invited to participate in human culture. Without the necessary social experience with a loving caregiver, the child's nervous system will not develop properly. As described in Chapter 1, the brain's emotional maturation relies on the way in which the infant relates to the caregiver's nervous system in close interactions through affect regulation patterns. Through this relationship, the brain self-organizes, which creates a unique mind with the capacity to develop increasingly complex states.

The human brain is a biologically open system, which is capable of incorporating and integrating growing amounts of meaningful information; this makes the nervous system highly plastic, complex, and well organized. Even though the human brain is self-organizing, this process can only take place in a dyadic context, a process that involves two brain systems. The infant's immature nervous system has a limited capacity for self-organization, partly due to limits in information processing speed, motor control, and the capacity of the sensory and associative areas (Tronick, 1998).

The interpersonal relationship fosters a unique pattern of neural circuits, and thus, every human brain is unique, the product of both genes and environment. The infant's responses to stimuli activate certain neurons, which form circuits and neural patterns. When this pattern is later reactivated, it engages in a constant process of change that modifies and reinforces the original pattern. Once a neural circuit has been established, it is easily reactivated through implicit (unconscious) memory tracks.

The self-organization of the infant's nervous system takes place within finely tuned microinteractions with a caregiver, and these early interactive experiences form the child's basic internal representations. Schore (1994) distinguished between interactive affect regulation and autoregulation as the components of self-regulation. The infant's innate functions are autoregulatory, meaning that the nervous system is regulated through deep-seated innate subcortical functions that, through the infant's interaction with the environment, become increasingly self-regulating. The autoregulatory functions become increasingly self-regulating through active learning in interactive situations, which promotes the brain's ability to self-organize. Autoregulation is the innate condition for engaging in dyadic self-regulation, and Sroufe (1996), among others, described how regulation goes from being largely dyadic to being individual. The goal of self-regulation is to be both oneself and in contact with the other, which is the precondition for the subsequent emergence of the empathy capacity and mentalization functions. The infant's dependence on the caregiver's regulatory functions is gradually replaced by the internalized capacity for self-regulation; the child's capacity for understanding mental states develops through the brain's self-organization. The literature uses many different terms to describe the capacity to understand and reflect on mental states in oneself and others, including metacognition, metacognitive monitoring, mentalized affectivity, theory of mind, mentalization, and so on. For simplicity's sake, in this context I have chosen to use the last term. In this chapter, I describe how the infant's biological makeup is a precondition for engaging in interaction with a primary caregiver. I also describe how the relationship affects the child's capacity for establishing attachment, helps develop the child's identity, and prepares the nervous system for engaging in mentalizing behavior. In the first section, I review the physiological conditions for personality maturation.

The Hidden Regulators

Myron Hofer, who is a professor of developmental psychobiology, has studied parent-infant relationships for years, including various patterns of the long-term effect of maternal behavior on the offspring's sensitivity to stress and disease and the role of maternal separation. Through studies of mammalian (especially rodent) attachment behavior, he has studied the hidden regulatory processes of attachment relationships as evident, for example, when infant rats are separated from their mothers. Hofer (1984a, 1984b, 1990, 1995) found that separation can be associated with the loss of various components in the young animal's relationship with the mother such as feeding, body temperature, and tactile and olfactory stimulation.

When infant rats are separated from their mothers and kept warm, their resting pulse drops to the same level as that of separated infant rats at normal room temperature. The difference between the two groups of separated rats is that the infant rats in the warmer environment become hyperactive, while the ones that are kept at normal room temperature become depressive. When the infant rats are with their mothers but do not receive nourishment for many hours their activity response is normal, but their resting pulse drops, as if they had been separated. Hofer concluded that the lower heart rate, which is related to the loss of milk, is probably due to a lack of "fuel" in the organism, while hyperactivity or depressiveness is related to the loss of tactile stimulation. Infant rats that receive milk through a feeding tube can be regulated to practically any resting pulse, depending on how much milk they consume during the 24 hours of their separation.

When the infant rats are kept warm and receive irregular tactile stimulation, corresponding to the natural care cycle, it is possible to regulate their activation levels. The more tactile stimulation the infant rats receive, the closer to normal is their activation level. The infant rats use tactile, temperature, and olfactory stimuli from the mother's body to maintain contact and to locate and grasp her teats. When the infant rats are separated from their mothers for more than 24 hours, their sleep cycle is disturbed, and dream sleep is reduced significantly. There is also a drop in the production of growth hormones, which is reestablished to normal levels if the infant rats are allowed to engage in brief interactions with nonnursing females and receive tactile stimulation.

Early permanent separation of infant rats from their mothers can produce long-term changes in the rats' sensitivity to stress later in life. For
example, Hofer (1975) found a substantial increase in severe immobilization behavior and stomach ulcers in 30-day-old rats that had been
separated from their mothers before they were 15 days old. A lack of
early caregiver regulation of the rats' nervous system was found to pre-
dispose for stress regulation disorders when the rats got older. Hofer
points out that many of the cognitive and physical changes that occur,
for example, in human grieving are surprisingly similar to those seen in
acute sensory deprivation of infant rats. Physiological functions involving the circulatory system, sleep/wake cycles, appetite, energy, and crying are all disturbed when infant rats are separated from their caregiver
for an extended period.

Like human infants, infant mice and rats respond with attachment
calls (ultrasonic cries in the case of mice and rats) when they are separated from their caregiver. Fear of strangers, which occurs in human infants around the age of 6 months, is a behavioral system that differs from
the attachment system, and which develops far later in rats, dogs, primates, and humans. Infant rats, for example, are not afraid of strangers
until they are around 25 days old. Hofer believed that the development
of the attachment systems and the formation of attachment patterns are
driven by the early regulatory interactions through hidden physiological
regulators. The physiological or homeostatic state that is achieved when
the infant engages in appropriate interactions with the caregiver is experienced as a pleasant state and emotionally safe. The opioid system (the
body's internal morphine system) is a powerful biological system that
plays a key role in caregiver-infant interaction and rewards attachment
processes.

The hidden regulators play a key role in early human relationships, as
they do in other mammals, and some continue to be in effect into adulthood. Field et al. (1986) found these hidden regulators in their study of
40 preterm children born before the 36th week of gestation and weigh-
ing less than 53 ounces (1,500 grams). Half the children were given tactile and kinesthetic stimulation for periods of 15 minutes a day for 2
weeks. Both the stimulated group and the control group were largely
identical with regard to initial weight, age, and total calorie intake. The
stimulated babies gained around 0.9 ounces (25 grams), while the control group only gained some 0.56 ounces (16 grams) per day. The babies

in the stimulated group developed faster and were released from hospital 6 days earlier than the control group.

Hofer pointed out that the regulating interactions and the hidden regulators that emerge in early infancy shape the internal representations and become an organizing mental structure for motivation and affect. The caregiving regulators control the neural systems that initiate arousal regulation, sleep/wake cycles, hunger/satiety, temperature regulation, reward, and motivation. The early hidden regulators and their interweaving with internal representations may explain why separation involves such profound and intense emotions of anxiety, anger, and despair, even in adults.

The level of physiological regulation in the early caregiver-infant relationship helps shape personality and determine the individual's future vulnerability to stress. The individual regulation processes form the basis for emotional states and the formation of internal representations. The basic regulation processes, however, come under increasing hierarchical control due to the maturation of the nervous system. As Fonagy (2003) pointed out, Hofer's research demonstrates that the evolutionary survival value of the close relationship with the caregiver goes far beyond mere protection and can be expanded to include a regulation of the infant's physiological and behavioral system. Attachment is not an end in itself but a system that evolution has used to carry out essential physiological and psychological tasks. Fonagy pointed out that Hofer's restating of attachment to regulatory processes offers a different explanation of the necessity of attachment. What is lost with separation is a long-term opportunity to develop a regulatory mechanism for assessing and reorganizing mental content. Attachment is a process that creates a complex and adaptive behavioral system, where certain mental functions are specifically human. As the development of the biological regulators in infant rats depends on the caregiver-infant unit, later mentalizing functions (see Chapter 3) in humans develop through repeated interactions between mother and child.

Among others, Hofer was inspired by John Bowlby, who was one of the first to suggest that infants and young children have innate needs for a warm, close, and lasting relationship with one caregiver, and that a lack of attachment can cause severe and permanent damage to the personality. In the following section I offer a brief outline of the basis of attachment theory.

Exploration and Attachment Behavior

Bowlby argued that attachment developed through evolution and emerged at the time when mammals needed to familiarize themselves with their environment in order to get by, as they were no longer able to survive on instinctive dictates alone. The attachment system improves the infant's chances of survival by allowing the child's immature nervous system to draw on the caregivers' more mature functions to organize the child's life processes. The caregivers' parental response is encoded in the child's procedural memory as expectations that help the child feel safe. This required mammals to rely on their mothers as a source of protection and of the knowledge needed to maximize their chances of survival. Human offspring require parental care for a very long time, and the human attachment system is highly complex. The attachment system is built into the child's interaction with the caregivers, and psychosocial development and the development of attachment are closely related (Allen, 2002; Herman & van der Kolk, 1987; Papousek & Papousek, 1981).

As mentioned earlier, in humans we distinguish between attachment patterns and attachment behavior. Attachment behavior can be observed when the child seeks reassurance, care, and comfort. Attachment patterns develop through a process where the child has at least one caregiver who provides basic and necessary care, and who interacts with the child. The child's and caregiver's ability to engage in attuned interaction promotes the child's ability to attach in a way that is unique to primates. The attachment bond develops gradually through the interaction, which means that at an early stage the infant prefers the primary caregiver over others. Once the attachment relationship has been formed, it is lasting, even in the face of subsequent separation. Attachment behavior is activated when the infant is separated from the caregiver, and research has shown that the stronger the attachment to certain attachment figures, the greater the likelihood of subsequent attachments with others (Mortensen, 2001).

According to Bowlby and Ainsworth, the infant is in a preattachment state until the age of approximately 3 months, mainly because the sensory and cognitive systems are not yet mature enough for the infant to identify specific external objects as attachment figures. As the sensorimotor system matures and connects with the deeper area of the prefrontal cortex (cingulate gyrus), attachment behavior develops, observable through the infant's separation anxiety and approach behavior around the age of 6 months. Even if the parents frighten the child, after the age of 6 months the child will nevertheless develop attachment behavior and seek the parents. Before the age of 3 months, the infant does not perceive whether or not the caregiver offers a secure base, so the choice of attachment object is not corrected with regard to security and survival, and the infant attaches even if the parents are perceived as frightening. An infant seeks to attune with a caregiver but is unable to assess her appropriateness. The infant attaches to anyone who is available (Kraemer, 1992; Lewis, Amini, & Lannon, 2001; Neumann, 1994).

Most mammals respond with attachment behavior when the mother disappears. In lower mammals, such as rats, attachment behavior is triggered when the mother abandons the infant for a prolonged period. The attachment system is only one of multiple behavior systems, and the relationship between the attachment system and the exploration system is particularly important. Ainsworth (1972) believed that there is a dynamic equilibrium between attachment and exploration, and that infants use the attachment figure as a secure base for exploration. If the infant is sick, tired, or scared, or if the attachment figure is suddenly absent, the exploration behavior is absent. If the child is fit, and the attachment figure is present, the child is more likely to engage in exploration behavior. Thus, it is biologically determined that attachment behavior is more important than exploration behavior. The balance between attachment and exploration is partially regulated by the sense of fear. A frightened child will display more attachment behavior and seek protection to enhance the chances of survival. Thus, attachment behavior serves a survival purpose. When the child feels safe, he gradually moves away from the secure base and independently explores the environment (Smith, 2003).

Most children form attachments with more than one person, but there is a limit to the number of attachment relationships. The attachment figures are placed in a hierarchy, and all caregivers are not treated the same. An attachment hierarchy means that the child prefers one main attachment figure when it comes to seeking comfort and security; Bowlby called this phenomenon monotropy (Smith, 2003). If the primary caregiver is absent, the child will approach someone else and eventually a stranger (Bretherton, 1980). The factors that determine which caregiver is most primary include the amount of time spent with the infant, the quality of the care, the caregiver's emotional investment in the child, and so on (Cassidy, 1999; Colin, 1996; Fonagy, 2001). If the caregiver disappears, the child may dismantle the emotional bonds and form new attachment bonds with someone who is willing and has the resources to provide care. A child who fails to distinguish between primary attachment relationships and others is likely to have a severe attachment disorder. The child may be attached to a caregiver without developing attachment behavior. This is evident, for example, in children who were raised by unpredictable and abusive parents.

Usually, the mother is the person who spends the most time with the infant, and thus she often becomes the target of the attachment behavior. Under normal circumstances parents will feel a strong urge to hold, comfort, protect, and feed the infant. To some extent, the parents' behavior adheres to a predetermined pattern, but social and cultural perceptions determine the actual expression of this behavior. Attachment and relationships are formed when caregiver and infant engage in attunement through present moments (Schore, 1994; Tetzchner, 2002; Trevarthen, 1993a, 1993b).

The Infant's Biological Capacity for Communicating and Forming Attachments

Infants are social beings, and our social disposition is part of the human genetic makeup. Infants have a biological capacity that enables them to participate in social interaction and communication, for example through imitation. As mentioned in Chapter 1, there appears to be an innate structure in the central nervous system for imitating behavior, which is supported by a particular category of neurons called mirror neurons. The ability to imitate emotional expressions and facial movements helps the infant discover his own humanity and forms the basis for identity development (Gallese, 2001). The mirror neurons were first discovered in the premotor cortex, but Fogassi et al. (2005) also found the neurons to be present in the base of the parietal lobes and therefore believed that the mirror neurons in this area may be responsible for not only encoding and mirroring motor action but also for understanding the other person's intent with the action. This ability remains useful throughout life. For example, when our mouth movements mimic another's, we gain insight into what the other person is doing. Bråten (2006) mentions that when we engage in mirroring, we involve ourselves in the other person's action as if we were seated in the center of the other person's body. This involvement means that we sometimes virtually try to come to the other's assistance, unwittingly and involuntarily. This happens, for example, if we are watching a high jumper and flex our muscles when he jumps, or when we lean in to "help" the tightrope walker balance. Autistic children probably have a defect in the innate preference for and imitation of human behavior, as they are much more prone to copy behavior and fail to distinguish between human movements and objects in motion. In a clinical anecdote, Bråten (2006) explained how a mother raises her palms toward her baby, who responds by raising his palms, so that the palms connect as in the patty-cake game. The infant does what the mother does, so we would call it imitation. The infant sees the mother's palms but not the backs of her hands. When he raises his hands toward hers, he sees the backs of his own hands but does not place the backs of his hands against her palms. According to Stern, autistic children will turn their hands so that they see the palms of their own hands, while typically developing infants incorporate the caregiver's point of view and mirror her action, touching their own palms to hers. When autistic children copy, they only achieve a partial share of the caregiver's experience (Stern, 2004). Bråten described how people with autism have difficulty mirroring objects and lack the ability for intersubjective empathy, because they are unable to involve themselves in someone else's movement based on that person's body position. This is an innate ability in typically developing infants.

The child not only imitates the expression but also perceives that the expression corresponds to a particular sensory impression or background emotion or vitality affect. This is because the components of the nervous system that link imitation and sensory impression are already fully developed in the seventh month of gestation. Newborn children are able to perform the same facial muscle movements as adults, but they are unable to combine them into facial expressions until the age of around 3–4 months. Only around the age of 6 months are children able to express themselves through the primary emotions that were originally defined by Darwin: joy, anger, anxiety, panic, sadness, surprise, and disgust (Beebe & Lachmann, 2002; Meltzoff, 1993; Trevarthen, 1993a, 1993b).

The variation of emotional dyadic interactions between caregiver and infant are imprinted in the child's developing nervous system and trigger characteristic psychobiological patterns. The dyadic relationship provides the brain with stimuli that lead to the development and differentiation of brain circuits. The first imprinting experiences, which occur immediately after birth, involve olfactory and tactile impressions. This imprinting experience produces the first representations of the mother in the form of olfactory and tactile models, but visual experiences soon take on a key role in the imprinting process (Schore, 1994).

The brain self-regulates and self-organizes through the emotionally attuned communication between caregiver and child, which continues to transform to ever higher levels with the ongoing maturation of the brain. In this communication, the caregiver senses and modulates the infant's motor, nonverbal, and affective expressions, and the communication experiences serve to fine-tune the infant's neural circuitry. In an appropriate contact, the caregiver infers the infant's emotional state based on external behavior; she interacts with the infant and in this process shapes the nervous system's capacity for self-organization. The diversity of interactions between caregiver and infant is imprinted in the child's nervous system. Regardless of the changes in the relationship during the child's development, the caregiver remains an external regulator for the child's internal affective state. The caregiver's active involvement in emotional interactions with the infant is the basis for the formation of internal representations of her as a mother (Rutter & Rutter, 1993; Schore, 1994; Siegel, 1999; Stern, 1985; Trevarthen, 1990).

The nervous system develops in light of the adaptation between internal motivations and external realities. Here it should be noted that the internal motivation is driven by the child's basic needs, where the affects signal a state of need. As Sørensen (2006) pointed out, affect is different from need. Need satisfaction is the objective, and affect regulation, along with physical care, is the means for achieving this objective. As mentioned earlier, the infant's nervous system is biologically adapted to develop in an affectively regulated interaction with a mature nervous system; this is how the child gets to know the environment and achieves need satisfaction. The infant's nervous system will go far to engage with the caregiver's nervous system, and when the infant's needs for mutual affect regulation are met, the child has a sense of pleasure and vitality. The infant's cognitive and emotional skills develop through this emotional communication (Aitken & Trevarthen, 1997; Siegel, 1999). On a neuroaffective level, the caregiver's regulation has a direct impact on the child's biochemical growth processes and promotes the development of new structures. This happens regardless of whether the child was raised in an environment where his needs were met in an emotionally attuned contact or in an environment characterized by abuse or neglect (Beebe & Lachmann, 2002; Perry, 2002; Schore, 1994).

The Neural Basis of Physiobiological and Psychobiological Attunement

The innate capacity for communication enables the infant to adapt to or synchronize with the caregiver's nervous system. This is probably mediated by oscillating neurons and mirror neurons in the nervous system. When caregiver and infant engage in moments of meeting, they move with temporal coordination and thus share an aspect of each other's experience. The infant quickly recognizes events that have common temporal structure. As mentioned earlier, Trevarthen's (1993a, 1993b) experiment demonstrated that an infant prefers synchronization between speech and lip movements, and a lack of synchronization with the caregiver will make the child distressed.

As mentioned earlier, Sander (1977) suggested that the basis for the infant's ability to self-regulate develops during the first few weeks of life through physiobiological regulation, and that the feeling of connectedness springs from the mutual influence of caregiver and infant on one another. The reticular activation system in the brain stem contains neurons that create a temporal structure for brain activity while the child is still in the womb. The production of neurotransmitters in this system controls the activation, receptiveness, and plasticity of the nervous system. The reticular activation system controls sensorimotor activity, selective attention, and curiosity. Motivation stems from an interaction between the reticular activation system, the diencephalon, and the limbic system. The synchronized interaction between caregiver and infant produces joint motivation and attention, and through this experience the infant develops a repertoire of social interactions to draw on in all later interpersonal relationships (Kraemer, 1992; Trevarthen, 1989, 1990).

Physiobiological and psychobiological attunement is the result of the mutual regulation of arousal between caregiver and infant, as the caregiver modulates the infant's energy state through attunement. This requires that the caregiver is sensitive to changes in the infant's states, and that the infant responds to her attempts at activating or reducing arousal. The infant has an innate capacity for creating physiological rhythms in relation to states such as sleep, drowsiness, attention, tension, and so on. These rhythms arise through fluctuations in arousal states that are regulated by the reticular activation system in the brain stem, and it is these rhythms or cycles that lead to the development of self-regulation systems through synchronized attunement (Schore, 1994, 2000; Trevarthen, 1993b).

At any given moment the brain forms a new pattern of neural activity, depending on the current interaction with the environment. For example, when a mother smiles at her child, the child's nervous system forms one pattern of neural activity. When they burst out laughing together, a new pattern is formed, and so on. Neural patterns arise in interaction with the environment, and neural patterns that are established through recurring experiences and high emotional intensity reactivate more easily. Recurring experiences help the nervous system self-organize and achieve stability.

The caregiver's sensitivity to the infant's signals is important for synchronized attunement. When moments of meeting occur, the child's neural circuits coordinate deep into the autonomic and limbic regions of the brain, which in addition to developing the emotional regions of the nervous system also serve to fine-tune bodily functions such as heart rate, breathing, digestion, and so on. Since synchronized attunement takes place in the limbic areas of the brain, the dyadic communication may be referred to as limbic resonance. As mentioned earlier, synchronized attunement or limbic resonance plays a key role in the development of the nervous system and thus also in identity development. The attachment behavior that is evident at the age of 6–9 months develops through affective attunement; it lets the child practice and coordinate attunement processes and thus supports the maturation of brain circuitry (Schore, 2003a).

In humans, achieving limbic resonance requires that an internal state can be expressed externally. Primates are the only animals with sufficiently sophisticated fine motor functions in the face to enable the use of a huge variety of facial expressions. These expressions are partially controlled by cranial nerves in the brain stem. The cranial nerves are connected to circuitry that involves the diencephalon and the limbic system (including the insula and the amygdala) and later connects with an area deep inside the frontal lobes: the orbitofrontal cortex, which enables us to feel and understand facial expressions. Primate and human brains are organized to associate the perception of gaze contact and facial expressions with emotions and meaning, and emotional expressions are communicated facially.

The ability to imitate enables the child to mimic subtle physical responses in the caregiver's facial expression moment by moment and attune with them. The child imitates subtle nuances in postures and facial expressions, and thanks to functions that connect both the brain stem and areas deep in the parietal lobes to the body, including the proprioceptive sense, the infant is able to associate his body sensations with the caregiver. When the infant uses imitation to synchronize with the caregiver's state through body sensations, he develops a sense of the caregiver's emotional state, which is a precursor of empathy. Limbic resonance requires sufficient calm and receptiveness for emotional signals from the other to be perceived and mimicked in the brain stem and the limbic system. Strong reactions, such as angry outbursts, render limbic resonance impossible.

Vitality Affects and Categorical Emotions

As mentioned earlier, the infant has an innate capacity for constructing physiological rhythms or cycles that spring from fluctuations in arousal states that are regulated in the reticular activation system in the brain stem. Over time, these fluctuations develop into the category of affective states that Stern (1985) called vitality affects.

Imitation behavior is the biological foundation for understanding other people's actions, but if all we were capable of was imitating each other, we would merely create mirror images with no possibility of personal differentiation. Therefore, Stern studied how infants adapt to someone else's behavior without formal imitation, and he found that intensity, timing, and shape were the three factors behind the synchronization. By *intensity* he referred to forcefulness; by *timing* he referred to rhythm and duration; and by *shape* he referred to tone of voice, body language, and so on. Stern pointed out that we cannot experience someone else's internal state through intensity, timing, and shape; however, having a sense of someone else's emotional behavior implies that our perception of timing, intensity, and form is transformed into what he calls vitality affects. Vitality affects can best be captured through kinesthetic terms such as surging, bursting, explosive, crescendo, decrescendo, and such. From the moment of birth, the child is exposed to body sensations every day, such as breathing, sucking, feeling hungry, moving, falling asleep, and so on, each with their own vitality affect and temporal form. Vitality affects are associated with being alive, being within one's body, and sensing that feelings well up and fade away (Stern, 1984, 2004).

Vitality affects, which Damasio (1994, 1998) called background emotions springing from the "background states" of the body, emerge constantly and connect with associative networks on higher hierarchic levels of the nervous system. Vitality affects tell the infant whether an emotional quality is pleasant or unpleasant, and they are perceived in the interaction between one's own behavior and body sensations and by observing, testing, and responding to other people's behavior patterns.

We perceive other people's internal states through their vitality, activation level, and discrete affective sensations, such as joy, sadness, anger, and so on. Vitality affects lead to instant changes in emotional states, and in the caregiver-infant relationship they are expressed in a wide variety of parental acts, such as the way the child is picked up, fed, diapered, has his hair brushed, and so on. The child senses the caregiver's way of performing an act as vitality affects. Through the proprioceptive sense the vitality affects give the infant an inner sense or intuition about the caregiver's internal state, which leads to a feeling of connectedness and promotes the ability to establish an attuned connection. The relationship is formed by the multitude of attuned interactions, and if the child fails to develop a basic ability to give and acquire human expressions in an attuned manner, there will be no joint attunement and thus no empathy (Stern, 1984, 1985).

When a sense is activated by something outside the organism, we receive a signal that this is not part of the organism as well as a signal from the site in the body that is activated. The infant perceives sensations bodily. The sensation generates a bodily reaction, depending on what it is that is seen or felt. Damasio argues that the infant does not differentiate between the different senses but instead perceives through an entire body that is moving and sensing. This holistic body sense continues to be implicitly (unconsciously) present in the adult. Vitality affects cannot be reduced to arousal, because they constitute activation patterns over time (Mathiesen, 2004). Vitality affects are also not synonymous with the innate primary emotions that Darwin described, and which are now referred to as categorical affects. Categorical affects are associated with certain facial expressions, which are social signals that are understood by everybody, regardless of their environment and culture. Stern (2004) clearly stated that there is no link between vitality affects and categorical affects, although other researchers disagree. Among others, Neisser (1993) described categorical affects as vitality affects that merge into differentiated internal states. Vitality affects exist in an uninterrupted process, while categorical affects are not present all the time. The link between vitality affects and categorical affects remains theoretically vague. Based on Neisser's view, a neuroaffective understanding of the difference between vitality affects and categorical affects would be that vitality affects that reach a certain arousal level activate the facial cranial nerves, and the emotional moods register in the facial expression as categorical affects. Vitality affects are sensed in a constant flow of varying sensations, which are occasionally expressed so strongly that the facial cranial nerves are activated. The more complex emotions, which are based on vitality affects and categorical affects, presuppose an exchange between the limbic system and the neocortex.

In early mother-infant interaction, facial and bodily expressions are decoded through categorical affects. Any emotional expression characterizes a categorical affect combined with qualities from the underlying vitality affects. Both vitality affects and categorical affects exist on the brain stem level and are controlled by higher neural systems, and the differentiation of categorical affects does not become clear until around the age of 2 months. Thus, the vitality affects are dominant at birth, while the categorical affects are not differentiated until a few months later. Vitality affects give the categorical affect a certain degree of vitality, which may be exaggerated or restrained, that is, more or less intense. The vitality affects color the expression of the categorical affects. One's way of being angry, happy, or sad is a blend of vitality affects and categorical affects. For example, anger can be rushing, sadness can be gnawing, and something can be exciting and arousing because it is associated with a hint of fear (Sørensen, 2006).

The Early Imprinting of Interaction Experiences, Attachment, and the Formation of Internal Representations

In the 1950s and 1960s, Bowlby developed the concept of internal working models, which is now often referred to as internal representations. Bowlby assumed that infants establish internal representations of their world and attachment figures while simultaneously developing complementary internal representations of their own self, based partially on their perceptions about how valued or devalued, competent or incompetent they are in the eyes of the attachment figure (Smith, 2003). In this section I discuss the early imprinting of interaction experiences, which develop into internal representations.

Bowlby based his concept of internal working models on the way in which wasps navigate. Wasps form an internal model of surroundings, which enables them to navigate without constantly having to develop new routes from scratch. Bowlby believed that while wasps and many other species rely on this principle, there must be more sophisticated models for people to enter into close relationships and develop a sense of another person's likely response. The earliest attachment experiences are acquired through imprinting, but as the brain matures the child gradually becomes able to preserve images of internal representations (Karen, 1998).

Internal working models or internal representations, to use the term that is more common today, are constructed through the self-experience of being with others, initially with the caregiver. The presence of internal representations means that children are able to form expectations, adjust their interactions, and control future interactions. By paying attention to their own state, infants are able to recognize themselves in interactions with caregivers, which is the condition for entering into and re-creating new relationships. When an infant imitates the caregiver and acts and feels like her in the given moment, the infant will begin to form a representation of how he feels inside while being with the caregiver in that particular way. Internal representations are formed on the basis of perceiving oneself as involved in human interactions, and they consist of memories of interactions with others. They are made possible by the cross-modal ability to integrate and coordinate sensations, perceptions, affects, and so on. Internal representations are nonverbal and deal with acting and being, and they are templates for being with another person.

Key to the internal representations is the affective state that characterizes the representations and gives them value (Emde, 1989; Fonagy et
al., 2002; Schore, 1994; Stern, 1997).

As mentioned earlier, Stern (1985) has pointed out that it is the combination of joy and interest that motivates attachment, and that these
two factors are the main indicators of affective attunement. The infant is
attached through the caregiver's psychobiologically attuned regulation,
which not only reduces negative affect but also increases the likelihood
of positive affect. Affective regulation involves an intensification of positive emotions, which is a prerequisite for the development of a more
complex self-organization. Regulated affective interactions with a familiar and predictable primary caregiver not only produce a sense of being
secure, they also promote a positively charged curiosity that vitalizes the
explorative behavior with regard to new social interactions. Positive
emotions are essential for the child's development because they produce
social involvement and an interest in an expanding world. With sufficiently positive emotional exchanges and an emotionally available caregiver, the infant will develop curiosity and a positive sense of increased
mastery and control. When activated, these psychophysiological need
states will prevail over ordinary need states; for example, the child will
prefer social play and the stimulation from joy over satisfying a hunger
need (Emde, 1989; Schore, 1994; Stern, 1990). Left to their own devices,
infants will not be able to push themselves into the necessary high-
arousal states, such as the experience of high-intensity joy and laughter
that is required to stimulate the nervous system. Similarly, the relationship with the caregiver promotes the possibility of an emotional sense of
feeling delimitation, feeling attachment, feeling loved, and so on (Neisser, 1993).

The reticular activation system in the brain stem, which is responsible
for regulating arousal, matures exactly during the period when mother
and infant attune emotionally with one another. The infant's nervous
system is being trained to handle a growing level of arousal, for example,
through play and laughter, which means that the nervous system develops a higher degree of resilience as well as a capacity for self-regulation.
The regulation of most of the neurotransmitters also matures in early
infancy and is probably experience dependent. The excitement stemming from seeing the caregiver's happy face is probably triggered by a
release of dopamine, a neurotransmitter that is associated with reward.

Dopamine stimulates the opioid system (the body's internal morphine system), which in turn activates the dopamine circuits. Dopamine facilitates the establishment of neural connections, and it is vitalizing and promotes the maturation of the limbic and prefrontal regions. The activation of the opioid system increases both the caregiver's and the infant's happiness and encourages play behavior (Schore, 1994, 2003a).

The infant is constantly examining the environment in order to become familiar with it, beginning with sensorimotor programs of behavior such as sucking, gripping, listening, vocalizing, and moving arms and joints. The sensorimotor programs create the first mental representations of the caregiver, partly through the ability to adapt through imitation. The infant's imagery and internal representations are determined to a high degree by the sort of experiences that infant has through supported and attuned communication with the caregivers. The child's sense of self is shaped by previous and current attunements and misattunements (Stern, 1984). In other words, the child's early relational experiences shape an internal representation that organizes and governs emotions, behavior, attention, memory, and cognition, which merges into what we call attachment. Bowlby's (1973) theory is based on the assumption that the child's expectations of attachment figures stem from actual interaction experiences. A child with a secure attachment will be less disposed to acute or chronic fear and will be able to explore the world and achieve separation in a healthy and natural way. If the internal representation involves an insecure attachment the child will not have the sense of a secure base, and the development of normal behavior such as play behavior, curiosity, and social interactions will be impaired.

People with different attachment histories have different behavior patterns and brain structures, and the internal representations are a long-term factor in the personality structure (Main, Kaplan, & Cassidy, 1985). Cumulative dyadic and triadic interaction experiences shape the internal representations that gradually develop into a template or pattern for adaptive behavior. The internal representations are not static models but develop and change with altered life conditions together with close caregivers, reorganizing and developing, as memory does with new learning. Internal representations are formed in the infant's interactions with the environment and through the infant's ability to reorganize patterns, to form expectations of what is predictable and different, and to categorize these differences (Beebe & Lachmann, 2002; Karr-Morse &

Wiley, 1997; Siegel, 1999). The child's contact with the caregiver re-volves around mutual regulation, and these experiences shape the child's internal representations. Emotional states can be associated with the in-fant's imprinting during early experiences, and experiences later in life, for example separation experiences, may involve fragments of sensa-tions that stem from the earliest experiences. Attachment formation consists of internal representations that are imprinted in our nervous system as the result of interactions with the primary caregivers and the infant's expectations of the relationship. Secure attachment is associ-ated with physiological encoding of the experience that physiological homeostasis can be reestablished with appropriate support from the caregiver (Hofer, 1995; Schore, 1994).

Internal representations are shaped by the child's history and, as the brain matures and object permanence develops, the child becomes able to preserve internal representations even in the absence of the original situation. As Schibbye (2005) pointed out, internal representations re-flect a sort of internalization process where intersubjective relationships turn intrasubjective, for example, with the internalization of the emo-tional experience of being praised or humiliated by a parent. The child shapes the internal representations from within and contributes with his own interpretation and subjective perceptions of the interaction. For ex-ample, a child may have a stern internal representation that has become part of the himself through representations of relationships that involve him. The internal representations contribute to an understanding of the environment, make it more predictable, and are crucial for the child's management of all future relationships. The child may have separate at-tachment strategies in relation to separate caregivers, and different rela-tionships may shape the child's neurobiological state in relation to different interactions. The activation of a specific neurological circuit under the presence of a specific relationship is an adaptive process that demonstrates the child's mental flexibility.

From External Regulation to a Self-Organizing Nervous System

Right from birth, all regulating interactions with the environment have self-regulating consequences. During infancy, the child's affects are regulated by the mother, but the child becomes increasingly capable of regulating his own emotions.

Based on the caregiver's external regulation, the child gradually develops the capacity for self-regulation as the nervous system matures. In a stable, competently regulated, dyadic system between child and caregiver, the externally regulated interaction experiences gradually lead to the development of self-regulation and internal coping strategies that are incorporated into the child's psychological organization (Sander, 1988). Depending on the caregiver, the child, and the dyad, the child will be more or less able to handle his own self-regulating processes, and over time the harmony of the regulation may be preserved or improved, or it may deteriorate. Different nervous systems have different degrees of flexibility or rigidity, and the child becomes increasingly capable of taking the initiative to alter his own states, which may alter the relationship. When the child has the experience of being able to affect the relationship through his own actions, self-regulation becomes a more active intersubjective skill. As the child develops, he organizes a higher degree of internal experience or mentalizing functions that are important for self-regulation.

Through balanced emotional stimulation, the caregiver facilitates the growth of neural circuits in and among autonomic, limbic, and cortical structures in the child's brain; these circuits mediate self-regulating functions. Regulatory skills promote the continued expansion of arousal, affects, and the complexity of the brain. Expanding neural circuitry makes it possible to intensify affects, which in turn connect and lead to the development of even more complex emotions. Expanded affect regulation patterns lead to increased self-understanding (Schore, 1994). The child's autonomic nervous system is sensitive, and the caregiver has a direct influence on rhythms of activity and passivity. Her rhythmic attention and attunement with the infant serve to regulate neurochemical and hormonal functions, and the child's autonomic nervous system, which matures in early infancy, is particularly sensitive to changes in temporal structures. The caregiver's patterns of attunement, misattunement, social engagement, and disengagement are very important for the maturation of sympathetic and parasympathetic components of the child's autonomic nervous system. The autonomic nervous system plays a key role in intensifying and maintaining affects and in modulating their intensity. When the autonomic nervous system matures and connects with the orbitofrontal cortex, the child is able to modulate his own affects. Through the caregiver's attuned contact with the child, the autonomic nervous system develops from primitive autonomic regulation into a flexible self-regulating system. The autonomic nervous system develops through the ability to communicate via facial expressions, gaze contact, vocalization, and gestures. Intersubjective regulation causes a shift from passive to active coping and self-regulating skills (Porges, 1995, 1996, 1997; Schore, 2002, 2003a).

As mentioned earlier, joy-filled caregiver-infant contact is regulated via the dopamine system and the opioid system. The attachment system expands through positively regulated, synchronized play experiences. This excitement stimulates the stress hormones and noradrenaline-based activity in the child's sympathetic nervous system. When the mother soothes and comforts the child, the parasympathetic nervous system is activated through a regulation of the child's oxytocin level due to sensory stimuli such as facial expressions, tone of voice, and touch expressing warmth and recognizability. Oxytocin, opioids, stress hormones, and noradrenalin are all involved in attachment behavior (Schore, 2003b; Uvnäs-Moberg, 1997). When attachment behavior triggers the release of endogenous opioids, discomfort is reduced, and the sense of satisfaction is increased. When emotional regulation is effective, the nervous system organizes coherently, but when it fails, the brain's complexity and capacity for self-organization are reduced. The effects of misattunement are borne by the child, but the inadequacy arises through the interaction. Massive and chronic misattunement or lack of attunement causes affective disorders, which I discuss in Chapter 4. When arousal levels and joy-filled transactions intensify, the limbic circuits are activated and integrate with the orbitofrontal cortex, among other areas. The infant requires extensive external support to be able to regulate arousal, and gradually learns to alleviate unpleasant arousal states without outside assistance.

Through the caregiver's interaction with the infant's innate biological abilities, the caregiver can create temporary or long-term changes in the neurotransmitter system. For example, studies of deprived monkeys have shown that the attachment system requires psychobiological regulation. Among other findings, monkeys that were raised by surrogate mothers have an underdeveloped serotonin and noradrenaline circuit. This condition results in hypersensitivity to noradrenaline and an elevated stress response. Serotonin calms the nervous system, while nora-drenaline heightens attention. The infant's release of the stress hormone cortisol is modulated by the caregiver's behavior, and when the caregiver is absent or fails to respond to the child's attempts at getting attention, the child enters a state of despair. When the child is exposed to stress, the hypothalamus releases a stress hormone (corticotropin-releasing factor, CRF), which activates another hormone in the pituitary gland (adrenocorticotropic hormone, ACTH), which triggers the production of cortisol in the adrenal gland (hypothalamus-pituitary-adrenal, HPA, re-action). Cortisol adds energy to enable the organism to overcome the stress (Gerhardt, 2004). The caregiver's contact with the child acts to instantly inhibit the child's stress response, and the child's exploratory behavior increases. The caregiver's ability to interpret and respond to the child's signals affects the child's own stress modulation. Stephen Suomi, who has done intensive studies into attachment behavior in rhe-sus monkeys, found that the stress system (the HPA system) is activated when infant rhesus monkeys are separated from their mothers, and that reunion and comforting lead to a drastic drop in heart rate (Anders & Zeanah, 1984; Hofer, 1983, 1984a; Karr-Morse & Wiley, 1997; Kraemer, 1992; Schore, 1994; Suomi, 2000).

Arousal Regulation, Optimal Frustration, and the Development of the Nervous System

As mentioned earlier, the child develops psychological agility and strength through interactions that take him or her from positive to negative and back to positive affect, and the child learns to handle stressful situa-tions through misattunements, gradually developing the ability to self-regulate out of these states with support from the caregiver. Dyadic reparative transactions offer comfort, and arousal regulation makes re-union possible. In the long term, this promotes the child's sense of being able to self-regulate to overcome unpleasant experiences. The ability to repair misattunements and thus reestablish broken attachment bonds relies on a reactivation of the attachment system. An essential and chal-lenging aspect of caregiving is to help the child contain growing amounts of intense affective arousal while making sure to comfort the child be-fore he is emotionally overwhelmed (see Fig. 2.1). To be able to perform

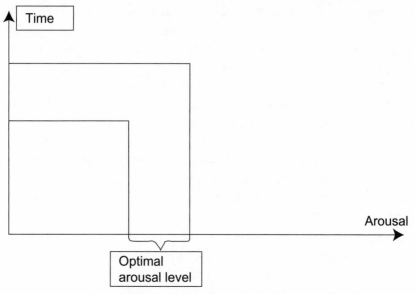

Figure 2.1. Optimal arousal level

these regulatory functions, the caregiver must be able to take a containing and maintaining role in relation to the infant's stressful state and
avoid being overwhelmed by the child's frustration (Schore, 1994,
2003b).

During the first year of life, the infant develops growing tolerance to
increasing amounts of arousal and uses the communicative experiences
with the caregiver to regulate his internal states. The development of the
nervous system depends on the child receiving sufficient and relevant
stimulation for the various regions to be activated. Both excessive and
insufficient levels of arousal will impair the development process (Neisser, 1993; Schore, 1994).

A child who experiences optimal frustration, and who in repairing
misattunements is able to control tension by approaching the mother to
be comforted, will develop a flexible and adaptive nervous system that is
capable of managing stressful experiences. However, if the child is raised
in an unpredictable environment characterized by abuse and neglect,
the nervous system is likely to remain poorly organized with a tendency
to become chaotic. Our psychological development is affected by good
as well as bad experiences, and certain experiences may have a protective effect even if they feel negative when they happen. The ability to

cope with stressful situations comes from living through and overcoming them, not from avoiding them (Perry, 1994; Rutter & Rutter, 1993). For example, when the child begins to be physically active and is able to get around independently, the mother should inhibit or reduce the child's arousal. At this time the caregiver-infant contact goes from being supportive to being more inhibiting and socializing (Izard, 1991).

When children are able to apply more cognitive strategies, they will begin to form an impression of the causes of comfort and discomfort and of the responses or behaviors required to achieve comfort and avoid or reduce discomfort. A child who is rarely soothed or comforted will have difficulty developing methods for self-soothing and will have fewer possibilities for self-regulation. Children who are exposed to chronic and high levels of anger that are not balanced and modified or who are exposed to unpredictable attacks will fail to develop effective coping strategies in relation to these high levels of arousal. In these situations, the child may opt for coping strategies that let him or her maintain integrity, but which involve behavior that others describe as maladaptive, inappropriate, or psychologically dysfunctional.

All nervous systems have a tolerance level where the intensity of arousal can be handled without major disruption. If thinking or behavior is disturbed, for example, if the arousal level exceeds the tolerance level, the child will devote energy to overcoming the stressful state. Some children have a low tolerance level, while others can tolerate high levels of arousal without experiencing discomfort or disorders of attention. The tolerance level may also vary with the state of the nervous system at any given moment and with the social context. For example, the child is more tolerant of stressful situations when surrounded by secure caregivers. Beyond the tolerance level, psychological functions are impaired, and activity is overtaken by the subcortical areas. For example, the autonomic nervous system triggers sympathetic activation; this acts through the stress system to cause inner discomfort and physical tension, which may in turn trigger inappropriate emotional behavior. If these states are intensified, higher cognitive functions will be impaired, such as abstract thinking and self-reflection. When the child has developed self-regulating skills, the cortical processes may inhibit the activation of the limbic system and thus prevent inappropriate emotional impulses from being expressed (Cozolino, 2000).

The development of arousal-regulating capacities, self-organization, and coping strategies across a variety of situations depends on the caregivers, temperamental factors, vulnerability factors, and so on. Securely attached children seem to be resilient to stress activation. For example, the number of cortisol receptors in the hippocampus increases when rats and monkeys grow up in a nurturing and stimulating environment with adequate maternal behavior, and these animals display less fearful behavior and lower noradrenaline and adrenaline levels in relation to stressors (Cicchetti & Tucker, 1994; Gunnar & Barr, 1998; Hofer, 1984a).

None of us are born with the ability to regulate emotional reactions. It is an essential process to learn to handle arousal states, so that the nervous system can enter a state of high arousal without disintegrating, that is, regressing to lower levels of functioning. The attachment system is an open biosocial homeostatic regulatory system, and it is crucial for a young infant to have a caregiver who can offer protection from states that he is not yet able to handle or regulate. If the caregiver is not able to support the infant when he disintegrates, the infant is forced into innate autonomic regulation, which is anxiety provoking. The caregiver's ability to sense momentary changes in the infant's mental states and to support the child's self-regulation is essential for personality development.

Early Interaction Experience as the Basis for Mentalization

The human nervous system develops on the basis of an early relationship, and the ability to mentalize, that is, to understand one's own as well as other people's emotions, can only develop within a relationship. The ability to interpret other people's behavior requires the ability to perceive other people's desires and needs. Communication relies on the caregiver's and the child's ability to understand one another's intentions, and the basis for this ability precedes the development of language functions. The child is born into a social world and will, in all likelihood, be involved in social interactions. The child's perception of reality is constructed within a community, and some situations are so unambiguously good or threatening from the infant's perspective that he needs no help defining them. Other situations are so unclear that adults are the only reliable source for the child to rely on in grasping them (Tetzchner, 2002).

The caregiver's understanding of the child's signals promotes secure attachment, and the caregiver's attunement with the child's mental state indicates that the adult is able to regulate the child's internal state. Wilfred Bion (1962) emphasized the importance of the mother's capacity to mentally contain and acknowledge the infant and his intentions. Secure attachment means that the caregiver is able to symbolize the child's internal state, and a secure attachment with a mother figure predicts a good mentalizing capacity in the child. Fonagy (2001) points out that mentalization capacity relies on the caregiver's ability to infer the infant's subtle needs and attune to them emotionally. Ideally, the caregiver is able to handle the child's distress while also communicating an understanding of the cause for the distress by accepting the child's affective state without being overwhelmed by the child's emotions. She is able to combine positive emotional communication with a normally negative emotional state, for example, by pretending that she is angry but with a positive, warm twinkle in her eye. The emotional message that contradicts the distress while also displaying it can act as a secure and containing base for the infant. Recurring interactions with a mother who is able to reflect, contain, and soothe distress will enhance the infant's ability to tolerate negative affect states and increase the child's confidence that the need for external support for self-regulation will be met.

Through intersubjective communication, mentalization develops into an intrapsychic ability that only emerges fully in the context of a secure attachment relationship (Fonagy et al., 1995). Based on two decades of research, Fonagy and Target (2002) have shown that secure attachment in early childhood enables the mentalization capacity to develop along the paths that have been prepared through evolution. There is a strong link between secure attachment and the development of capacities that require curiosity, the ability to play, symbolic skills, frustration tolerance, ego strength, ego control, social cognitive skills, self-awareness, and so on. Thus, secure attachment promotes the development of the key self-regulating mechanisms in the brain that enable us to self-regulate and empathize. The mentalization capacity develops on several different levels (see Fig. 2.2): in the insula and the amygdala, in the orbitofrontal cortex, and between areas deep inside the prefrontal cortex (medial frontal, orbitofrontal, and dorsolateral regions). Development on the insula-amygdala level involves an intuitive and bodily sense of one's own emotions, while the orbitofrontal cortex level has to do with

Figure 2.2. The child's emotional progress

empathy. Due to connections between structures in the prefrontal cortex, the child is able to associate affects with a capacity for perceiving, predicting, and recognizing other people's emotions (Fonagy, 2003).

Attachment researchers such as Bretherton, Bates, Benigni, Camaioni, and Volterra (1979) and Main (1993) saw the degree of harmony in the parent-child relationship as a key factor for the development of symbolic mental functions and argue that secure attachment liberates the necessary resources for the child to develop cognitive symbolic functions. Fonagy and Target (1996) said that playing makes the child aware of the distinction between an internal experience and an external reality. For example, when the father pretends to be a dangerous troll, the realistic setting for the relationship has been temporarily suspended, which lets the child test ideas, roles, and perspectives that gradually contribute to an expanded ability to understand oneself in relation to others. The mental mechanism is important in determining which phenotype is expressed, since it is not the child's observable behavior or objective environment that determines the genetic expression but rather the child's assessment of the social environment. The mentalization capacity is profoundly affected by the child's previous experiences. As Fonagy and Target (2002) pointed out, human attachment confers a crucial survival benefit as it allows us to develop social intelligence and sense-making abilities. Self-reflection and the ability to reflect on other people's motives, actions, and so on develop through the earliest relationships, even if they do not become evident until later in life. Reflections on one's own internal states can be a powerful source of understanding how or what someone else might feel. Our capacity for mentalization creates consistency and distinctions between internal and external experiential worlds and enables us to maintain an understanding of someone else's perspective and distinguish between our own and someone else's perceptions (Hart, 2008).

Feeling that others feel one's feelings and are able to respond appropriately to one's communication are vital for the development of secure attachment and for the brain's self-organization and development. The mentalization capacity is crucial for the development of close relationships throughout life and lets us strengthen and intensify emotional bonds (Fonagy et al., 2002; Siegel, 1999).

Summary

The child's nervous system and personality mature through countless subtle processes of attunement and misattunement and joy-filled experiences that unfold in the child's interaction with the primary caregivers. The caregivers' love, empathy with, and understanding of the child determine the child's behavior and lay the foundation for ways of being together that further the child's psychological survival, and which help shape the child's personality. In this chapter I have described the role of the caregiver's early interactions with the child in relation to the development of the nervous system. In the next chapter I review the child's developmental stage or levels of mental organization and their development process in close interactions, initially with the caregivers and later in other important relationships.

CHAPTER THREE

Psychodynamic Levels of Mental Organization

From birth onwards, the infant is using its expanding coping capacities to interact with the social environment.

Schore (2001a, p. 11)

We have also learned that the developmental course of infancy is not linear. There are normative times of qualitative change or transformation, sometimes referred to as times of biobehavioral shift. These have been noted to take place at two to three months, six to nine months, around one year, and at eighteen to twenty-one months.

Robert Emde (1989, p. 40)

Between 1949 and 1990, neurologist Paul MacLean (1967, 1970, 1973, 1990) developed his controversial theory of the "triune brain." (see Fig. 3.1) This theory proposes a brain structure in three tiers, which he viewed as quantum leaps in the evolution of the human brain. He believed that the human brain has evolved over millions of years from the bottom up, with higher centers evolving as superstructures to lower, older parts. MacLean believed that there is a difference in kind between the chemical and structural properties of the three tiers, and that they represent distinct evolutionary levels. They are mutually connected through massive nerve paths and act as three brains in one. He uses the term triune to express that the whole is greater than the sum of its parts, because their mutual exchange means that each of the three brain structures contains more information than it would if it operated in isolation. Even if the three brain structures are closely related, each brain struc-

The neomammalian brain handles
mental and cognitive reasoning. This
part of the brain contains the centers that
fuse and make sense of perceptions and
enable complex emotions.

The paleomammalian brain refines basic
affects, such as anxiety and anger, and
thus enables the development of social
emotions and expanded memory functions.

The reptilian brain regulates basic bodily
functions, works instinctively, and handles
basic motor planning and basic affects,
including seeking certain aspects of anxiety
behavior, and aggression.

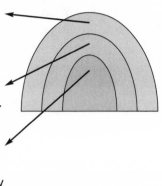

Figure 3.1. The triune brain, with a description of the
different levels of mental organization.

ture is capable of functioning partially independently. However, the
boundaries between the three structures are not clearly defined, and it is
difficult to locate a function as belonging exclusively within one brain
structure or another. MacLean divided the three brain structures into
three different forms of mentation, with the most primitive layer performing protomentation, the middle layer emotomentation, and the third
layer ratiomentation. He referred to the most primitive layer as the reptilian brain, because vital reptilian functions correspond to functions
deep inside the brain stem and the diencephalon. This part of the brain
regulates basic bodily functions, works instinctively, and handles basic
motor planning and basic affects, including seeking, certain aspects of
anxiety behavior, and aggression. The second layer he called the paleomammalian (older mammalian) brain or the limbic system. This part of
the brain refines basic affects, such as anxiety and anger, and thus enables the development of social emotions and expanded memory functions. Both the reptilian brain and the paleomammalian brain lack the
neural circuits required for verbal communication. The third layer he
called the neomammalian brain; it consists of the neocortex, which handles mental and cognitive reasoning. This part of the brain contains the
centers that fuse and make sense of perceptions and enable complex

emotions. It expands an emotion by adding our thoughts about the emotion and enables us to symbolize, inhibit impulses, and imagine what others feel.

Both Luria and Freud were inspired by the neurophysiologist Hughlings Jackson, who in the early 1900s stated that the human brain consists of a hierarchy of functional levels, and that through discrete developmental stages the structures that develop early in life are progressively replaced by later-emerging structures, which thus expand the complexity of the brain. The functions that were present on the preceding levels become subordinate to the higher and later-developing levels (Schore, 2003b). John Bowlby has emphasized that the brain's hierarchical structure provides increased adaptability and efficiency but that it also makes the nervous system more vulnerable, as it increases the risk of errors that will make the subsequent system less efficient (Mortensen, 2001). Development does not simply consist of adding new capacities; it is in fact a transformation of organization or capacities in accordance with the regularities in the hierarchical integration of the brain. Both before and after birth, brain development is a process of organization, disorganization, and reorganization, and there can be no reorganization without disorganization. The brain's development process goes from a relatively global state and lack of differentiation to a state of increased differentiation and hierarchical integration (Cicchetti, Toth, & Lynch, 1995; Schore, 1994).

There is no single body of research that covers the growth of the nervous system in childhood. But combined findings have identified certain growth periods. Some researchers, including Fischer and Rose (1994), call for caution, pointing out that we do not yet have sufficient data to draw clear-cut conclusions. Chugani, Phelps, and Mazziotta's (1987) research, one of the few research materials to describe the growth periods of the nervous system through positron emission tomography (PET) scans, shows that in infants under 5 weeks of age the most active parts of the brain are the sensory cortex, the thalamus, brain stem structures, and the vermis in the cerebellum; this selection of areas corresponds largely to the area that MacLean called the protomentation level. Initially, vision is handled by subcortical visual structures, and the primary visual cortex does not become active until the age of 2–3 months. Around 3 months, areas in the parietal, temporal, and occipital cortices, the bas-

8-month-old infants' development level:
Activation of the frontal and occipital
cortices is initiated.

3-month-old infants' development level:
Parietal, temporal, and occipital cortices,
the basal ganglia, and the cerebellum.

5-week-old infants' developmental level:
The sensory cortex, the thalamus, brain
stem structures, and the vermis in the
cerebellum.

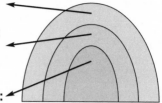

Figure 3.2. The triune brain based on Chugani et al.'s theory
of developmental progression.

al ganglia, and the cerebellum are activated, corresponding largely to the
area that MacLean referred to as the seat of emotomentation. At this
time the child begins to be capable of volitional control of motor functions and vision. At 8 months of age, the frontal and occipital cortices are
activated, and the development of ratiomentation begins (see Fig. 3.2).

Chugani et al.'s (1987) study is often quoted, but it should be noted
that the subjects were 29 children aged 5 days to 15 years, all suffering
from some form of epilepsy (Bruer, 1999). According to Schore (2002),
MRI studies reveal that the brain volume increases rapidly during the
first 2 years of life, and that the brain's anatomy at the age of 2 years resembles the adult brain anatomy. All the main bundles of nerve fibers
have been formed when the child is 3 years old, and children under 2
years of age have a larger volume in the right than in the left hemisphere.
The sensorimotor areas of the cortex develop before the associative areas. The brain is fully developed around the age of 20–23 years. A Swed-
ish study of children and youth aged 1–21 years found that their nervous
systems showed growth periods at the age of 1–2 years, 7–8 years, 11–12
years, and 14–15 years (Fischer & Rose, 1994).

The amygdala, which is located deep inside the limbic system, is active from birth, and at the time of birth the infant has developed the
startle response and an impulse-based temperament. The cingulate
gyrus, which forms the top of the limbic system, develops at the age of

3–9 months, which means that from this time on, the infant is able to share joy-filled states. At this time the infant also begins to show clear separation behavior, typically at the age of 6–8 months. Here it should be noted that fear-based anxiety, which is amygdala-driven, differs from separation anxiety, since fear is present from birth, while separation anxiety does not occur until the maturation of the cingulate gyrus and hence has a different neurobiological basis (Panksepp, 1998). The orbitofrontal cortex in the prefrontal cortex begins to mature around the age of 8–12 months, which supports the infant's ability to inhibit behavior and regulate emotions; this is also the time when object permanence develops. The orbitofrontal cortex receives sensory input from all sensory modalities and lays the foundation for a subsequent organization of abstract representations. It is the only cortical structure that is directly connected to the hypothalamus, the amygdala, and the reticular activation system in the brain stem (which regulates arousal), and thanks to these connections it is able to modulate behavior and basic needs. Development is not complete until around the age of 20 years, and the prefrontal cortex increasingly gains overall control of other areas of the cortex (Schore, 1994, 2001c). The development of facial recognition and the smile is an example of the infant's emerging functions. For example, a newborn child has endogenous smiles, while the social smile does not emerge until the age of 4–6 weeks. For several months the infant smiles indiscriminately at everyone, but around the age of 6–8 months the infant only smiles at familiar faces, while strangers' faces often trigger fear and crying (Hansen, 2002).

At birth, only certain neural circuits are fully functioning; most are under development, and a few are undifferentiated. The mental organization levels do not change linearly during childhood, but there are huge changes and qualitative shifts at times. Human development takes place in periods of rapid behavioral reorganization, initially evident as a fleeting reaction or behavior under very specific circumstances. Later, behavior becomes increasingly reliable, and specific behaviors are displayed more frequently. During the first 2 years of life, there are substantial changes in the child's subjective perception of the self and others. Organizational changes in the child's nervous system and in the caregivers' interpretation of the child mutually promote each other. Once a mental organization has been formed, it remains active throughout life (Beebe & Lachmann, 2002; Emde, 1989; Sroufe, 1979; Stern, 1985;).

In the following I review the child's levels of mental organization in the light of a variety of theories and observations of children's psychological development and behavior through different stages in life, and I link the observations with theories on neuroaffective development.

The Domain of the Sense of Being in the World, Age 0–2 Months

During the first few months of life the nervous system is still immature, and as Chugani et al.'s (1987) PET scans illustrated, the most active regions at this time are located in the brain stem and deep inside the limbic system. The earliest types of affective behavior are generally physiologically conditioned, that is, they are bodily reactions, triggered by stimulation that affects the autonomic nervous system. Affects develop from states of dissatisfaction or discomfort (Mathiesen, 2004). In the following, I look at the functions the child has to learn to master at this level of mental organization. This period corresponds to the sense of self that Daniel Stern has called the emergent self, where the infant begins to perceive meaning and wholes on a sensory level.

Perception and Sensation

The infant prefers the mother's voice immediately after birth and quickly develops a preference for her individual scent. This distinction intensifies and refines the infant's innate search for closeness and communication with her. The importance of this sense is soon trumped by tactile stimulation. Touch and the development of the kinesthetic sense are crucial for the child's gradual development of a sense of his own existence and boundaries. Even though some senses are more important for the infant than others, newborn children have sensory capacities that enable them to sense and perceive their environment, and right from birth they are partially able to use all their sensory modalities, including vision, hearing, smell, touch, and so on. Cross-modal or amodal perception and vitality affects develop within the first 3 weeks of life and enable the infant to perceive sensory wholes and coherence. Even at this early stage, the infant's experiential world is colored by the specific vitality affects that are awakened, and the vitality affects help the infant orient himself in the world. To have a sense of self or a sense of being in the world, the infant must have a body sense via proprioceptive feedback, internal patterns of tension, and affective qualities that are initially based on vitality affects (Stern, 1985).

The newborn infant does not have separate sensory units based on motor functions, affects, and cognition; these functions are differentiated and only integrate later. Initially, the infant's sense of being goes through the body, as the infant uses his body and receives care (Brodén, 1991). The infant experiences or expresses affects in relation to internal bodily sensations (such as hunger) and in response to touch, tactile sensations, sudden movements, or rapid shifts in position. The loss of physical support or the sense of falling triggers an instant sensory alarm reaction in newborn children, which is activated through deep subcortical areas (including the amygdala and the hypothalamus), and which is expressed through screaming and crying (Joseph, 1993).

As mentioned earlier, Fonagy (2005) noted that a newborn child enjoys engaging in directly imitative behavior, and that infants prefer acts that are part of their own behavioral repertoire. At this time, infants spend a great deal of time paying attention to acts that are a perfect match to their own body movements. At an early stage these observations promote differentiation between the child and the external world. For example, an infant observes that even if he moves an arm, the chair remains in place. In this way, infants build a primary representation of their body as an object that is separate from the surroundings. It is through their own acts that infants begins to appear to themselves and develop a sense of existence and of being. When an infant is engaged in motor activity, such as touching herself, the infant records the signals that are sensed inside the body (proprioceptive signals) as well as the sensory feedback from the part of the body that is being touched—information that differs from when the caregiver touches the infant. In this way, the infant begins to distinguish her own acts from those of others and to distinguish between self and other (Gergely & Watson, 1996, 1999; Schibbye, 2005; Watson, 1994).

Social Functions

The infant's interactions with the caregiver have a powerful effect on what the infant learns and experiences. The caregiver's way of holding the infant, moving, touching, and speaking to the infant, and so on, generates a pattern that triggers a response within the infant. If the infant is exposed to insensitive handling with abrupt movements that are not attuned with the infant's state, innate autoregulatory survival functions in the autonomic nervous system will be activated, either through a parasympathetic response of "going dead" or "freeze" or through sympathetic activation, which triggers negative avoidance reactions and crying.

During this early period the caregiver's time is spent regulating and stabilizing the infant's sleep and hunger, and much of the social interaction takes place through physiobiological regulation, as mentioned earlier. In the regulation the interaction is about soothing and calming, which means modulating vitality affects, among other things, and the caregiver attempts to help the infant transition between the various states in an early and basic form of affect regulation. At this time the infant has not yet developed coping strategies or any psychological defense strategies as protection from the world (Stern, 1985).

During the first 2 months of life, the infant's need for sleep changes, and the child spends more and more time awake. Furthermore, a rhythm is gradually established where the infant is more alert during the day. At this time, the caregiver often sees the infant becoming more interested in contact and in playing. Gaze contact is expanded, the social smile is established, and the infant begins to vocalize socially a few weeks after the social smile has been established. Bower (1977) noted that the social smile emerges 46 weeks after conception, that is, at the age of 1.5–2 months. The endogenous smile emerges during dream sleep as a fleeting feature. Gradually, the smile begins to be triggered by soothing stimulation, often when the infant is asleep or tired, but eventually also when she is awake and alert (Emde, 1989; Sroufe, 1979).

When the infant is awake, she is very interested in and receptive to external stimulation and spends a great deal of time following sounds and visible objects. The infant finds the human face fascinating, and normally caregiver and child have frequent facial and gaze contact. From around week 6 the infant is able to fixate visually on the caregiver's eyes and to maintain gaze fixation, as her eyes expand and light up. The caregiver develops a firm sense that she is the one the infant is looking at, and that the infant responds to her communication (Stern, 1977).

From the outset, the caregiver helps make the infant's actions meaningful through interpretative behavior, and parents treat their children as comprehensible and meaningful beings. A 1-month-old infant is able to associate different types of interactions with different caregivers, and even if the infant has not yet developed a critical sense in relation to the caregivers, the caregivers quickly come to seem predictable to the infant (Stern, 1985).

By the end of the first few months of life the infant is able to engage in simple protoconversations, looking intentionally at the mother, brow furrowed and jaw dropping as signs of concentrated attention, smiling and recognizing the mother's imitative sounds and her smile. Hand movements are often precisely synchronized with lip and tongue movements to shape an integrated expressive act that matches the vocalization, and the infant appears to attune with the caregiver (Trevarthen, 1990).

Neuroaffective Development

At this time, the infant's nervous system is fragile and requires external regulation to avoid being overwhelmed. The infant's cortisol level remains low during the first few months of life, as long as the caregiver is able to support the infant's nervous system through touch, rocking, comforting, and food. The nervous system is unstable and reactive, and cortisol levels can climb dramatically if the infant does not receive the necessary regulation. An infant who is attuned with the caregiver is able to handle more arousal, and it takes more to trigger cortisol production (Gerhardt, 2004; Gunnar & Donzella, 2002).

As mentioned earlier, the caregiver's patterns of attunement, misattunement, social engagement, and disengagement play a key role for the maturation of sympathetic and parasympathetic components in the infant's autonomic nervous system. The autonomic nervous system is essential in intensifying and maintaining affects and in modulating their intensity. Porges (1995, 1996, 1997) has described how the autonomic nervous system develops through the ability to communicate via facial expressions, gaze contact, vocalization, and gestures. The development of the basic regulation of the autonomic functions helps the infant regulate and coordinate arousal level and maintain attention. The infant will experience passing states of discomfort, such as crying, and disengage from the interaction. Through attuned contact with the caregiver, the infant acquires strategies for self-soothing and achieving equilibrium. The imitative behavior lets the infant learn to maintain attention for longer intervals of time, provided the caregiver is able to maintain the infant's fleeting attention through her calm and joy-filled vitality. This enhances the infant's basic capacity for controlling attention.

As we saw in Chugani et al.'s (1987) research, the primary sensory cortex is active from birth. This area plays a key role in the processing of tactile and kinesthetic sensations (Chugani, 1997). The sensory input that emerges in the contact with the mother is involved in shaping and activating neural growth, and by touching the infant the mother provides a tactile stimulation that is pleasant and promotes development, facilitating a lasting balance in the stress response system. Touch stimuli help trigger self-soothing behaviors through the hormone oxytocin, and among other functions the stimulation bolsters the connections between the hypothalamus and the amygdala in the limbic system. Positive and negative sensations are processed in the amygdala and send messages to nuclei in the hypothalamus, which regulates the autonomic nervous system (Panksepp, 1998; Schore, 1994; Uvnäs-Moberg, 1998).

The sense of equilibrium (the vestibular system) is myelinated before birth, and together with the development of the vermis in the cerebellum and structures deep inside the parietal lobes, such as the insula, this gives infants a sense of their own body position in relation to the environment and the ability to coordinate their motor functions. The caregiver's cradling and rocking helps soothe the infant (Anders, 1989), and with the input of these movements, the vermis develops and modulates the production of several neurochemical substances (e.g., noradrenaline and dopamine). The infant actively seeks as much skin stimulation as possible, a prominence that is only later surpassed by visual stimulation.

The amygdala, which in early childhood regulates the intuitive emotions and later acts as the fear center of the nervous system, is active from birth and matures during the first months of life. The maturation of the amygdala develops the infant's ability to share emotional experiences and associate them with external events. In the womb and right after birth the child orients toward familiar stimulations and forms attachments with the people who are there for the child, regardless of their behavior. The infant will seek out the familiar, even if it is unpleasant. This is no doubt the reason why the infant keeps approaching a familiar but abusive parent even while responding with stress and fear. The stress and fear response will not be evident in the infant's response pattern until the child is a few months old, as this is the time when the amygdala is mature enough for aversive learning (Trevarthen, 1989).

Around the age of 2 months there is a qualitative shift in the infant's attention functions. The child's smile and vision become more intentional, and the interaction changes from physiobiological to psychobiological regulation.

The Domain of Interactions and Protoconversation, Age 2–6 Months

Chugani et al. (1987) found that around the age of 2–3 months areas are activated in the parietal, temporal, and occipital cortex, the basal ganglia, and the cerebellum that enable the infant to perform volitional control over motor functions and vision, among other things. Stern referred to ages 2–6 months as an intensely social period in life. During this period the infant develops the feeling of connectedness and pleasure in the contact, which constitutes a sort of emotional reservoir for human bonding. This period corresponds to the sense of self that Stern calls the core self, where the infant begins to sense a distinction between self and environment. The sense of a core self includes a sense of being one coherent physical entity with boundaries and a center that is the source of action. The infant perceives emotions as related to the self, which is a precursor of self-differentiation. During this period certain areas in the limbic system become more active, and the infant begins to be capable of fear and anger responses.

In the 2–6-month period, protoconversations begin to emerge, as the infant acquires the basic nonverbal building blocks of human interaction. The infant also begins to have varied interaction experiences with different caregivers and learns to adapt to different social situations and explore new conditions (Rye, 1997; Stern, 1990).

Perception, Motor Functions, and Sensation

Toward the end of the third month the infant begins to take an interest in objects; this is made possible by far better hand-eye coordination (Stern, 1977). Even so, the 3–4-month-old child's hand is only able to handle one object at a time, and if a child's attention is attracted to something else, he will drop the object he is holding. The infant has difficulty maintaining attention and in communication exchanges is only able to focus on one element at a time. At the age of 2–6 months the infant develops both motor and memory capacities, becomes increasingly curious about the environment, is motivated to examine and learn, and is able to hold onto information for longer intervals. Infants discover that they are able to cause things to happen, both in relation to other people and in relation to the physical world, and they have volitional control over their own acts, which is a crucial element in distinguishing between self and other. Infants develop a sense of coherence, that is, a sense of physical cohesion and a sense that experiences that move together in time are linked (Olson & Strauss, 1984; Stern, 1985).

The infant is able to selectively recognize the parents as early as the age of 2 months in a precursor of attachment behavior, but clear attachment behavior is not evident until around 6–8 months. Despite being able to recognize the parents at 3 months, the infant mostly smiles in interactions without differentiating between strange and familiar faces; only around 5–6 months does the infant draw a clear distinction (Tetzchner, 2002). Four-month-old infants spend more time looking at happy and angry faces than they do looking at neutral faces, but by age 5 months the infant begins to distinguish between sad, scared, and angry faces. Laughter is the most intense expression of positive affect and requires far more arousal than smiling. Laughter is rarely seen before 4 months, although smiles and vocalization are common much sooner. At first, the infant laughs when exposed to powerful stimuli, such as being lifted up into the air; a little later, the infant may laugh at more subtle events such as being tickled or seeing the mother do something funny (Sroufe, 1979, 1996; Tetzchner, 2002).

Protoconversation and Joint Attention

As mentioned earlier, during this period the infant becomes less bound to imitation and gradually begins to select actions in response to communication. Imitation continues to be important, as it provides the mutual regulation of affects. Interactions at this age level consist of nonverbal dialogues, and the child's ability to prefer stimuli that are not imitation but rather protoconversation further develop ability to understand other people's behavior as different from his own and to internalize the perception of others as separate from himself. When an infant begins to respond to communication rather than simply imitating, he begins to develop a sense of being separate from the caregiver by virtue of acting and experiencing differently. Previously, the infant's vitality affects were dominant, but now the infant's internal states are easier to respond to due to the development of categorical affects. The infant begins to expect a response to his actions. From the age of 3–4 months, the infant's repertoire of mutual exchanges of expressions expands, and the purpose of the contact seems to be the achievement of mutual attention and joy. Protoconversations unfold and are regulated in a fashion similar to adult conversations. During this period the caregiver exaggerates the behavior patterns that are elicited by the infant in a way both sufficiently stereotyped and sufficiently varied to hold the infant's attention (Beebe & Lachmann, 2002; Stern, 1977).

Around the age of 5–6 months, the infant develops an even stronger sense of self; for example, she begins to take an interest in gazing at herself in mirrors and examining herself. The child begins to develop a sense of humor, sharing joy-filled moments from mutual experiences and responding with laughter to the caregiver's joy-filled teasing. During this period the infant learns to invite the caregiver to play and to initiate interactions. The infant becomes an expert at initiating, maintaining, avoiding, and ending the flow of a social exchange. The infant begins to develop a sense that she can be involved in regulating interactions and emotions, and that experiences are her own. The infant's sense of being involved in regulating the interaction creates a new basis for developing an understanding of other people's mental states (Fonagy et al., 2002; Stern, 1985; Trevarthen, 1993b).

The 6-month-old infant shows an emergent ability to follow someone else's gaze; the infant looks toward the same object as the adult but stops at the first object that grabs her attention. Only some months later is the infant able to maintain attention. In addition to the stabilization of the autonomic nervous system, basic self-regulation and maintenance of attention require support in maintaining a joint focus through the caregiver's attuned and close contact (Tetzchner, 2002).

Internal Representations and Triadic Interactions

Stern (1977) described how at this age the infant learns to master most of the caregiver's signals and is thus able to perform movements in parallel to hers in a sort of biologically determined choreography of general social interactions. It is during this period that the infant begins to develop internal representations, that is, self-experiences of being with others that enable the infant to have expectations, adjust interactions, and direct future interactions, even if these interactions are beyond the infant's control. The internal representations are formed as the infant acquires schemas for various human emotional expressions and signals, stores the dialogue patterns, and forms a more complex image of the caregiver (Smith, 2001; Sroufe, 1989b; Stern, 1985). The internal representations are organized in the course of the first 6 months through timing, affective attunement, and the regulation of arousal. Infants as young as 3 months have internally represented events, but these are not yet stabilized. Only around the age of 6 months does the infant organize his social capacity in relatively characteristic ways (Beebe & Lachmann, 2002).

Once the infant has incorporated the basic experiences concerning the caregiver's behavior, objects become interesting. The child begins to examine and manipulate objects and seeks to draw the caregiver's attention to the object in relation to emotions and actions. The social triangulation with an object helps develop the child's ability to feel secure and supported when a third object comes between the two, and later this third object is replaced with other persons. As the contact becomes triadic, the interaction between the caregiver and the infant changes, as the caregiver is no longer the sole focus of the child's attention. The point at this stage is to learn about the nature of objects and to learn to deal with triads, not just dyadic relations. Researchers have found that children as young as 3–6 months begin to form a triadic intersubjectivity that includes the mother, the father, and themselves. For example, when the infant plays with dad, and something joy-filled and surprising occurs between them, the infant is likely to turn toward the mother, as if to check that she has noticed (Øvreeide & Hafstad, 1996; Stern, 2004).

Neuroaffective Development

MRI studies have shown that there is a rapid metabolic change in the primary visual cortex around the age of 8 weeks. The development of the occipital cortex enables the infant to register a much larger number of visual stimuli, including the caregiver's emotionally expressive facial expressions. The visual impressions are linked to the limbic system, and this connection plays an essential role in the ability to maintain mutual visual gaze contact and emotional regulation, which is crucial for the formation of relationships throughout life. By the end of the third month nerve fibers in visual cortex develop further (Austin, 1998), which means that the infant's visual world is no longer limited to a radius of approximately 8 inches. Now the child's visual reach is almost as wide as an adult's, although depth perception and the ability to judge distances are not yet fully developed. Face-to-face interactions begin when the infant is around 2 months old, and the child is able to follow the caregiver as she moves away, comes closer again, and moves around the room (Schore, 2003a, Yamada et al., 1997, 2000).

Through the exchange of gaze the infant develops increasing control over the autonomic nervous system. The mutually regulated gaze contact increases sympathetic arousal, and when the infant looks away to avoid contact, parasympathetic activity increases. During this period parts of the cingulate gyrus develop, an area involved in play, separation behavior, laughter, and crying. Because the front part of the cingulate gyrus is so closely connected to the amygdala and the hypothalamus, the infant is now able to be aware of emotions and attune with others, and the ability to control and balance the arousal level develops further. During this period, the cingulate gyrus connects with the parietal regions, which intensifies the deep emotional sensations that are sensed through the body, and which help regulate subtle nuances in social interactions (Donaldson, 1987; Gerhardt, 2004; Rothbart, Evans, & Ahadi, 2000; Schore, 1994, 2003a, 2003b; Trevarthen, 1989).

During this period the infant's sleep pattern becomes more stable, and the natural cortisol rhythm stabilizes, with the highest level occurring in the morning. Only around the age of 4 years does the child have a cortisol rhythm that resembles an adult's (Gerhardt, 2004).

From Interaction to Relationship: The Domain of Relationship Formation, Age 6–12 Months

Chugani et al. (1987) found that the medial part of the frontal lobes and the association areas are activated around the age of 8 months. During this period, self-perception is associated with subjective and mental experiences corresponding to the sense of self that Stern calls the intersubjective self. The child experiences having her own subjective center for emotions, motives, desires, and intentions and sees that others have such a center too, and that experiences can be shared with others. The child's muscles grow stronger, and the motor cortex develops further; this enables the child to move around independently and leads to an expanded sense of cause and effect, the ability to predict events, and an understanding that persons and objects have permanence. Until this age level, emotional memories have probably mainly been processed and stored by the amygdala as wordless, implicit (unconscious) templates.

Until the age of 7 months, the child is not able to move an object from one hand to the other, and the child will not move an object across the body's midline. The child also has difficulty when offered a new object to the same hand and will bump into the new object with a closed hand. Gradually, the child refines these skills but still has difficulty when both hands are full and she wants to accept a new object. Only around the age of 12 months has the child solved this problem, probably thanks to the maturation of the prefrontal regions. At this time, the child will be able to make a choice when offered two different toys, rather than trying to grasp them both (Donaldson, 1987).

Communicative Reference and Attention Control

At 6 months, the infant shows clear behavioral intent. The infant reaches for things that he wants and begins to display more volitional anger responses. At 8–10 months of age, the child will address the caregiver for assistance with a form of communicative intent. Initially, the child looks back and forth between the object and an adult while reaching for something that is out of reach. Later, the child begins to point while vocalizing or looking at the adult.

The child begins to display a repertoire of gestures aimed at making others engage in the attention that he wants, and the child checks the caregiver's facial expression before doing something that seems uncertain or risky. Around the age of 10 months, the infant seeks emotional information from the caregiver as help in interpreting the environment. For example, if the child falls, he will look up at the mother's face to find out how to feel. If the mother expresses anxiety or concern the child cries, but if she is smiling the child may laugh instead. In a well-known experiment where the child has to cross what appears to be a dangerous gap to reach a tempting object, the child checks the mother's face; if her mimicry shows signs of concern or fear, the child does not proceed, but if her mimicry indicates that it is safe to cross, the child dares to explore the obstacle. Thus, the child uses the caregiver to regulate his own emotional states and behaviors. During this period the child relies on the mother's facial expression when exploring and seeks her support. Her failure to approve of this development will inhibit the child's curiosity and sense of security in relation to exploring the world (Davidson & Fox, 1982; Emde, 1984, 1989; Hofer, 1983; Schore, 2001a; Stern, 2004).

Around the age of 9 months, the child is able to maintain focus without being distracted by other stimuli and to find what the adult is looking at, provided the object is within the child's field of vision. The ability to follow the caregiver's gaze direction is not fully in place until around the age of 12 months. This further develops the child's capacity for joint attention. The child begins to point while looking at the caregiver to check whether she is looking at the object that the child is focused on. If she does not share the child's focus of attention, the two may either be brought together or remain isolated (Tetzchner, 2002).

The ability to orient and to shift one's attention to specific stimuli and the ability to maintain focus develops in a slow and gradual process during the first year of life. The directed control of attention, that is, the ability to inhibit a dominant reaction to perform a less dominant one develops during the course of the second year.

Attachment Behavior

From around the age of 7 months, the infant's behavior becomes increasingly goal oriented and based on familiar patterns of organization. Around 6–8 months the infant begins to display fear toward strangers. The relationship with the caregiver becomes a part of the child's internal organization that is not easily replaced, and it is difficult for others to take the caregiver's place and give the infant the necessary stimulation. The caregiver becomes a sort of base, and when, for example, the child is tired or feels insecure, he will turn to the caregiver. Separation behavior occurs when the child is introduced to new situations or unfamiliar persons, and when the caregiver leaves the child. Similarly, the child displays reunion behavior when she returns. The child begins to inhibit behavior and disengage when exposed to new and threatening situations and unfamiliar people. The child's internal representations are modeled on the relationship, and the child's self-image is based on the way the child perceives himself as seen through the caregiver's eyes. For example, an unwanted child will probably have a general feeling of not having any justification and of being unloved (Sroufe, 1989b; Sroufe, Cooper & Deltart, 1992).

Archaic Empathy and Primary Mentalization

At 7–9 months of age, the child begins to discover that physical events are based on underlying mental states, emotions, motives, and intents, and that states of mind can be grasped and compared. The child begins to be able to attribute intents and motivations to others and develops a sense of how well his own emotional state matches someone else's. The child begins to pick up states of mind in the caregiver and to regulate accordingly. The child has the experience of having an internal life with emotions, motives, and intentions and sees that this is true of other people as well. Internal experiences can be shared with others, and it becomes possible to share joint attention, intentions, and affective states. When the child begins to be able to engage in affective attunement, he feels that it is possible to establish a field of resonance with the caregiver. The child notices when an experience can be shared with the caregiver, and when it remains isolated (Stern, 1985).

At this age level, loose associations determine the flow of consciousness, emotions take the place of other emotions, and events that appear to be linked in time produce associations and internal coherence. The child is emotionally associative and does not distinguish between external and internal realities. Freud called this primary process thinking. The French psychoanalyst Pierre Luquet used the term primary mentalization about primary process thinking, and the term secondary mentalization about secondary process thinking, that is, the symbolic and reflexive capacity (Fonagy, 2001). The child's ability to understand his own and others' mental states, that is, the ability to mentalize, is based on the maturation of the prefrontal cortex, which is not initiated until after the age of 12 months. In the present context, I use the term mentalization about the phenomenon that Luquet calls secondary mentalization. Prior to the development of secondary mentalization, the internal representations are partial and tied to specific situations and physical causality, which distorts them and makes projections unavoidable. For example, when the child sees the mother getting angry because he is crying, he is unable to preserve the image of the mother as nice; instead, the child associates his crying with the mother's angry face in the specific situation, with no understanding of the contextual nature of the situation. Fonagy (1991) believes that the ability to convert primary mentalization to secondary mentalization helps mature primitive defense mechanisms into more sophisticated forms. Impulse inhibition and the suppression of needs at the age of 12–18 months mark the first step in the transition from primary to secondary mentalization, but secondary mentalization is not fully developed until the age of 3–4 years, when the defense mechanisms develop into more mature forms. For example, denial and splitting are both immature defense strategies that reflect primary mentalization with an inability to self-reflect, while more mature defense mechanisms such as repression and sublimation only emerge once secondary mentalization has developed. Later in this chapter, in the section about self-protection strategies, I describe the development of defense mechanisms on the various levels of mental organization.

Secondary Intersubjectivity

At this time, the child is capable of entering into more advanced forms of intersubjectivity, where the shared mental states can contain specific intentions, and the child is increasingly able to interpret other people's intentions and convey his own. Intersubjectivity is often so highly synchronized and embedded in a joint attention focus that it lets the infant see an object from the caregiver's point of view. It is often emotionally charged, and in the dyad the caregiver can affect the infant's mood modification, influencing what the infant feels, how much, and whether the infant should feel anything in relation to certain objects in the environment (Schore, 2003a; Stern, 1977, 2004).

Initially, intersubjectivity is a one-way process, but after the age of 12 months the child develops a more generalized understanding of others and is able, on an increasingly advanced cognitive level, to form internal representations of other people's mental states. The child learns to enter into two-way intersubjectivity by knowing that the other person knows what the child knows, and so on. Eventually, the development of intersubjectivity enables self-reflection and intersubjective awareness (Stern, 2004).

Neuroaffective Development

At the age of 6–8 months, the display of attachment behavior, that is, fear of strangers, is a sign that areas in the cingulate gyrus have connected with the autonomic nervous system. In particular, the maturation of the frontal part of the cingulate gyrus lets it assume control over activity that was previously mainly controlled by the amygdala. At 9–12 months, the child begins to move away from and return to the caregiver, first by crawling and later by walking. The attachment patterns that the child formed in the early contact are evident and reflect, for example, the quality of the relationship between the caregivers and the child, among other things with regard to the child's confidence in receiving assistance and cooperating (Schore, 2003a; Stern, 1995, 2004).

During the first 7–9 months of life, the child depends on the caregiver's presence for regulation. It is only when object permanence has developed, thanks to the maturation of the orbitofrontal cortex, that the child begins to be able to maintain internal representations of the interactions with the caregiver, even when she is not currently present. As Sørensen (2005) pointed out, there is a difference between emotional object permanence and the cognitive object permanence that Piaget described in relation to the child's mental development. The object permanence concerning inanimate objects that Piaget finds in the child around the age of 18–20 months is not a prerequisite for developing emotional object permanence. The role of object permanence in relation to personality development has to do with emotions, not with primary perception and cognition. Object permanence begins to develop at the age of 7–9 months but is not fully developed until the age of 3 years. As Mortensen (2001), among others, pointed out, achieving mature forms of object permanence is a lifelong endeavor. When emergent object permanence begins to develop, the child enjoys playing with the permanence of objects, as in the game of peekaboo. At 7–9 months of age, the child is often able to sit upright and to crawl, begins to be able to move around independently, and, thanks to object permanence, objects are no longer "out of sight, out of mind" (Emde, 1989; Sroufe, 1989a; Stern, 1977, 1985).

The maturation of the orbitofrontal cortex enables the child to form a mental image of others, an ability that is a prerequisite for emotional object permanence. With the development of the orbitofrontal region, the child begins to perceive continuity between past, present, and future, a crucial feature that distinguishes interaction from relationship. The child is able to preserve interactions over time, that is, to enter into relationships. At this time, any dysfunction in the contact between child and caregiver will begin to be evident as a relational disorder that the child will bring into other relations as well.

The internal representation that replaces the caregiver when she is absent helps the child achieve impulse inhibition and self-soothing. The child begins to be able to establish transitional objects to aid self-regulation and emotional relief by imitating the interaction with the caregiver. By establishing internal representations of the caregiver, the child can preserve an internal image of her to guide his behavior (Bråten, 1993).

The memory capacity changes considerably after the first year of life due to the maturation of the hippocampus and the orbitofrontal development, which represents the transition from recognition to recall (Schacter & Moscovitch, 1984). Recognition is present in functions that merely require an intact hippocampus function, while recall requires an activation of the prefrontal cortex. The maturation of the hippocampus also supports the child's self-regulating mechanisms, protecting the nervous system from being under- or overstimulated (Goldman-Rakic, 1987; Schore, 1994).

From the age of 10–12 months, the infant is able to handle increasing levels of joy and excitement in the dyadic contact with the caregiver and a lasting feeling of joy or happiness. The joy-filled experiences help develop the basis of pride, and during this time there is a substantial increase in positive affect and a reduction of negative affect. The child engages in agitated, unmodulated dopamine-based activity with boundless energy that conveys excited behavior and gives the child a sense of being the center of the world. This is a manic and self-centered period, which occurs just before the connection between the limbic system and the orbitofrontal cortex is sufficiently established. The high levels of arousal are initiated through sympathetic activity and lead to an increased resting pulse, which is reduced once the orbitofrontal cortex is capable of inhibiting the sympathetic arousal. It is the activity in the reticular activation system in the brain stem that triggers the amount of arousal required to give the child this boundless energy and the ability to be constantly active. For example, injury in the orbitofrontal cortex in monkeys will cause hyperactivity, and the maturation of the orbitofrontal cortex stops the child's tendency toward constant motor activity (Hofer, 1984b; Schore, 1994; Sroufe, 1979). This inhibition begins around the age of 12 months and affects the child's development from 12 to 18 months.

Narcissistic Deflation: The Domain of Emergent Socialization, Age 12–18 months

At the age of 12–18 months, when the child's omnipotent excitement and narcissistic joy are at their peak, the orbitofrontal cortex develops further, which contributes to the self-regulation of affect. At the age of 12 months, the child is able to inhibit certain impulses in order to realize others, and the child has a sense of different options. As the orbitofrontal cortex develops, the first presymbolic representations emerge, mediating the emergent capacity for affect regulation, and the child begins to construct mental representations of possible future states.

At 12 months, children are very interested in their own mirror image. They enjoy touching the mirror, maybe smiling at it, looking behind the mirror in a search for the child they see, and so on. At this time a child does not know that the mirror reflects a representation of himself. Only around the age of 20 months does the child recognize himself in a mirror and have a sufficient sense of self not to point at his own image as if the mirror were showing another child. If a child has a red spot on her nose, before the age of 18–20 months she will attempt to rub the spot off the child in the mirror; only after this age will she rub the spot off her own nose. A 12-month-old child still has difficulty distinguishing between her own and other people's emotions despite a clear sense of self. For example, a child will often begin to cry if the caregiver hurts herself or examine his own fingers when another child hurts her fingers. At the age of 14 months, the child begins to perceive someone else's pain and tries to help, for example by going to the adults for help. Only at the age of 20–24 months will the child attempt to comfort the other person or display other forms of caring behavior (Karr-Morse & Wiley, 1997).

While the ability to preserve internal images is established around the age of 12 months, the ability to hold mental representations of other people's mental representations only develops around 18 months. This is one more step on the path to a more mature form of object permanence that only emerges much later, which involves perceiving oneself and others as constant entities regardless of which state of mind characterizes the child or the other person. The child is still a long way from being able to preserve permanence in a way that does not leave him or her at the mercy of his or her emotions. The precursor of this form of understanding emerges through imitation behavior, protoconversations, and affective attunement and develops with the maturation of the orbitofrontal cortex (Baron-Cohen, 1995). The ability to hold mental representations of other people's mental representations further develops children's self-differentiation, as it enables them to distinguish between their own and someone else's experiences and internal representations. Children begin to develop a sense of how they are perceived by others and to see things from other people's perspectives. Mentalization enables us to imagine and understand someone else's internal experiences, which is the basis of empathy and compassion (Schibbye, 2005).

At the age of 14–20 months the child begins to separate physically and psychologically from the caregiver. At this stage, compared with an insecurely attached child, a securely attached child is more autonomous and more likely to call for the caregiver's attention when challenged beyond his capabilities. A secure attachment relationship is a prerequisite for autonomy. During this period the child begins to develop his own volition but is still keen to make sure that the relationship remains intact and is reestablished. The child develops a sense of permanence in the relationship, and by developing coping strategies in relation to recovery from misattunements the child develops competences that enhance his self-esteem (Sroufe, 1989a).

Language Development and Social Functions

At the age of 15–18 months, the child develops a greater awareness of the possibility of conveying experiences to others through linguistic meaning and context. The child begins to display emotions such as pride and embarrassment and to demand objects with statements such as "That's mine." Language development is rooted in dialogue and personal experience, and words draw their meaning from actual interaction experiences. The child begins to use gestures at the same time as he speaks his first words.

During the second year of life, the role of the caregiver changes from caregiving to socialization, and the caregivers display behavior that make the child inhibit unlimited exploration, aggression, and so on. At 12–18 months, the child inhabits a self-centered world and is puzzled to discover that others may have different thoughts and emotions. For example, the child does not understand that the mother is unable to feel what the child feels (Fonagy, 2005). Tulkin and Kagan's (1972) research showed that for mothers of 10-month-old infants, 90% of their physical and verbal behavior involves love, play, and care, while only 5% involves inhibiting the child from continuing specific activities. At 14 months, the child spends approximately 6 hours a day in stimulation-seeking, explorative play. Interactions with the caregiver are characterized by a higher ratio of social interventions than play behavior, which facilitates the growth of the inhibiting structure in the orbitofrontal cortex. On average, mothers of 12–17-month-old children express a prohibition once every 9 minutes, which requires a high degree of impulse control from the child.

Shame and Regulating the Shame Response: Narcissistic Deflation

Feelings of shame or embarrassment begin to emerge around the age of 12–14 months (Schore, 1994, 2003b). When shame occurs it immediately inhibits the child's curiosity and pleasure and stops explorative behavior. The development of shame is an innate biological capacity that is seen in all social predator mammals (such as canines), but not in social prey mammals (such as rabbits). Like humans, canine mothers also shame their offspring if they fail to adapt to the group.

When the caregiver wants the child to stop a particular behavior, she uses stress-inducing gazes, facial expressions, or vocalizations. Shame is activated during the caregiver's presence through misattunement, and the child experiences the sudden shift from high to low arousal as an unpleasant negative affect state. The shaming mechanism regulates the child's omnipotent, grandiose, manic, agitated, and excited state and requires a deflation of the child's feeling of omnipotence, that is, a mechanism that is capable of reducing the child's arousal and promoting development of a more balanced self (see Fig. 3.3). Shame is a biological mechanism that helps develop an internal value system, and which serves an essential regulating function that lets the caregiver effectively

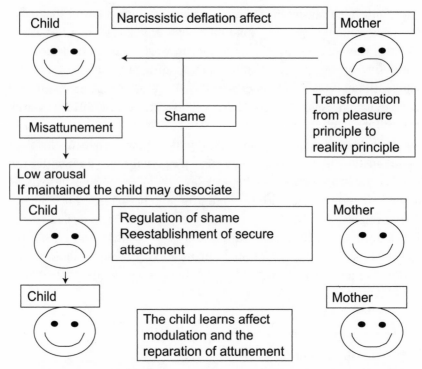

Figure 3.3. The narcissism of 15–16-month-old children is particularly vulnerable to deflation. When the joy-filled, excited child unexpectedly encounters a face express-ing misattunement, the result is a narcissistic deflation affect. The child is thrust into a low-arousal sate, which he is unable to autoregulate. Shame represents the rapid shift from a positive high-arousal state to a negative low-arousal state.

socialize her offspring. Shame experiences are important for achieving self-regulation and a superego structure.

When the caregiver begins to inhibit the child's explorative behavior, the result is often a clash of wills, and the child is frustrated. At this stage, the caregiver must be able to tolerate and contain stressful misat-tunements and communicate the paradoxical message that even though the child is important and his needs and interests are special, these needs are no more amazing and unique than anybody else's. This form of misattunement between caregiver and child is important for the child's differentiation and eventual independence from the caregiver and en-ables the child to develop self-regulating skills (Schore, 1994).

Even though shame promotes development, it is a powerful experience, and the intensity and duration needs to be regulated. Prolonged states of shame are harmful, and even if the infant is capable of modulating negative emotional states, these states will continue to escalate in intensity and duration if the caregiver does not assist the child in this modulation. Keeping the child in a state of shame for a prolonged period can cause damage that may later develop into a personality disorder. At this level of development the child is not able to self-regulate the painful state without the caregiver's assistance; the child depends on her support to modulate and relieve the negative affective state. Shame is a powerful regulator in the relationship, and the child seeks reunion by looking at and reaching for the caregiver. If she responds, is emotionally available, and supports the child's affect regulation, attunement can be resumed. This attunement process transforms the child's narcissistic rage to more mature forms of aggression. Shame reparation is important for delicate regulatory skills in social interactions with others, for example, in balancing one's own needs with those of others (Schore, 1994, 2003a).

Neuroaffective Understanding of the Shame Response

The caregiver's altered status as an agent of socialization contributes to the maturation of the orbitofrontal cortex, which handles the regulation of emotional states. The development of shame requires a certain level of cortisol. Slightly elevated cortisol increases concentration and facilitates the growth of noradrenaline-based connections from the brain stem to the prefrontal cortex. Noradrenaline probably helps mature the orbitofrontal cortex, and at the same time the orbitofrontal cortex connects with deep subcortical structures such as the hypothalamus, which regulates the autonomic nervous system, among other functions. The caregiver's prohibition leads to an inhibition of high-arousal states (among other functions, it inhibits the production of dopamine and opioids), which reduces the child's sense of grandiosity and joy-filled activity, which in turn facilitates impulse inhibition (Schore, 1994, 2003a).

By frustrating and satisfying the child in a flexible and balanced manner, the caregiver helps the child handle the shame regulation process (narcissistic deflation). This corresponds to the Freudian understanding of the transformation from the pleasure principle to the reality principle, which inhibits the child's self-centered and selfish behavior and perceptions. Many children must have a highly mature orbitofrontal cortex before they are capable of impulse control and of engaging in a process where emotions can be managed internally, which is yet another step toward psychological maturity. The caregiver must repeatedly offer support that is not humiliating but may be frustrating in relation to the child's grandiose illusion. Ideally, this deflation should happen gradually rather than in a sudden and overwhelming manner, since the child's nervous system is fragile (Schore, 1994).

As mentioned earlier, the narcissistic deflation effect serves to mature the orbitofrontal cortex, which connects to the autonomic nervous system; this makes it possible to inhibit arousal and activate impulse inhibition. Stimulation of the orbitofrontal cortex activates the parasympathetic nervous system, which in turn inhibits the stress hormone system (Schore, 2003a), while sudden shifts from sympathetic to parasympathetic activity cause immobilization and the production of cortisol. The narcissistic deflation effect develops the internalized shame effect, the sense of embarrassment and regret that becomes a factor in self-regulation. Orbitofrontal maturity marks the end of the narcissistic period, and by the end of the second year of life, the child will be able to self-regulate hyperactive states.

It is not necessary for the caregiver to use shame as a strategic form of parenting, as it is often unavoidable because the child's elevated dopamine level at this age draws the child into unbounded exploratory behavior. Without access to the caregiver's affect-regulating function, the child does not have an avenue for displaying a more volitional form of affect regulation. Unless the child is assisted in activating a shame response, the child will remain in a grandiose or omnipotent state; a child who is kept in a shame response will remain in a dysphoric and helpless state. Unpredictable caregivers keep the child in an unregulated state of grandiosity and helplessness. Shame differs from humiliation: Humiliation is associated with interactions that involve the parents' anger and failure to repair the misattunement. As mentioned earlier, the brain requires a certain level of cortisol to develop shame, but a chronically elevated level will disrupt the child's self-regulating functions. If the caregiver is unable to help the child repair the misattunement, a chronically elevated level of cortisol is maintained. In that case, the beneficial effects of this hormone in promoting the development of concentration and the inhibiting functions of the orbitofrontal cortex may be lost, as cortisol regulation breaks down. When a child is repeatedly placed in humiliating situations over time, there is an overactivation of cortisol, and the system breakdown activates both primitive parasympathetic components ("going dead" or freeze behavior) and increased sympathetic activity (fight or flight), which can have catastrophic consequences for brain development. Normally, sympathetic and parasympathetic structures are connected in a mutually integrated circuitry that is activated antagonistically or reciprocally. This reciprocal connection may be disrupted, and thus, for example, the child may attack someone without being psychologically present in the act. In its most extreme consequence, this corresponds to committing an affectless murder (Schore, 1994; Siegel, 1999).

The internalized self-regulated shame effect only develops if the dyad between caregiver and child until this point has been satisfactory. If the child's dopamine-based circuits are not sufficiently activated, noradrenaline-based inhibition will fail to occur, and the sense of shame that forms the basis of guilt and morals will not be activated. Thus, the child must be able to tolerate high levels of arousal for the feeling of shame to develop, something I examine in more detail in Chapter 5.

The Domain of Verbal and Cognitive Processing, Age 1½–2 Years

At the age of 1½–2 years the child's internal representations become more sophisticated, which is a prerequisite for a complex imagination and for the ability to empathize with someone else's mental states and emotions. The child's verbalization skills also undergo substantial development.

At that age, the basic neural connections between the limbic system and the orbitofrontal cortex are fully developed, and the emotional and impulse-inhibiting system integrates with the not yet fully developed prefrontal cortex and parts of the left hemisphere, which is the seat of language development, among other functions. The child becomes capable of internalizing shame, which will play a key role in regulating emotional expressions and social interactions (Trevarthen, 1993a, 1993b). During this period the child becomes increasingly autonomous and independent and physically able to roam ever farther away from the primary caregiver. It is also during this period that the child begins to establish more profound relationships with many other people besides the primary caregivers, and secondary caregivers become increasingly important for the child's ongoing development of internal representations. During this phase the child actively approaches other adults and children and experiments with contact. The child tests different qualities of alliances with the parents; for example, the child may experiment by holding the father close and pushing the mother away, and vice versa. This period corresponds to the sense of self that Stern calls the verbal self, where self-perception is related to linguistic meaning and context. It is only at this point that we can truly speak of a capacity for empathy.

Language Development and Play Ability

The child begins to be able to use two-word sentences, and development is based on linking emotions, internal representations, and language. For example, a mother may tell her 18-month-old child that she will leave briefly and that in the meantime the child should play with his teddy bear. When the mother leaves, the child will look toward the door, restraining his tears, and then turn to the teddy bear and repeat what the mother said in his own words. He will hold the teddy bear as if to comfort it, soothing it by explaining that Mommy is going to be back soon. When the mother returns, the child will be able to tell her what happened. The child is able to use language and play to modulate and control emotional expressions and experiences and to regulate himself through private speech (Emde, 1984, 1989; Sroufe, 1979). At 18 months, the child begins to be able to use symbols, which further develops play ability. At this point the child is able to communicate about himself to others, and begins to develop the capacity for symbolic play, such as pretend games. A study of 21-month-old children found that they had no problem using a building block as a bar of soap when they were washing their teddy bears, but subsequently they had great difficulty pretending that the block was a piece of bread when they were asked to feed the bears. At 28 months, only half the children had difficulty using the block as a bar of soap and then later as food (Harris, 1994; Neisser, 1993; Stern, 1985).

Around the age of 1½ years the child is able to engage in role-playing and tries to express other people's emotions, mimicry, and speech. When the caregiver helps the child engage in pretend play, for example by giving the doll a cup of tea or a bath, the child cooperates by accepting the mother's contributions. The child is able to engage in parallel play without much cooperation and has limited ability to add new play elements. Only when the child develops the awareness that others have a different center for their subjective experiences is the child able to assume someone else's role and engage in role-playing; this occurs around the age of 4 years (Neisser, 1993; Trevarthen, 1993a, 1993b).

Winnicott said that in mutual play the child makes experiences about "me" versus "not-me," and that it is through play that the spontaneous activity of the personality can be creatively expressed. Gammelgaard (2004) pointed out that if play development does not take off, the child will fail to achieve a sense of belonging within himself and as an adult he will lack a secure inner base as the source of his thoughts, emotions, and actions. A child who fails to develop play ability may either be tied to the concrete—"everything is real"—or withdraw to a pretend world that has no link to reality. Play is a means of mastering the gap between the inner and outer world.

Self-Regulation and Sense of Self

At the age of 1½–2 years the child has frequent mood swings and begins to be aware of the obstacles involved in trying to master the world. The child is able to express anger with a different form of directedness than before and may respond with unprovoked anger. At this time the child has far greater control over emotional experiences and expressions and is able to plan behavior. Moderate levels of shame help the child regulate his relationship with the world and act as a signal for change and self-correction. The child begins to be able to sense when his arousal level should be inhibited and may break off a behavior that is otherwise satisfying but which bothers someone else.

At this time the child develops the ability to feel empathy. The child displays prosocial and altruistic behavior such as approaching someone who is upset or in need, offering comfort or assistance. The child is able to regulate his own negative affect and also to regulate others' affect, for example, by assuming roles and taking other people's perspective despite his own mood state. The child's previous experiences of being with a regulating and comforting caregiver have been incorporated into his internal representations, and the child copies the caregiver if someone else—or the child himself—needs to be comforted. Self-calming and soothing behavior shows how various psychological structures can be represented simultaneously; for example, the child may be unhappy while using an internal representation to comfort himself (Izard, 1971, 1991; Schore, 1994).

Hoffman described an example that illustrates the gradual development of the child's capacity for empathy and shows how children at different ages respond when they observe other children. In a case of emotional contagion, the 0–6-month-old infant who sees a crying child begins to cry as well, responding to human distress as if it were his own. The 9–12-month-old child who sees another child fall down and get hurt will begin to cry and crawl toward the caregiver to be comforted, as if he had fallen down himself. The 12–15-month-old child who sees another child hurt her fingers may imitate and put his own fingers in his mouth to see if it helps. The child is able to distinguish his own state from the other child's, but not until the age of 15–18 months will he be able to fetch his teddy bear and hand it to the crying peer for comfort (Sørensen, 2006). Children aged 12–15 months cannot distinguish their own needs from others' and believe that everybody wants the same, while an 18-month-old child understands that others have wants that may be different and may even be opposite to his own. One aspect of empathy is the understanding that even if one does not have the same feeling, one may still sympathize with and understand someone else's feelings (Gopnik, Meltzoff, & Kuhl, 1999).

The ability to use symbols is important for the development of the mentalizing capacity, because the ability to distinguish between the symbol and the object marks the beginning of the mental ability to differentiate the self. The child's episodic memory develops and thus the child is able to organize specific events in time sequences, which later lets the child recall memories and use them as a basis for acting. The child's ability to delimit and differentiate and to relate to himself is evident, for example, in the ability to identify himself as an object in a mirror, as described previously, by pointing to a red mark on his own forehead rather than pointing to the red spot in the mirror. Children begin to use the word *I* to refer to themselves and to perceive themselves and others as either boys or girls (Schibbye, 2005).

Sexual identity develops late in gestation and continues to develop until the age of 1½ years. In Freud's understanding of psychosexual development, this corresponds to the Oedipal phase, although in his theory this period begins at the age of 4–5 years. When the child has reached the latency period, the level of circulating sex hormones drops until prepuberty (Schore, 1994). The narcissistic deflation period and the maturation of the sensory system in the sexual organs coincide in time. The child becomes more interested in touching and presenting the sexual organs, and joy-filled contact can lead to excitement in the genital areas and stimulate sexual feelings—a phenomenon that should not be confused with adult sexuality. In light of the timing there is reason to assume that the maturation of the feeling of shame is involved in regulating the social aspects of sexuality.

Neuroaffective Development

The dorsolateral prefrontal cortex matures around age 1½–2 years, which enables the child to develop more complex symbolic representations. The child is now able to recall previous events and experiences that may help him modulate affects. After age 1½, the memory functions develop; for example, the child is able to recall more complex memories. The explicit memory system and the connections between the hippocampus in the limbic system and the prefrontal regions are now mature enough that the child can relate to previous memories and be in the present while holding expectations of the future. The child is now able to maintain a stated desire about what the reality ought to be, even if the facts say otherwise. Object permanence develops further, which enables the child to begin to exist in an emotionally charged world without being at the mercy of his emotions. The world grows gradually more permanent, regardless of the child's and the other's state of mind or emotion (Sørensen, 2005).

The development of the dorsolateral prefrontal cortex forms the basis for the emergent working memory, and the child begins to be able to choose between options and to maintain focus longer. This form of attention requires a controlled suppression of alternatives in favor of a specific focus of attention. This attention system is used to resolve conflicts of attention or action, correct mistakes, and plan new actions. Neurophysiological studies have located the executive control capacity (the ability to make plans and control behavior, judgment, goal attainment, and so on) in the brain's medial (front part of the cingulate gyrus) and lateral prefrontal regions. For example, research has shown that negative emotion in adults is associated with intense activation of the amygdala but is modulated by the front part of the cingulate gyrus. This form of attention control lets the child follow internally determined priorities, focus attention as needed, and inhibit behavior in an appropriate manner. It also enables the child to achieve psychological intimacy, which lets the child sense someone else's emotions and thoughts without being overwhelmed by the other's distress or discomfort (Fonagy & Target, 2002).

The executive control system is an active system that differs from a more primitive behavior-inhibiting system that Gray (Beauchaine, 2001) labeled the behavioral inhibition system (BIS) and a reward or behavioral activation system (BAS). These two systems are initiated by limbic structures in interaction with the sympathetic nervous system and are thus not under volitional control (see Chapter 6, the section on depression, p. 247). Normally, the balance between the fear of punishment and the attraction of the new and unfamiliar or of rewarding situations is controlled by the balance between BAS and BIS. The BAS-BIS complex connects to the front part of the cingulate gyrus, which may moderate the effect of early activation processes and promote self-control. Fonagy and Target (2002) assumed that the capacity for directed attention is necessary for the development of the mentalization function, both because the development of directed attention control and sophisticated mentalization functions coincide in time, and because brain scans suggest that the structures in charge of mentalization and those in charge of directed control are located close together or even overlapping. Similarly, optimal self-control requires a certain capacity for attention control.

The integration of the parietal regions and the limbic system with the orbitofrontal and dorsolateral prefrontal cortices brings emotional and cognitive intelligence together. Emotional resonance means that on an emotional level the child is able to put himself in someone else's place, which is associated with activity in the orbitofrontal cortex, while a cognitive understanding of someone else's state is more related to activity in the dorsolateral prefrontal cortex. The ability to predict and perceive someone else's feelings emerges when these two regions connect. The mental or cognitive function of putting oneself in someone else's place develops after the age of 1½ years (Cozolino, 2000; Donaldson, 1987; Fonagy et al., 2002; Schore, 1994, 2003a). According to Schore (1994), the right hemisphere is dominant during the first 3 years of life. The left hemisphere begins its growth spurt around age 1½, at which time language development really takes off. At this age, there is a slow and gradual shift from right-hemisphere dominance to left-hemisphere dominance. This reflects a shift from emotional dependence on close attachment figures to increased cognitive and motor control and verbalization capacity, all of which are primary functions of the left hemisphere (Tucker, 1992).

Around the age of 2 years, the basic personality structure is fully developed, and the subsequent development is about the integration and development of motor, mental, and cognitive functions. The dorsolateral prefrontal cortex is the brain region that takes longest to myelinate and develop.

Understanding Other Minds and the Domain of the Narrative, Age 2–4 Years

At ages 2–4 years, the child develops a more complex and abstract understanding of others, also with regard to grasping ambivalent or contradictory emotions. The child may begin to refer to himself as a subject who is felt from the inside and may begin to engage in dialogues with his internal representations. At the same time, the child is able to see himself as an object that can be perceived by others and to predict and perceive other people's emotions thanks to additional maturation of the prefrontal cortex, in particular the dorsolateral prefrontal area, and in the connection between the right and left hemispheres (Schore, 2001a). This period corresponds to Stern's description of the narrative sense of self, and the sense of self at this level revolves around finding meaning and coherence within an autobiography.

Language Development

The acquisition of language expands the child's experiential world with almost limitless possibilities for interpersonal exchange. In addition to understanding and producing language, the child begins to be able to objectify himself, and the development of secondary mentalization leads to a capacity for self-reflection. The child now has a new means of communication, allowing him to engage in the joint creation of meaning with the sense that he and the other have different and separate perceptions of the world that can be communicated verbally. Language lets the child create narratives, here understood as stories about events, experiences, and so on from the child's life, and communicate about things and people that are not currently present.

At the age of 2–4 years, the child begins to relate to the difference between personal and official knowledge. Stern emphasized that language has tremendous importance for the child's ongoing development but adds that there is also a risk that language "drives a wedge between two simultaneous forms of interpersonal experience: as it is lived and as it is verbally represented. . . . [T]o the extent that events in the domain of verbal relatedness are held to be what has really happened, experiences in these other domains suffer an alienation" (1985, pp. 162–163). The part that is captured by language will always be separate from the original nonverbal experience, and the verbal representation of the self in the left hemisphere can be very different and detached from the experiential representation in the right hemisphere.

Narratives

Children's language is characterized by overly generalized categories or very specific experiences, and children's understanding of events has an emotional and self-centered logic. The 2-year-old child is characterized by primary process thinking, and powerful experiences, positive as well as negative, are often surrounded by a private and confabulated mind-set, which means that memory gaps are often filled with made-up material, without the child noticing the difference between actually remembered and made-up content. The child has difficulty distinguishing between relevant and irrelevant, and in telling a coherent story often imitates other people's stories. At this age level, everyday experiences are recreated through an endless number of simple narratives that are used in everyday speech. Bruner (1990) described that on average there are eight and a half narratives per hour; three quarters of them are told by the mother, and a quarter of the narratives are about something that the child is doing. The narratives are often a retelling of the child's behavior, and they are rarely neutral but seek to convey a particular inter-pretation and to justify the parent's actions. At this time children learn that their actions are influenced by what they relate about their behav-ior, and how. Narratives are not simply explanatory; they are also rhe-torical, as the child asks a large number of questions without necessarily expecting answers to all of them. During the third year of life, the child begins to be able to distinguish between true and false and between commonly occurring or singular events (Bruner, 1990).

Language offers a new symbol and memory system, and through nar-rative structures and play children seek to make sense of events and increasingly begin to express their emotions verbally. Through these narratives children find meaning and coherence, for example by telling their own stories and talking about themselves in their own words. The autobiography is based on the caregivers' presentation of reality, as a child sees himself from the parents' perspective. The narratives help shape the child's self-identity but also allow the child to position himself within a story. The primary function of the narrative story is to organize experiences that may in themselves be incoherent or chaotic. Words that are value laden or describe internal states often continue to carry special meaning throughout life, because emotions and words are linked at an early age, in the close contact with the caregivers (Bruner, 1986; Stern, 1985).

Mentalization

As mentioned earlier, mentalization refers to the ability to understand mental states, that is, to reflect on one's own and others' thoughts and feelings. Mentalization develops successively from primary to secondary mentalization (the latter is what is generally referred to as mentalization in this book). At age 12–18 months, there is a shift where impulses are no longer necessarily acted out, and emotions can be managed internal-ly. This is a step toward secondary mentalization, but it is not until the age of 4 years, approximately, that mentalization is fully developed, where children develop the symbolic capacity to think about their own thinking and reactions (Fonagy, 2001).

The primary mentalization capacity develops when the insula, the amygdala, and the deeper regions in the frontal lobes (the orbitofrontal cortex) mature. Secondary mentalization results from maturation of the medial sections of the prefrontal cortex (including the front part of the cingulate gyrus), the dorsolateral prefrontal cortex, and the corpus callosum and through additional maturation of the same structures in the left hemisphere, which inhibit primary mentalization. Prior to the development of secondary mentalization, the internal representations are partial (see Chapter 3, the section on archaic empathy and primary mentalization) and tied to specific situations and physical causality, which distorts them and makes projections unavoidable. Secondary mentalization makes it possible to separate emotions from action and relate to the difference between internal thought processes and external reality. The child may feel anger without hitting anyone and begins to be able to verbalize emotional states, for example by expressing anger verbally.

From around the age of 3–4 years, the child begins to be able to see that other people's experiences are different, and that others may be wrong or even lie. The child is also able to predict that others may have erroneous assumptions. The child is able to reflect on other people's internal mental states. Mentalization makes it possible to assess one's own as well as other people's thought models, plan activities, and evaluate, reevaluate, and predict events. It is only at this age level that the working memory begins to develop, which enables the child to integrate mentalization with cognition on a sophisticated abstract level (Schibbye, 2005).

There are strong indications of a link between the child's ability to assess and understand other people's thoughts and feelings and the child's experiences with joint pretend play. Social understanding develops through conflict resolution situations that require the child to consider someone else's point of view as part of the negotiations and through the child's recurring experiences with sharing, arguing, and negotiating in a pretend world with others where the child encounters other people's individual opinions and perspectives. The child's social understanding also develops in conversations about emotions and mental states, especially with the caregivers (Dunn, 1996).

The ability to transform primary mentalization into secondary mentalization helps primitive defense mechanisms mature to more advanced levels, and the nervous system begins to function as a dynamic system with a repressed subconscious. Thus, the nervous system is able to use repression, sublimation, intellectualization, and displacement as self-protection strategies, unlike the more primitive protection strategies associated with primary mentalization (including denial, idealization, projection, projective identification, introjection, and splitting) (Schore, 2003b). The initiation of the internalization process and thus the acquisition of secondary mentalization and an understanding of other minds depend on the degree of consistency and security in early relationships and an adequate psychological function in the caregivers (Fonagy, 1991; Gergely & Watson, 1999).

Guilt

Shame has to do with the child's being and develops before guilt; shame is a prerequisite for the development of guilt. Because it is difficult for the child to separate thoughts from actions, he may feel guilty about thoughts as well as actions. Feelings of guilt do not develop until after the child has acquired language. This has caused Schore (1994), among others, to point out that while shame is a right-hemisphere function, guilt is a left-hemisphere function. During the first 3 years of life, the right hemisphere is dominant. The 2–4-year-old child continues to be self-centered and feel that the world revolves around him, but that implies not only that the child is the champion of the world but that the child is also the guilty party if something goes wrong. Feelings of guilt, embarrassment, and envy develop around the age of 3 years; at this time the cognitive skills grow more complex. Feeling guilty requires an awareness of norms and an understanding that others require compliance with these norms. It is this understanding, among other things, that later develops into a moral sense. Similarly, a sense of embarrassment requires an awareness of other people's potential views of one's behavior, which is based on imagination (Øvreeide, 2002; Rutter & Rutter, 1993; Sroufe, 1979; van der Kolk, 1987).

Adaptive Behavior

Around the age of 2 years, children are able to adapt their behavior in certain situations, for example, by not showing emotions that they have learned are unacceptable, an ability that we continue to rely on throughout life. Children begin to be able to understand complex social situations, and with increasing cognitive maturity learn to hide their internal state from other people's critical and insensitive reactions. The difference between the right and left hemispheres becomes more evident as children learn to maintain two different states: a private internal state and a socially adapted behavior. Already at the age of 2½ years, children may begin to deny wrongdoing, even when it is quite obvious who is responsible.

As a child's mental and cognitive abilities mature, he gets better at arguing when he is angry or unhappy. At the age of 3 years, there are dramatic changes in the child's way of referring to mental states, and the child is far less at the mercy of his emotions. Children around age 2½ are unable to use reasoning when they are angry or upset, unlike 4-year-old children (Dunn, Slomkowski, Donelan-McCall, & Herrera, 1995). Around the age of 4 years, children may begin to offer reasons for violating rules, which probably shows the left hemisphere interpreting behavior that was initiated in the right hemisphere. The left hemisphere attempts to relate to a social context, and children strive to understand themselves and resolve the problems that arise in the social context. They find ways of cooperating and securing other people's acceptance, which contributes to a growing sense of self. At an early stage, children are interested in comparing their own capabilities with others' and actively seek to construct morals. At the age of 4 years children are able to present others with an erroneous perception of a situation even when they know the right solution. For example, studies show that 4-year-olds have no problem pointing to the wrong box to tease a villain who is out to steal someone else's reward, while 3-year-olds honestly tell the villain where the reward is (Siegel, 1999; Tetzchner, 2002; Turiel, 1998).

Reduction of Attachment Behavior and Expansion of Social Relations

Around the age of 3–4 years, children become gradually less dependent on the physical presence of attachment figures and able to understand and accept reasons for the parents' absence. Separation anxiety will break through if the parents' absence is unpredictable, inexplicable, or frightening. Thus, the attachment has not been weakened, but the child is better at maintaining relationships as internal representations during time spent away from the attachment figures. Already by age 2, interactions with peers are expanding, and at age 4 the child begins to form friendships and prefers some children over others. The child's play ability develops, and he no longer plays parallel to others but engages much more in joint play structured around a joint process. About half of 4-year-olds have a special relationship with one other child with whom they spend more than 30% of their time (Hinde, Titmus, Easton, & Tamplin, 1985).

Neuroaffective Development

According to Schore (1994), the orbitofrontal cortex is larger in the right hemisphere, while the dorsolateral prefrontal cortex is larger in the left hemisphere, and these two systems only begin to cooperate between the third and fourth years of a child's life. Davidson (1994a, 1994b) argued that the inhibition of negative affect is due to the dorsolateral cortex in the left hemisphere dampening right-hemisphere affective activity. Each hemisphere is able to form independent self-representations, and they do not merge until the child is 3 years old, when there is significant myelination in the corpus callosum. This growth causes a transfer of dominance from the right hemisphere to the left. Explicit memory and narratives can be recalled through the language functions in the left hemisphere, and experiences that are stored implicitly in the right hemisphere may be inaccessible to the left hemisphere. The left hemisphere begins to be able to inhibit the implicit functions of the right hemisphere, which in a psychoanalytic understanding is characterized as repression. The left hemisphere relies on explicit verbal functions, while the right hemisphere relies on implicit nonverbal functions.

Both the right and left hemispheres continue growing, at different rates, and the prefrontal cortex continues to organize. During the third year of life there is a qualitative shift in children's understanding and attention, and thanks to the development of secondary mentalization children begin to be able to handle various mental states, both in themselves and in relationships with others. Understanding others requires the ability to imagine that one is someone else as well as the ability to distinguish reality from imagination. This ability requires the ongoing development of the connection between the orbitofrontal cortex and the dorsolateral prefrontal cortex as well as development of the dorsolateral prefrontal cortex in both hemispheres. Secondary mentalization enables an emergent capacity for self-reflection, and children begin to be able to regulate themselves and to show concern for others. The maturation of the connections between the orbitofrontal and dorsolateral prefrontal cortices enhances the ability to handle interpretations and develop opinions about others (Fonagy, 1991, 2003; Schore, 1994). As mentioned earlier, it is not until the age of 3–4 years that a child is able to distinguish between thoughts and action or reality and fantasy and to process more complex states. Four-year-old children quickly perceive the difference between real life and pretense; for example, the 4-year-old child laughs when Dad pretends to be a clown, while the 2-year-old is astonished and has difficulty getting the joke because of the limited ability to grasp the difference between real life and fantasy (Fonagy et al., 2002; Rutter & Rutter, 1993). This is probably because secondary mentalization is only fully developed when the dorsolateral prefrontal cortex and the corpus callosum have matured further.

The Domain of Symbolization, Age 4–7 Years

Between ages 4 and 7, the prefrontal cortex and the corpus callosum continue to organize. In particular, the dorsolateral prefrontal cortex has a prolonged growth period that stretches beyond puberty. In late childhood, cognitive and emotional development form increasingly complex connections horizontally as well as vertically throughout the nervous system. The emotional structures in the limbic system and in the orbitofrontal cortex integrate far more with the parietal regions and the dorsolateral prefrontal cortex, and the child begins to develop the ability to interpret emotions (Schore, 2003a).

The Use of Symbols

The 6–7-year-old child begins to be able to convey experiences in more coherent narratives but still needs playlike activities to convey experiences with subtlety and complexity. Symbols become increasingly important and useful in the intuitive sharing of information in relation to an interpreted reality. Behavior is controlled to a higher degree by the child's integrated moral understanding, although impulses still break through easily. Until age 7, children use self-speech to control their own behavior and often speak out loud, reminding themselves how to do a task or solve a problem. When the private speech disappears, the child has become better at controlling arousal states. At this age the child's inner life begins to be dominated by thoughts rather than visualization through action or verbalization. The child begins to be able to reconstruct tasks, and flexibility and creativity increase, which lets the child manipulate tasks and achieve new goals without first learning a task from scratch (Barkley, 1998; Øvreeide, 2002; Trevarthen, 1993a).

Expansion of the Mentalization Capacity

An expansion of the mentalization capacity can be characterized as Fonagy's (2003) interpersonal interpretative mechanism (IIM), the precursor of the capacity for self-reflection. IIM contains no representations of experiences; rather, it is a mechanism for processing new experiences. It is a collection of neurocognitive mechanisms and probably an extension of the lower mentalizing functions. While early mentalization is more closely related to emotions via the orbitofrontal cortex, IIM is associated with other areas in the medial section of the prefrontal cortex in cooperation with the dorsolateral prefrontal cortex. This marks a difference between the emotional and the cognitive understanding of someone else's emotions, similar to the difference in being held in the other person's heart or in their thoughts. It is only at this time that children begin to be able to relate to themselves in thinking. As Gammelgaard (2004) pointed out, imagination and creativity are not sufficient for the development of the empathy capacity. It is only through empathy that we can reflect on ourselves. It is by seeing ourselves through someone else's eyes that we become aware, on a higher level of consciousness, that we have a self that is separate from the other's self.

When the child is 4–6 years old, IIM is still only emergent. The 4–6-year-old child follows rules in a concrete way, and rules are perceived as inviolable authority, not yet as a set of guidelines created on the basis of a common understanding. Children do not distinguish between accidental and intentional acts; it is the consequences that matter. Their concrete consequence and rule-based morals can make them feel guilty about acts they had no influence on. Children will feel like an active participant in everything they are involved in, whether voluntarily, under force, or through manipulation, and thus will feel guilty if something goes wrong or they fail to comply with acceptable norms. Children are self-centered and blame themselves for whatever happens (Øvreeide,

2002). For example, if a curious child approaches a situation that has an unfortunate outcome, the child is easy prey to feelings of guilt, even if the acts and the control lay entirely with someone else.

At this age, the child begins to be able to understand complex and abstract action plans behind unspoken intentions or misleading behavior that hide the real intent. The child is increasingly able to maintain focus, and there is a further increase in the child's ability to talk about and recognize emotions. The child is now able to begin to make plans and think ahead and begins to be able to use perceptive skills (Goleman, 2003). When a group of 3-year-old children expect a box to contain candy, and instead it contains crayons, the children expect their peers, who are waiting outside, to believe that the box contains crayons. The 3-year-olds' own experience prevails over the perception of other children's perspective, and the children do not understand that they have received additional information that has affected their perception. However, 4- and 5-year-olds say that their peers waiting outside will expect to find candy in the box. At this age level, the children understand that other people's internal expectations are based on their particular experiences, and thus they are able to represent an erroneous perception in the other. From the age of 6 years, mentalization develops further, and the child is able to represent the other's perception of a third person's inner world. This ability to grasp someone else's perception of a third person's perceptions enables a child, for example, to imagine how the mother perceives the father's experience (Schibbye, 2005). At the age of 6–7 years, the child's perspective expands, and the child's self-centered view is dismantled, in part due to a growing ability to differentiate between different points of view. Children begin to be able to manipulate their thoughts actively and to regulate in accordance with their considerations. They are able to assess other people's expectations and to tell a story from someone else's perspective. A child under 6 years of age, for example, has difficulty explaining to someone else what to do, since young children have a limited ability to see something logically or cognitively from someone else's point of view. After age 6, children develop the empathic capacity to grasp not only other people's immediate emotions but also their general experiences and life conditions (Bertelsen, 1994; Dunn, 1987).

Mentalization is mostly an implicit (unconscious) function, like riding a bicycle. Only when the capacity is fully developed is mentalization something that we engage in all the time, and the child constantly seeks to understand and respond to other people's wishes, expectations, and emotions to influence their behavior. The expanded mentalization capacity makes other people's behavior comprehensible and predictable, and the self-reflective function makes the child's behavior more intelligent. The ability to influence one's own actions rests on one's ability to process and reflect on one's own as well as other people's emotions, actions, desires, and so on (Fonagy, Target, & Gergely, 2000). If emotions remain unsymbolized they cannot be processed explicitly (consciously) and verbally. In that case they are either lived or processed nonverbally, for example, in the form of psychosomatic symptoms; they cannot develop through a cognitive feedback system, and a child will have difficulty sensing himself on a mental, reflective level (Gerhardt, 2004).

Social Functions

The ongoing development of the right hemisphere is experience-dependent, and synchronized interactions between peers rely on the maturation of neural structures in the right hemisphere. The ability to create affective attunement and resonance with other children depends on the ability to read faces and prosody unconsciously and effectively, to engage in resonance with other people's states, to communicate emotionally, and to self-regulate affects. At this time, the child must be able to cope with new environments and deal with the stressors that may occur, for example, when disagreeing with others. At this age, the child is able to engage in symbolic play and in collaborative interactions with peers.

Abstraction and the Domain of Logical Thinking, Age 7–13 Years

From the age of 7 years, the child is able to form higher cognitive abstractions and symbols. Toward the end of this age phase, the more mature types of identity formation begin to emerge: self-reflection, self-objectification, the interpretation of social contexts, and the choice of strategies and social roles. The child's thinking is more logical, and the child is able to enter into varying roles, using countless simultaneous perspectives. These developmental gains must be seen in relation to developments in the prefrontal cortex and parietal regions.

Cognitive Integration

Gestures, symbols, and verbalization are more closely connected and organized at this age level. Gestures develop from instinctive and imitative behavior that is acquired through cross-modal transfer. Gestures connect with language and later with the formation of symbols, both depending on the cortical maturation of the parietal lobes and the prefrontal cortex. Both these areas are not fully mature until the age of 10–14 years. For example, a 4-year-old will use pantomime before describing a hammer; a 10-year-old will use pantomime while explaining how the hammer is used; and a 14-year-old will use gestures selectively, presenting particular gestures in relation to certain words, coordinating the two systems of communication (Joseph, 1993). During this period, implicit knowledge should integrate with abstract cognitive functions on higher levels of mentalization.

The expansion of the mentalization capacity means that the child begins to be able to put feelings into words—the feelings are reflected cognitively, but this requires that the child has access to autonomic and limbic structures for the cognitive reflections to connect with vitality affects and categorical affects, among other aspects. Cognitive reflection is a linguistic form of knowledge in the sense that there are words and concepts for describing the knowledge that has been acquired (Schibbye, 2005). During this period the child becomes able to integrate mentalization with higher cognitive functions, but the emotions may also become detached from cognitive reflection.

Working Memory

At the age of 7–13 years, the child develops a real capacity for hypothetical thinking, understanding probabilities, shaping ideals, and testing possibilities. The child is increasingly able to tune out neural background noise and maintain a working memory, which facilitates skills that suppress or govern emotions. This enables the child to process a situation efficiently or initiate a new response as the situation requires. The prefrontal cortex gives the self the flexibility and time to consider a situation without being at the mercy of impulses.

The maturation of the working memory develops the child's capacity for self-reflection. At this point, identity formation depends on the capacity for social reflection and introspection, and the child's own identity stands out more clearly. The development of children's self-image at this age level requires that children understand that they are involved in both constructing and interpreting their own stories (Fonagy et al., 2002; Frønes, 1994; Hobson, 1993; Neisser, 1993; van der Kolk, 1987).

The expansion of the mentalizing function is evident, for example, in children's view of friendships at various age levels. Youniss (1980) interviewed children at three age levels about friendships. The youngest group, the 6–8-year-olds, emphasized play relations and sharing. The middle group, the 9–11-year-olds, were more interested in the reciprocity that is implicit in attachment relationships, the sort of help that friends can give each other, and the confidence that others will help, for example, by caring if one is lonely. The oldest group, the 12–14-year-olds, viewed close friendships as relationships characterized by rapport, the ability to cooperate, reciprocity, and mutual trust, for example, in relation to talking about one's feelings and being understood.

Conscience and Morals

Around the age of 9–10 years, children understand that rules are social constructs based on agreements, and that morals are common human regulations that are open to change and negotiation (see Fig. 3.4). A child increasingly discovers that other people's feelings are not only affected by the consequences of his actions but also by the feelings and nonverbal reactions that he elicits in others. Pride and guilt become essential, not just by virtue of other people's views but based on the child's own internal sense of responsibility. At age 8–10, children begin to develop a conscience; thus, a negative emotion can be directed at their own actions, and they assess their own intentionality (Øvreeide, 2002;

Shame: the sense of discomfort or embarrassment
↓
Guilt: the sense of having done something wrong
↓
Morals: thoughts about what is right and wrong

Figure 3.4. Shame—guilt—morals

Tetzchner, 2002), for example, when their thoughts about others trigger a bad conscience.

Around age 12, children gain far greater insight into their own emotions, and the cognitive reflection means that they develop internal representations that may be mutually contradictory and ambivalent. Children are no longer restricted to a single aspect of a problem but are able to draw on a variety of simultaneous perspectives, also in their relations with others. At this age level, children can clearly distinguish perceived reality from fantastical (perhaps made-up) stories governed by desires and a search for social affirmation both from themselves and from others, and they are able to relate to different aspects of their own personality. Children are far better at considering the intention behind an act and dealing with contradictory emotions toward others (Øvreeide, 2002; Tetzchner, 2002).

Actual Selves and Ideal Selves

During this age period, children think about their own qualities and compare themselves with others; this becomes a key aspect of self-perception. At this time, children not only develop a sense of what they are like but also of what they would like to be. Until the age of 7–8 years, a child is governed by her ideas about what others want her to do. In relation to 6-year-olds, 12-year-olds perceive a much bigger difference between what they think their parents think they are like, and what they think the parents would want them to be. For example, a 10-year-old who does not do her homework might think that her parents think that she is lazy and want her to be different. A big discrepancy between the actual self and the ideal self will lead to emotional difficulties for the child. The maturation of the prefrontal cortex lets children develop more mature coping strategies that give them a sense of being in control of their life (Tetzchner, 2002).

By the age of 12 years, the child has more permanently internalized his or her countless interactions with significant caregivers. For example, it is often at this age that psychiatrists begin to distinguish between relational disorders and personality disorders. The experiences and internal representations that a child has formed through close relationships begin to play out on an internal psychological level, something that culminates around puberty when the child begins to detach from the parents. At this time the plasticity of the subcortical structures is reduced, neural pathways become more permanently specialized, and it is increasingly difficult to unlearn and change habits; for example, by the age of 12 years it is difficult to acquire a new language without an accent. At this time, peer and group relations become essential; the child bonds with peers and leaves the parents' environment behind in order to establish psychological autonomy and explore other close emotional bonds. In this manner, the child learns to get by in more advanced social relations. Even if the peer group plays a key role, and the child breaks the bonds of dependency, the family continues to function as a secure base (Frønes, 1994; van der Kolk, 1987).

The Domain of Individuation: Puberty

Puberty is often described as the child's second big chance, and during this period intimacy and friendship relations may take over the family's status as role models to some extent. Adolescent individuation and group formation are important aspects of youth, and the peer group is used as a means of transition between the dependency of the family and emotional maturity. The peer group often provides a sense of belonging and acceptance that is no longer possible in the family (van der Kolk, 1987). The transition between youth and adulthood is a stressful period, when young people often need to mark their separation from the parents and experiment with their identity. Many young people are boundary-seeking and engage in risky situations, something that is also common in other mammals.

Recent studies suggest that the understanding of others continues to develop throughout puberty, which enhances social competence. A well-developing 12-year-old is able to consider hypotheses and thus possible alternatives and to process predictions intellectually without any direct link to the real-life situation. The adolescent is able to present events and experiences in a temporally coherent and logical structure; this is related to the development of cognitive skills that are not necessarily associated with mentalizing functions, and which therefore become more separate. It is only toward the end of puberty that teenagers are able to distinguish between the ideal and the practically feasible as two different categories that cannot always be expected to match (Øvreeide, 2002).

Neuroaffective Development During the Teenage Years

The teenage brain is undergoing rapid change and is therefore both anatomically and neurochemically different from an adult brain. Among other things, there is an age-specific change in the dopamine balance between limbic areas and the prefrontal cortex, which controls the motivation system in relation to determining which stimuli are deemed relevant (Spear, 2000). The activation of sexual hormones initiates sexuality and interest in the opposite sex. Until puberty, the testosterone level is approximately three times higher in boys than in girls, but during puberty testosterone reaches a level that is about 15 times higher in boys. Girls produce about twice as much estrogen as boys until puberty and then about eight times more (Stein, 1987). The release of sex hormones during prepuberty stimulates neurons to increase the number of synaptic connections, and during puberty there is a renewed period of pruning and specialization (parcellation) in the gray matter of the brain, particularly in the cerebellum and in the parietal, frontal, and temporal lobes. This process is believed to reorganize neural circuits and to help stabilize the nervous system; as a result, the brain comes to rely far more on acquired patterns. In the corpus callosum the synaptic connections are strengthened, which means that the transfer of information between the two hemispheres is boosted; this enhances cooperation between the emotional and holistic hemisphere and the creative, symbolic, and linguistic hemisphere (Giedd, 2002; Giedd et al., 1999; Purves et al., 2001).

The increase in gray matter peaks in the prefrontal cortex at the age of 11 years in girls and 12 years in boys. This is followed by a pruning process where excess neurons or synaptic connections die (apoptosis). The same process begins in the temporal lobes at age 16. The prefrontal cortex is not fully mature until around the age of 20–23 years. Giedd (2002) has considered whether the increase in gray matter during puberty is due to a new wave of synaptic connections. If that is the case, puberty may prove to be another critical development phase, where teenage activities may help guide a selective pruning in the cortical regions. The increased release of sex hormones probably has an organizing effect on brain structures and thus on feminine and masculine behavior (Bruer, 1999; Schore, 2001a; Sowell & Jernigan, 1998). The cerebellum also changes, both in volume and shape, during childhood and youth.

The cerebellum is not fully myelinated until age 22 years, and thus, the ability to balance affective and cognitive processes and to navigate in a complicated social life develops slowly.

During puberty, the limbic system activates more frequently in relation to emotional stimuli than it does in adults. For example, when teenagers look at emotional facial expressions, the amygdala activates far more than the prefrontal cortex, while in adults the reverse is the case. This means that teenagers respond far more emotionally to facial expressions than adults, who process them more rationally. Teenagers have more difficulty identifying frightened faces; instead, these faces are often described as sad, shocked, or angry. It seems that functions in the orbitofrontal cortex are inhibited during this period, which often leads to big mood swings in teenagers' behavior (Schore, 2003a; Yurgelun-Todd, 2002).

The orbitofrontal cortex and amygdala are the most plastic areas of the cortex, and they are capable of continued synaptic growth. At this time, the teenager is bombarded with neural and environmental changes, and it takes a robust and stable nervous system to preserve continuity. Puberty demands a highly robust and integrated nervous system that is capable of balancing the autonomic nervous system, so that the high degree of insecurity and stress that characterizes this critical period of transition can be regulated and tolerated. There is probably a link between the neural changes that take place during the teenage years and the emergence of certain psychopathological disorders (Schore, 2003a).

The massive reorganization of personality during puberty leads to countless psychobiological changes that are only surpassed by developments during the first 2 years of life. After a relatively long period of slow growth during childhood there is a developmental transformation. Rakic, Bourgeois, and Goldman-Rakic (1994) have calculated that primates lose some 30,000 synapses per second throughout the cortex during puberty, which comes to an ultimate loss of almost half the synapses per neuron in the cortex. A similar overproduction and pruning is seen in the human cortex (Huttenlocher, 1984). The massive reorganization during this period renders the teenager's nervous system fragile. Teenagers' reactions are far more "limbic," and during this period the need-inhibiting structures in the orbitofrontal cortex lose their strength. This means that teenagers are not always able to predict the consequences of their actions and may wind up in situations that are not very well considered.

The specialization process in the prefrontal cortex enables a further development of the teenager's focus of attention; impulse inhibition becomes more effective, and planning and structuring become more sophisticated (Spear, 2000).

Self-Protection Strategies

In Chapter 2 we saw how the interaction between caregiver and infant consists of attunement as well as misattunement. Sometimes children are overwhelmed and have to come up with ways of protecting themselves. These defense mechanisms develop successively into increasingly complex and sophisticated strategies, and I will now describe the development of self-protection strategies on the different levels of mental organization.

Schibbye (2005) mentioned that a neglected and complicated area in dynamic psychology is to put defense mechanisms into a relational perspective. Basic anxiety and the associated protection strategies are part of the personality structure in a number of ways and develop within the relationship with the caregiver to enable an infant to protect both himself and the relationship. Gradually, defense mechanisms become autonomic, nonvolitional strategies that are applied independently of the context where they developed. In this section I make a small attempt at expanding the understanding of Freud's theory on defense mechanisms as a way of balancing an intrapsychic system and at placing defense mechanisms into a relational context. I view defense mechanisms as self-protection strategies that probably form the basis of a fundamental and evolutionary anxiety in relation to the threat of being abandoned, invaded, or overwhelmed, and I therefore use the term self-protection strategies rather than defense mechanisms.

Freud viewed defense mechanisms as the ego's means of warding off anxiety and being overwhelmed. The defense mechanisms are customarily divided into two categories: successful defenses, where the impulse is released; and failed defenses, where the impulse continues, as it lacks release and merely becomes more intense. Freud assumed that the buildup of tension might result from internal tension stemming from the drives (e.g., sexuality) or from the superego (e.g., feelings of guilt). He viewed the defense mechanisms as the ego's way of balancing the satisfaction of drives and the superego's acceptance of the drives in order to secure a culturally acceptable release.

Self-protection strategies are as essential to our psychological survival as the body's immune system is to our physical survival. Self-protection strategies are tasked with balancing the nervous system on the current level of mental organization, for example, when there is a conflict between the child and the environment. Self-protection strategies serve to maintain a form of equilibrium in the psychological structure and as protection against overwhelming stimuli when the nervous system has reached its arousal capacity. The various self-protection strategies are activated successively as the nervous system matures. Self-protection strategies are indispensible, but they may remain immature or appear incomprehensible, for example, when the child has been forced to relate to avoidant or unstable caregivers. The purpose of self-protection strategies is to protect the child from unbearable psychological pain or chaos. A given self-protection strategy may be appropriate at one time in the child's life but inappropriate at another time, and thus psychological defenses may develop in inappropriate ways that cause problems with adaptation.

Psychodynamic theories do not usually distinguish between regression and defense mechanisms. In the current context, defense mechanisms are characterized as psychological self-protection strategies, while regression only occurs when more advanced self-protection strategies fail. Self-protection strategies are appropriate, among other things, because they dampen painful and unpleasant feelings and thus provide pain relief. For example, when the nervous system is exposed to a stressful situation that it cannot handle, it will regress to a previous level to handle the conflict with a minimum of discomfort. Regression means reverting to earlier self-protection strategies that enable the nervous system to manage the conflict. Psychological resilience is conditioned by the capacity of the nervous system to stabilize the arousal level, preserving a sense of security, and enabling the nervous system to handle stressful situations without resorting to self-protection strategies. Psychological resilience reflects the integration of neural arousal-regulating with emotional and cognitive networks, which keeps the activation of mature forms of self-protection strategies to a minimum.

A child with an immature and unintegrated nervous system will rely on basic and more immature self-protection strategies. Immature forms of self-protection strategies often distort reality and weaken the more mature psychological functions because they developed to protect the child at early levels of mental organization.

Self-protection strategies mature successively; like the rest of the nervous system, they are hierarchical and established on various levels in the nervous system. As we saw with the development of the self, we preserve the earliest forms of self-protection strategies, but they are gradually overtaken by more mature forms. If a more mature strategy fails to provide the necessary protection, the nervous system will seek self-protection on a lower level. Thus, a mature nervous system will have a wide repertoire of self-protection strategies on many different levels, while an immature nervous system will only have a few strategies available. The more highly developed the nervous system is, the wider the repertoire. On a basic level, self-protection consists of unreflected implicit (unconscious) processes. On a more mature level, the child may have repressed unpleasant and threatening experiences; in a Freudian sense this is referred to as the dynamic unconscious. As mentioned earlier, the self-protection strategies are fully or partially implicit (unconscious) and cannot be integrated with structures in the prefrontal cortex. The unintegrated and nonreflected emotions play out as intrapsychic or

Protecting ego integrity
Repression, intellectualization, sublimation, and displacement.

Protecting the relationship with others
Late: Projective identification, splitting, and introjection.
Early: Denial, idealization, projection.

Protecting the survival of the organism
Sympathetic fight-or-flight behavior or vegetative parasympathetic activity, which causes an immobilization response.

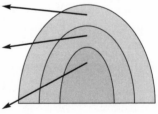

Figure 3.5. Self-protection strategies in the triune brain

interpersonal dramas outside the influence of the prefrontal cortex. The various self-protection strategies can be illustrated with Paul McLean's model of the triune brain with its levels of protomentation, emotomentation, and ratiomentation.

Self-Protection Strategies on the Level of Protomentation and Early Emotomentation

The early or primitive self-protection strategies are innate. They are autonomically regulated and consist of parasympathetic (calming) and sympathetic (activating) activity and may be associated with the regulation that takes place in connection with the activation of an innate fight-or-flight system or a freeze system (immobilization). When these systems are activated, a child is inaccessible to his surroundings and thus outside the reach of contact. Self-protection strategies on a reptilian level serve to protect the organism in situations that are deemed to be threatening.

When children are able to engage in protoconversations, on a basic level they become able to self-regulate, and thus the earliest self-protection strategies develop. At an early stage of life, infants are able to withdraw from unpleasant situations; this involves an early denial of situations that are unbearable. Infants withdraw to their own inner world, turn away, or restrict their field of attention. If this protection strategy proves ineffective, an infant falls back on autoregulating self-protection strategies. In the slightly older infant this self-protection strategy is evident both as denial and as idealization. For example, in some cases the child will be able to remember a traumatic incident but not the emotions that were originally associated with it, and the child may, for example, talk about an incident without becoming emotional. Winnicott argued that due to the child's early self-protection strategies, abuse and other trauma cannot be defined as external events. In early childhood, traumas belong to the external world, but the child gains psychological protection from the fact that external traumas appear, in a psychological sense, as projections. In adults, infantile traumas will appear internal because they have become events that are part of a complex internal psychological structure (Gammelgaard, 2004). Before the development of affective attunement at the age of 6–9 months, the infant has no sense of his own inner world or of this inner world as the source of frustration. Instead, the infant aims this frustration at the environment and blames the environment for the frustration. For example, an infant gets upset and blames the table leg if she tripped on it. Projection is a self-protection strategy that develops early during the phase of emotomentation.

Self-Protection Strategies on the Level of Late Emotomentation

On the level of late emotomentation, the infant's internal representations are often fragmented and divided. Through interactions with the caregiver, the infant identifies with her, among other things through affective attunement, and at this time the infant has difficulty differentiating emotionally between what belongs to the caregiver and what belongs to the infant himself. Self-protection strategies on a limbic level serve to protect the relationship. The infant begins to be able to achieve a form of defensive exclusion of emotions; for example, when attachment behavior is activated the infant may choose not to respond, but he is not yet able to place the emotion within himself or with the caregiver. The infant has not yet developed object permanence and therefore relates to the interaction as it appears here and now. The internal representations are divided and may be either good or bad, and the infant has no ability to merge them into complete representations. During the second half of the first year of life, the infant develops the capacity for introjection and projective identification. Only then can the nervous system, in accordance with the pleasure principle, make a distinction that lets the good parts belong to the system, while the bad parts are assigned to the external world (Gammelgaard, 2004).

Melanie Klein viewed projective identification as an important primitive defense mechanism. Originally, she defined projective identification as the projection of unwanted psychological material onto another important person with whom the child then identified. Projective identification works in two ways: In the secure relationship, the mother incorporates some of the infant's emotions in order to return them to the infant on a level that the infant can handle, and she responds to the infant's projective identifications. In the insecure relationship, where the caregiver is incapable of engaging in an attuned affect-regulating process and receive the infant's emotional communication, the infant will not be able to safely project valuable parts of himself onto the mother. In projective identification it can be difficult to tell who is the sender and who is the recipient of emotions. Just before the infant reaches narcissistic deflation, he is in a phase of omnipotence. When shame begins to emerge, omnipotence is easily deflated; the infant no longer feels that the world revolves only around him but also takes on experiences that he is not to blame for. At this time, the child cannot differentiate between what belongs to others and what belongs to himself. Thus, the infant risks introjecting other people's conflicts or mishaps, simply because he or she was present or otherwise involved.

Self-Protection Strategies on the Level of Ratiomentation

On the level of ratiomentation, the infant has developed object permanence, and the prefrontal cortex has developed a mentalizing capacity. Self-protection strategies on this level are aimed at protecting the ego. Freud believed that the contrast between subject and object only emerges once the infant's thinking is able to reproduce a notion about something that is not present here and now, and which may no longer exist in the world (Gammelgaard, 2004). On this level, self-protection is about isolating the affect; the emotional content of the experience can be separated out, even if the experience is consciously known. On this level of mental organization, self-protection strategies include repression, sublimation, intellectualization, and displacement. These self-protection mechanisms do not develop until the prefrontal cortex has expanded sufficiently or until the language regions in the left hemisphere have connected with the right hemisphere and are able to regulate emotionality in the right hemisphere.

Repression means that a thought or a feeling is excluded from consciousness. Repression can have negative consequences because the nervous system expends a great deal of mental energy on keeping forbidden thoughts and feelings from entering consciousness. Repression involves pushing both the content of the conflict and the associated emotion out of explicit consciousness.

Mature defenses such as humor and intellectualization make it possible to reduce powerful emotions, remain in attuned contact with others, and maintain one's sense of reality. Sublimation and displacement allow the nervous system to convert affects and displace them, making it possible to handle powerful grief or pain on a level that the psyche can manage. Balanced inhibition through the prefrontal cortex is normally an appropriate self-protection strategy, provided the inhibition does not go too far in suppressing the pressure of emotions from the subcortical regions. A moderate inhibition of the impulse pressure means that emotions do not get the upper hand and thus prevents the nervous system from regressing.

Summary

Personality development is closely associated with emotional interactions between caregiver and child that promote the development of identity and self-reflection. At any age level, newly developed skills and competencies present a potential for new psychological opportunities as well as obstacles. The reorganization of the various levels of mental organization leads to the possibility of increased flexibility or increased vulnerability in the form of rigidity or chaos. The internal representations continue to differentiate and develop throughout the life span and change in response to the environmental shifts that the child experiences, from the adaptation that takes place in kindergarten to the school context and relationships with friends and peers (Cicchetti et al., 1995; Sroufe, 1979).

The developing child becomes more self-regulating and plays an increasingly active role in his own regulation process. Many parts of the brain consist of regions characterized by plasticity and remain capable of developing synaptic connections throughout the life span. Right-hemispheric capacities are essential for processing emotional information and regulating bodily states, and they are crucial for our ongoing personality development. Capacities in the right hemisphere connect with narratives and socially acceptable behavior as the left hemisphere matures. Basic personality formation, which takes place early in the child's life, is essential for ongoing personality development, but even if the nervous system is more plastic in childhood than it is later on, personality development continues throughout life, achieving increasing maturity, sophistication, and balance in interaction with neural growth (Sroufe, 1989a).

In Chapters 1–3 I have discussed the interaction with caregivers and the child's levels of mental organization on different age levels. This organization is described in light of what might be called normal or typical development. In the next three chapters I look at deviations from typical development, partly from a relational perspective and partly from an intrapsychic and neuroaffective perspective. I round off this review with a systematic description of the ways in which abnormal development can lead to psychological dysfunctions in the personality structure of children as well as adults.

PART TWO

—ᴍᴍ—

A Neuroaffective Perspective on Attachment and Relational Disorders

CHAPTER FOUR

Dysregulation and Misattunement in the Dyadic Interaction

> *When the development of an infant is observed with a clinical eye*
> *one sees . . . characteristic patterns and some variant patterns. . . .*
> *When there are deviations, it is the relationship with the caregiv-*
> *ers and not the infant alone that appears deviant. Often it is not*
> *even clear which variations are the most likely precursors of later*
> *pathology. And at each successive age, everything seems differ-*
> *ent, yet everything feels exactly the same, clinically.*
>
> Daniel Stern (1985, p. 186)

The formation of attachments is crucial in interpersonal relationships, and practically all developmental psychologists agree that the most basic relational disorders occur if parents are unable to derive happiness or joy from spending time with their baby. Adult clients who have suffered severe abuse often say that the worst thing that happened to them was not feeling loved. Regardless of what sort of mutual attunement and psychobiological rhythm that caregiver and child engage in, this structure, organization, or rhythm will be incorporated into the child's developing nervous system. A lack of accord between the caregiver's experience and actions and the child's needs and states will lead to relational disorders.

As mentioned in Chapter 1, the interaction pattern between caregiver and infant consists of the caregiver's and the infant's contributions, which together make up the intersubjective interaction. Developments in infant research have taken several different paths. Some theories describe an understanding of the infant's internal, subjective experiences and development; other theories study the infant's competencies and development based on objective behavioral descriptions; others again deal mainly with the infant's interactions and mutual regulation with the caregiver; and some look at the child's attachment and relationships. Infant research does not yet have a combined understanding of these different levels and approaches, but hopefully within the next few years we will be able to merge developmental theories and place innate competences, physio- and psychobiological regulation, interaction, and the consequent internal representations and attachment and relational patterns that are the basis for personality formation into a larger context.

In the three previous chapters I have discussed how attunement and misattunement are necessary and frequent occurrences in well-regulated interactions, and what role they play in regulating the child's nervous system and personality development. Chapters 4 through 6 describe dysregulation patterns, their neuroaffective impact on personality development, and their potential for developing into psychological disorders. This chapter looks at long-term misattunement as an obstacle to the child's ability to engage in social interactions with others and as a potential source of developmental impairment or arrested development.

The Impact of Severe and Prolonged Dysregulation

Normally, the child has the capacity to modulate low-level negative affect states, provided they are moderate. The infant's nervous system is not sufficiently developed to handle negative states that escalate in intensity, frequency, and duration. An infant who has to remain for a prolonged period in a state of negative affect or is not met in an attuned affect is likely at particular risk of developing psychological disorders. The caregiver's involvement in the infant's affect regulation is important for the child's shift from negative affective states back to positive states, and as mentioned earlier, the infant learns to modulate affective states through the caregiver's ability to regulate her own affect in relation to the infant (Schore, 2000).

In the 1960s Mary Ainsworth pointed out that the deprivation of care falls into three categories: insufficiency, distortion through neglect, and discontinuity. These three categories are often mixed up, which makes it difficult to differentiate and study the individual aspects (Karen, 1998).

Winnicott (1960) emphasized that inadequate maternal behavior constitutes a threat to the child's psychological health, and the child is forced to dissociate with the risk of developing what he called a false self. The child's lack of coping strategies will cause him to engage in innate autoregulating behavior, where he is no longer able to establish self-regulation. The child is no longer able to interact with the external environment and is closed off to attachment communication and interactive regulation (Schore, 2003a).

Daniel Stern, Colwyn Trevarthen, and Edward Tronick's video recordings of microinteractions between mothers and babies have revealed how early and how easily the interaction becomes a part of the baby's communicative repertoire. Through the daily contact the microinteractions come to form ever larger wholes, which can eventually be characterized as relational or attachment patterns. It is these attachment patterns, among other things, that Mary Ainsworth and Mary Main studied and categorized. A moderate stress level enhances learning, but stressors that exceed the capacity of the nervous system have the opposite effect. If the stimulus level is constantly too low the infant soon loses interest, and if the stimulus level is too high the infant turns away or cries. In the early stages of life, relational and attachment disorders appear as disturbances in the regulation of sleep, food, and so on, not as a psychological disorder in the infant. Whether the infant is exposed to excessive levels of arousal, in the case of abuse, or inadequate levels of arousal, in deprivation or neglect, the consequences for the development of the nervous system can be dire. A lack of attunement or constant misattunements will expose the infant to frequent negative affect states with no influence on his own regulation and situation. An infant who is frequently abandoned to an escalation of arousal states without regulation of the affective state will eventually become traumatized (Bradley, 2000; Fonagy et al., 2002).

The Parents' Personality Structure, Internal Representations, and Mentalization Capacity in Relation to Dysregulation

Even though the infant has organizing skills from the outset, no infant is able to develop organizing skills and competencies without the support of the primary caregivers. An infant may temporarily adjust to the absence of intersubjective relations, but if the caregiver is not able to change, and no one else is available, the consequences for the infant will be catastrophic. The infant needs loving and caring adults to feel worthy of love and for the nervous system to develop (Cicchetti et al., 1995; Emde, 1989; Stern, 1985). Whether the child's personality development is abnormal or healthy depends on the caregiver's ability to be emotionally available, to attune with the infant, and to be open to the infant's innate competencies on the child's terms.

The Caregiver's History

Studies with monkeys have shown that primates that grew up in total isolation usually show parental incompetence, with insufficient caregiving behavior when they become mothers themselves. There are, however, large individual differences in these monkey mothers' ability to cope, as approximately one third of the deprived monkey mothers display normal care for their offspring (Suomi, 1991). The other two thirds are uncaring, neglect their offspring, and even attack them. They either withdraw from others or are unpredictably vicious, and when the hierarchical order is to be determined, these monkeys engage in fighting without acknowledging defeat. They engage in self-harming behavior, for example, by biting themselves, banging their heads against the wall, and so on. Periodically, they eat and drink to excess and have difficulty regulating their sleep cycle. They do not learn to discriminate between social stimuli, such as different facial expressions, probably because they lack the early experience of synchronicity between themselves and their mothers and the associated social expressions. Their behavior gives the impression of an unintegrated nervous system.

Suomi's (1991) studies have shown that the effect of severe social understimulation in primates is reversible if the isolation has lasted less than a year. He also found that young deprived monkeys to some extent were able to compensate for their psychological damage by later growing up with peers. The isolated infant monkeys were unable to initiate contact, but they gradually developed play ability and other interaction skills, and after a few weeks they did begin to initiate play and other interactions. As adolescents and adults the isolated monkeys had largely normal behaviors, but in new and stressful situations they responded with the same sort of stereotypical behavior that they had displayed during their isolation. They also displayed major behavioral difficulties if they were returned to isolation.

The monkey studies have led to the assumption that dysregulated attachment in human infants will also lead to a subsequent abnormal caregiving capacity, and much research has been devoted to studying the effect of parents' personality structures, internal representations, and mentalization capacity in their interactions with their children. Thus, it seems that the caregiver's ability to interact with her baby stems from factors that developed long before the baby is born. The mother's bond with the child emerges in a complicated process that is related to the internal representations that she has developed through her attachment with her own parents. Izard (1991), Main et al. (1985), and Main (1990) have demonstrated how the caregiver's manner of affective expression predicts aspects of the attachment pattern that develops between her and the coming child. Parents who are able to describe their emotions and considerations when they talk about their own childhood attachment experiences are able to distinguish their own needs from the child's needs and are capable of containing and responding to the child's mental state. This predicts a high likelihood that the infant will develop a safe or secure attachment with them.

Caregivers With an Unmodulated Nervous System

Parents who have suffered massive neglect or abuse in childhood, and who have lived without a closely attuned contact, have often lacked the opportunity to develop self-regulating functions and object permanence. These parents' immature nervous system is often emotionally unstable and socially dysfunctional. That is, they are incapable of affective regulation in stressful situations; their mentalization capacity is inadequate; and in all likelihood they will not be able to promote their own child's self-regulation. The parents' unmodulated nervous system will be characterized by internal conflicts, sudden mood swings, and difficulty achieving affect regulation—elements they will inevitably bring into the interaction with their infant. One father described his internal experience as an alien feeling where something exploded, and he disappeared through a tunnel without being able to stop the process. His facial expression was filled with rage, and he was extremely tense. Occasionally he hit his children, and sometimes he yelled at them, filled with a rage that he was unable to control. Afterward he attempted to deny the rage, and sometimes he felt shame and refused to speak about the incidents (Siegel, 1999).

Parents with a low frustration threshold will often attempt to resolve misattunements through external acts without engaging in empathic contact with the child. They often feel that they are losing the fight with the child and end up in a power struggle where they either seek to keep the child from getting the upper hand or become defeatist and allow the child to gain control (Bradley, 2000). Many abused parents have little understanding of the child's needs or age, and they respond with power, control, and rejection or with passivity and indifference. Often the parents feel that the child is trying to control them. These parents have difficulty being consistent and often hit their children in anger, frustration, and irritation. Some of these parents do not seem to regret their actions or understand the child's pain. Punishment is not used to dampen the child's behavior but occurs randomly and unpredictably when the parents' frustration and powerlessness run high. Parents who have difficulty managing their own self-regulation are overwhelmed; they quickly lose control over themselves, and they often have rigid coping strategies (Cicchetti et al., 1995; Crittenden, 1988).

Caregivers' Ability to Tolerate Their Own Negative Emotions

Bowlby did not think that the parents' negative feelings toward the child were necessarily harmful; he also believed that such emotions occur from time to time in most parents. In his view, it is more important that parents are able to tolerate their own negative emotions instead of denying them. A dismissive mother is often filled with feelings of anger, rejection, and abuse, which drown out her positive feelings toward the child. By contrast, a mother who is too indulgent will be too accepting of unacceptable behavior in the infant, for example, aggressive impulse breakthroughs or spiteful reactions. According to Bowlby, the denial of certain emotions is a serious matter, since these parents will often act without reflecting on their actions and attribute feelings to the infant that in fact are their own. The parents may find it so difficult to distinguish their own needs from the child's and be so distanced from their own emotions that they are incapable of sensing the child's emotions. Hence, they often tend to project their own negative feelings onto the infant, which forces the infant to view himself as worthless and unloved. Some caregivers reduce their own discomfort by trying to make the child behave in a certain way to match their own needs. For example, if the caregiver is unable to deal with her own anger, she may place it in the infant and engage in an interaction that makes the infant angry and spiteful (Schibbye, 2005). Among others, Fonagy et al. (1995, 1997) and Main et al. (1985) have described how the infant is only able to develop a secure attachment if the parents are able to reflect on what it is that makes them harbor negative feelings toward their child.

Activation of the Caregiver's Internal Representations

In all forms of contact, internal representations are activated, including the caregivers' interactions with the infant. The neglect and abuse that the parents suffered in previous relationships are relived as internal representations that link previous neglect and abuse with current parenting behavior. For example, if the mother perceives the infant's normal tendency to avert his gaze to regulate arousal as a sign of rejection, she may break off the interaction a little too soon, before the infant is ready to quit. In that scenario the infant will receive insufficient stimulation. Caregivers with unresolved traumas often form defensive strategies to avoid being overwhelmed by painful emotions, and they may have to distance themselves from the infant's needs to avoid feeling psychological pain (Karen, 1998; Stern, 1985). This may lead to a chronically insecure relationship (Fonagy et al., 1995).

Most internal representations are implicit (unconscious) and exist on a lower level of mental organization. The caregiver may perceive the infant as hostile and treat the child with anger without being consciously aware of it, and thus, the infant's responses to this provocation meet her expectations of the hostile character of the infant. Even if anger or grief has not been consciously acknowledged, the feelings do not go away but are maintained implicitly and continue to have an effect. For example, the caregiver may act in subtle ways to provoke the child's anger when her own anger threatens to overwhelm her. She may live out her anger through the child or convert her depression to negative qualities in the child, defining the child as annoying, demanding, and so on. In this way, the caregiver's negative feelings turn into dysfunction in the child.

Fonagy (2001) mentions that it may sometimes be hard to spot what went wrong in a relationship when an infant responds with an insecure attachment, and the caregivers are neither particularly abusive nor neglectful nor have a mental illness. Sometimes the key is that the caregiver is not emotionally available to the infant. The child has not had an opportunity to engage in an affectively attuned contact, which is a prerequisite for developing internal representations of one's own internal sensations. When the caregiver aims her hatred, disgust, and so on at the infant in implicit or subtle ways, the infant forms a self-image based on the caregiver's way of containing the infant. For example, if an infant bites the mother's breast because he is excited and happy, the caregiver may feel anxiety and disgust. If this type of experience occurs frequently, it may affect the infant's understanding of his own state, for example, as excited joy is associated with anger and rejection.

All parents want to love their child, but it may be difficult for them to find this love if they were not loved and seen through a sensitive parental contact, met on their own conditions and with their needs (Cicchetti et al., 1995; Karen, 1998). Crittenden (1983) emphasizes that mothers who neglect their children desperately wish to avoid having the children removed from the home and placed in foster care. They are attached to the children in their own way, which is hard to identify until the threat of separation appears, and even then, outsiders may find it hard to identify.

The Impact of the Caregivers' Poor Mentalization Capacity

As early as 1971, Winnicott said that the caregiver's responses in the normal caregiver-infant contact relate to the infant's state. For example, if the caregiver sees that the infant is distressed, she will comfort the child and thus reduce the child's stress level. The problems arise when her face expresses her own feelings and perceptions, not the child's, and when she is dismissive or intrusive. The child loses the sense of owning his own affect and becomes unable to understand and interpret the other's experience and behavior. The caregiver's state of mind becomes part of the child's self, and the child misses the opportunity to understand his own feelings. If the caregiver is able to self-regulate emotionally and distinguish her own needs, affects, and intentions from the child's, she will be able to regulate the infant without confusing her needs and affects with the child's, or vice versa. When the caregiver is unable to tell the difference between herself and the child, she is incapable of regulating the child's states. This leads to dysregulation and pain in the child that the caregiver cannot comprehend. The caregiver's response to the infant is internalized and becomes part of the infant's self-image. The caregivers play a crucial role for the child's possibility of developing self-reflection (Schibbye, 2005; Sørensen, 2006).

In a nonattuned contact, the caregiver is unable to manage the infant's distress in a way that makes the infant feel contained and understood. Fonagy (2001) said that parents who are unable to reflect on the infant's internal experiences and respond to them deprive the infant of a fundamental psychological structure that the child needs to construct a sense of self. Accepting the child's mental content has a containing function (Bion, 1967). Caregivers with an inadequate mentalizing capacity will repeat their own history in relationships with their children. The caregiver's mentalization capacity reflects her self-perception and self-understanding and thus also her view of her child. The child's mentalization capacity depends on the caregiver's ability to perceive that the infant's responses are not only about the infant but also about her.

The crucial prerequisite for a mature empathic capacity is the caregiver's ability to deal with her own state as well as the infant's, which may be different from hers. The display of "raw" emotions, when the caregiver is unable to distinguish between her own state and the child's and when she lives out her feelings in an unattuned and insensitive manner, is testimony to inadequately developed higher cortical functions and highly activated limbic structures. When the caregiver is unable to distinguish between her own needs and the infant's, the infant is unable to separate emotionally from the caregiver and thus fails to develop a self. The raw emotions may be positive or negative, but the infant can handle more joy and care than disgust, anger, and sadness. Completely unregulated joy, for example, in a manic caregiver, may, however, be very destructive for the infant. When the caregiver is unable to sense the infant's subjective state and denies his feelings, for example by refusing to believe that he is anxious and had a nightmare when he comes to her for comfort, or when she fuses with his state without being able to self-regulate, for example if she becomes just as scared as the child when he has nightmares, the child lacks an opportunity to receive the caregiver's support in self-regulating. In the latter example, she takes over the child's affect and becomes the center herself, which may result in the child having to comfort the caregiver. If the caregiver loses her temper and gets angry, the child is not seen and comforted. The child is abandoned and left to autoregulate while also having to manage the anxiety in the dyadic contact. The child is scared of the caregiver's anger, and that makes the amygdala, particularly in the right hemisphere, sensitive to future fear states (Sørensen, 2006).

Mary Main (1993) argues that the transfer of a secure attachment and the differences in the child's attachment patterns are closely related to the quality of the caregiver's mentalization capacity. She argues that the caregivers' incapacity to distinguish their own feelings from others' and to understand their own feelings leads to vulnerability in infants and young children. Main developed a semistructured interview called the Adult Attachment Interview, which asks parents about attachment relationships in their childhood and the influence that they believe their early relationships have had on their own development. Based on these interviews she uncovered three patterns. First, some parents were autonomous and secure, and were able to offer a clear and coherent account of early attachment, regardless of whether the attachment experiences had been satisfying. They had no problem remembering particular events when they had been concerned about incidents concerning attachment. Second, preoccupied parents had many conflicted attachment-related childhood memories and were unable to organize them into a coherent image. They often had difficulty recalling incidents that caused sadness, and they had little insight into the effect that attachment-relevant experiences had had on their development. Third, dismissing parents expressed that they did not remember much about their relationships with their parents in childhood and tended to idealize their parents on a general level and to describe incidents of rejection when they did manage to remember specific incidents.

A study of a group of single mothers living under stressful conditions in the form of unemployment, criminality, psychiatric illness, and so on found that the children were far more likely to have a secure attachment if the mother was able to reflect on her own as well as her child's mental states (Fonagy & Target, 2003). Fonagy et al. (1995) developed what they call a vulnerability/resilience model, based on studies showing that caregivers' mentalizing capacity is particularly important when the infant is exposed to stress or inappropriate interaction patterns. Mothers living in isolation and extremely stressful conditions who had a high mentalization capacity all had securely attached children, while mothers living in similarly stressful conditions and isolation who had a poor mentalizing capacity had children with an insecure attachment. In a sense, the mothers' mentalizing capacity enabled the children to develop a mentalizing capacity themselves and helped them escape a negative social legacy (Fonagy, 1999c). Mentalizing skills seem to be biologically prepared and are released spontaneously unless the development is hampered by the dual setback of the lack of a secure attachment and abusive experiences on the part of the attachment figure.

The Role of the Infant's Inherent Conditions in Relation to Dysregulation

Genetic factors and various influences during pregnancy mean that all infants are unique; this is evident already during gestation and early infancy. It is expressed, for example, in the infant's regulation of arousal and activation levels, ability to engage in attunement, attention capacity, mood states, and so on. Belsky (1996) found that the risk of the infant developing an insecure attachment pattern increases with the number of risk factors present, for example, in the form of poor psychological function in the parents and a difficult temperament in the infant. Studies have shown that the infant's temperament and the caregiver's personality each have less importance than their mutual match. Thus, it is necessary to know something about the infant's temperament as well as the caregiver's personality to predict the quality of the resulting attachment (Smith, 2003).

In the 1960s, when Mary Ainsworth was studying attachment patterns, Stella Chess, among others, was interested in the infant's inherent conditions and the interaction of these qualities with the environment. Children who later showed emotional or behavioral difficulties were often born with a temperament that was difficult to regulate. Chess also found that a child with an easy temperament might develop problems, since such a child, who has an easy time interacting with others and is good at adapting, is more likely to imitate the caregivers' dysfunctional sides. Chess found a large number of cases where the parents' and the infant's temperaments seemed to be a poor match. She did not think that the child's temperament sealed his fate; rather, she interpreted the responses to mean that certain children required a more sensitive attunement and more interactions with the caregiver. The problematic interaction could either be exacerbated or improved, depending on the interaction between the infant and the caregiver and on the effect of external factors, such as peers and teachers, on the relationship (Chess & Thomas, 1982; Karen, 1998).

A number of innate components affect relational development. Brazelton developed the Neonatal Behavioral Assessment Scale, which examines the infant's capacity for protecting himself against external impressions, for going from one state to another, and for self-consoling. Naturally, the likelihood of developing a relational disorder is greater if the infant has a congenital impairment that makes it more difficult for the caregiver to interpret the infant's needs and to attune with the infant (Madsen, 1996; Stern, 1985).

Dysregulation Patterns

In early infancy, a child may have regulation disorders but not yet have developed symptoms of internal psychological disorders (Stern, 1985). Repeated lab studies, including some carried out by Colwyn Trevarthen and Edward Tronick, have found that when infants are unable to engage in a stable attuned contact with a primary caregiver, they withdraw from interaction and either become distressed and expresse discomfort or seek self-stimulation. They develop stereotypical behavior patterns that are not adjusted in relation to the environment. They develop difficulties picking up positive as well as negative signals from the environment, and their nervous system regresses to innate or previously acquired behavior patterns. The nervous system organizes through close contact between caregiver and infant, provided the environment is predictable and stable. An infant with a fragile and chronically stressed nervous system will often be hard to interpret and tend to respond negatively or unpredictably, which often causes the adults around the infant to become insecure and correcting. The infant needs to meet appreciation, which requires that the caregiver is emotionally available and able to understand the infant's needs. It is this appreciation that gives infants a sense of being entitled to their own emotions.

Anders (1989) distinguished between degrees of disorders in the relationship between children and parents, ranging from temporary behavioral disorders to rigid and prolonged interaction patterns that are constantly activated in caregiver-infant interactions. The interaction patterns may change over the course of the child's development. The caregivers may be good at stimulating the child at one age level, but when the child grows older and begins to make demands, the caregivers are not always able to meet the child's developmental needs. For example, when the child becomes more physically active and defies the caregivers, their role changes and takes on a stronger socializing component. If the caregivers have difficulty handling this transition, they may indulge the child's desires in an attempt to stop the pestering, which may cause the child to get stuck in an omnipotent position, where he finds it hard to comply with other people's demands. The opposite may also occur, where the caregivers become excessively angry, which makes the child feel wrong and unloved when displaying autonomy (Cozolino, 2000; Siegel, 1999).

Overstimulation is just as harmful to a child as understimulation. The mutual interaction between caregiver and child unfolds through adapted levels of activity, where the caregiver does not stimulate the child too much or too little. The child's self-regulation strategies are adapted to the compromise between the need to maintain the engagement with the caregiver and the need to protect his integrity by keeping arousal on an acceptable level. Both negative and positive affect can constitute a level of overarousal that violates the child's integrity, which poses problems for self-regulation. When the child is exposed to overwhelming experiences or overstimulation that he is unable to attune with the caregiver, he stops seeking joint attention and trying to share experiences with the caregiver. Failure to terminate an interaction sequence when the child disengages disturbs the mutual character of the interaction and makes it hard for the child to calm down (Beebe & Lachmann, 2002; Belsky, Rovine, & Taylor, 1984; Øvreeide, 2002; Sander, 1985).

Contact Disorders

When the child stops seeking joint attention and taking the initiative to share experiences, he develops a contact disorder. Contact disorders may result from a variety of causes, as the child organizes communication based on the received response. For example, in the beginning of a contact exchange, when the caregiver fails to observe the child's focus of attention and involvement, when she interprets the child's initiatives negatively or fails to take the necessary time to allow the child to find his focus of attention and respond, when she fails to wait for the child's response, when she does not help the child expand his focus, and when she fails to support the child's concentration, the result is frustration in both parties, and the child soon loses interest in the environment. The caregiver communicates through tiny microevents that are all significant if they are repeated often enough (Øvreeide & Hafstad, 1996).

A contact disorder may stem from a variety of causes. For example, if there are several important caregivers around the child who are either replaced frequently or who are dismissing or expressionless, the infant will not be able to engage with predictable contact patterns. The infant will not be able to organize in an attuned contact and initiate interactions with an expectation of what is going to happen. The infant will attempt to adapt to the varying interaction patterns to match the varying responses that the caregivers provide but will do so at the cost of self-regulating and identity-forming skills. A number of studies have found that highly variant caregiving patterns in institutions and foster care are a frequent cause of attention-deficit/hyperactivity disorder (ADHD; Fonagy, 2001).

A child with unreliable parents will attempt to maintain trust and preserve a form of control in unpredictable situations. The unbearable reality that the child cannot alter or escape from is instead altered in the child's mind, for example through dissociation, which I discuss in Chapter 5. If the child's boundaries are constantly violated, the child does not develop a sense of a generational hierarchy and fails to learn to sense his own boundaries. All forms of reverse generational hierarchies, where the child has to take care of the parents, will force the child into a premature independence process that exceeds the child's maturity level. Simultaneously, this situation traps the child in a distorted dependency relationship with the parents, as the child worries about the parents (Øvreeide, 2002; Sørensen, 2005).

The Caregiver's Influence on Dysregulation Patterns

Every child is unique, and the caregiver must respond to the child's actual needs. A fearful child, for example, requires a different response than an active and outgoing child, and a tired child requires a different response than a bored one. The caregiver's internal representations are crucial for the way in which she relates to her unique child. A dismissing caregiver, for example, may fail to mirror the child's distress because she does not have the capacity to form a coherent image of the child's mental state. An overregulating mother may represent the child's internal experiences with a high degree of clarity but fail to attune with the child on the child's terms, and an ambivalent mother may be so vague or contradictory that the child is unable to communicate.

When the infant's signals result in intervention or rejection, the infant will learn to inhibit his behavior. Intervening, dismissing, and ambivalent caregivers all use affective signals that are confusing. For example, the caregiver's mimicry may display an affect that signals a desire for closeness, but when the infant responds, he is met with rejection. When the infant is unable to predict the caregiver's behavior, the child becomes insecure and responds by being frightened or angry and becomes incapable of organizing his behavior (Crittenden, 1994, 1995; Fonagy, 2001).

Overregulation

Emma is 9 years old and in a therapy session with her mother. The mother repeatedly states that she is very concerned that Emma is unable to take care of herself. She says that she has always been worried that Emma did not eat enough, and as a baby she was difficult to feed. Emma did not sense satiety, so sometimes she ate so much that she was sick afterward. Emma was not enrolled in daycare because the mother did not think that she could handle it. Emma wants to wear skimpy T-shirts like her friends, but she is not allowed to, because the mother is worried what might happen. Although the mother feels sorry for Emma, she feels she has to check, for example, by asking her to lift up her shirt before she goes off to school, to be sure that she is not cheating. The mother says that Emma often expresses opinions that she does not actually believe in. During the session, Emma says that she does not like her class teacher, and the mother takes over and says that the teacher is really nice.

This very intervening mother lacks respect for her child as a separate person. She tries to impose her will on the daughter, shape her according to her standards or needs, with no regard for the girl's mood, desires, and such (Anders, 1989). Controlling and intrusive behavior from the caregiver is one of the most common causes of overstimulation and includes interference with the child's self-regulating behavior. Initially, the child may try to adapt through avoidance maneuvers, for example, by dampening his signals. If overstimulation by the primary caregiver is a daily occurrence, the child will form a generalized expectation of overstimulation and will respond defensively, also in interactions with other people (Beebe & Lachmann, 2002).

Minuchin, Rosman, and Baner (1978) have described the overregulating relationship as enmeshed. The relationship is characterized by inadequate boundaries between the child and the caregiver, and the caregiver acts on her own ideas and needs, dictating the child's identity and the role he must play. The contact is schematic; the caregiver does not listen to the child's signals and needs and is incapable of promoting the child's self-regulation and rhythm. At first glance, the caregiver's interactions with the child seem caring and warm with a clear distribution of responsibility between caregiver and child, but often an observation of the microinteraction reveals that the caregiver is completely out of touch with the infant's initiatives and needs. The caregiver's overregulating behavior is often a cover for vulnerability in relation to feeling helpless and a fear of losing control. The caregiver does not always sense her own insecurity when she is with the child but does what any good mother should do for her child. When the child attempts to establish communication on his own terms or, at a later stage in development, seeks some form of joint understanding or agreement, the mother feels threatened, and the experience may cause her to rigidly cling to her reality. In her way of relating to the child, she appears to do what the child wants, but she does it in a way that denies the child's reality. "Thus, the mother's response is not simply a takeover but also a denial of the child's reality" (Sørensen, 1996, p. 81; translated for this edition). The child attunes with the mother in a way that ensures attachment, but it is not based on the child's own affective experience. To engage in intersubjective sharing with the caregiver, the child has to adapt his behavior and thus his experiences to match the mother's needs. When the attunement is taken over by the caregiver, the child becomes uncertain of his internal reality. The child has difficulty creating psychological space and differentiating, and the relationship risks becoming symbiotic. When the caregiver places aspects of her affective life in the child, the child's ability to develop self-boundaries is hampered (Schibbye, 2005).

If the caregiver is chronically overregulating, the child is imprinted with the experience that emotional facial expressions are irrelevant in communication with others and incapable of affecting the external world, and the child will gradually stop showing affective facial expressions. A child who is always led by the hand without being entitled to a proper dialogue will not be able to explore the environment, make his own experiences, or have his own emotions. Such a child will retreat into a passive acceptance of the conditions that he is offered, like a kitten that goes limp and silent when its mother picks it up by the scruff of the neck (Brodén, 1991; Neisser, 1993; Stern, 1985).

Underregulation

Mona is 1½ years old, and in the contact with her, Mona's mother seems low on mimicry, annoyed, unfocused, and absent. During the observed lunch, the mother seems uncertain whether she will be able to hold Mona's attention, even though she sits at the table calm and attentive. Mona is often corrected for no reason, and the mother does not contact her in any other way. Mona constantly pays attention to the mother's facial expression and tries hard to follow along. The mother seems insecure as Mona eventually becomes restless and unfocused, and Mona is immediately asked to straighten up. At no point does the mother engage in any vitalizing contact with Mona

The caregiver may be so absent that she fails to notice the child, let alone demonstrate that she has understood the child's signals (Smith, 2003). She does not respond to the infant's initiatives, and the mutual involvement is low. The child is often left to himself or indiscriminately left with others; the caregiver may forget about the child, and the caregiver's face is often expressionless, eye contact is vague, and she avoids close contact when she is with her child. The caregiver often expresses discomfort at physical contact and psychological warmth, and when the child does not need her support she turns away or gets involved in a way that is not helpful to the child (Mortensen, 2001). In extreme cases the caregiver may be completely emotionally closed off and lack the emotional presence that is necessary for attunement and sharing. Even though the caregiver does provide basic care, and everything looks normal, upon closer inspection there is no emotional contact. In other words, it is hard to discern the interaction that causes the child to seem so distant and sad (Schibbye, 2005).

A child's reaction depends on his innate temperament. For example, an active and outgoing child who is frequently understimulated will become more active in her attempts at eliciting a response from the caregiver, while a passive and introverted child will be quicker to give up and develop an absent and depressive pattern. A mother who is depressed or compulsively obsessed with thoughts that are unrelated to the child will not be able to engage in the vitalizing contact that is required to capture the infant's fleeting attention, or she will fail to notice the infant's invitations. Thus, the interaction will lack nuanced attunement. When the child fails to receive sufficient joy-filled stimulation, he is not encouraged to engage in the vitalization and joy that are required to develop the nervous system, and due to the lack of high-arousal experiences the nervous system is not trained and expanded to manage increasing levels of arousal.

Maladaptive and Chaotic Regulation

Kevin is 6 years old; he has a slight speech impediment. When the therapist asks him a question, his mother interrupts and does not let him finish. The mother is in constant activity, moving about and speaking in a loud, shrill voice. She is competing with her son for the therapist's attention, and Kevin becomes physically restless and boundaryless. She constantly comments on what Kevin is doing and praises him highly, only to correct him and scold him the next moment. This leads to constant discussions and arguments between them. During dinner, the mother suddenly decides that Kevin should do his language training, and Kevin is unable to focus on dinner or on the language training.

When the caregiver is unable to achieve timing or synchronization or engage in varying regulation patterns with the child, the regulation is maladaptive. If the caregiver's response is correct and maybe positive but lacks timing and synchronization, the infant will be confused, object, and withdraw from the contact.

In relation to maladaptive regulation, Stern (1977) talked about inauthentic attunement. Inauthentic attunement is characterized by a mismatch between verbal messages and body language. For example, the caregiver may correct the child in a friendly and cheerful tone of voice, which means that the child is unable to interpret the message. The child does not understand what the mother wants, and whether she means what she says, and her emotional expression is difficult to interpret.

Maladaptive regulation may also consist of so-called paradoxical stimulation, where the caregiver is vitalizing and attentive without engaging in attuned contact. When the infant is ready for contact the caregiver disengages, and when the infant disengages she seeks his attention. Paradoxical stimulation may involve the caregiver stimulating the infant only when he is hurt or has an unpleasant experience. Thus, the infant's main moments of joy and vitality are associated with an immediately preceding unpleasant feeling. Bateson's double-bind theory can be characterized as paradoxical stimulation and also as ambivalent attachment. For example, a mother's message of wanting a kiss while she is also sending a metamessage of anger and disgust may constitute a double bind, because the infant is stuck with no possible response, since the child is wrong whether he responds to the message or the metamessage. The result of a double bind may be confusion, uncertainty, and, in extreme case, borderline states and psychosis (Anders, 1989; Neisser, 1993; Schibbye, 2005; Stern, 1985).

Chaotic regulation represents an extreme form of irregular regulation, where the regulation in the interaction is so varying that it can be difficult to perceive a pattern (Anders, 1989). In an interaction where the caregivers' contact with the child is unpredictable and frightening, the child has no support for creating rhythms and regulation. Furthermore, the interaction does not make sense in a way that lets the child regulate in relation to the parents' input. The child receives no support in calming down or any help with orientation or attention control, and the parents may even make the child insecure through angry, aggressive, and threatening behavior. Unregulated parental expressions of rage and contempt may evoke intense feelings of worthlessness and humiliation in the child.

A child who is exposed to chaotic regulation will scan the parents' faces carefully from a young age, attempting to decode what the parents will do and to find meaning and predictability. The child is not met on his conditions and often has never seen the parents expressing anticipation and joy. Some of these children will attune as "good" when the parents are nice and attentive and see themselves as "bad" when the parents are mean and cold. Later, these children's ambivalence, their mistrust of others, and unprovoked hostile attacks will elicit negative responses. As Sroufe concluded, "You get an empathic child not by trying to teach the child and admonish the child, you get an empathic child by being empathic with the child. The child's understanding of relationships can only be from the relationships he's experienced" (quoted in Karen, 1998, p. 195).

The regulation, dysregulation, attunement, misattunement, and so on that the child experiences through everyday microinteraction experiences become part of the child's internal representations, and at an early age the child displays various relational patterns and patterns of communication both in interactions with the caregiver and later also in interactions with other caregivers and peers.

The Child's Attachment Behavior and Relational Strategies in Connection With Dysregulation

Relational disorders are often understood in the light of attachment theories, including John Bowlby's and Mary Ainsworth's research. Ainsworth studied the child's relationship with the primary caregiver in an attachment context and hence called the child's responses attachment patterns. Interaction patterns are discernible in all the child's interactions with the caregiver, from diaper changing to feeding. The relationship is the sum of the interactions that occur between caregiver and child. Perhaps the term attachment patterns could be replaced with interaction patterns or interaction strategies to avoid confusion with the term attachment disorder, which is often used for severely abused or neglected children who have suffered early damage. In the following, however, I have chosen to maintain the original term attachment patterns, and use the term relational disorder generally for disorders in children who have an insecure attachment pattern.

In severe cases, a child who fails to establish a regulated rhythm in interactions with a primary caregiver will develop an attachment disorder or a relational disorder, which makes it impossible for the child to form relevant attachments with others in the future. With the exception of the victims of severe abuse, a child will always seek attachment, splitting off internal emotional states and excluding and denying certain experiences from the intersubjective field to maintain the attachment (Stern, 1985). When the relationship with the caregiver is characterized by anxiety, hatred, and shame, the child's exploratory behavior, ideas, and constructive thoughts are suppressed. The stressful experiences force the child to develop self-protection strategies, and the child will often be anxious. Attachment research shows that childhood anxiety develops in relations with adults who are unable to help them handle tension, chaotic confusion, and pain.

As early as the 1950s, Robertson and Bowlby identified three phases of separation response: protest, which is related to separation anxiety; despair, which is related to grief; and denial, which is related to defense mechanisms (Ainsworth, 1993). Bowlby said, "All of us, from the cradle to the grave, are happiest when life is organized as a series of excursions, long or short, from the secure base provided by our attachment figure(s)" (1988, p. 62). Attachment theories deal with closeness and security on the one hand and exploratory curiosity on the other. The interaction is observable, among other places, in the child's attunement with the caregiver in insecure situations that elicit the child's attachment behavior. Bowlby pointed out that attachment is an inherent feature in all social mammals, and that attachment behavior develops, even when the child is exposed to severe maltreatment and punishment from attachment figures. He considered attachment the prerequisite for curiosity and exploratory behavior. When attachment behavior is activated because the child feels unsafe, exploratory behavior stops; once the child feels safe again, the attachment behavior is switched off, and the exploratory behavior is resumed. With the exception of extreme cases, human as well as animal infants become clingy when they are scared or upset, and if there is no other option they will cling to their abuser. Thus, the attachment relationship is assessed through attachment behavior or, in extreme cases, through the lack of attachment behavior as the child relates to the parents in insecure situations.

Attachment Behavior

From around the age of 6–8 months the infant responds with attachment behavior when separated from the primary caregiver; this is labeled separation anxiety. The critical or sensitive period for the formation of specific attachment relationships stretches over a longer period in infancy. Before the age of 6–8 months the infant is able to switch attachment figure, and even secure attachment relationships may become inhibited. Attachment behavior serves the biological function of providing safety and security and requires no additional rewards to develop. Secure attachment relationships promote independence and counteract dependence, and attachment behavior manifests more frequently when the child is tired, sad, or scared.

Attachment behavior is most obvious in 12–30-month-old infants when they are separated from their primary caregivers and in the time following reunion. Attachment behavior consists of three phases: protest, despair, and denial. If the child is separated from the parents for a prolonged period, for example, if the child is institutionalized, placed in foster care, or relocated repeatedly, the child will eventually detach, as if loving care no longer mattered. The child needs certain stimuli for attachment to develop, and a child who has been deprived of caregiving contact from a primary adult will fail to develop attachment behavior. Thus, attachment behavior is detached or suppressed under special and extremely deprived circumstances. For example, in the case of early emotional damage, the child develops a permanent detachment, acting indifferent to the caregivers' presence and displaying superficial interaction that lacks any depth (Smith, 2003).

The Romanian Orphans

In a study of children who had been adopted from Romanian institutions after the age of 8 months, only 37% were assessed as securely attached to their adoptive parents even many years after the adoption took place, while 66% of those who were adopted before the age of 4–6 months were assessed as securely attached, which corresponds largely to the normal population. Most of the Romanian adoptees who were 8 months or older before they were adopted displayed an atypical, insecure attachment pattern, and they were described as uncritical, superficial, indiscriminately friendly, and with diffuse, unselective attachment relationships that lacked reciprocity. The children did not come to adults for assistance and comfort and were able to leave the adoptive parents without any distress. Tizard (1977) characterized indiscriminate friendliness as a behavioral pattern that appears when children will contact any adult without the caution that is seen in normal children. At an early age, abused or neglected and institutionalized children display a lack of response to social interactions and insensitivity to social boundaries. It appears that when the attachment process runs off course in children who have been institutionalized since a young age, the consequences can be very severe indeed. According to Chisholm (1998) and Marcovitch et al. (1997), children who are offered adequate care before and around the age of 4–6 months will be able to develop a secure attachment pattern, while adoptive and foster parents of children who were adopted or put into foster care after this age often report greater difficulties with the child's attachment. The Romanian children who were classified as disorganized retained that classification at the age of 3 years, and their social behavior continued to be severely deviant at age 8 (Chisholm, 1998). As these figures show, not all of the children developed an insecure attachment pattern. It appears that the causal relationship is multifactorial, and that it takes a combination of vulnerability factors for a child to develop an attachment disorder, relating to both the child's innate competencies and the care environment. In families where the child's vulnerable nervous system does not engage in adequate interactions with the caregivers, for example, due to the caregivers' stress or lack of understanding of the child's signals, the child may develop attachment or relational disorders. Fonagy (2005) pointed out that there appears to be a difference between the findings of the Canadian studies of Romanian orphans done by Megan Gunnar et al. and the British studies done by Michael Rutter et al., with the Canadian studies being far more pessimistic. The Canadian studies found that children who were adopted after the age of approximately 6 months showed signs of early emotional damage regardless of the subsequent childhood environment, while the British studies found that one isolated risk factor did not incur any increased risk of psychopathology; instead, the British studies argued that it takes a combination of risk factors to increase the likelihood of future problems (Belsky, Rosenberger, & Crnic, 1995; Rutter, 1985).

Many studies have found that the probability of developing an uninhibited attachment pattern has more to do with the length of time the child has been institutionalized than with the length of time spent with the adoptive family (O'Connor et al., 2000). Studies of children who were raised in institutions have found that being in an environment with warm,

attentive caregivers is not sufficient for developing an attachment relationship, because the children lack a primary caregiver. Children who
were raised in institutions are often clingy, indiscriminate, attention-
seeking, and ingratiating toward strangers without the ability to form
deeper attachments. These features seem to persist; a study of the same
children 6 years later found that in addition to the indiscriminate behavior they also tended to be restless, disobedient, and unpopular (Rutter &
Rutter, 1993). Some studies have found that children who were placed
in residential institutions where they were stimulated and received care,
without, however, being offered an attachment figure, may over time
form an attachment with adoptive parents, provided they were adopted
by the age of 2 years (Hodges, 1996).

Other studies have shown that adopted children from Romanian institutions often have massive emotional and cognitive difficulties. The cognitive difficulties include problems with structuring and organization
(executive functions) as well as rigid and very concrete thinking. The
children often have difficulties with concentration, attention regulation,
and inhibiting control functions. It appears that the executive functions,
which reflect frontal lobe development, are highly sensitive to early experiences (Hofer & Sullivan, 2001). Chugani et al. (2001) did PET scans
of 10 adopted Romanian children and found that deprivation-related
changes in the neural structure are associated more with specific than
with general difficulties in brain structures. Characteristic behavioral
symptoms at the time of adoption were the absence of crying, stereotypical and self-destructive behavior, and social difficulties, probably all
related to a dysfunction in the limbic areas, the brain region that conditions our emotional development. This study suggests that limbic and
frontal functions rely on early experiences, and that early damage is irreversible if the deprivation continues beyond the first year of life
(Chugani et al., 2001; Gunnar, 2001).

As described above, the studies are not in complete agreement. Probably, the institutionalized Romanian children have been exposed to severe deprivation in every area, and fortunately it is rare to see children
in Western European cultures who have suffered such massive and
chronic deprivation. In these countries we often see early emotional
damage where the child is not necessarily understimulated, for example,
with regard to motor or language functions. In my experience, children
with early emotional damage who are placed with adoptive or foster par-

ents after the age of 1–2 years do seem to have irreversible emotional damage regardless of the efforts of the foster or adoptive parents, but it should also be pointed out that there is very little research on useful treatment methods for these children. Studies of children who were exposed to deprivation or severe neglect or abuse have shown that emotional damage more clearly reversible before the age of 4 years, and that damage that is evident at the age of 4 years is normally also present at age 6 (Gunnar, 2001).

Attachment Disorders

Researchers in Fonagy's lab have worked with Edward Tronick's still face paradigm, where researchers instruct mothers to alternate between interacting with the infants and avoiding showing mimicry or responding to the infant's initiatives. The experiment showed that insecurely attached children spent a great deal of time looking at themselves, and they quickly became distressed and had difficulty maintaining contact with the mother, especially after the mother had been without facial expressions. These mothers were not able to share joy-filled interactions with their children in relation to a joint external world. When children are not offered a joy-filled interaction, they lose interest in the environment, which their knowledge about it. Fonagy pointed out that this is probably a main cause of understimulation and of the lower IQ of many children with attachment disorders. A child is unable to engage in the external world without the caregiver's involvement in present moments. When the child lacks an opportunity for engaging in joint affective attunement with her, the child is restricted to his own world (Fonagy, 2005).

Relational disorders are often viewed in relation to Mary Ainsworth's distribution of attachment patterns. Other researchers have observed various attachment disorders and divided them into categories. As of yet there is no complete classification of the various forms of relational disorders, and before I turn to Mary Ainsworth's classification, I will describe an alternative classification developed by Zeanah, Mammen, and Lieberman (1993). They described five attachment disorders: nonattached, indiscriminate, inhibited, aggressive, and role reversal. In the nonattached condition, the child has no preference for an attachment figure; this is also something we see in severely deprived institutionalized children. A child with indiscriminate attachment does not use the caregiver as a secure base, for example by checking with the caregiver in insecure situations. Instead the child indiscriminately goes to others for security and care, a feature of children with disturbed early attachment histories, for example children who were raised by severely abusive parents. This type of disorder has two subtypes: children who constantly engage in risky behavior, and children who seek indiscriminate contact and have social difficulties. In the inhibited attachment disorder we find children who lack curiosity and who remain with the attachment figure instead of engaging in age-relevant exploratory behavior. This behavior is common in children who cling to the caregiver and in compulsively subservient children who have learned to consent and to fulfill the caregiver's wishes. Aggressive attachment disorder is common in children aged 1½–2 years. These children often have anxiety symptoms that are neglected due to the child's aggressiveness. The aggression is either directed at the child himself in the form of self-harming behavior or at the attachment figure and is expressed in severe and prolonged impulse breakthroughs in the face of minor frustrations. Children with role reversal attachment disorder (reverse generational hierarchy) are often controlling and either comfort the caregiver or control and punish her.

Ainsworth's Attachment Types

The most widely recognized classification of attachment patterns is the one developed by Mary Ainsworth based on John Bowlby's attachment theory. Ainsworth worked with Bowlby for a limited period and did a very thorough study of attachment patterns. She began developing her research as part of a smaller project in Uganda but later systematized her empirical research in a Baltimore study, where she developed four scales to describe mothers' interactions with their infants. The Baltimore study originally included 23 white middle-class families who were recruited through pediatricians.

Ainsworth believed that humans are biologically disposed to engage in attachment relationships, which are acquired patterns that have developed, among other reasons, to reduce anxiety and enhance our adaptation to our primary caregivers. Her hypothesis was that the infant first has to know the mother well before being ready to explore other people. According to Ainsworth, the confidence and openness that the infant is able to meet the world with is determined by how safe and secure the infant felt in relation to the mother. Ainsworth developed what she called the strange situation test, where the infant's reactions were observed when mother and child were together, when the mother left, when the infant was alone, when a stranger entered, and when the mother returned. The test lasted 21 minutes, divided into periods of approximately 3 minutes each. Ainsworth was interested in the infant's exploratory behavior during the mother's and the stranger's presence. The situation consisted of eight episodes that proceeded in a standardized sequence. The first three episodes were introductory and not stressful. The first stressful event was introduced during the third episode, when a female stranger entered who calmly sat down in a chair and conversed with the mother and then slowly approached the infant, inviting him or her to play. Episode 4 consisted of the first separation phase as the mother left the room. Episode 5 consisted of the first reunion phase when the mother waited in the doorway for a moment to allow the infant to mobilize a spontaneous response. In the sixth episode the infant was alone, and the observation concerned the infant's response to separation. In the seventh episode the stranger returned, while in the eight episode the mother returned, and after observation of the reunion the test concluded (Ainsworth, Bell, & Stayton, 1971; Ainsworth, Blehar, Waters, & Wall, 1978).

Ainsworth's (1972) thesis was that an infant who is able to use the mother as a secure base for inquisitive behavior will be able to move away freely and will choose to return to her from time to time. Ainsworth's purpose with the experiment was to find the balance between attachment and exploration behavior in 1-year-old infants. She classified the infants according to two criteria based on their tendency to explore their environment when they were with the mother, with a stranger, or on their own, and how they treated the mother, especially when she returned after a brief separation. As expected, she found that the infants explored the environment more actively when they were alone with the mother. Ainsworth said that the switch back and forth between exploration and attachment behavior will be disturbed if the infant feels that the caregiver is psychologically unavailable and unable to attune.

The strange situation test was the first standardized method for assessing the quality of the attachment relationship between infant and caregiver. Ainsworth identified three attachment types: secure, insecure avoidant, and insecure ambivalent. In particular, the infant's responses during the reunion with the mother were indicative of the attachment type. Later, Mary Main added one more category: disorganized attachment. Ainsworth defined the three attachment types and Main the fourth as follows:

Type A: Children with anxious, avoidant, or resistant attachment show few apparent signs of distress when the mother leaves and ignores her when she gets back. Many of the infants treat the stranger with more friendliness than the mother, and their play behavior is tense and inhibited.

Type B: Infants with a secure attachment play actively and happily and seek contact with the mother when she returns, even if they may be distressed while she is gone. They let themselves be consoled and resume their play when she returns.

Type C: Infants with an ambivalent attachment are upset when the mother leaves and are difficult to console when she returns. They seek contact but are also aggressive and resistant, and their play behavior is inhibited.

Type D: Infants with a disorganized attachment have failed to develop coherent strategies for handling the stress of separation but display a variety of behaviors when they reunite with the mother, including anxiety, freezing, and possibly ritualized, compulsive behavior.

A common feature for the infants in the groups with disorders (A, C, and D) is insecure attachment. These infants seem to lack both secure attachment and a sense of being rooted in themselves. They do not feel that the mother is able to help them regulate moods, for example, by reducing anxiety, distress, and discomfort (Schibbye, 2005).

In Ainsworth's study, 55–65% of the infants had a secure attachment pattern, 20–30% had an insecure avoidant attachment pattern, and 5–15% had an insecure ambivalent attachment pattern. Also, 15–25% of the infants were difficult to classify. Therefore, Main and Solomon (1986) reviewed video recordings of 55 infants aged 12–20 months who had been observed in the strange situation and who had been put aside as impossible to classify. All these infants displayed disorganized or disoriented behavior in the strange situation to a degree that they seemed to lack an attachment strategy, even when they were secure. Studies have looked at the relative distribution of attachment patterns in several parts of the world, and there appears to be a relatively higher share of avoidant attachments in Western Europe and of ambivalent attachments in Israel and Japan. Studies in the United States have found that more than 85% of the children who are removed from their parents due to abuse have a disorganized attachment pattern (Karen, 1998). Studies of institutionalized Romanian children identified no children with an insecure avoidant attachment pattern, although the children displayed difficulties with both internalization and externalization. In the avoidant attachment pattern the child learns to avoid expressing an attachment need to avoid the risk of rejection, but in an institutionalized setting that is probably not a helpful behavioral strategy (Marcovitch et al., 1997).

The infant may display different attachment patterns toward different caregivers, for example a secure attachment with one caregiver and an anxious attachment with another. The pattern that develops in the interaction with the mother, however, is often the dominant pattern. Over time, the infant develops a more uniform attachment pattern; for example, 6-year-olds with different attachment forms for their two parents have a more uniform and integrated pattern when they reach adolescence and adulthood. The attachment patterns described by Ainsworth and Main have been confirmed in countless studies in different cultures and in infants in different age groups (Mortensen, 2001; Sroufe, 1989b).

As Smith (2003) pointed out, Ainsworth's Baltimore study is only useful for forming hypotheses, not for testing them, because the selection was too small. Similarly, with three or four primary attachment categories, the classification is so coarse that one risks pressing one's observations of individual differences into a rigid, predetermined format, failing to take into account that children's needs in many cases only partially match a certain category. The strange situation measures attachment through an assessment of the infant's use of the attachment figure as a secure base. Its limitation is that it leaves out other important functional aspects such as the infant's temperament in interactions with the caregiver, coping and self-regulating skills, and the way in which these skills lead to the maturation of the neural internal representations in an ongoing process of change. Thus, Ainsworth and Main's classification is only a guideline, not an absolute.

Avoidant/Resistant Attachment Pattern

Simone is 9 years old, and her mother feels that Simone has always kept her distance from her; for example, she has never wanted to sit

in her mother's lap. The mother thinks that Simone is "daddy's girl,"
a notion that the father rejects. Simone likes her maternal grandpar-
ents, and the mother does not understand why Simone prefers them.
The mother is plagued by severe anxiety, is quick to take offense, and
has an unstable mood. She says that Simone tries to console her when
she has panic attacks, and that she is so afraid of being rejected by
Simone that she herself becomes dismissing. In their interactions Si-
mone seems sullen and dismissing, but out of the corner of her eye
she remains constantly aware of her mother's every move.

In the avoidant attachment pattern the infant shows no apparent response when the mother leaves or returns. Ainsworth found that the
mother's behavior was often characterized by distance and rejection.
The mother had difficulty attuning with the infant; her speech was unrelated to her mimicry; and she had difficulty relating to the infant on his
developmental level in various situations. The infant received no consolation from the mother, and the broken attachment bond was not repaired in a satisfactory manner. The infant's oppositional or avoidant
behavior provoked the mother and caused a lack of consistent boundary
setting, which further exacerbated the conflict.

Crittenden (1995) observed that when the mother was avoidant or
failed to attune with the infant, the infant was compliant and submitted
to the adult. Faced with a possibly hostile and demanding caregiver,
many of these infants try to do everything right to avoid rejection.

The infant will restrain his emotions either to deny their existence or
to avoid expressing them lest they upset the mother. Some of these infants engage in excessive and compulsive caring, and infants with an insecure or avoidant attachment may appear cool, proper, and polite. The
child attempts to keep the parents at a distance, staying busily engaged
with toys and avoiding contact with the parents.

Isabella and Belsky (1991) distinguished between avoidant and resistant attachment patterns and argue that the avoidant attachment pattern is established as a defense against insensitive and intrusive behavior.
While the avoidant pattern often seems to be caused by an obsessive
mother who is unable to modulate her affect, the resistant attachment
pattern seems to have more to do with maternal underinvolvement,
where the infant either responds with ambivalence and anger or with
passivity and helplessness stemming from the inability to connect with
her.

The infant's temperament seems to play an important role for the nature of the attachment pattern. Sroufe identified three types of avoidant attachment patterns: the projecting child who constructs stories, the shy, isolated child who seems emotionally flat, and the disturbed child with twitches, daydreams, and repetitive stereotypical activities. These children often seek negative attention and generally seem insecure (Bradley, 2000; Karen, 1998; Siegel, 1999; Stern, 1985).

The avoidant attachment pattern may develop through both overstimulation and understimulation. At one end of the spectrum are extremely manipulative caregivers who, for example, deny the child's helplessness and focus only on the child's strengths. In doing so, they deprive the child of an opportunity for reality testing, which causes the child to develop unrealistic ideas about himself and his abilities. At the other end of the spectrum is the extremely passive mother who, for example, allows the child to initiate contact, to which the mother then responds. The mother makes herself available to the child without direction or guidance, and she avoids misattunements as well as the repair of misattunements. For example, parents who are unable to develop a generational hierarchy force the child to try to find coping strategies that involve taking an emotional responsibility that is more than the child can handle.

Even if the child appears to be able to handle the avoidant behavior, research shows that the child's nervous system is under considerable internal pressure when interacting with the caregiver. The stress response system is activated, the heart rate is increased, and the child appears to have difficulty modulating affect. The child attempts to suppress negative affect, avoids engaging in the relationship to avoid adding to the distance, and seeks to avoid negative contact. When the child needs care, he will attempt to dampen the biologically based attachment need, which leaves the nervous system in an overwhelmingly stressful state. The child perceives the mother's presence but is guarded and under considerable stress. The child inhibits the impulse to approach the mother and assumes a stance of anxious waiting until the dangerous moment has passed. Depending on temperament, the child often assumes either an overcompensating tense position or a passive position.

Ambivalent Attachment Pattern

Camilla is 12 years old, and her mother has contacted social services because she is incapable of controlling Camilla. She says that

Camilla refuses to listen and will not go to school. She has tantrums, throws the furniture around, steals, lies, hits and shoves, and is verbally abusive. On the other hand, Camilla will not leave her mother alone; she clings to her and threatens to kill herself if she has to be separated from her mother. Their relationship has always been characterized by power struggles. The mother is a slight, quiet woman, while Camilla is big and robust. When the mother cautiously asks Camilla a question, Camilla gives an irritated and reproachful reply, scolding her mother. When Camilla is showing her room, she slams the door in her mother's face and reproachfully asks her whether she is listening at the door. Embarrassed, the mother laughs at the psychologist who witnesses the incident and says that Camilla is so sweet when she speaks.

In the ambivalent attachment pattern, the infant responds by approaching the mother when she returns, but the mother has difficulty consoling the child, and it takes a long time before the child is able to focus on playing again. The infant is less active in exploration, plays less, and responds with objections and clingy behavior when the mother is about to leave. Just as the mother has difficulty consoling the child, the child has difficulty letting himself be consoled, and instead of resuming contact with the mother when she returns, the child is either passively complaining or aggressive and kicking (Schibbye, 2005).

The mother's behavior is often unpredictably exuberant, and the infant may suddenly and without prior warning become the object of lavish attention with kisses and hugs. She wants to connect with the infant in a way that does not always match the infant's needs, and she is unable to perceive and respect the infant's signals, which makes the contact overwhelming and emotionally invasive. In some cases the mother is both resistant and invasive. For example, when the mother is governed by random impulses, suffers from mood swings, and easily becomes aggressive, she fails to meet the infant's needs for love and care. At other times, the mother's facial expressions show anger or a lack of engagement, which is noted by the infant. Immature parents with weak impulse control are unable to attune with the infant, and the infant responds by simultaneously approaching and withdrawing. The consequence may be that the mother holds the infant by force, using her power to demonstrate her superiority.

The ambivalent pattern is evident in some depressed mothers because they are aware of their inadequacy and lack of closeness and hence tend to try to attune with the child through sudden impulses. The child's signals are occasionally attuned but just as often ignored. To seize the mother's interest and joy-filled attention the infant must adjust to her varying emotions. If the mother is unpredictable the child becomes dependent on her, possessive, immature, and infantile.

Both children with avoidant attachment and those with ambivalent attachment have rigid and inflexible personalities, and many have difficulty managing their impulsivity and frustration in stressful situations. They have difficulty engaging in symbolic play and attuning with others, which disrupts their capacity to develop self-reflection later. They do not develop curiosity and autonomy and lack confidence. The ambivalent children mix intimacy with hostility and are often sweet or ingratiating when they want to accomplish something but become highly hostile if things do not go their way. They try desperately to gain influence over their mother by constantly seizing her attention (Karen, 1998).

Disorganized Attachment Pattern

Matt, age 2 years, has been placed in a family institution together with his mother. Matt is described as a restless boy with no capacity for concentration. His mother is incapable of planning and looking out for Matt's most basic needs, such as establishing a regular bedtime and mealtimes. She meets Matt with negative expectations, threats, inconsistencies, and contradictory replies. When Matt hurts himself she does not comfort him but seems indifferent, ridiculing him. She is dismissive toward Matt's severe sleep anxiety. Matt is indiscriminate and without positive expectations. He is easily startled and seems anxious. When addressed he tries to ignore the contact or raises his arms to protect himself. When he is with the mother he is a quiet, introverted boy with a serious expression, and he shows neither joy nor sadness. With others, by contrast, he seems angry, pent up, and without expectations, and he is violent and destructive toward other children. His mother likes to be close to him physically, but he pushes her away, and his body goes rigid. Matt has a high degree of respect for his father but also seems to be afraid of him.

In the disorganized attachment pattern the child's behavior is contradictory, chaotic, and consists of unintegrated behavioral strategies. For example, the child may initially approach the mother, then back away and maybe, in severe cases, walk in circles before going into a trancelike freeze state. The child may also avoid gaze contact and begin to rock back and forth. The interaction is usually followed up by paradoxical communication on the part of the mother, as she simultaneously signals the child to come to her and to stay away. Her behavior is confusing, and she seems threatening or frightened. The child is unable to organize in relation to her behavior and cannot use her to be comforted and calmed. She often scares the child. Children who are exposed to physical, sexual, or emotional abuse develop disorganized relational strategies, and unpredictable communication leads to an inadequate self-regulating capacity. When the child is reunited with the mother, the child is unable to modulate his fear because she is frequently the source of the fear (Main & Hesse, 1990). The child's only chance is to enter into a trancelike state corresponding to the freeze behavior associated with activation of the innate autoregulated nervous system, as described earlier.

The child's disorganized attachment pattern activates an old evolutionary reaction pattern because the child, rather than finding security with the parents, becomes distressed. The child's biological capacity means that he or she will inevitably seek the primary caregivers when feeling insecure. Any parental behavior that makes the child anxious confronts him with an impossible paradox, where the child is unable to approach, shift attention, or flee. The child becomes incapable of developing optimum coping strategies for handling this emotional challenge, and some disorganized children try to control or dominate the caregiver by humiliating her or acting subserviently and dismissive, or through role reversal where the child displays caring and parenting behavior (Karen, 1998; Schore, 2001b).

The disorganized pattern often stems from disorders in the caregiver, who appears frightening or frightened, helpless, or extremely affectively misattuned; thus, these parents are very immature, substance abusers, or mentally ill (Fonagy, 2005). These parents often have little or no empathy and mentalization capacity and lack representations of self and other. Massively chaotic and unpredictable behavior in the parents may lead to the development of a disorganized attachment pattern. These parents' sudden emotional shifts are not usually caused by actions in the external world but by internal psychological processes, which are often reality distorted. Thus, there is no relationship between their reactions and the infant's behavior, and the infant is unable to form rhythms and engage in expectation-based behavior. The child's nervous system grows accustomed to an unpredictable environment. The infant's frozen or dissociated state offers a sense of inner calm because the opioid system is activated, but this state probably corresponds to the frozen dissociative state that an animal experiences in the final stage of the survival struggle when physical survival is unlikely. That creates an immense and terrifying distance between the infant and the caregivers. "As the parent disappears into rage, the child becomes lost in terror" (Siegel, 1999, p. 284).

Chaotic and unpredictable parents often meet the child with unpredictable friendliness or aggression and contempt. A child who is met with contempt is filled with a feeling of being humiliated and of "shame-rage." The child encounters the aggressive communication in the caregivers' terrifying eyes and in their state of unmodulated narcissistic rage. By not attuning with the child, the caregivers fail to support the child in regulating the painful negative affective state. These experiences are stored as internal representations, and when the child experiences stressful states later in life, the experience will reactivate a representation of the parents' humiliating and mocking faces and trigger the dissociative state where the parents originally left the infant. The combination of unregulated primary narcissism and narcissistic rage, resulting from a humiliating parental attitude, leads to contempt for others and a lack of empathy. These children are unable to convert internal representations to stable representations of themselves and others. The disorganized infant is often sensitive to the caregiver's mental state and behavior, but due to the caregiver's unpredictable behavior the infant is unable to engage in a rhythm of self-organization but remains dysregulated and lacks internal coherence (Fonagy, 2001).

Schore (2001b) pointed out that the infant is better off with an insecure and predictable attachment pattern, because it is easier to adjust to a relational (albeit inappropriate) pattern than a disorganized attachment pattern, where there is no predictable behavior to adjust to. Even though a rigid and fixed relational strategy is a limited strategy, it is better than having no strategy at all.

General Comments About Insecurely Attached Children

An unattuned, insecurely attached child is not curious, has a low fear threshold, and has difficulty self-soothing. At the age of 2 years, when this child is exposed to problem situations, he or she is easily frustrated, distressed, and negative even in the face of simple problems. The child's behavior often elicits threats, anger, or insensitive demands, and often a pattern emerges where the child engages in power struggles that take over problem solving. Because the child has no expectation that the caregiver will be emotionally available in stressful situations, he rarely seeks help from the caregiver, even in difficult situations. The child only sporadically engages in problem solving, and the caregiver is either ignored or met with expressions of anger. By observing one of the participants in the relationship it is possible to draw up an assessment that captures important aspects of the relationship, since both parties' behavior reflects expectations and emotions that have built up over time (Sroufe & Fleeson, 1986). Children with an avoidant attachment pattern often have rigid interaction experiences that tend to reduce their emotional experiences and expressions. Children with an ambivalent attachment pattern will have experiences involving chronic dysregulation, which makes it difficult for them to regulate themselves and often causes them to dramatize. Children with a disorganized attachment pattern are unpredictable and often display maladaptive responses without an external cause.

Attachment patterns develop through early intersubjective contact between caregiver and infant. Numerous studies and theories have been published concerning how attachment patterns become part of the child's personality structure later in life and describing the child's communicative repertoire in subsequent interpersonal relations. In the following sections I look at the role of dysregulation patterns in relation to personality development and the child's communication with other people besides the caregivers.

The Role of the Dysregulation Pattern in the Development of a Communicative Repertoire

Relationships and attachment develop in an intersubjective context and are initially dyadic. The dyadic relationship is gradually embedded in internal representations. These internal representations become part of the person's overall history of diverse and varied interactions and relationships, which promotes a sense of having a social network and a world of shared experiences and acts as a resource for strengthening friendship bonds. Relational interviews with 10-year-old children and their parents show that children with early secure attachment patterns are quick to develop relationally oriented strategies, for example, by seeking help or consolation, while children with an early avoidant attachment pattern reply that they mostly keep to themselves and try to solve problems on their own without outside help. According to Grossmann and Grossmann (1993) and Main and Cassidy (1988), the initially established attachment pattern remains stable over a 5–10-year period in 80% of the cases.

Securely attached children are able to handle conflicted and contradictory emotions, while children with a history of insecure attachment only direct their attention at selected elements of emotional responses. Crittenden (1995) argued that securely attached children are balanced with regard to using affect and cognition, while children with an avoidant attachment pattern ward off emotions and rely on cognitive strategies, and children with an ambivalent attachment pattern rely on strategies that are primarily emotionally directed.

Mary Ainsworth's Attachment Categories

A common criticism of Mary Ainsworth is that the strange situation represents too narrow a slice of behavior to serve as the basis for assessing the quality of attachment on an individual level and, further, that her theory does not lend itself to discerning the link between attachment and the child's subsequent development (Smith, 2003). When the child interacts, it is not only the attachment system but the full range of behavior that is activated in the intersubjective relationship between caregiver and child. In many situations the attachment system is not activated, since this behavior occurs only when the child feels insecure. Crittenden (1992a, 1992b, 2000) argued that several categories should be included in the assessment of the child's attachment behavior, including the child's behavioral pattern, capacity for affect regulation, and use of a secure base in relation to the attachment figure's behavior. She also argued that the child's level of maturity affects the development of coping strategies. It is her assumption that the child will gradually become capable of altering the quality of the attachment relationship, as the child's emotional behavior and mental maturity change with age and expand the child's competencies.

However, Sroufe (Sroufe, 1996; Sroufe & Egeland, 1991) and others believed that early attachment experiences create expectations about the responses of other people that the child interacts with, because the child will generalize and internalize experiences from early interaction with the caregiver. Through the early interactions the infant forms internal representations of interactions, which affect the child's motivation, emotions, and subsequent interpretation of attachment-relevant experiences. He argued that ongoing support from the caregiver is also important for maintaining and refining the foundation that was established in the initial attachment. Bowlby, for example, emphasized that children's adjustment is always a product of both the child's history and the current circumstances, and that the early relationship is essential, not only in shaping future relationships but also in helping the child develop a system for mental processing, which gradually shapes internal representations of the child himself as well as others. We need a great deal of additional research to be able to reach conclusions about the role of attachment patterns in relation to psychopathology and about the categorization of psychopathology (Fonagy, 2001). As Smith (2003) pointed out, it is important to note that the existing research does not enable us to fully assess the role of early security and the quality of subsequent care in relation to the child's subsequent communicative repertoire.

Consequences of Secure and Insecure Attachment History

Unstable affect regulation limits the child's behavioral repertoire and often leads to rigid thought patterns that disrupt the child's interactions with others. Social difficulties are often the result of an inability to regulate negative emotions, direct one's attention away from troubling stimuli, suppress impulsive reactions, plan ahead and focus on problems, understand, interpret, and assess social information, and control one's behavior (Fonagy, 2001). Main found that children who were insecurely attached to their caregiver at age 6 had a reduced capacity for self-reflection and were unable to have thoughts about emotions and thoughts. At the age of 10 years, these children had difficulty recalling the past, and their capacity for self-reflection and complex thinking was severely reduced. These personality patterns may be severely entrenched, but they depend on how extreme the child's insecure pattern with the parent is, and whether the child has other attachment figures who seem secure (Main, 1993).

Grossmann and Grossmann (1990) found that children with a history of secure attachment concentrated better, had a better capacity for planning, were more relaxed, and were friendlier toward other children than children with a history of insecure attachment, who often seemed unpredictable and restless and were involved in conflicts. The quality of the attachment often predicts the child's later social skills, capacity for affect regulation, self-perception, understanding of friendship, and confidence (Bretherton, Golby, & Cho, 1997). Even at the age of 18 months, a securely attached infant seeks less physical contact because he is able to attune with the caregiver at a distance, and her presence supports the infant's play and curiosity. When the child is 2 years old, he turns to the caregiver when a problem exceeds his resources; the child is aware of verbal and nonverbal signals and is sensitive to her wishes. Urban et al. found in their research that 1-year-olds with a secure attachment pattern are better functioning than same-age children with an insecure attachment pattern 5, 9, and 14 years later (Schibbye, 2005).

The Role of Attachment Patterns for the Development of Mentalization

Fonagy et al. (1995, 1997) emphasized the significant connection between secure attachment patterns and general symbolic capacities, especially with regard to expanded mentalization. For example, a borderline issue may be the result of inadequate affective attunement, which is already evident at the age of 6–12 months. As mentioned earlier, appropriate attachment processes are crucial for the mentalization capacity to develop along the paths that have been prepared throughout evolution. Fonagy and Target (2002) pointed to studies showing a modest correlation between an early attachment pattern and a later personality pattern. However, there is a strong correlation between secure attachment and the presence of a robust mentalization capacity. It is not quite clear what is meant by "personality pattern" in this context, and whether or not the authors operate with a distinction between personality pattern and communicative repertoire. Fonagy (2003) concluded that it is not attachment as such that predicts good personality properties; rather, attachment security in the caregiver-infant relationship during the first year of life enables the nervous system to develop the structures that develop mentalizing functions. Severely insecure attachment patterns may jeopardize the development of the processing skills required to manage social relations, self-regulate in stressful situations, and process emotionally charged information.

In a severely insecure attachment pattern the child adjusts to the caregiver's confused or incomprehensible behavior and has no opportunity to develop an understanding of his own and other people's inner experiential world and mental content. As a result, the child fails to develop the ability to distinguish between his own and other people's experiences and to perceive himself and others as reflective. The child will perceive any rejections on the part of the mother as a feeling of being unloved, and her rejection becomes part of the child's sense of self. When the child fails to develop a capacity for mentalization at the age of 3–4 years, he develops a sense that the caregiver's and other people's behavior is arbitrary and unpredictable and is unable to see the connection between his own expressions and the caregiver's response. The child does not understand that there is a link between actions and certain perceptions, needs, and desires and is consequently unable to understand or predict other people's reactions (Fonagy & Target, 1996; Target & Fonagy, 1996). Without the capacity to understand and distinguish it is difficult for the infant to develop a sense of being able to organize and regulate himself and the relationship with the mother. The infant is unable to understand other people's feelings, interpret their behavior, and predict their actions. The infant places his own mental content in the other, and when the infant feels pain, for example, he has no sense that the other does not also feel pain, and vice versa. The infant supposes that others have the same experiences as he does (Schibbye, 2005).

Joint pretend play helps develop mentalization (Fonagy et al., 2002). Children with relational disorders often engage only sporadically in pretend play, and their ability to participate in pretend play is limited and poor, despite normal intelligence. Their play behavior often lacks complexity, and there is an absence of pretend play involving others. The child is often either hostile and aggressive without provocation, with a general tendency toward negative interactions with peers, or extremely adaptive at the cost of developing a personal identity (Sroufe, 1989a). The rigid internal representations in anxious children are often self-fulfilling, since a child who expects to be rejected often ignores or misinterprets social interactions due to mistrust.

Relational Disorders as Psychological Risk States

Relational disorders can be considered psychological risk states that arise as a result of recurring regulation and interaction disturbances. Attachment patterns may change over time, for example from insecure to secure, when the infant engages in a close relationship with a responsive caregiver who offers an opportunity for changing the attachment pattern. Thanks to the plasticity of the nervous system, the child's internal representations may be altered through interactions with other significant caregivers. The infant's brain has a high degree of plasticity and a significant capacity for compensation and reparation, and the nervous system has inherent reparative capacities that seek to achieve self-healing. As long as the child's inappropriate attachment patterns have not been too severe and persistent, it is possible to utilize the brain's capacity for seeking harmony (Allen, 2002).

Research has not demonstrated a direct link between the nature of psychosocial disorders and specific damage in childhood development, and it remains an open question whether it ever will. It does appear, however, that a disorganized attachment pattern carries a greater risk of subsequent psychological disorders than other insecure attachment patterns (Fonagy, 2001). The human ability to handle social and environmental stress varies on an individual basis, and the infant's innate temperament and potential play an important role for the response of the child's nervous system to the environment. An attachment pattern that changes from secure to insecure, for example, is strongly correlated with powerful negative life events such as the loss of a parent, abuse, or severe somatic illness. Virtually all research supports the importance of having an early opportunity to form a close and secure attachment with a primary caregiver who cares about the child and provides adequate attention and care (Karen, 1998).

Children from a secure relationship are often treated in a more straightforward manner, with the expectation that they will obey, comply with rules, and show age-appropriate behavior. Children with relational disorders are often treated with more discipline and control. There are fewer expectations that they will obey, and they are often treated distantly and arouse other people's anger more easily. Through his communicative repertoire the child attempts to attune with others, and if a preschool or school teacher responds in kind, the child has no opportunity to change his communication but is instead confirmed in this inappropriate interaction without receiving the necessary support (Sroufe, 1989a). Many children with insecure attachment relationships have few adjustment strategies. They are not able to reflect on their own situation and understand other people's intentions, and they have trouble modulating their own behavior. These children often have many frustrating experiences, and their inadequate social coping strategies are often put under pressure in preschool and school contexts. A child who is unable to decode social interactions or express emotions will fail to grasp what goes on in interactions with peers. When the child is unable to attune emotionally and is unclear in communication, the child will see other children responding in ways that seem incomprehensible and experience rejection without knowing the cause. The child does not have a sense of control over the way he is treated by others. Children with relational disorders are reactive to internal and external stimulation, overreact to frustration, and have difficulty tolerating anxiety and distress. They often have a raised sensory sensitivity, suffer from perceptual distortions, and often attribute magical properties to events or actions that lie outside their control. These children have an inner sense of insecurity. When exposed to stress they have few resources for coping with the situation, and their nervous system is fragile (Cicchetti et al., 1995; van der Kolk, 1987).

Avoidant Pattern of Communication

Chas is 14 years old, and during our conversation he hides behind his cap, only sporadically engaging in gaze contact. He mostly seems expressionless, but when he talks about what makes him happy he smiles and is vitalized. One-on-one contact seems overwhelming to him, and he often laughs inappropriately. He is keen to adjust to his environment and appears to accept rules without discussion, and it is difficult to gain a real impression of who he is. He may express that he feels angry inside but explains that there is no point in showing it, since it only leads to conflict, and he never has his way anyway. He does not like to be around large groups or crowds because he feels that people stare at him. He is most comfortable at home on his own, but at the same time he finds this state of affairs upsetting. He waits for other people to take the initiative and make the first move, and he does not contribute to dialogue. He scans his surroundings and seems good at decoding what is expected of him and at engaging in conventional behavior.

The avoidant pattern of communication may be affected by earlier experiences where the child was involved in either an overregulating or underregulating interaction pattern. The child has an internal vitality that is rarely expressed and tones down his emotional side. The child has learned that his own needs and feelings are irrelevant but scans other people's feelings and regulates accordingly. The child directs energy at predicting and attuning with other people's mood states and needs. This lets the child avoid experiences of anxiety but also leads to a lack of identity that cuts him off from sensing his own emotions. The child has difficulty engaging in a separation process, is not spontaneous, often seems uninvolved, and is incapable of engaging in contact development because he tries instead to act as the other person's mirror (Cozolino, 2000).

If the child has failed to develop strategies for being vitalized through other caregivers, he will withdraw, and when he needs support and comforting, the acquired self-reliance isolates the child from benefiting from support and assistance from others. The child rarely displays spontaneous responses, often rejects contact, and often uses logical, analytical thinking that lacks emotional resonance, self-reflection, depth, subtlety, and vitality. The child feels lonely and is hungry for contact but unable to reach out to others.

The child's avoidant pattern of communication makes others withdraw because the contact offers no reward. The child has difficulty communicating and interpreting emotional signals; he knows how to handle cognition but not affect. The child does not dare to get close to others and often goes around by himself. For example, the child has learned to choke back anger and has difficulty expressing grief. In a situation where a child has to grieve, he will turn the anger on himself and may become depressive (Karen, 1998; van der Kolk & McFarlane, 1996). The child has learned that articulating or displaying emotions associated with an activation of the attachment system may have unfortunate consequences. Some of these children strive for compulsive perfectionism at the risk of denying emotions such as anger and grief, which in its most extreme consequence may lead to suicidal behavior. Crittenden (1995) pointed out that when those with an avoidant attachment pattern commit suicide, there are rarely signs or warnings that reveal their despair, and after their death there may be some uncertainty about the motivation.

Ambivalent Pattern of Communication

Marie is an intelligent 15-year-old who has lived with a foster family for about 1 year. When she is at ease, she is well-spoken, relaxed, and calm. She quickly settled in with the foster family, but after 3 months she became temperamental, slamming doors and constantly wanting to be heard. She often argues with her mother on the phone, and afterward she rocks back and forth, banging a steel brush into her head until it causes small cuts. She blames others for everything, distorts reality, and will take words out of context, twisting the content. She does not like to see others upset, and once when her foster mother was distressed, Marie described it as the worst thing she had ever experienced. She likes to get attention constantly, and even the slightest correction or reprimand makes her angry. Marie would like to return home to live with her mother but seems to be scared when the prospect begins to seem realistic. She often complains about physical ailments and seeks attention by talking about how bad she feels, constantly seeking affirmation. She has an ambivalent relationship to authorities and does her best to break down the asymmetry in the relationship. She is able to reflect on her maladaptive sides when she is at ease, but when her emotions are aroused, she projects and becomes impulsive and immature.

A child who has developed an ambivalent pattern of communication often appears anxious and contact seeking and has difficulty with self-regulation. The child is intensely focused on decoding the relational aspect rather than the content of the contact. The child has frequent experiences of approaching others but being rejected and left in a stressful state, clinging to others in an attempt to achieve self-organization. The child is often whiny, angry, and impossible to satisfy, has difficulty relaxing in an emotional contact, and always seems guarded and appears to be moving away. The child unwillingly drives others away with mixed signals and by being very difficult to please. The child does not feel able to get close enough to others, and due to a strong need for encouragement and acceptance, a constant desire for contact, a desire to possess others, and constant feelings of jealousy the child may have difficulty relating to others. The child is so attention seeking and so obsessed with having his own needs met that he pays no attention to other people's needs. A child with an ambivalent pattern of communication is often so afraid of either being expelled or swallowed up that his aggression is distorted or expressed as passive aggression. The child often has powerful and intense impulse breakthroughs in relations with close attachment figures. The child develops a dependency on other potential attachment figures while simultaneously waging war on them. Ambivalent children have an internal sense of insecurity toward close relations and direct much of their energy to keeping tabs on the caregiver's whereabouts, what she is doing, and whether everything is in order while at the same time being unable to handle being close to her.

Disorganized Pattern of Communication

Sam is 7 years old, and in immediate contact he seems like a sensible, polite, and somewhat precocious boy. At first he is hesitant and reluctant; he appears hectic and nervous and speaks at a high pitch. His gaze is shifty, and he has trouble maintaining concentration for long. He is aware of the adult's facial expression and responds to even small misattunements; as long as the adult shows him a happy expression he seems secure. However, he quickly grows insecure and responds by becoming agitated and nervous. As the contact develops, he drops the polite attitude, becomes less tense, and tends to test boundaries. He alternates from moment to moment between an immature boundary-testing contact, shouting cuss words, sticking out his tongue, and hiding, and seeking an immature form of closeness, engaging in peekaboo games while, without knowing the psychologist very well, saying that he loves her and inviting a hug.

The self-regulating capacities of the disorganized child are chaotic and unpredictable, and the child often has severe difficulty with affect regulation, behavioral problems, and attention deficit disorders. The child

often has a hostile and aggressive attitude to peers, which makes relations difficult (Cicchetti et al., 1995; Fonagy, 2001). The child often responds with impulse breakthroughs or tantrums and extremely regressive
behavior. This reveals the chaotic internal world, which reflects the lack
of predictability that the parents have displayed. The child is so used to
hostile or unpredictable responses that the anxiety capacity is activated
as soon as others approach. The child has a fragmented image of his own
history and is unable to reflect or form narratives about his life.

The child often has a well-developed capacity for scanning a situation
from moment to moment, constantly maintaining a sense of the position
of objects in the environment. This scanner function has developed on
the basis of fear, and it is important for the child to constantly monitor
other people's mental state to avoid punishment. The internal representations do not develop into positive comforting figures but instead into
incomprehensible representations that are quick to spark anxiety. The
child does not develop the capacity to use internal representations in
self-organization; he decodes other people's external behavior without
having developed a capacity for seeing behind the expressions and sensing another person's internal mental state. The child learns to engage in
here-and-now-oriented interactions on the level of protoconversations
but does not develop the ability to engage in affective attunement. Since
the child is locked into decoding other people's external behavior here
and now, the child is not capable of maintaining a relationship over time,
even if he continues to be attached to the close caregivers (Fonagy et al.,
2002; Siegel, 1999). The mentalizing function that develops in the orbitofrontal cortex, and which is responsible for maintaining social relations
and the capacity for empathy, among other functions, fails to develop,
which means that the child is unable to form internal representations of
other people's mental states (Fonagy, 2003).

Summary

The field of developmental psychology has not yet coalesced into a coherent theory of development but takes a variety of approaches, ranging
from microinteractions, regulation, attachment, or relational patterns to
the way in which these patterns form internal representations which develop our personality. A family life consists of many complex structures

and behaviors, which may be difficult to capture, as they are often subtle and nonverbal. Often, combination phenomena emerge, where the various interaction patterns become impossible to discern.

Some parents are so damaged by their own childhood experiences that they have no parenting capacity to draw on, and some parents deny or are incapable of understanding a child's difficulties. Even parents with limited or no parenting capacity will try to protect their children from the unpleasant experiences that they themselves endured. Regardless of how dissociated or defensive the parents are, and regardless of how limited their parenting capacity is, the vast majority still have a capacity for loving their child. Regardless of how much neglect or abuse the child has suffered, the primary caregiver is still the child's attachment figure. The child does not have any option other than to incorporate her responses and shape herself accordingly. Attachment confers a survival value because events of abuse are brief and atypical in comparison with the infant's constant need for protection and nutrition.

John Bowlby said,

> No longer are the desire for food or sexual satisfaction regarded as the sole engines of personal intimacy. Instead, an urge to keep proximity or accessibility to someone seen as stronger or wiser, and who if responsive is deeply loved, comes to be recognized as . . . having a vital role to play in life. Not only does its effective operation bring with it a strong feeling of security and contentment, but its temporary or long-term frustration causes acute or chronic anxiety and discontent. When seen in this light, the urge to keep proximity is to be respected, valued, and nurtured as making for potential strength, instead of being looked down upon, as so often hitherto, as a sign of inherent weakness. This radical shift in valuation, with its far-reaching influence on how we perceive and treat other people, especially those whose attachment needs have been and still are unmet, is, I believe, the single most important consequence of the change of conceptual framework. (1993, p. 293)

In this chapter I have described how interaction patterns between caregiver and child fuse into relational and communication patterns that can be assessed and understood through Ainsworth's and Main's attachment categories. The child incorporates attachment patterns through internal representations to form the communicative repertoire that the child will later unfold in interactions with other adults and peers, although, according to Fonagy and Target (2002), it is difficult to document a direct link between attachment and personality patterns. It is difficult to categorize behavior without losing too much detail and subtlety. On the other hand, it is important to try to ascertain whether the interactive dances that the child engages in with significant caregivers have an impact on mental health and mental disorders. At this stage, developmental psychology has not yet become a unified theory, and it will probably continue to develop for many years to come. The next chapter describes how inappropriate attachment patterns in the child's interpersonal contact can probably develop into neuroaffective disorders on an intrapsychic level.

CHAPTER FIVE

Disorders in
Neuroaffective Development

*When infants are not in homeostatic balance or are emotionally
dysregulated (e.g., they are distressed), they are at the mercy of
these states. Until these states are brought under control, infants
must devote all their regulatory resources to reorganizing them.
While infants are doing that, they can do nothing else.*

Edward Tronick and Katherine Weinberg (1997, p. 56)

As early as 1889, Pierre Janét speculated whether the maturation of the
nervous system might stop at a certain point in development, incapable
of progressing and adding new elements. He claimed that the psychological consequence of trauma is a breakdown in adaptive and attuned
mental processes, which lead to insufficient integration of the self. If the
nervous system remains in an autonomically regulated state, it will shut
out external stimuli, close in on itself, and become unreceptive to interpersonal communication. If this state becomes chronic, the nervous
system will shut out emotional arousal, for example, stemming from unfamiliar stimuli in the limbic system, and similarly, the sophisticated processing areas in the prefrontal cortex will block out any complex cognitive
and affective information, thus hindering cognitive and emotional development. Under normal circumstances, traumatized children will adapt to
their surroundings, but they are easily affected by minor stressors and
respond differently. Many authors have pointed out that the inability to
regulate emotions is one of the most profound and potentially permanent consequences of early neglect or abuse (Schore, 2001b, 2002b; van
der Kolk, 1994, 1996c; van der Kolk & Fisler, 1994; van der Kolk & Mc-
Farlane, 1996).

Relational traumatization has a considerable negative effect on the development of the infant brain, much more so than traumatization caused by nonhuman factors such as natural disasters. Traumatization within early relationships has particularly severe consequences and may have a lifelong impact on brain development. As development progresses, earlier behaviors are hierarchically integrated into more complex behaviors. As new behavioral capacities develop, earlier capacities become subordinate to more mature forms of behavior, but the earlier forms remain potentially active. In stressful situations, earlier forms of functioning will emerge, and the latest patterns to become integrated are more vulnerable to dysfunction and more susceptible to being replaced by less differentiated forms. Sometimes, a maladaptive adjustment pattern may be latent and only emerge in periods with increased stress. Similarly, earlier forms of functioning may be available as an element in current behavior as part of the child's ongoing adjustment. At times, this behavior will be appropriate for environmental adjustment; at times it may impede further development. The presence of less differentiated early forms of functioning do not necessarily lead to psychopathological behavior but is more likely to be reflected as rigidity, anxiety, attention deficit, or hyperactivity, which may disrupt the ongoing adjustment process (Santostefano, 1978; Sroufe & Rutter, 1984).

In the previous chapter, I reviewed how long-term dysregulation and misattunement can cause various relational disorders on an interpersonal level. In this chapter, I address the impact of long-term severe dysregulation and misattunement on an intrapsychic and neuroaffective level.

The Child's Response to the Loss or Lack of an Attachment Person

The powerful instinctive need for attachment is common to all primates, and this need means that neglect or abuse can cause severe psychological disorders. For example, Harlow (1958, 1959) found that when a baby rhesus monkey is separated from its mother, its only goal is to reattach with her. When the monkey cannot see its mother it is scared and reduces its activity; occasionally it enters a freezing state where it sits completely motionless for long periods. When an infant monkey is separated from its mother, opioid-sensitive neurons are inhibited, which makes the monkey cry out for the mother and display attachment behavior. The reduction in opioid-sensitive circuits enables the motor systems to produce vocalizations (Kalin, 1993).

Even when an infant stops directing the need for contact at an emotionally unavailable caregiver, the attachment need has not been extinguished; it has been downregulated and inhibited (Sroufe, Fox, & Pancake, 1983). The infant calls out for the attachment figure by screaming and crying, which are vocal expressions of survival anxiety. An infant who is left alone in this situation or whose crying results in unpredictable responses or abuse will never learn how it feels to preserve or regain one's balance through external comforting. Bowlby (1979) pointed out that when a mother is annoyed and critical and frustrates the infant, the child gets not only angry and aggressive but also greedy for care. Bowlby proposed that one of the reasons why emotionally cold criminals lack superego control is that their feelings of love have never been allowed to develop, or that a primitive narcissistic rage has taken over. The infant can handle long separations without developing emotionally flat behavior. It is deprived separation, where the child does not have a chance to develop attachment with anyone, that is destructive. If the infant does not have an alternative mother figure to replace the original mother figure, and if the infant is not able to keep the memory of her alive, or if a series of maternal replacements have not allowed the infant to attach with any of them, the infant becomes unattached. An unattached infant fails to establish a secure base, develops mistrust, bitterness, protest, and depression, and relates indiscriminately to others (Karen, 1998).

Robertson and Bowlby (1952) described a particular sequence in children's reactions to the absence of the attachment figure. The protest phase sets in immediately after separation and may last anywhere from a few hours to weeks or even months. During this period the child cries and searches for the attachment figure. When the child enters the phase of despair, the child is preoccupied with the lost caregiver but spends less time searching. Crying becomes monotonous or quiets down, and the child becomes passive, loses appetite, and does not demand anything from the environment. Gradually the child begins to show more interest in others and resumes eating. Attachment behavior is not activated in relation to the attachment figure from whom the child was separated, and if the child sees the attachment figure, he remains passive, without showing any initiative or interest. If the child loses his attachment figures repeatedly, he will gradually invest less in new possible attachment figures and begin to contact everybody indiscriminately. This is an appropriate strategy in an environment with few potential attachment relationships. The child takes what he can get; this is very different from the clingy behavior of a child who refuses to let go of the caregiver, which is characteristic of children who are the victims of abuse. During the protest phase the child's autonomic nervous system responds with sympathetic activation, while the subsequent phase of despair is a parasympathetic reaction (explained in the following section). Despair is a passive state that occurs in stressful situations where active coping strategies are not possible. When the caregivers are unable to support the child in regulating sympathetic and parasympathetic activity, the development of a nervous system that is capable of handling elevated levels of sympathetic arousal and stimulation is hampered. The protest phase is the earliest manifestation of the anxiety of annihilation (Schore, 2003b).

An abusive or neglecting mother often has a vulnerable nervous system that has difficulty handling even minor stress experiences. For example, she may freeze and shut down when she hears the infant screaming. After the protest phase with sympathetic activation (crying), the child engages in parasympathetic inhibition, where the protest, crying, and screaming die down, and the child matches the mother's state. Schore (2001b) noted that this is the key factor in affective disorders, as abuse or deprivation early in life result in a chronic sensitivity in the stress response system, even in response to mild levels of stress. A child with an innately fragile nervous system who is raised in an environment with insufficient stimulation, emotional attunement, and unpredictable responses will suffer damage to the limbic system and prefrontal cortex and will be at constant risk of disintegration. Kohut (1984) has suggested that the fragmentation of the self represents the most profound anxiety conceivable. The child will not be able to cope with the stressful, chaotic events that occur in all human relationships. The nervous system becomes rigid and unable to attune with the environment. The child devotes energy to defensive strategies as a means of protection against interactions that might potentially trigger a disorganized state. The child's nervous system attempts to avoid novel situations and fails to develop the coping strategies for new and challenging situations that are necessary for developing the self-organization capacity of the nervous system (Schore, 2003a).

Polan and Hofer (1999) have suggested that the attachment bond is not lost when the child is exposed to a disorganized contact with the caregiver; instead, the child loses the possibility of developing a higher order of regulatory mechanisms, including the capacity for assessing and reorganizing mental content. The neural structures that form the basis for the mentalization capacity develop through multiple attunements, misattunements, and reparation of misattunements with the caregiver; when children are able to distinguish their own psychological states from those of others, they are ready to engage in meaningful interpersonal relationships. Misattunements leave their mark on the brain stem level (e.g., in PAG), because they lead to a registration of discomfort, pain, and abandonment. When children are incapable of distinguishing between psychological states, due to either relational or innate disorders, their capacity to maintain a clear distinction between self and other is weak, and their mentalization capacity remains immature and unsymbolized, which means that they are incapable of distinguishing between their own and others' motives and needs, putting themselves in someone else's place, and converting the basic self-protection strategies into more mature forms, such as repression (Fonagy, 2003).

The Infant's Response to Insecure Attachment Patterns

As previously described in a discussion of hidden regulators, Hofer (1984a, 1987) found that reestablishing a single motherlike factor made it possible to avert a single physiological aspect of despair without influencing the others. For example, the mother's body heat controls the infant monkey's activity level, while her tactile stimulation determines its growth hormone levels. Milk reestablishes the heart rate, and periodic feeding modulates sleep-wake cycles. In this manner, the mother constantly adjusts the infant's physiology, and when she is not present, the infant loses all of his organizing channels at once, and the physiology collapses, which thrusts the infant into a chaos of hopelessness. When mammals are separated from their attachment figure, their physiological regulation is disturbed, which can be measured physiologically and probably also triggers strong psychological pain (Lewis et al., 2001).

Humans are essentially mammals, although we have a far more so-phisticated mental capacity. Since we also have a limbic system, it is easy to imagine that our responses to attachment in many ways resemble those of other mammals. In addition to the serious consequences that all mammals risk when being abandoned by their caregiver, early abuse or deprivation in humans seem to have a particularly damaging effect on our higher mental functions, especially when an infant is exposed to se-vere deprivation or a disorganized attachment pattern. Watt (2005) has pointed out that severe abuse or deprivation can cause far-reaching and largely irreversible damage to the nervous system, probably due to mas-sive neurochemical disturbances that result from a lack of regulation in the caregiver-child relationship. The limbic system and the area above it (the cingulate gyrus and the orbitofrontal cortex) help regulate struc-tures deep inside the brain stem. These structures mature and stabilize in close caregiver-child interaction.

The Biological Organization of Insecure Attachment Patterns

Many studies have shown that children have an increased heart rate when exposed to separation in the strange situation (Donovan & Leavitt, 1985). Children with a secure attachment pattern have a slightly reduced heart rate when they begin to play, while this reaction is absent in chil-dren with an avoidant or resistant attachment pattern, whose stress lev-el seems permanently elevated. There have been a number of studies of the cortisol level in children in the strange situation, but the findings have been somewhat contradictory. Typically, the caregiver is the first person that the infant has to adapt to, and the child appears to develop emotional and neurobiological disorders in several areas when the attachment is disturbed. These include the child's capacity for self-organization, sensorimotor integration, and control over emotional and sensorimotor behavior. The child's internal representations of the rela-tionship with the caregiver are involved in self-regulation and become a regulator for the child's neurochemistry. For example, securely attached children rely on the caregiver to reduce their stress, while children with an insecure avoidant attachment pattern have experiences where the caregiver either fails to respond or makes an inappropriate response to their discomfort. Consequently, they will tend to try to regulate the stress level themselves by down-toning their affects at the cost of attunement and identity development. Insecure ambivalent children have experienced the caregiver as unstable and will therefore try to increase their attachment behavior, which sometimes leads to a reduced stress level. Children with a disorganized form of attachment lack a strategy for self-regulation and hence also for the reduction of stress in interactions with the caregiver (Smith, 2003).

Several studies suggest that when the child is exposed to inadequate care the result may be structural changes to the prefrontal cortex involving a change in the asymmetry between the two hemispheres, which has consequences for later developing behavior and affect. This seems to be characteristic of children of depressive mothers. Mothers with depressive symptoms seem to have difficulty providing optimum stimulation for their children, and they show fewer positive and more negative affects when interacting with their infants. As a result, these infants seem to have difficulty developing appropriate arousal regulation strategies. Dawson (1994) and Dawson, Frey, Panagiotides, Osterling, and Hessl (1997) found that infants of depressive mothers showed reduced left-hemisphere activity both generally and when they interacted with their mothers, which is probably associated with reduced positive approach behavior, for example, joy over playing together with the mother, and increased negative behavior, for example, by attracting the mother's attention when she is busy doing something else. Several infant studies have found that right-hemisphere frontal activation increases when the child responds with withdrawal emotions such as crying, distress, and disgust, and increased left-hemisphere frontal activation in approach behavior and joy-filled emotions (Davidson, 1994a, 1994b; Davidson & Fox, 1982, 1988, 1989).

Dawson's research found that during the first few years of life the child is particularly sensitive to maternal depression because this is a time when the frontal lobes are undergoing significant growth. Dawson et al. (1997, 1999) found that children whose mothers had had severe depressive symptoms while the child was 18–24 months old had an increased risk of developing anxiety symptoms in comparison with 5-year-old children with depressive mothers, who were not at risk. Dawson et al. concluded that the child's approach and withdrawal behavior, seen in combination with characteristic prefrontal activation, depends on the mother's behavior, not whether she is depressive. The depressive mothers' infants were less affectionate, and the children found it harder to self-activate. Instead they focused on their mothers, used gestures and vocalization to get her attention, wanted to sit on her lap, had trouble maintaining attention, and were aggressive toward her when her attention was directed at something else. Dawson et al.'s studies found that depressive mothers' infants both express negative affect more frequently and have difficulty regulating intense negative emotions, which is evident both in their behavior and in their brain activity. These children have failed to develop adaptive strategies for affect regulation.

Davidson (1994) pointed out that the asymmetrical pattern seems to become apparent when the mother is negative in her contact, is emotionally unavailable, fails to provide a relevant response to the child's initiatives and affective states, is out of synch, or consistently violates the child's boundaries. Negative experiences strengthen neural networks that are associated with negative affect, which means that the prefrontal inhibition mechanisms and the abstract mentalizing functions are not stimulated, and the child is governed by his immediate needs and incapable of reflecting on his behavior (Perry, 1994). Teicher (2002) pointed out that in children who have suffered massive neglect, it seems that the right hemisphere is more developed than the left—as if the development has not managed to cross over to the left hemisphere. According to Schore (1994, 2003a), intense emotional states will be mediated through the right hemisphere, and the child will not be able to form narratives and understand his reactions because the verbalization and interpretation of emotions require that structures in the left hemisphere are well-developed and sufficiently linked with the right hemisphere through the anterior commissure and the corpus callosum.

In Chugani et al.'s (2001) study of institutionalized Romanian children, PET scans showed diminished glucose activity in the orbitofrontal cortex, the amygdala, the hippocampus, and the brain stem in both hemispheres, all structures that regulate stress management. When damage in these areas occurs during infancy, the result seems to be a loss of social behavior, development of motor stereotypes, reduced gaze contact, and lack of mimicry. The autonomic nervous system, the limbic structures (amygdala, hippocampus), the cingulate gyrus, and the insula play important roles for the development of attachment behavior and object permanence. Neurobiological studies have found that damage to areas in the amygdala during early infancy causes serious changes in emotionality (Schore, 2003a). Blair, Morris, Frith, Perrett, and Dolan

(1999) pointed out that asocial boys with severe emotional disorders are unable to identify frightened and sad facial expressions but have no similar problems with aggressive expressions. When the children are presented with frightening stimuli, the amygdala is not activated as it is in typical children. Damasio (1994, 1998) described that the ability to put oneself in someone else's place, for example by describing what a person in a photo feels based on the person's facial expression, rests on functions in the limbic system and in the parietal lobe (the insula region) in the right hemisphere, which initiates emotional responses and associates them with body sensations. It appears that severe regulation disorders cause disturbances in this particular area.

Neurotransmitter Regulation in Insecure Relationships

Neurotransmitter balancing begins in the womb. Maternal substance abuse during pregnancy will harm the unborn child, and animal studies have shown that pregnant mothers who are exposed to stress affect their unborn child through stress hormones. The child's nervous system may be more or less vulnerable or resilient at birth due to experiences in the womb and thus more or less vulnerable or resilient to insensitive parenting. Greater vulnerability from birth may lead to difficulties with self-regulation if the child is raised by a caregiver who fails to respond or who is unable to attune with the child (Suomi, 1999).

In relation to neglect or abuse, researchers have focused particularly on the balancing of neurotransmitters such as noradrenaline, dopamine, and serotonin. Under normal childhood conditions these substances are usually in balance, but in the case of social deprivation and inadequate conditions they are imbalanced. It appears that in a neurobiological sense, the attachment system organizes the more primitive neurochemical systems, which regulate stress, among other functions; this affects the child's neurobiological regulation in later interactions and other situations (Kraemer, 1992; Smith, 2003). Dysfunctions in the noradrenaline-serotonin-dopamine balance seem to be critical as these systems continue to develop after birth, especially in mammals (Goldman-Rakic & Brown, 1982). These neurotransmitters seem to be associated with attention functions, stress responses, circadian rhythms, and neural plasticity.

Young monkeys who grew up either in total isolation or with surrogate mothers have a low level of noradrenaline and show a despair response to separation. Drugs that reduce the synthesis of noradrenaline and dopamine also increase the likelihood of activating the despair response. Thus, a reduced noradrenaline level is associated with an increased risk of a despair response, whether the cause is a reaction to the environment or neurochemical in nature (Kraemer, 1992). Growing up in an environment without a caregiver is an unpredictable, uncontrollable, and inescapable situation, and this type of stress will reduce the noradrenaline level in the brain. Normally, the noradrenaline level is high right after birth, but in deprived infant monkeys the level drops quickly, even if the monkey is offered a surrogate mother. The stress response system is disturbed and remains unstable over time and in turn appears to disturb certain circuit connections, including the connection between the amygdala and the hippocampus, which is involved in shaping polymodal connections to other brain regions such as the orbitofrontal cortex, which regulates emotional and social behavior. Thus, disturbances in the stress response system disrupt connections to the cognitive structures that would normally regulate emotional behavior. One effect of a low level of noradrenaline is to make it difficult for the child to maintain attention, motivation, and persistence, which in turn inhibits the child's adaptive capacity.

The lack of joy-filled stimuli limits the development of dopamine receptors, which may hamper the capacity for joy, reward, and positive affect in the prefrontal cortex, among other places, an area that is normally densely packed with this type of neurons (Depue, Luciana, Arbisi, Collins, & Leon, 1994; Martin, 1997). For example, animal cubs that have been exposed to early stressful experiences have permanent changes in the function of dopamine receptors, especially in the cortical regions, and there is a remarkable reduction in the number of dopamine receptors in the dopamine-producing regions in the brain stem (Clarke et al., 1996; Lewis, Gluck, Beauchamp, Keresztury, & Mailman, 1990). A child who experiences a great deal of rewarding contact, and who may be genetically equipped with a high number of dopamine receptors from birth, will have a positive approach to life (Gerhardt, 2004). The serotonin level is also regulated through the early caregiver-child interaction. A low serotonin level is associated with aggressive and depressive behavior because this neurotransmitter balances emotions (Davidson,

Putnam, & Larson, 2000; Rosenblum et al., 1994; Suomi, Seaman, & Lewis, 1978).

The Autonomic Nervous System as a Stress Regulator

The autonomic nervous system is a part of the nervous system that connects the central nervous system to internal organs, blood vessels, and sweat glands. It acts outside volitional control to regulate functions in these organ systems. Affects are controlled by the communication between the autonomic nervous system and the central nervous system. Without the autonomic nervous system, we would not be able to sense emotions, because emotions and assessments are anchored in the body. The autonomic nervous system consists of two systems: sympathetic and parasympathetic. The sympathetic nervous system controls the activation of the nervous system in response to threats and other forms of high-energy activation. The parasympathetic nervous system is a vegetative system, which acts to promote the digestive process and lower the heart rate, among other functions. These functions are regulated reflexively, and the two nervous systems have opposite functions. Normally, the sympathetic and the parasympathetic systems alternate between predominantly sympathetic and predominantly parasympathetic activation (Hart, 2008).

The Polyvagal Theory

Stephen Porges (1995, 1997, 2001) developed the polyvagal theory, which revolves around the autonomic nervous system and is based on Darwin's theories, among other things. According to the polyvagal theory, the autonomic nervous system regulates in relation to three different evolutionarily developed behavioral strategies. The first strategy is characterized by the activation of a primitive, unmyelinated vagal system that promotes digestion and responds to impulses by suppressing metabolic activity; this system is called the vegetative vagal system. This primitive vagal activation corresponds to immobilization behavior (freeze). The second level is based on the sympathetic nervous system, which is capable of increasing metabolic activity and inhibiting the influence of the primitive vagal system on the intestinal system. The sympathetic nervous system mobilizes behavior that is necessary for fight or flight. The third level is unique to mammals and is characterized by a myelinated vagal system that is quickly able to regulate the heart rate, and which promotes engagement and disengagement in relation to the environment. This system is called the mammalian vagal system.

The autonomic nervous system is important for our capacity to regulate stress situations, typically through the myelinated vagal system. If the nervous system is overburdened it regresses into an autonomic regulation of fight-or-flight or immobilization behavior. In traumatic situations the child responds first with sympathetic activation (fight or flight). If the child is not supported in downregulating, the primitive unmyelinated vagal system is activated; this is a passive state, which is characterized by an increase in opioids and cortisol. The activation of the unmyelinated vagal system leads to a reduction in heart rate, blood pressure, and metabolic activity despite increases in the amount of circulating noradrenaline and adrenaline. The intensified parasympathetic activation makes it possible to maintain an internal equilibrium despite the sympathetic activation. Porges (1997) described that the sudden and lightning-quick shift from a failed fight-or-flight strategy, which requires massive sympathetic activation, to immobilization is associated with the primitive vagal system. In the traumatized state, which may be prolonged, both the sympathetic and the parasympathetic nervous systems are highly active (Schore, 2002a). When the nervous system engages in autonomic regulation, it is no longer able to regulate through social contact. Thus, it is important not to burden the nervous system beyond its capacity.

The mammalian vagal system is developed and activated during the first 3 months of life when the child is in a secure and securely attuned contact with the caregiver. Any perceived discomfort and insecurity will jeopardize the development of the child's self-regulating skills, as the child's nervous system is locked into an autoregulated state that is beyond the child's influence. The brain stem functions, which balance social behavior, are not under cortical control. An inadequate development of the mammalian vagal system probably causes damage to deep-lying limbic structures, which results in flat affect, attention-deficit disorders, hypersensitivity, and problems with affect regulation. These types of symptoms are common in many children with developmental disorders. A downregulation of the myelinated vagal system prevents the maturation of neural structures that are associated with social behavior and relational contact (Hart, 2008).

Cortical regulation of the autonomic nervous system can only take place when the child perceives the environment as secure. The mammalian vagal system in particular has strong connections to the orbitofrontal cortex. If the environment does not feel secure, the nervous system will adapt to this situation and engage in autonomic regulation, and when self-regulating capacities are reduced, social skills are hampered because the child's nervous system is focused on managing insecure and frightening situations (Porges, 2001).

The Stress Response Systems SAM and HPA

A number of researchers have attempted to study the neurobiological structures involved in the attachment system. Among others, studies have measured calling behavior in baby monkeys that were separated from their mothers to discover whether the two stress response systems of the organism, HPA (hypothalamic-pituitary-adrenal) and SAM (sympathetic adrenomedullary), might offer an insight into the behavior patterns that have been observed in the strange situation. Both stress response systems are related to sympathetic activation. One system, SAM, is regulated by the hormone CRF (corticotropin-releasing factor). Among other functions, CRF serves to activate the release of noradrenaline and adrenaline, which activate the sympathetic nervous system, for example, in connection with the startle response. The release of adrenaline and noradrenaline facilitates the accessibility of energy for the body's vital organs; the effect is rapid but also short-lived, and thus the organism is quickly able to return to its normal state. The SAM system remains activated as long as the organism engages in activities where it is trying to overcome difficulties, for example, through the fight-or-flight response. The other stress response system, the HPA system, is activated by the hormone cortisol (Sapolsky, 1998; Schore, 2003a). The role of cortisol in the stress situation is to help extinguish sympathetic activation through a negative feedback process. Cortisol is released some minutes or hours after an event. The HPA system is activated when the organism stops engaging in activities that may alter its situation; for example, the HPA system is highly activated in states related to acquired or learned helplessness.

During the protest phase (SAM activation) heart rate and body temperature go up; in the despair phase, by comparison, the heart rate becomes arrhythmic and the breathing shallow (HPA activation). Animal studies have shown that in the despair phase, the cortisol level increases up to approximately six times the normal rate after only 30 minutes in isolation, at which time the animal stops complaining and curls up in a corner. It loses interest in food and drink, slumps, and has a depressed and sad facial expression.

Studies of the attachment and stress response system in monkeys found that the frequency and duration of calling behavior were markedly higher when the monkey mother was placed in an adjacent cage where the infant monkey could hear her, compared with the infant monkey who was in total isolation, who was much calmer. The completely isolated infant monkey had a markedly elevated cortisol level (HPA activation) compared with the partially isolated infant monkey, which displayed a strong stress response (SAM activation). Activation of the HPA system appears to be more prominent in situations where the behavioral coping strategies are not available. Compliant animals are characterized by extreme withdrawal, apathy, depressive behavior, and a lack of active coping strategies. By contrast, repressed animals that actively try to manage and avoid potential confrontations with a dominant animal show elevated stress response levels in the sympathetic nervous system (the SAM system), which is associated with a chronically raised heart rate, but no long-term increase in cortisol (Spangler & Grossmann, 1993).

The stress response system (HPA) is complex and has not yet been fully explored. Schore (2002) has suggested that prolonged periods of sympathetic activity lead to an excessive cortisol response to trauma, while chronic and intense vegetative vagal activity is associated with low cortisol levels. One effect of elevated cortisol levels is cell death in the hippocampus, while prolonged activation of the vegetative vagal system causes an extremely low cortisol level, which causes damage to the limbic structures. Extremely traumatic states in early infancy may lead to reduced cortisol levels in adulthood. Both understimulation and overstimulation cause stress and either elevated or reduced cortisol levels.

Cortisol Regulation

Cortisol can be traced in blood, urine, and saliva, and hence the analysis of saliva samples has become a common method for measuring stress levels. Normally, the release of cortisol follows the circadian rhythm. Levels go up during the last few hours of a sleep cycle, peak in the early morning, drop quickly after the person wakes up, and continue to decrease gradually throughout the day. The child gradually develops a rhythmic variation, and the adult pattern is in place around the age of 2 years. Already at the age of 3 months, the cortisol level peaks in the morning (Smith, 2003). Cortisol affects most organs and tissues. It suppresses immune responses and increases the level of circulating glucose. Children with a chronically increased or reduced cortisol level have a harder time focusing and maintaining attention (Glaser, 2004).

Small everyday temporary elevations in cortisol levels as a result of acute stressors improve the child's ability to concentrate and to handle stressful experiences competently, with regard to both physiological and behavioral challenges. Chronic stress in early developmental stages in mammals, including humans, may either cause chronic stress activation or reduced emotionality, which leads to highly negative emotionality or passive avoidance behavior. In children with an insecure attachment pattern, the mother's presence has not been as effective in regulating the stress response system as it has in children with a secure attachment. The caregiver's inability to regulate the child's stress response and the child's feelings of being overwhelmed in relation to the insecure attachment pattern may result in high recurring cortisol levels during early development. In some children, over time the chronically elevated cortisol level seems to cause a reduced activation of the stress response system and thus of cortisol. The reduced stress response activation appears to cause the child to develop intense conflicts with his or her environment as the child becomes impulse governed and lacks empathy and understanding of how his responses might affect others. A raised cortisol level is associated with anxiety and fear; for example, the cortisol level is high in students while they are taking exams. In stressful situations, a high cortisol level is associated with competent responses. It is still unclear how we might distinguish between children in whom an elevated stress response activity signals fear, anxiety, and vulnerability and children in whom it indicates a higher social and emotional competence.

Heightened stress response reactivity seems to imply better emotional competencies when the cortisol level is regulated in relation to individual stressors. Thus, the child's cortisol level is increased in the stressful situation, but once the situation is over it is downregulated. Perhaps evolution has ensured that after a prolonged and extreme elevation in cortisol, the stress response system is downregulated as a protective measure against the negative neural consequences of raised cortisol levels; however, this protection comes at a socioemotional cost. When the nervous system has been exposed to a high cortisol level for a while, receptors shut down; this happens when the stressful situation is pervasive. A rapid regulation of cortisol levels in connection with stressful events seems to be related to the child's perception of previous situations of coping. Thus, good social skills seem to be associated with strong stress responsiveness in relation to social conflicts with rapid subsequent downregulation (Hart, Gunnar, & Cicchetti, 1995).

Consequences of a Chronically Imbalanced Stress Response System

Chronically elevated or disturbed cortisol levels are often associated with neglect or abuse and chronic stress activation. For example, Sapolsky (1998) found that baboons at the lower levels of the hierarchy have elevated cortisol levels. Additionally, when the dominance hierarchy is unstable or new, the entire baboon group shows elevated cortisol levels. Unpredictable, stressful experiences are particularly likely to cause high stress levels in the nervous system; for example, rats are not traumatized if they hear a warning sound before an electric shock. The rat learns when something bad is going to occur, and the rest of the time it is able to relax. Rats that are able to prepare or feel that they have some degree of influence on the electric shock are not traumatized. It is of no importance whether the rat is in fact in control—it is the rat's perception of the situation that reduces the stress response. If a rat has been exposed to recurring uncontrolled stressors, it will continue to be affected by the lack of predictability for a long time; for example, it will have difficulty acquiring avoidance behavior. Martin Seligman found that when rats were in a cage where they could not escape electric shocks, they eventually resigned and withdrew to a state of hopelessness. When the electric shocks stopped, these rats behaved as if they had lost all hope and strength, and they stopped trying to escape; the researchers character- ized this as learned helplessness (Seligman & Beagley, 1975). The rats were unable to handle ordinary life events such as competing for food or avoiding social aggression. The sense of control is exceedingly important in relation to motivation and psychological coping. The traumatized, helpless animals often displayed self-harming behavior, loss of sleep, el- evated cortisol levels, and disturbed levels of noradrenaline, serotonin, and dopamine. As mentioned earlier, disturbances in these neurotrans- mitter levels are associated with irritability, depression, aggression, and violent behavior (Perry, 1994; van der Kolk, 1987).

In infant rats, prolonged separation from the caregivers causes ele- vated stress response activity and causes a lifelong increase in stress reactivity. There is considerable difference in the sensitivity of the in- dividual rats in relation to previous stressful experiences, which sug- gests that the long-term effect stems from a combination of genetic vulnerability and environmental responses (Chugani, 1999; Chugani et al., 2001).

Early Care and Cortisol Regulation

Myron Hofer's studies with rats showed that there is undoubtedly a critical period during which the stress response system (HPA) is estab- lished. Studies of institutionalized Romanian children have produced similar findings. Gunnar et al.'s study found that the longer the children had been institutionalized, the more disturbed was their cortisol rhythm. Failure to reduce the cortisol level in the evening represents a dysregu- lation of the stress response system, but it was impossible to say whether the cause was inadequate care, malnutrition, inadequate stimulation, so- matic illness, physical abuse, and so on. Infants who were adopted after the age of 4 months continued to have elevated levels and disturbances in the circadian variation of cortisol levels after adoption, while children who were adopted before the age of 4 months had normal, rhythmic cor- tisol levels. It appears that the HPA system is established around the age of 6 months. In the first months of life, the cortisol response is variable, but after this age it appears to stabilize (Chisholm, Carter, Ames, & Mor- ison, 1995; Gunnar, Morison, Chisholm, & Schuder, 2001; Lewis & Ram- say, 1995).

Early care seems to have a strong impact on the establishment of the density of cortisol receptors in the hippocampus in the limbic system, and the hippocampus has a modulating function on the autonomic nervous system, among other elements. When the child does not receive adequate stimulation in infancy, the hippocampus will not form a sufficient number of cortisol receptors, and consequently it will not be able to downregulate stress hormones in stressful situations and thus protect the neocortex from under- or overstimulation. Chronic activation of the stress response system and thus excessive cortisol release over a prolonged period at a sensitive time in infancy weakens the hippocampus through a loss of neurons, and its ability to control the release of stress hormones is impaired. This might help explain memory problems in children and adults who have been exposed to chronic stress, as the hippocampus plays a key role for our short-term memory. An impaired hippocampus function means that the cortisol level is not downregulated, and elevated levels of cortisol reduce the serotonin level. If the function of the hippocampus is impaired, there is nothing to balance the effect from the amygdala (Allen, 2002; Hart et al., 1995).

The HPA System and Attachment Patterns

Spangler and Schieche (1998) studied individual differences in the stress response system (HPA) in children with different attachment patterns. They saw secure attachment as a buffer against elevated stress response in separation from the caregiver. They found a particularly increased HPA stress response in children with an ambivalent and disorganized attachment pattern. By contrast, they did not find an activation of the HPA system in children with an avoidant attachment pattern; their explanation is that these children have developed an appropriate and effective coping strategy to avoid or reduce the risk of rejection when they need contact. In the strange situation all the children had an increased heart rate when they were separated from their mothers, even the children who did not appear to care about her absence. Thus, it seems that the HPA system is only activated when the child is unable to find relevant behavioral strategies. From an attachment perspective, establishing contact after separation from the mother is the only adaptive behavioral strategy for emotional reorganization. Ambivalent and disorganized children will try to regulate their unstable emotional state by seeking to be close to someone, but they will not be able to use the mother as a source of security and emotional regulation. A study found that these children had elevated cortisol levels even before the strange situation was initiated. It seems that the ambivalent and disorganized children's attachment system is constantly activated, and they cannot effectively use the mother as a secure attachment figure.

Gunnar, Mangelsdorf, Larson, and Hertsgaard (1989) noted that a secure attachment relationship is capable of balancing less adaptive temperamental dispositions. Gunnar et al. observed that the HPA system was activated in inhibited children with insecure attachment but not in inhibited children with secure attachment. Thus, inhibited children with an avoidant attachment pattern also have an elevated cortisol level. They concluded that there is a connection between HPA activation, attachment security, and temperament. In securely attached children, crying and negative expressions are not related to physiological stress. Crying in securely attached children is not associated with physiological arousal, because it serves as an effective coping function, in contrast to insecurely attached children, who have limited coping strategies that often fail to lead to behavioral regulation. When crying cannot be used as an effective coping strategy in regulating attachment behavior, crying instead activates the child's stress response system and is not associated with soothing and comforting as it is in children with a secure attachment pattern (Spangler & Schieche, 1998).

Studies have also found that insecure attachment patterns can cause high emotional reactivity as well as the opposite: low emotional reactivity. A child who is unable to self-regulate will quickly reach an elevated arousal level. This activates the stress response system and causes elevated noradrenaline and cortisol activation, which keeps the child in a tense emotional state. Being exposed to chronic and severe stress over a prolonged period may give rise to an antiarousal or downregulation mechanism, which means that the stress response system (HPA) is no longer activated, and the cortisol level remains low (Gunnar & Vazquez, 2001). That may lead to a state of emotional paralysis and dissociation and feelings of emptiness and alienation. The child adapts passively, fails to respond to stressful situations, and denies painful events. Unfortunately, this downregulation extinguishes all emotions, and the child no longer responds to joy-filled stimuli either, even if he may put on a happy face (Cicchetti & Tucker, 1994).

Hyperarousal and Dissociation

Hyperarousal and dissociation develop in the absence of appropriate responses from the child's caregivers or as a result of severe traumatization. Serious misattunements and traumatization not only leave the child with an insecure attachment but also trigger chaotic changes in the nervous system. Children with a disorganized attachment pattern, who are often exposed to traumatic experiences, are particularly quick to respond with a heightened alarm response. The caregiver is unable to modulate the child's arousal level but often induces extreme levels of stimulation— either too high, in the case of abuse, or too low, in the case of deprivation. The early stage of a threat experience triggers an alarm response that involves the sympathetic aspect of the autonomic nervous system. If the caregiver does not help the child regulate the state but instead exacerbates the pain, the child will escalate into a pattern of extreme hyperarousal. Even if the child shows obvious signs of needing help, the caregiver continues to intensify the state. When the child has been in this state without support for some time, he will dissociate; the child will stop taking an interest in stimuli in the external world and retreat to an internal world instead.

The child necessarily seeks the caregiver when alarmed, so any parental behavior that frightens the child will create a paradoxical situation, as approach, a shift in attention, or flight are all impossible. The child develops a sort of synchronicity with the mother's dysregulated state, which is imprinted onto the autonomic and limbic structures. The caregiver's disorganized behavior means that she often has dramatic mood swings including exuberance, panic states, and rage. A child who is constantly bombarded with stressful experiences will be unable to establish equilibrium, which has severe consequences for the nervous system, since all the child's mental energy will be directed at pursuing a state of equilibrium on the brain stem level (Schore, 1994, 2001b).

If the nervous system fails to activate a reciprocal regulation of the autonomic nervous system, both the sympathetic (energy-expanding) and the parasympathetic (energy-inhibiting) system will be activated. This happens, for example, when the infant sees the mother's aggressive face. This leads to a chaotic state in the nervous system and is associated with a disorganized attachment pattern. Schore (1994, 2003b) suggested that the child can become locked into a chronic stress state, where both the sympathetic and the parasympathetic systems are hyperactivated. This occurs when the sympathetic and parasympathetic nervous systems are activated simultaneously, as is the case, for example, in situations of shame and humiliation. If the autonomic nervous system cannot be balanced the result is chronic dysregulation, which means that the nervous system can be simultaneously hyperactive and downregulated. Naturally, this might help explain how certain antisocial personalities are able to kill someone and then explain that it felt as if they were watching the event on film (Schore, 1994, 2003b).

Sometimes the opioid system is activated in the downregulated state, which alters the perception of painful stimuli, the sense of time and place, and the sense of reality. In the sympathetic fight-or-flight state the stress hormones are activated, the noradrenaline-based system is elevated, and the serotonin level is reduced, which leads to a state of hyperactivity, alertness, and irritability. Long-term activation of noradrenaline results in an increase in hyperarousal, tension, and a heightened unmodulated startle response, which produces a sense that the world is a dangerous place that requires constant vigilance. In extreme and prolonged activation of the sympathetic nervous system, the opioid system can be activated, probably as an evolutionary means of achieving pain reduction in connection with prolonged fight-or-flight situations. In stressful situations a parallel increase in noradrenaline and dopamine levels causes a sense of vigilance and a tendency toward paranoid and perceptual disorders (Cozolino, 2000). There is a pronounced gender difference in the response patterns in relation to trauma, as women are more likely to rely on a vegetative parasympathetic pattern, while men tend to use a sympathetic hyperarousal pattern. This is evident, among other things, in the fact that boys tend to display hyperarousal disorders in the form of impulsiveness, aggression, attention-deficit disorder, and external behavior, while girls are more likely to respond with hyperarousal disorders in the form of anxiety, panic attacks, and dysphoria. Males are more likely to respond with a sympathetic fight-or-flight pattern, while females are more likely to respond with a parasympathetic freeze response (Hart 2008; Perry, 1990, 1994; Schore, 1994).

Autoregulation

In extreme stress states the child's more advanced levels of function-ing disappear, and the child regresses and leaves management of the stress states to primitive levels. When the infant is exposed to more stimulation than his nervous system can handle, he switches from a reg-ulation system that interacts with the parents to an autoregulating sys-tem. Here, the autoregulating system is defined in light of the polyvagal theory about the two basic, innate self-protection strategies, where the child strikes a balance that does not require contact with the caregiver; these strategies are based on the vegetative vagal system and the sym-pathetic nervous system (see the section on polyvagal theory). Chronic states of hyperarousal or dissociation only occur if the child is exposed to chronic stress states, where he relies on the vegetative vagal system or the sympathetic nervous system for prolonged periods.

When the child stops taking an interest in external stimuli and avoids contact, limits affect, submits, and loses the ability to act, these are all signs of an activation of the vegetative vagal system. The freeze state occurs in hopeless stressful situations, where the child strives to avoid being noticed. The child will always initially engage the sympathetic hy-perarousal state and attempt to use his limited behavioral repertoire to attract the caregiver's attention, which is an appropriate strategy when the caregiver is an accessible source of warmth, comfort, and protection. If the child fails to receive support for regulation through the sympa-thetic hyperarousal defense, the nervous system enters a freeze state. If the child's nervous system is maintained in a freeze state, the child will dissociate, which involves numbness, avoidant behavior, and a reduction of affect. The child cuts himself off from external stimuli and retreats into an internal world. Traumatized children are often observed to have a glassy gaze, and they are passive and lack initiative. In the passive parasympathetic state, the amount of endogenous opioids is sometimes increased, which reduces pain, causes immobilization, and inhibits cries for help. The stress response system has evolved to ensure survival in critical situations, and in relation to chronic stressful experiences this activation causes irreversible changes (Perry, 1994; Perry, Pollard, Blakely, Baker, & Vigilante, 1995; Schore, 2001b).

When the child is in an autoregulated state, that is, either a hyper-arousal or a freeze state, he is unable to self-regulate affectively and directs all his resources at reorganizing. The disorganized state becomes a pattern that is activated in more and more situations; it is generalized, so that even slight stimuli such as loud noises or voices will activate the alarm response. The child's stress response capacity is activated over and over again, and everyday stressors that would not previously have triggered a response now elicit excessive reactivity. These children are hyperreactive and hypersensitive, and the fear states gradually develop into a character feature. A primitive recognition of a simple movement, mimicry, posture, and so on may set off an avalanche that triggers a response from the child's nervous system. Because this state has been activated so many times, the nervous system is activated in response to even minor incidents that might remind the child of previous traumas or rejection. The child develops an extreme degree of vulnerability and may respond in ways that are unpredictable and incomprehensible to others. The child goes rapidly from feeling slightly uncomfortable to feeling threatened or terrorized, and even positive affects such as joy and enthusiasm may cause the nervous system to dissociate. If the stress response is constantly activated it becomes hyperactive and hypersensitive—or it breaks down. Even minor transgressions can cause the child's nervous system to disintegrate. Some children with this type of difficulty may function well in isolated and well-defined situations where the anxiety response is not activated, but the child's ability to integrate states is often so limited that even the slightest ambiguity or ambivalence can cause disintegration.

At an early state the nervous system adapts to an unpredictable environment, and for a child growing up in violent and chaotic surroundings it is appropriate to be hypersensitive to external stimuli, to be constantly vigilant and potentially ready to respond. Unfortunately, these survival strategies are counterproductive when the environment changes. The child has spent so much time in a state of fear that he will focus on nonverbal features and be unable to relax. Children who are in a chronic state of sympathetic hyperarousal often have an increased muscle tone, slightly raised temperature, difficulties with affect regulation, and generalized anxiety. By contrast, children in an autoregulated parasympathetic state have reduced muscle tone, a lower heart rate, and an affective flatness that is often experienced as a depersonalization or an out-of-body experience. Stress responses are functional in emergency situations, but a chronic stimulation of the stress system is harmful. When a child who is unable to self-regulate is exposed to situations that reactivate earlier trauma, the child will dissociate with no ability to sense emotions (Bradley, 2000).

Lack of Self-Regulation and Attention Deficit Disorder

Severe abuse and deprivation appear to interfere with the child's development process and lead to chronic changes that cause a wide range of symptoms in the nervous system, such as an inability to distinguish between internal and external reality, dissociation, and a lack of mentalization. Early experiences of overwhelming anxiety, for example, may permanently alter sensitivity to stimuli related to the trauma. It can be difficult to extinguish deep subcortical patterns once they have been activated. A child who has had frightening and traumatizing experiences early in life remains in a chronic state of hypersensitivity where it can be difficult to find the necessary calm to incorporate new social experiences and develop cognitively. The child is unable to self-regulate, feels out of control, does not experience that others can help him calm down, and often has a low threshold of tolerance. The child's nervous system is fragile, partly due to the lack of organizing capacity and partly due to a lack of practice handling high and increasing levels of arousal. The child is hypersensitive to high levels of arousal, whether they stem from anger or joy. When the arousal level is too high, the nervous system disintegrates and engages in autoregulated parasympathetic or sympathetic activation, depending on the child's innate tendency. That makes it difficult for the nervous system to build self-regulating skills and to achieve adaptive and flexible functioning in the future. All emotional categories and sensory perceptions have the capacity to cause disintegration when the arousal level exceeds a certain threshold (Bradley, 2000).

The child's self-perception is based on the capacity to regulate internal states and behavioral responses, for example in relation to external stressors. Studies concerning PTSD (post-traumatic stress disorder) have found that the younger the child is when the traumatic event takes place, the greater the risk that the child will develop chronic difficulties with regulating emotions such as anger, anxiety, and sexual impulses. Stimuli may trigger danger responses even if they are not directly related to the traumatic event. The child loses the ability to focus on relevant stimuli, develops attention problems, and becomes unable to inhibit impulses once they are activated (van der Kolk, 1987).

A child who is forced to deal with constant stress situations perceives the world differently than children who are secure. An overactivation of the autonomic nervous system and the limbic system makes attention control a difficult task. The ability to focus one's attention is necessary for future learning and adaptation and for driving development forward (Brazelton, 1984). Brain stem structures have partly taken over control and respond reflexively and impulsively—and in many cases aggressively—to perceived threats (Perry, 1994).

The Impact of Dysregulation on Brain Development

As mentioned earlier, adult monkeys raised by mothers that were unable to provide appropriately stable, attuned, and predictable contact show lifelong changes in neurotransmitters such as noradrenaline, serotonin, and dopamine. These changes cause them to lose their capacity to modulate aggression, and they become erratic, unpredictable, chaotic, and vicious (Lewis et al., 2001). The brain's circuits are shaped through a natural selection of connections that match environmental data. In the early caregiver-child contact the child attunes with the caregiver's dysregulated state, which is incorporated into the child's nervous system. For example, if the child is in a chronic stress state, synaptic connections are reduced in number, which leads to an ineffective regulation of the autonomic nervous system and its interactions with higher centers, including the limbic system and the orbitofrontal cortex. The self-regulation of the nervous system becomes unstable, and its capacity for change and development later in life is reduced. The dominance of subcortical activity may prolong protest and rage responses or cause extreme passivity and depression (Schore, 1994, 2002).

As mentioned earlier, disturbances in neurochemical signals during infancy may stem either from inadequate care (deprivation) or abuse. Inadequate and dysfunctional stimulation impairs the necessary pruning and specialization of neurons and neural circuits, which in turn impairs the capacity to organize experiences. Abuse may activate the anxiety response, which causes the child's nervous system to dissociate. Both abuse and deprivation have an almost invisible toxic effect on a developing nervous system. For example, a child who is exposed to abuse develops an alarm response that alters the structure and functions of the brain to form adaptive responses to survival-related information. Even if the alarm response facilitates survival, chronic stress experiences cause the nervous system to become either hyper- or hyporeactive. This leads to exaggerated or diminished alertness, causes the startle response to activate more quickly than normal or not at all, and leads to affect lability, anxiety, and so on. The earlier and the more extensive the abuse, the more severe the consequences for the child's development, and the bigger the risk that the child will have difficulty developing self-regulation strategies. A neural system that activates frequently practices responding to certain stimuli, just as practicing the piano serves to mature the neural circuits involved in playing it. The more threat-related behavior the child experiences, the more activation there is of the neural systems involved in overcoming this type of experience. The degree and nature of specific responses will vary from person to person (Perry, 2001; Perry et al., 1995; Schwarz & Perry, 1994).

Emotional Reactivity and Stress-Related Impulse Breakthroughs

Constant sympathetic activation leads to primitive responses and impulse breakthroughs. The more prolonged the stress activation, the more unregulated the nervous system. Chronically elevated stress hormone levels during infancy probably cause permanent functional damage to the microarchitecture of the limbic systems and to the circuit connections to the orbitofrontal cortex. The orbitofrontal cortex is in charge of impulse inhibition and the general control of all affect-regulating structures, and inadequate organization of autonomic control through orbitofrontal structures prevents the coordination of the autonomic system and its capacity for reciprocal functioning. Even small disturbances may develop into intense stress states that are perceived as rapid shifts to negative affective states (Schore, 2003a, 2003b) and cause the child to lose the ability to self-regulate. Disturbances in the limbic system seem to affect the development of certain functions in the orbitofrontal cortex, which in addition to impulse inhibition are also in charge of object permanence and the capacity for associating internal images with emotions, for distinguishing one's own needs from those of others, for reality correction, for mentalization, and thus for adapting behavior in relation to social norms (Gerhardt, 2004).

Stress sensitivity is an appropriate strategy when an individual has to be ready to respond quickly to danger. However, like all other adaptive responses, hypersensitivity in the stress system may be inappropriate, and minor frustrations may lead to aggressive outbursts. This leads to negative responses from the environment, which in turn activate the stress response system and destroy relationships. Neural systems form strong connections between associated tracks and generalize specific events, especially in relation to threatening stimuli. In evolutionary terms, this strategy is appropriate, but it also makes us vulnerable. For example, if a child has a history with traumatic experiences, an elevated heart rate that is caused by a harmless experience can trigger an alarm response in the brain stem and cause a panic attack. The child is in a constant state of anxiety because the nervous system has become hypersensitive to sympathetic activation, and the child will not know what caused the panic state (Perry, 1999).

An elevated activation of stress hormones over a prolonged period adjusts the nervous system to constant vigilance. The amygdala, which is constantly scanning the environment for possible threats, is a structure that is quickly kindled. As a result, it gradually becomes self-activating once it has been stimulated for a prolonged period. The amygdala is activated by the release of noradrenaline, and chronic activation means that it is activated by even minor stimuli and has trouble downregulating its reactivity (Vyas, Mitra, Shankaranarayana Rao, & Chattarji, 2002). LeDoux (2001) has documented that if the amygdala is self-activating, and if the function of the hippocampus is partially impaired due to increased cortisol activation, the person will respond with frequent and incomprehensible anxiety responses. The hippocampus, the frontal part of the cingulate gyrus, and the prefrontal cortex are able to prevent the release of stress hormones and inhibit amygdaloid fear conditioning. When the hippocampus and areas in the frontal lobes fail to activate sufficiently to inhibit anxiety impulses, the hyperactive amygdala becomes a permanent problem that may be difficult to alleviate (Perry & Azad, 1999, 2001; Scaer, 2001; Teicher, 2002).

When the orbitofrontal cortex is not sufficiently capable of inhibiting impulses from the subcortical systems, the consequences may involve not only increased anxiety but also increased aggression, because the fear system in many regards is parallel to the rage system. The balance between fight and flight behavior is determined by nuclei located in various regions in the amygdala. The circuits project to the hypothalamus before terminating in the PAG system in the brain stem, which perceives discomfort and activates motor programs. Both an impaired and a hyperactive amygdala can lead to aggression. Schore (2003a, 2003b) described two forms of aggression: "hot-blooded" and "cold-blooded." The rage system is characterized as hot-blooded aggression; it is associated with displays of temper and agitation triggered by contact and occurs in connection with a hyperactive amygdala. Stimulation of certain areas in the hypothalamus may trigger a different form of rage: cold-blooded rage, which is more instinctive and less emotional, and which occurs in connection with reduced activity of the amygdala. The cold form of aggression is primarily associated with hunting behavior and actually has little to do with anger and rage; instead, it is a need-based mechanism that activates dopamine (Solms & Turnbull, 2002; Sørensen, 2006). When animals defend their territory they rely on hot-blooded rage, while the hunting instinct that is applied in assaults or attacks, for example, is a case of cold-blooded rage. An increase in anxiety activates the amygdala and leads to the release of noradrenaline, which under normal circumstances serves to suppress the parasympathetic system and feelings of pleasure. The hunting instinct, which only activates the hypothalamus without the simultaneous amygdala activation, probably releases both noradrenaline and dopamine, which activates feelings of hyperactive energy and pleasure (Panksepp, 1998). Cold-blooded rage occurs when the amygdala fails to activate, and thus, children with damage to the amygdala respond with this type of rage. Siegel (2005) has documented that these two aggression systems are closely linked, and the activation of one form of aggression inhibits the other (Sørensen, 2006). Cold-blooded rage may be associated with a form of counterphobic response, where the assault on an innocent victim leads to some sort of high or rush due to sudden dopamine-based activation, which in turn activates the opioid system. Sympathetically activated dissociation probably serves as a protection against a vague sense of anxiety, which can be achieved, for example, by threatening and frightening others. The nervous system always strives for equilibrium at any cost (Hart, 2008).

Dysregulation in the Child's Mental Organizations

As mentioned earlier, the child's nervous system is shaped by events that take place while the child is still in the womb. For example, it appears that maternal stress during pregnancy can lead to raised cortisol levels in the child and vague or ambiguous stress responses. As mentioned earlier, traumatic experiences and lack of attunement during infancy also have severe consequences for the subcortical brain structures that are in charge of basic regulatory capacities. The disturbance of regulatory capacities impairs the child's ability to develop the necessary flexibility to adapt to new and challenging situations and to develop new coping and self-protection strategies. Dysregulation of basic autonomic structures are woven into the brain's fundamental neurochemical regulation and render the nervous system fragile, prone to disorganization, and incapable of handling raised levels of arousal. The child will also have difficulty defending against future stressors. Development forms mental organizations that build on one another, and what happens in the initial stages of development will echo throughout the subsequent stages (see Fig. 5.1).

For example, negative experiences during gestation such as chronic maternal stress or substance abuse will affect the development of brain stem and midbrain structures, which in turn will influence the development of limbic and cortical regions, and so on (Cicchetti & Tucker, 1994).

0–2 Months

Matt is 11 years old and has been raised by a mother with a serious substance abuse problem. When he was put into foster care at 5 years of age he was a little, observant boy, hard to gauge. Today he seems generally insecure and suspicious. He lacks facial expressions, and his mood never changes, except when he is seized by a sudden anger that may erupt for no apparent reason. He thinks everybody is his friend, and he only forms superficial contacts. He has always overeaten and has had difficulty dressing appropriately for the seasons. When he was caught stealing candy in the local supermarket he was unashamed but explained objectively what had happened. When he becomes chaotic he throws everything around, yells curse words and

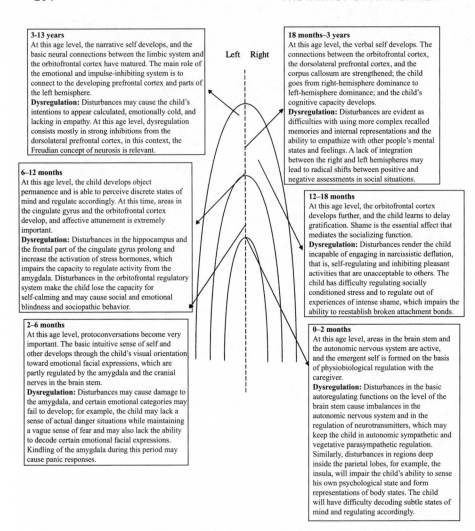

3-13 years
At this age level, the narrative self develops, and the basic neural connections between the limbic system and the orbitofrontal cortex have matured. The main role of the emotional and impulse-inhibiting system is to connect to the developing prefrontal cortex and parts of the left hemisphere.
Dysregulation: Disturbances may cause the child's intentions to appear calculated, emotionally cold, and lacking in empathy. At this age level, dysregulation consists mostly in strong inhibitions from the dorsolateral prefrontal cortex, in this context, the Freudian concept of neurosis is relevant.

Left   Right

18 months–3 years
At this age level, the verbal self develops. The connections between the orbitofrontal cortex, the dorsolateral prefrontal cortex, and the corpus callosum are strengthened; the child goes from right-hemisphere dominance to left-hemisphere dominance; and the child's cognitive capacity develops.
Dysregulation: Disturbances are evident as difficulties with using more complex recalled memories and internal representations and the ability to empathize with other people's mental states and feelings. A lack of integration between the right and left hemispheres may lead to radical shifts between positive and negative assessments in social situations.

6–12 months
At this age level, the child develops object permanence and is able to perceive discrete states of mind and regulate accordingly. At this time, areas in the cingulate gyrus and the orbitofrontal cortex develop, and affective attunement is extremely important.
Dysregulation: Disturbances in the hippocampus and the frontal part of the cingulate gyrus prolong and increase the activation of stress hormones, which impairs the capacity to regulate activity from the amygdala. Disturbances in the orbitofrontal regulatory system make the child lose the capacity for self-calming and may cause social and emotional blindness and sociopathic behavior.

12–18 months
At this age level, the orbitofrontal cortex develops further, and the child learns to delay gratification. Shame is the essential affect that mediates the socializing function.
Dysregulation: Disturbances render the child incapable of engaging in narcissistic deflation, that is, self-regulating and inhibiting pleasant activities that are unacceptable to others. The child has difficulty regulating socially conditioned stress and to regulate out of experiences of intense shame, which impairs the ability to reestablish broken attachment bonds.

2–6 months
At this age level, protoconversations become very important. The basic intuitive sense of self and other develops through the child's visual orientation toward emotional facial expressions, which are partly regulated by the amygdala and the cranial nerves in the brain stem.
Dysregulation: Disturbances may cause damage to the amygdala, and certain emotional categories may fail to develop; for example, the child may lack a sense of actual danger situations while maintaining a vague sense of fear and may also lack the ability to decode certain emotional facial expressions. Kindling of the amygdala during this period may cause panic responses.

0–2 months
At this age level, areas in the brain stem and the autonomic nervous system are active, and the emergent self is formed on the basis of physiobiological regulation with the caregiver.
Dysregulation: Disturbances in the basic autoregulating functions on the level of the brain stem cause imbalances in the autonomic nervous system and in the regulation of neurotransmitters, which may keep the child in autonomic sympathetic and vegetative parasympathetic regulation. Similarly, disturbances in regions deep inside the parietal lobes, for example, the insula, will impair the child's ability to sense his own psychological state and form representations of body states. The child will have difficulty decoding subtle states of mind and regulating accordingly.

Figure 5.1. Overview of the development and dysfunctions of the brain structures

offensive remarks, and then goes on to speak gibberish. Next, he lies down on the floor, crawling and shouting inarticulately before eventually curling up in a fetal position. He has a severe attention deficit disorder and gets angry and resistant when he is met with demands.

The emergent self is formed in the period just prior to birth and through the first 2 months after birth based on the caregiver's physiobiological regulation. Severe dysregulation may disturb the child's basic autoregulatory functions on the brain stem level, which, among other effects, causes an imbalance in the autonomic nervous system and in the regulation of neurotransmitters. Disturbances on this level lock the child into autonomic sympathetic and vegetative parasympathetic regulation. In cases of severe abuse or neglect with a substantial lack of regulation, the nervous system will fail to develop more complex self-protection strategies. Being stuck in a vegetative vagal system contributes to severe emotional disorders related to feelings of emptiness and freezing. If the child does not perceive the environment as secure and fails to experience an attuned contact that stimulates the development of the mammalian vagal system, the nervous system will be unable to self-regulate and is kept in a fragile autoregulated state, in constant danger of freezing or fight-or-flight activation. The mammalian vagal system is poorly developed during the first 3 months of life, and the child will seek self-protection in innate strategies when he fails to achieve protection through contact with the caregivers.

In the sympathetic state the child engages in fight-or-flight behavior or attack. In the parasympathetic freeze state anxiety and pain disappear, and the organism engages in a calming numbness caused by the release of opioids. By assuming the fetal position the child shuts off external stimuli (Krystal, 1988; Papousek & Papousek, 1975; Schore, 1994). The shift from self-regulation into a prolonged autoregulating state can cause damage to the developing limbic system, which is still fragile. The child's only coping strategy in connection with stress situations is to rely on innate self-protection strategies. The earliest and most basic self-protection system consists of an activation of the autonomic nervous system; in severe cases this may cause dissociation on a deep subcortical level, which leads to an inability to feel pain, feel hunger or satiety, cold or warmth, and so on.

Development in certain areas in the parietal lobes, such as the insula, appears to be disturbed, which impairs the child's ability to sense and produce images of his own psychological state and create representations of body states (disturbances of the proprioceptive sense). The child has difficulty interpreting complex states of mind and regulating accordingly. This means that the child will have difficulty intuitively empathizing with others as well as a limited capacity for affective self-regulation (Schore, 2001b). The nervous system loses the ability to integrate deeper sensory functions, and when the child is in the vegetative parasympathetic state, a defensive exclusion occurs of the signals that normally trigger attachment behavior. The child attaches indiscriminately to others, which is seen, for example in children who have been exposed to early emotional frustration. Thus, disturbances in deep subcortical structures, for example, the amygdala, appear to impair the development of structures such as the cingulate gyrus and the orbitofrontal cortex. Activation of these two structures affects attachment behavior and feelings of shame, as we will see in the section on the 6–12 month age level.

2–6 Months

Twelve-year-old Kyle is generally an anxious boy, who is afraid to sleep with the light off and always keeps a knife next to his bed. In relation to others he is provoking, and he attacks others at the slightest disagreement. He has difficulty controlling his arousal level, and even joy can make him overexcited. For example, when he is looking forward to a visit to a circus, he gets unhinged, makes strange noises, burps constantly, and keeps singing the same song for a week, driving other people mad. He likes being with younger children whom he can manage and control, but he might also threaten them when he wants things his way. He has no empathy and recently stole a cell phone from a girl the same age as himself; he threatened her with a knife and pressed his elbow so hard against her throat that she was unable to breathe, even though he likes the girl. When confronted with the incident he became angry and reproachful.

At the age of 2–6 months the core self develops, and the child begins to develop a sense of having his own needs. During this period, there is a shift from physiobiological to psychobiological regulation, and protoconversations become very important. The lack of reciprocity in the child's relationships at this age level disturbs the development of a sense of self and the ability to sense others intuitively. Inadequately attuned interactions with the caregiver early in life seem to render the child unable to sense himself or others emotionally, and the child uses denial in relation to anything that is difficult or incomprehensible. Severe traumatic experiences during this period may damage the amygdala and cause certain emotional categories to fail to develop; for example, the child may lose the sense of actual danger while maintaining a vague sense of fear, and the ability to interpret certain emotional facial expressions, such as grief, may be lost.

In early infancy the child's fleeting attention requires support, and through this contact the child learns to maintain focus. Disturbances at this stage will compromise the child's ability to engage in attuned social interactions, maintain focus, and adapt to social situations. The child fails to establish a sense of what feels important and is drawn toward fleeting stimuli without being able to choose. Severe dysregulation at this age may prevent the child from developing a sense of the delimitation between self and the external world or a sense of his own needs.

Both under- and overstimulation and overwhelming experiences can make the amygdala more active, and the child will begin to display clear fear and anger responses. Excessive kindling of the amygdala during this period may cause panic responses later in life where the child is unable to control anxiety impulses. This is seen, for example, in children who respond with heightened startle responses and who panic quickly.

6–12 Months

Marie is a 16-year-old girl whose moods can change from moment to moment. When she gets upset or is in a bad mood, it takes a long time for her mood state to change, and the bad mood lingers throughout the house. She is a very likeable girl. She is often very sweet when she feels good, and she wants to help with cooking and often asks if she can help. When she feels bad, she becomes argumentative and tries to make the other person angry and upset. Her foster mother describes her as unpredictable; one moment she may express hatred and contempt, only to praise the same person highly the next moment, without giving any impression that she is aware of the contrast. When she speaks with her foster care consultant, she sometimes seems desperately miserable and says that her one and biggest wish is to move back in with her birth mother; however, when she is actually with her birth mother she cannot stand being with her. She is popular among other girls her age, because they find her good to confide in, but they are confused by her sudden mood swings and by the fact that she will use very ugly words about them and then deny saying them the next moment.

At the age of 6–12 months the intersubjective self develops, and the child develops object permanence and learns to interpret discrete states of mind and regulate accordingly. At this time, areas in the lower part of the prefrontal cortex (the cingulate gyrus and the orbitofrontal cortex) and affective attunement are crucial. The inability to regulate affect intensity is one of the most severe symptoms in children who have suffered abuse or neglect; among other things, this involves disturbances in the orbitofrontal regulation system that make the child lose the capacity for self-calming. Damasio (1994) has described how the consequences of damage to the human orbitofrontal cortex involve difficulty with delayed gratification and problems with (secondary) mentalization.

When the child fails to make the caregiver's face light up, and the caregiver is unable to engage in affective attunement with the child, the dopamine circuit fails to activate sufficiently, which impairs the development of a healthy feeling of grandiosity in the child and makes it difficult for the nervous system to climb to the next mental level. If the formation of connections between the limbic system and the prefrontal cortex is inhibited, emotions remain primitive and undifferentiated with no access to the more complex affect-regulating system, and emotions cannot be processed on a cognitive level. In this situation, the capacity of the nervous system to develop affect regulation in relation to internal and symbolic representations is impaired (Kalin, 1993; Schore, 1994).

Insufficient maturation of limbic structures probably makes it difficult for the child to integrate different internal representations of the caregiver into one person. The child's object permanence is still immature, and the child's internal representation of the caregiver is conditioned by the varying representations of the caregiver in the present. The child is unable to form a constant internal representation of the caregiver, for example, as a lovable person who may sometimes be annoying. The internal representations remain fragmented or partial. The lack of consistency between internal representations undoubtedly impairs the child's ability to develop mentalization, and the child is not able to develop more mature forms of self-organization.

A child who is exposed to massive dysregulation at this age forms weak internal representations of other people's mental states. When another's current mental state mixes with one's own, a sort of projective identification develops that emerges in an insecure relationship, where the caregiver is unable to engage in an attuned affect-regulating process (see Chapter 3, the section on self-protection strategies on the level of ratiomentation, p. 121). That makes it difficult for the child to distinguish between internal states. Due to projective identification, the affective experiences that have not been symbolically coded, and which cannot yet be communicated verbally, are carried into the child's later relationships (Schore, 2006c). For example, 9-year-old Annette's class teacher says that Annette lacks boundaries between imagination and reality and an internal sense of right and wrong, and that she is unable to empathize with other people's needs. Fonagy et al. (2002) mentioned that an inability to mentalize can lead to a vague fear of suffering a mental breakdown. The child is trapped in emotional states, unable to regulate his way out. The nervous system is in constant danger of stress activation, because unstructured social situations require an understanding of other people's mental states. The child has difficulty predicting other people's behavior, because it is difficult for the child to distinguish between himself and others and to distinguish between true and false.

Among other consequences, the lack of mentalizing functions will cause a tendency for impulse breakthroughs, isolation, psychosomatic reactions, overeating, and so on (Schore, 2001b; Teicher, Ito, & Glod, 1996).

12–18 Months

Jack is a 10-year-old boy with a keen sense of justice. He is incapable of seeing any fault with himself and never apologizes for anything. He always gets angry if things do not go exactly as he wants them to, and he speaks to his mother as if she were his peer. The mother's cohabiting boyfriend thinks that Jack is hard on his mother; he is bossy and unable to delay gratification. When someone speaks with Jack about other people's negative perceptions of him or about how he upsets other people, he immediately becomes tearful, hides his face under his shirt, and seems offended, embarrassed, and humiliated. Even with sweat pouring off him, he will remain in this state until he receives help with neutralizing his mood. Afterward, the incident appears to be forgotten, and he is unable to describe what happened to him.

At this age level, the child learns to delay gratification, and shame is the essential affect that mediates the socializing function. Prior to this age level, the child is governed by immediate needs, probably due to the lack of inhibition of impulses from the prefrontal regions. Children aged 15–16 months are particularly vulnerable to narcissistic deflation, as discussed earlier. If the child remains in the shame-filled stress state for too long, the result may be dissociative damage, where parts of the child's psychological flow are shattered, because at this stage the child is unable to autoregulate the painful state without the caregiver's help. If the child has no opportunity to engage in narcissistic deflation because the caregiver fails to mark a misattunement, the child loses the ability to self-regulate and inhibit pleasant activities that are unacceptable in the eyes of others. The child has difficulty regulating socially conditioned stress and regulating out of intense feelings of shame, and this affects the child's ability to reestablish broken attachment bonds. The ability to tolerate experiences of negative affect is important for psychological flexibility and the capacity for self-regulation. The failure to develop narcissistic regulation, which otherwise emerges at exactly this stage in development, undermines the capacity for affect regulation to neutralize grandiosity and regulate excitement or narcissistic rage.

When the child is unable to regulate narcissistic deflation, the internal feeling of low arousal that occurs in shame is associated with a painful state that should be avoided. When shame remains unregulated, feelings cannot be expressed, partly because the mentalizing functions in the orbitofrontal cortex are disrupted. After a shame-filled misattunement, if the child does not receive support to reestablish attuned contact but is instead humiliated, mocked, and exposed to aggressive teasing by the caregiver, the child's narcissistic pain is maintained. This may make the child engage in a sympathetic state of excessive narcissistic rage or a parasympathetic state of submission. The child's explorative behavior is limited, and the child will focus on the caregiver's mood state instead of seeking separation. The child does not engage in the normal separation from the mother but attempts to establish a symbiotic relationship. Gradually, the child forms internal representations associated with shame and the experience of the other person's negative judgment. Frequent and prolonged misattunements will make the child believe that his needs are unacceptable and shameful, as in the case of 20-year-old Sheila, whose mother consistently told her she wished that Sheila had never been born, and that she was useless and always in the way. Sheila admired her mother and was very attached to her, and she felt like a dreadful person who deserved to be punished (Basch, 1985; Lewis, 1979).

Conversely, omnipotent children have never had the opportunity to engage in narcissistic deflation. They are often admired by their caregivers and are not supported in developing a realistic positive and negative self-image, and they do not experience the tension between desire and reality. The child has not been confronted and prevented from continuing inappropriate behavior, perhaps because the caregivers could not bear to see the child sad or angry. If the child does not receive support in downregulating high-arousal affect, the child's grandiose self or omnipotence will be strengthened. The child does not learn to regulate affect and defend against feelings of impotence. Some children who were raised without violence become violent nonetheless, because the parents failed to mark boundaries; intent on fulfilling the child's needs and preventing frustration, they subjugated themselves to the child. When the parents fail to impose their authority, the child loses the opportunity to self-regulate through the shame effect. The child responds with narcissistic rage every time the world does not fall into line or becomes dysphoric if the world fails to live up to the child's expectations. Although the parents are providing a great deal of emotional care, they are not promoting the development of psychological protection (Benjamin, 1996).

18 Months–3 Years

Sixteen-year-old Penny often complains about headaches and stomachaches, and she constructs various causes of her ailments that fail to coincide with real-life facts. Her somatization seems affected, and one moment she may complain loudly and seem to be in pain, while the next moment she may forget herself and begin to fool around and laugh with her girlfriends.

At this stage, the verbal self develops, and the sense of self is associated with linguistic meaning and consistency. The connections between the orbitofrontal cortex, the dorsolateral prefrontal cortex, and the corpus callosum are strengthened; the child goes from right-hemisphere dominance to left-hemisphere dominance, and his cognitive capacity develops. Dysfunctions at this age level appear as difficulties with the use of more complex memory recall and the ability to empathize and understand other people's mental states and emotions. The mentalizing capacity is attributed to the orbitofrontal and dorsolateral prefrontal cortices, mainly in the left hemisphere, and without the capacity for self-reflection and symbolic thinking, feelings and intentions can only be represented on a limbic level. A lack of integration between the right and left hemispheres may imply radical shifts between positive and negative assessments and big differences in social behavior. Left-side frontal activation is associated with inquisitive and explorative behavior and social interaction, while impaired left-side activation is associated with withdrawal, negative affect, and timidity. Impaired activation of the right frontal lobe leads to impulsivity and hyperactivity (Davidson, 1994; Hart, 2008).

When the child is unable to find a recognizable version of his own mental state in the caregiver, he misses an opportunity to achieve symbolic and verbal concepts about states. A child who has failed to receive recognizable and modified feedback to his affective states through attunement may later find it difficult to distinguish reality from imagination and psychological reality from physical reality. This may cause the child to use affect for purposes of manipulation rather than communication. Disturbances in the limbic system may mean that emotions are expressed through physical acts and bodily responses, for example psychosomatization, and so on.

As mentioned earlier, infants do not distinguish between external and internal reality. The child's capacity for understanding mental states in himself and others is based on the maturation of the prefrontal cortex. The integration of primary and secondary mentalization normally begins during the second year of life and is partially completed between the fifth and sixth years of life. When the child is unable to mentalize emotions, the development of an awareness of the distinction between psychological and physical reality is impaired (Fonagy, 1998a; Target & Fonagy, 1996). The child is aware of thoughts and feelings but does not reflect on them. Mentalization or reflexivity is a capacity that promotes decentering and the ability to see the other.

A child who grew up with abuse or neglect is often unable to perceive the caregivers' external expressions as a psychological reality and instead perceives them as concrete physical reality. This is evident, for example, in 10-year-old Lena, who orders her friends around without engaging in mutual play and without taking an interest in their desires or sharing her internal world with them. Most 2–4-year-old children will be aware of the difference between their own internal state and the outside world and other people's emotional states. Children who are surrounded by threats and actual trauma as well as children with caregivers who are withdrawn and unable to engage in affective attunement and vitalizing contact with the child have few opportunities to develop a distinction between internal and external reality.

Children who have been exposed to threats have such a strong need to focus on the external world and its physical and emotional dangers that there is no room for them to pay attention to themselves. Abuse forces the child to focus on the physical world and to be on guard against everything that happens because the caregivers' internal world is incomprehensible or painful. A child left alone will not have the necessary support to maintain attention, and for such children the caregivers' internal world is incomprehensible (Fonagy, 2001).

Unattuned stimulation at this time may mean that facial expressions, bodily states, and affective information that are implicitly processed in the right hemisphere are not transmitted sufficiently to the left hemisphere for semantic processing, and hence the child fails to develop the ability to put emotions and internal states into words (alexithymia). Impulse breakthroughs and an inability to structure and plan stem partly from dysfunctions in the prefrontal regions (Cozolino, 2000; Schore, 1994, 2001b, 2003b).

A child who suffered abuse or neglect and a lack of attunement will often be trapped in an egocentric universe and has difficulty changing perspective. Mutual play is difficult, and the child has failed to develop sufficient mental capacity and flexibility for resolving social conflicts and imagine alternatives; the child also has difficulty handling uncertainty and unpredictability. A child who is unable to self-organize and regulate affect will often engage in experiences where action is separated from intention. For example, the development of morality requires an ability to interpret one's world and carry out judgments that govern one's acts. If the child fails to do this, he will often be unable to reflect on emotionally charged situations and will not feel responsible and included. Violations of social norms often occur because the child is unable to understand a situation from another person's perspective. If the child fails to develop the ability to engage in shame affect, feelings such as guilt, embarrassment, and regret do not develop (Fonagy et al., 2002).

The acquisition of language, which begins around the age of 18 months, supports sharing and bonding. Children who have suffered severe abuse or neglect often use fewer words about emotional states and have a far more contextualized language. These children often speak in short sentences with few words; their stories lack an essential curiosity; the child is unable to prioritize and experiences are not organized in a narrative form, and the child is unable to communicate experiences. These children speak much less about their negative internal states, and during their second year of life, some develop the ability to present false positive affect and to inhibit negative affect in order to adapt to the caregiver (Cicchetti, 1991).

3–13 Years

Michael, age 26, explains that his parents were always subdued and appropriate, and they were upset when he and his brother reacted violently, talked back, or argued. Michael has always been well-mannered and polite with a tendency toward melancholy. He speaks softly and seems very controlled, and he has difficulty standing up for himself when he is unhappy about something. He complains about low self-esteem; he feels sad and is unable to feel happy that he has completed his law degree. Each time he completes a task or an assignment, even when he has received someone else's approval and acknowledgment, he hears an inner voice that constantly blames him for not being thorough or careful enough.

At this age level, the narrative self develops, and the basic neural connections between the limbic system and the orbitofrontal cortex are fully mature. The main task of the emotional and impulse-inhibiting system is to connect to the still developing prefrontal cortex and parts of the left hemisphere. If the orbitofrontal and dorsolateral prefrontal cortex fail to connect, the child's intentions may seem calculated, cold, and lacking in empathy. At this age level, dysregulation consists mainly of strong inhibitions from the dorsolateral prefrontal cortex; the Freudian concept of neurosis is relevant in this context. At this level, impulses that are rendered taboo through socialization are inhibited and associated with other situations or objects that the caregivers deem more acceptable, as for example when a child destroys a toy but is in fact furious with the parents.

From the age of 7 years, the parietal lobes and the prefrontal cortex are mature enough for children to form higher cognitive abstractions and symbols, draw on countless parallel perspectives, and handle varying and even contradictory internal representations. Children are actively able to manipulate thoughts, self-regulate considerations, and assess other people's expectations. At this time, children have a sense of what they are like as well as what they would like to be. A big discrepancy between actual self and ideal self poses emotional difficulties, since at this time relational difficulties move into an intrapsychic arena where they play out as internal representations that may be mutually conflicting and defy easy integration. At the age of 12 years, experiences and internal representations that a child has formed through close relationships become part of a more advanced personality.

Puberty

During the teenage years the nervous system embarks on an extensive development process after a relatively long period of slow growth. Although the teenage years may be potentially growth-promoting for some, for children with early developmental disorders this may be an emotionally overwhelming and disorganizing period of life. A nervous system that is unable to regulate and integrate due to early stressful experiences is vulnerable and has difficulty sustaining the huge neural changes that occur during this period. The nervous system has trouble regulating and inhibiting the powerful impulses coming from the subcortical structures and is thrust into varying levels of arousal. As mentioned earlier, in some cases the already fragile nervous system is unable to handle this massive restructuring, which leads to chaos and potential collapse (Schore, 2003b).

Over the years, there have been many considerations of the development of relational patterns into personality features. The next section outlines some considerations of how dysregulation patterns lead to a lack of integration and vulnerability in neural structures, which may eventually develop into personality disorders.

From Internal State to Personality Feature

If [an infant or child] follows a favorable course, he will grow up not only aware of the existence within himself of contradictory impulses but able to direct and control them, and the anxiety and guilt which they engender will be bearable. If his progress is less favorable, he will be beset by impulses over which he feels he has inadequate or even no control; as a result he will suffer acute anxiety regarding the safety of the persons he loves and be afraid, too, of the retribution which he believes will fall on his own head. (Bowlby, 1979, p. 5)

The hierarchical organization of the brain implies that the nervous system develops as distinct and separate entities, all interconnected and interrelated but capable of dissociating. When the regions fail to connect properly, stress will cause the nervous system to lose its coherence easily. For example, when information from the amygdala cannot pass up the vertical hierarchy to the orbitofrontal levels, the symptoms will appear on limbic, motor, and somatic levels and fail to integrate with mental representations in the prefrontal cortex. Memories that cannot be integrated on a semantic or linguistic level will organize on a more primitive level, for example, in visual imagery or somatic sensations. The child lacks an organizing cognitive capacity to attribute meaning to any traumatic experiences. Instead, the experiences are maintained in the implicit memory, the child unable to process the memories in daytime consciousness (Luu & Tucker, 1996; van der Kolk, 1987, 1996b).

The orbitofrontal cortex is in charge of the overall, central integrating regulation of affective processes, and dysfunctions in this region prevent self-organization and may produce various forms of disturbance in emotional regulation. Dissociations may occur between many different brain structures and on many levels in the hierarchical brain, a topic explored in more detail in Chapter 6. Dissociation on the brain stem level results in very basic difficulties with autonomic regulation and sensory impairment, for example, a lack of proprioceptive sensation. Dissociations in the limbic system result in impulse breakthroughs or easily triggered anxiety, while dissociations on the prefrontal level result in neurosis-like disturbances. These dissociations render the nervous system inflexible and prevent the development of an integrated sensation of the self over time and in relation to others. A dissociated nervous system prevents the coordination of neural circuit connections, and the integrative process of neural connections that is necessary for development is disturbed. The mentalization capacity, which is last to develop, and which is essential for the child's ability to understand complex interpersonal situations, is not sufficiently established. As a result, the child is flooded by internal representations that are not anchored in reality, and which the child is therefore unable to reflect on, and this comes to dominate the child's behavior (Fonagy, 1999b; Siegel, 1999).

Internal representations of the attachment figures are stored in the limbic and orbitofrontal regions, particularly in the right hemisphere. For the child to be able to verbalize and create narratives of these representations, the language areas in the left hemisphere must have access to the information. Children with severe relational disorders have not repressed their experiences, since repression requires an active inhibition on an orbitofrontal and dorsolateral level, especially in the left hemisphere. Early traumatic experiences lie buried deep in the implicit memory and thus elude symbolization or verbalization. Among other things, the left hemisphere attempts to build compensatory defensive functions that cut off overwhelmingly painful earlier experiences. Schore (2003b) pointed out that when the nervous system is exposed to events that are perceived as threatening, the right hemisphere regains dominance.

The instinctive need for attachment is common in all primates, and strong attachment bonds are associated with an elevated opioid level. Attachment is highly rewarding, even when the child's stress system is triggered by caregiver abuse. Children who have suffered severely traumatizing early experiences are quickly retraumatized when exposed to events that resemble the original traumatizing events. They wind up in the same psychological and mental state as they were then, helpless and without any chance of escape. The helplessness that the child was exposed to then prevents the child from seeking other support, and the child might seek a person who reminds him of the abusive attachment figure. The recognizable is more attractive than the unknown when facing a threat. Often, a child who has suffered abuse will engage in activities that resemble recognizable incidents. Every time the child suffers abuse later in life, he is engaging in a familiar cycle. The child's biochemistry is analogous to the biochemistry involved in substance abuse because the body releases opioids. This is a typical pattern in domestic abuse, for example, where a conflict with incidents of abuse will give the victim a simultaneous arousal of adrenaline and opioids that trigger feelings of anxiety, excitement, and a recognizable feeling of joy. The reunion that reestablishes the attachment bond in turn triggers a release of opioids, which constitutes a powerful "reward" that maintains the victim in a cycle of abuse (Scaer, 2001).

Summary

Van der Kolk and Fisler (1994) have stated that the loss of ability to regulate the intensity of emotions is by far the most severe effect of early trauma, abuse, and neglect. The internal states that the infant's and the young child's nervous system are exposed to eventually become personality features. Early relational traumatization and the coping strategies that the child develops in response to the trauma will influence the personality structure throughout life (Fox, Schmidt, Cathins, Rubin, & Coplan, 1996; Schore, 2001a, 2001b).

> As we shall see, the disorganizing effect of trauma and its lack of resolution can be passed from generation to generation. The emotional suffering, the stress-induced damage to cognitive functioning, the internal chaos of intrusive implicit memories, and the potential interpersonal violence created as a result of trauma produce ripple effects of devastation across the boundaries of time and human lives. (Siegel, 1999, p. 60)

CHAPTER SIX

Neuroaffective Developmental Symptom Descriptions

> *Blocks are structured patterns of behavior that represent unsatis-*
> *factory resolution, a compromise of childhood conflicts . . . life-*
> *denying and life-threatening situations that forced him to become*
> *"armored" as a means of survival.*
>
> Alexander Lowen (1976, p. 34)

In the mid-1980s, Allan Sroufe, Michael Rutter, Dante Cicchetti, and others pointed out the need for a new discipline to integrate developmental and psychiatric thinking. They saw a need for a new perspective on psychopathology, since the existing models were not yet able to explain how dysfunctions develop and are maintained. They wanted to understand psychopathology not only from the point of view of the mature brain but also in relation to those factors in early development that might cause developmental disorders in the neural circuits. As one of their goals, they wanted to study psychological disorders through a description of changes in the brain's functional organization based on the link between inappropriate childhood conditions and the development of the nervous system, regardless whether the disorder occurred in early childhood or late adolescence (Cicchetti et al., 1995; Cicchetti & Tucker, 1994; Emde & Sameroff, 1989; Sroufe & Rutter, 1984).

There seems to be a great deal of confusion and lack of consistency between psychodynamics and biology in relation to understanding psychological disorders, and there continues to be a lack of research into genetics, the influence of the close caregiving environment, and its effect on neurobiology. As Rutter, Silberg, O'Connor, and Simonoff (1999) pointed out, a great deal of research into personality disorders and various syndromes has aimed to prove the predominance of either genetic or environmentally reactive factors. So far, research has not provided convincing results for either point of view. Within both psychiatry and psychology, there has been considerable interest in making sense of the symptomatology of psychological disorders, and research efforts have often targeted either genetic or psychodynamic explanations. There is a close link between the effects of nature and nurture; no resources or weaknesses can unfold without a genetic predisposition, and genotype develops into phenotype through environmental influences. Nobel laureate and psychiatrist Eric Kandel (2005) pointed out that even the most highly socially conditioned disorder is essentially biological. All psychological disorders reflect specific changes in neurons and their synaptic connections. He further added that microbiological studies show that critical stages in development and learning have found that both genetic and developmental processes are involved in determining neural connections. Genetics alone cannot determine the variation in mental disorders; social and developmental factors are equally important. Both genetic combinations and social factors play a role in determining behavior and in modifying gene expression. Learning, including learning that causes maladaptive behavior, leads to changes in gene expression, in neural function, and in synaptic connections.

Although psychological disorders can be viewed in a multifactor perspective, in the following I focus on potential causal explanations through a dialogue between psychodynamic models of explanation and neuroaffective theories. At this point in time, the psychodynamic and neuroaffective theories are still so far apart that a convincing link and integration cannot be fully established. Accordingly, the following should only be seen as outlined hypotheses and propositions in need of ongoing development, refinement, and correction. With inspiration from Paul MacLean's model of the hierarchical and lateralized brain, this chapter attempts to view familiar mental disorders from a neuroaffective developmental point of view.

A Neuroaffective Developmental Understanding of Psychological Disorders

In explaining psychological disorders, some researchers point to the importance of early mother-child interactions, while others point to the high frequency of sexual and violent trauma in severe disorders such as borderline personality disorder; these two approaches make up, respectively, the mother-child interaction model and the trauma model (Gammelgaard, 2004). A common form of traumatization of the immature personality is an ongoing relationship that has a traumatizing effect due to a devastating lack of normal care; this may either be very stressful in the case of abuse and ambivalence or lead to insufficient development due to low arousal in the case of deprivation. Human psychological development is impossible without attachment, and neglect and abuse have a double effect when committed by the primary caregivers (Sørensen, 2005). The traumatic relationship is gradually integrated into the psychological system, and in adults infantile trauma, like all other events, has become part of a complicated psychological structure. The difficult task is to explain how certain external conditions are translated into internal psychological processes.

Psychological disorders arise as a combination of a genetic or innate disposition and environmental or psychosocial stressors, which activate an innate neurophysiological vulnerability. Among other effects, changes in the mother's hormone balance regulate genetic expression in the fetal brain, which affects the development and functioning of the nervous system. Freud described that early trauma has a far greater negative effect than trauma occurring later in life, because the nervous system is weak and immature with few and primitive defense strategies (Schore, 2003a). Dysregulation leads to a high likelihood of later identity-related or behavioral difficulties because the nervous system is prevented from unfolding its full potential. Maladaptive behavior patterns typically begin with maladaptive regulation patterns in early caregiver-child contact. Schore (2003a) described how a vulnerable and undeveloped nervous system that is exposed to inappropriate stimulation will tend to attempt to stabilize through dissociation. Children who have had to adapt to dysregulated patterns for a long time will have difficulty processing and integrating experiences due to dissociated brain patterns as well as difficulties with self-organization. Thus, even minor stressful experiences may traumatize the child by overwhelming the brain's ability to adapt because the nervous system is not sufficiently integrated to be able to balance the stressful state. Over time, the disorganized state will become a personality feature.

The child's way of processing life themes and the form that these themes take will change throughout the developmental stages, varying with the child's level of maturity. As humans, we have an innate capacity for self-organization; as the brain matures, this capacity develops in the hierarchical structures of the brain, here referred to as the mental organizations of the brain (Hart, 2008). Each mental organization is shaped by countless interactions and regulatory systems. The outcome of these regulatory exchanges will expand or restrict the capacity of the nervous system for biological and behavioral self-regulation (Sameroff, 1989). Attachment disorders and relational disorders belong on a different level than somatic illness, and understanding and treating psychopathology requires an ability to describe relationships. Relational disorders reflect a dynamic balance between the child's innate competencies and vulnerabilities and environmental factors. If this balance changes, the relational problems will change as well. If the external factors that cause the child's behavioral difficulties do not change, relational disorders may become internalized as personality problems that may be present for life. Adaptation strategies that serve the child well at one point in development may later disrupt the ability to achieve more flexible adaptation (Anders, 1989; Sroufe, 1989b; Sroufe & Rutter, 1984).

It is not relevant to talk about relational disorders in infants under the age of approximately 2 years, since their symptoms must be viewed as dysregulation between caregiver and infant. From the age of 2 years until puberty it is relevant to talk about relational disorders, as the child's psychological difficulties often consist of chronic disturbances in the relationship between caregiver and child, with the child increasingly contributing to the disturbance. The relational pattern has become part of the child's own internal representations, but it continues to be an open system that can be affected by changes in the relationship. Around puberty, the characterological patterns become more set, and it is only now that it is relevant to talk about actual personality disorders. At this stage, the mature personality is able to juggle the many different internal representations that provide the internal regulation, and which are not always compatible (Anders, 1989).

In any psychological or behavioral disorder, the problem may be located within the child, within the child's relationship with the caregivers, or in the caregiver's internal representations of the child. Each of these perspectives offers a particular diagnostic focus and invites a particular type of intervention. If the disorder is located within the child, the intervention will aim at dissolving the symptoms within the child; if the disorder is located in the interaction between the child and the caregiver, the intervention will revolve around relational therapy; and if the disorder is located in the caregivers' internal representations, the intervention will focus on individual therapy aimed at these representations. In childhood, the relationship is absolutely crucial for the child's psychological coping strategies, and the child lacks the psychological strength to either maintain an emotional disorder or overcome it without changes to the relationship (Emde & Sameroff, 1989).

In order to integrate the different perspectives of psychological and behavioral disorders it is necessary to assess whether a psychopathological state is the result of a relational disorder, or whether the disorder is innate, as, for example, in pervasive developmental disorders or in Down syndrome. It should also be assessed whether any innate pathologies may have caused a subsequent relational disorder. For example, a child with autism may have such weak signals that it requires a major effort from the caregiver to engage in a developing contact, and thus, the child may develop a relational disorder (Cicchetti et al., 1995).

It is impossible to understand relationships without assessing the child's developmental context. This requires a thorough evaluation of the child's relationship with the caregivers, based on both the current and early relationship, and an assessment of the parents, their childhood history, and their current life situation. Similarly, as the child grows older, the assessment must also include an assessment of the relational organization in the contexts that the child enters into, including home, school, and so on. Psychological development is defined by the child's level of mental organization; minor misattunements and their reparation will always occur and are indeed essential for the development process. Most children quickly overcome misattunements once their competence reaches a new area. For other children, obstacles seem to develop that hamper psychological maturation, and they develop a psychological or behavioral disorder. When a child's mental organization is changed, the caregivers have to adapt to the child's developmental level within a reasonable time span. If the caregivers are unable to adapt, relational disorders will result, and the child's psychological or behavioral difficulties become apparent. Anders (1989) suggested a spectrum of relational disorders ranging from minor to more serious to severe disorders. Relational disorders stem from a combination of the child's innate vulnerability and the degree and duration of the dysregulation (Anders, 1989; Emde &

Sameroff, 1989). Sørensen (1996, 2005) suggested that relational disorders may develop into personality features as quirks, as characteristics, and, eventually, as a psychiatric disorder. He pointed out that instead of viewing personality disorders as actual mental illnesses, we might speak of personality types that appear more or less pathological and of gradual transitions between a normal characteristic and odd and pathological forms.

The Resilience or Vulnerability of the Nervous System

Emotions such as anger, joy, grief, curiosity, and so on are neither positive nor negative but are colored by the intensity of the vitality affects. Thus, a person's way of being angry or happy reflects the collaboration between vitality affects and categorical affects, and all emotions across the spectrum may be either regulated or dysregulated. When emotions appear persistent or recur over prolonged periods of time, they are often considered personality features. When personality features become established in an extreme form in adults, the term personality disorder is often applied. When the intensity of the vitality affects exceeds a certain level it generally seems that an emotional hijacking may occur in relation to any category of affects, which involves an activation of limbic structures and a deactivation of neocortical structures (Sørensen, 2006). When the orbitofrontal and dorsolateral prefrontal regions are well developed, increased activation may instead downregulate emotional expressions and suppress the processing of impulses stemming from the subcortical regions.

All traumatic experiences cause psychological disorders because they force the nervous system to enter a rigid or chaotic state (Siegel, 2004). Every single experience is organized in neural circuits, and the psychological structure consists of patterns of experience that are under constant and ongoing development. Any interaction has the potential for a mutual capacity for self-regulation, and in the development process the child becomes increasingly capable of self-regulating and dampening arousal in connection with overstimulation, maintaining attention, and inhibiting behavioral expressions. During the first year of life, a major organizing process unfolds, and relational stances gradually become more stable, more characteristic, and more predictable. But no organization of relational stances or internal representations is ever completely fixed; there is always a potential for transforming internal representations, and the child or adult has a potential for developing other relational approaches (Beebe & Lachmann, 2002).

The child's relationship with close caregivers may lead to either development or stagnation. Regardless whether the nervous system is resilient or vulnerable, it is malleable. The nervous system attempts to balance itself and to engage in resonance with a more mature nervous system and thus develops additional agility or vulnerability, which affects its robustness later in life. The child's relation patterns are expressed in interactions with the caregivers, but the relational strategies become part of the child's internal representations and thus are also evident in the child's later relationships with others. Thus, early relational disorders have an immediate as well as a long-term effect. A high degree of vulnerability suggests that in relational contexts, the nervous system becomes rigid and quickly disintegrates, which is probably an important cause of psychological disorders. Disorders are typically most visible in emotionally challenging situations that require behavioral flexibility and affect regulation. Isolated incidents may alter a nervous system, but typically it is the daily dose of misattunements and inadequate regulation that become embedded in the child's behavioral repertoire. Individuals with mental illness lack the ability to regulate internal stress, which leads to an inappropriate activation or inhibition of neural circuits. A stable and flexible nervous system is able to return to a balanced state quickly after a stressful incident, while a rigid or vulnerable nervous system takes a long time to recuperate, regardless whether the flexibility or vulnerability is innate or environmentally reactive (Thelen, 1989). A nervous system that has adapted to an unpredictable or inappropriate environment through early experiences will maintain this once-adaptive response in new contexts. In a context that is free of unpredictability and external threats, the child's response will appear maladaptive and incomprehensible (Perry & Azad, 1999).

For infants with a high innate degree of neural vulnerability, who have difficulty self-regulating and interacting with the caregivers, it only takes low stress levels to develop subsequent psychopathology. A resilient infant will probably be able to tolerate higher levels of misattunements and relational stress before the nervous system disintegrates. Thus, there is no objective limit for the strength of the nervous system. The flexibility of the nervous system is determined by psychobiological af-

fect-regulating systems that are located in deep subcortical structures, among other places, and which regulate the maturation of later-
developing areas in the neocortex (Schore, 2003a).

Post-Traumatic Stress Disorder

Much of our knowledge about dissociation comes from the intense
research into PTSD that has been carried out over the past 15 years, including attempts to understand the state neurobiologically. For example,
Jacobs and Nadel (1985) said that new stressors can activate a latent
childhood fear. Fear that develops early in childhood, before the hippocampus is fully developed, is stored as implicit memories in circuits
outside the hippocampus. As the hippocampus develops, this fear is not
represented in explicit memory. When a new stressful experience releases large amounts of cortisol, which temporarily impairs the functioning of the hippocampus, the amygdala will activate an old childhood fear.
When the hippocampus is impaired, the trauma may be reactivated without any connection to time and place, which produces a sense that the
trauma exists in the present, and the child is kept in a fear state (van der
Kolk, 2000). There is increasing documentation that PTSD, which is triggered in relation to traumatic events later in life, occurs mostly in individuals who have experienced developmental trauma or dysregulation
(van der Kolk, 2000).

Van der Kolk (1996a, 1996b) stated that humans will try at any cost to
avoid a sense of meaninglessness or a lack of control; we have trouble
accepting experiences that make no sense and will do anything we can
to find a sense of meaning. The left-hemispheric prefrontal cortex is particularly involved in seeking meaning and consistency in conscious mental experiences, and in PTSD states, activation in the left prefrontal
cortex and Broca's area (speech articulation) is impaired. It is as if the
two hemispheres fail to connect, and the left hemisphere is unable to
make sense of the experiences and translate them into a narrative form.
Among other things, this may explain how a sense of panic can render us
speechless or inarticulate when we are confronted with something that
is overwhelming. PTSD involves a raised activation in the temporal lobe
in the right hemisphere; this implies increased activity in the hypothalamus and the amygdala, which may cause the immune response to overreact and the nervous system to react with aggressive outbursts and

panic attacks. The hippocampus and regions in the prefrontal cortex are deactivated, which deactivates our sense of time and place and our sense of object permanence. When the amygdala takes over, and the hippocampus is overburdened, the result may be limitations to our self-perception, and continuity in terms of time and place is lost, which causes a sense of disorientation.

In PTSD, the noradrenaline-based circuits activate much too easily, which constantly prepares the person to respond to fear situations, and the serotonin level is reduced. The elevated noradrenaline level causes panic attacks, among other effects. The dopamine-based circuits are involved in modulating stress responses in the orbitofrontal cortex, among other places, and a reduced dopamine level reduces joy and reward activation. PTSD leads to changes in affect regulation and cognitive discrimination; these are often chronic symptoms that resist treatment. PTSD consists of a constant stress level which, as an effect of long-term potentiation, may downregulate cortisol levels to protect the organism, and which causes a dissociation of parasympathetic and sympathetic activity (see the section on autonomic aggression). PTSD consists of mistaken learning of neurobiological patterns and overlearning of dissociative mechanisms. As Shalev noted, the combination of biological, psychological, and social mistaken learning and imprinting locks down developmental potential and acts as a biopsychosocial trap. Rather than adapting, the nervous system flares up, which has prompted van der Kolk to characterize PTSD as a psychobiological allergic reaction to stress (Sørensen, 2005).

Based on Paul MacLean's model of the triune brain (see Fig. 6.1), I will now classify a number of familiar psychological and behavioral disorders in relation to both developmental and neurological theories. Kernberg (Mortensen, 2001) has proposed a classification system based on his own theory of developmental psychology. He also works on the basis of the triune model, distinguishing between the main categories of psychotic, borderline, and neurotic personality structures. In the following, I describe a number of familiar psychopathological phenomena: dissociation, anxiety, aggression, depression, attention and kinesthetic disorders, and eating disorders based on the model presented below. I also explain how all of these disorders can be understood on three levels: autonomic, limbic, and prefrontal. In this context, dissociation is applied as an overarching category that makes it possible to understand the described

Affect-inhibiting prefrontal personality disorders
Prefrontal suppression of aggression
Secondary depression (neurotic depression)
Hysteriform disorders
Obsessive-compulsive disorders

Affect-regulating limbic personality disorders
Omnipotence
Narcissistic depression
Borderline personality disorders

Sensory-regulating autonomic personality disorders
Sympathetic dissociation: fight or flight
Parasympathetic dissociation: freeze
Anaclitic depression
Early emotional frustration (antisocial disorder)
Schizoid disorder

Figure 6.1. Personality disorders in the triune brain

psychopathological phenomena and psychological disorders on a neuroaffective level.

Dissociation

As Sørensen (2005) mentioned, dissociation is a common phenomenon; its opposite is association. In this sense, dissociation defines something that might be associated but is not. Dissociation is a human ability that lets us manipulate our daytime consciousness, deliberately as well as unconsciously, and thus enables us, for example, to handle anxiety or unbearable psychological pain. Dissociation is the way in which the nervous system maintains a stable self-image and worldview. Any dissociation implies psychological protection, and it is the context that determines whether it is appropriate or pathological. Threats to life and limb or a feeling of injustice or humiliation can make physical and psychological pain so powerful that emotions, sensations, and memories are split off. Dissociation occurs when one loses one's sense of having a safe haven to retreat to, either psychologically or physically, in the face of anxious emotions or experiences (van der Kolk, 1987).

The idea of dissociation stems from Pierre Janét, who in the late 1880s believed that some persons were genetically unprepared to handle overwhelming stress in connection with emotional trauma. He described that dissociated states were common in children and adults who in their childhood had been subjected to sexual or physical abuse. Mental functions stem from anatomically separate but neurally connected circuits, and Janét believed that severe traumatic experiences might dissolve the "mental glue" and cause the circuit connections to be torn apart. Powerful and deep dissociation might, for example, eliminate the ability to symbolize and fantasize, self-regulate affects, and moderate emotionality. In this case, the child's ability to process everyday conflicts is lost, and the ability to preserve comforting and rewarding experiences is impaired (van der Kolk, 1987).

The concept of dissociation is used to explain a variety of psychological mechanisms, and in its broadest sense the concept can be understood to mean a dissociation of the brain's integrative functions. Dissociation often refers to an inadequate integration of the different aspects of an experience and may consist of both a developmental and a traumatic block. Dissociation can occur in response to danger situations, psychologically overwhelming experiences, traumatic events, or specific brain damage or be the result of a developmental disturbance of the nervous system. Dissociation may be an everyday phenomenon, for example, when the organism responds to something that is potentially dangerous before the consciousness has had time to register what is going on. For example, Sørensen (2005) mentioned a television show (*Fear Factor*), where the theme was a competition about overcoming fear when placed in extreme situations. One woman had to put her hand into a glass jar filled with big spiders; her hand was barely in the jar before it came out again, as if it had a mind of its own. Determined to win the large cash prize, she tried repeatedly but never managed it. In this situation, the woman was probably a victim of her phylogenetic past when spiders posed a real danger, and lightning-quick amygdala-controlled reactions saved lives. Dissociation is always the result of the organism being overwhelmed. Dissociation can vary both in extent and in severity; for example, van der Kolk et al. classified dissociation as either primary, secondary, or tertiary. Similarly, dissociation can occur in any conceivable combination in relation to behavior, emotions, sensations, and knowledge (Sørensen, 2005).

The neural circuits consist of many parallel, interacting systems, and this structure makes the system prone to dissociation (Schacter, 1996). Anatomically, dissociation can occur in any part of the nervous system that consists of association neurons or polymodal circuits where subsystems that are normally in close communication begin to limit and delimit their level of functioning. Dissociative phenomena prevent the dissociated areas from integrating on the next developmental level. For example, Piaget (1973) explained that experiences that are not integrated on a verbal level will connect in subsystems that are wordless and associated with implicit (unconscious) memory. Dissociated experiences tend to remain unsymbolized, existing as a separate reality in the person's implicit world. Personality development consists of an integration of neural circuits, and psychopathological dissociation limits personality development (Siegel, 1999). For example, trauma may sever the connection between the implicit (unconscious) and explicit (conscious) memory systems, so that certain experiences are kept away from our daytime consciousness; this phenomenon is called repression (Schacter, 1996).

Normally, the concept of dissociation is understood in the context of neural connections that have become severed, and thus we lack a concept that covers undeveloped and poorly integrated circuit connections. At this point, we do not have a clear distinction between, on the one hand, the lack of integration of neural circuits due to understimulation and, on the other hand, neural circuits that were once connected but have become separated, either as the result of minor everyday stressors or highly traumatic experiences as in PTSD or as the result of a surgical procedure, for example, to remove a brain tumor.

In my opinion, dissociation can occur on all neural levels in both the hierarchical and lateralized structures of the brain, as there are association regions on many levels in the hierarchical brain. In the following sections I exemplify how dissociation can occur on an autonomic level, on a limbic level, between the right and left hemispheres, and between implicit and explicit memory.

Dissociation on the Level of the Brain Stem

Sympathetic dissociation: fight or flight. *Six-year-old Sean has always been very aggressive; he slams the doors in his mother's apartment and often loses his temper. He lacks concentration, is bossy, and has trouble calming down. When his mother insists on something, he gets angry, stamps his feet, and screams. When he is with other children, he bites and kicks them for no reason. When he is acting on affect it is impossible to make contact with him.*

Parasympathetic dissociation: freeze. *Ten-year-old Nicholas does not feel hunger or satiety and is a calm and happy boy. He is hard to gauge and has few mood shifts. He is never excited, has no emotional ups and downs, is never angry or annoyed, and never disagrees with anyone. He is a withdrawn, anonymous, sweet boy who lacks initiative.*

Sympathetic and parasympathetic dissociation. *Twelve-year-old Matt might suddenly flail around the room, screaming like a wild animal. In demanding situations he is threatening, screams, pushes around the furniture, throws his shoes, crawls on the floor, and makes loud noises. Eventually he begins to pull furniture together like a nest, rolls up in a fetal position, and closes his eyes.*

To quickly summarize the most primitive danger reactions of the nervous system: According to the polyvagal theory, the autonomic nervous system relies on three behavioral strategies to regulate: (1) activation of a vegetative vagal system, which is characterized by a primitive, unmyelinated parasympathetic system that responds to impulses by suppressing metabolic activity, corresponding to immobilization behavior (freeze); (2) activation of a sympathetic nervous system, which mobilizes the behavior that is necessary for fight or flight (fight-fright-flight); and (3) Activation of a mammalian vagal system, which supports engagement and disengagement with the environment and inhibits the two other levels through the "vagal brake." Children who are exposed to massive overstimulation, chaotic regulation, or massive dysregulated levels of arousal from an early age will dissociate into extreme levels of sympathetic hyperarousal or a freeze state that they are not able to regulate without assistance.

Immobilization states occur, for example, when animals in the wild are chased by a predator and suddenly drop down with soft muscles, playing dead. This strategy is appropriate as any movement will incite the predator to continue hunting, and because most carnivores are uninterested in dead carcasses. Ramachandran (2003) suggested that in humans this phenomenon is experienced as derealization and depersonalization disorders, where the world is perceived as unreal and dreamlike. Derealization means that the world does not seem real, while depersonalization means that the self does not feel real. Ramachandran described how the 19th-century British explorer David Livingstone was once attacked by a lion but felt neither pain nor fear; he felt as if he was not present in the situation and was instead watching the whole incident from a distance. Immobilization states often also trigger a strong alarm response and vigilance, which prepares the organism to perform the defense reactions necessary to engage in fight or flight. The person observes the world with an intense and alert gaze that is void of meaning, because the limbic system is no longer functioning.

If the child is kept in dissociation on the brain stem level, either in the sympathetic or the vegetative parasympathetic state, the mammalian vagal system fails to develop, and the child will have difficulty integrating affective states and developing basic self-regulation strategies. Over time, this means that the circuit connections between the hypothalamus, the amygdala, and the orbitofrontal cortex are inadequate, and when the higher centers in the central nervous system fail to regulate the autonomic nervous system sufficiently, the nervous system will regulate through primitive autoregulating functions. In everyday situations, the child responds with autonomic hyper- or hypoarosual states without a self-regulating capacity. In this way, events can lead to an inextinguishable alarm response, where simply becoming excited, regardless of the cause or the context, can be a trigger. Trauma research has long studied these responses, and it is common knowledge that highly traumatized persons live through temporary states of hyperactivity, aggressive outbursts, startle responses, flashbacks, and nightmares varying with paralysis, indifference, and withdrawal. It takes little psychological arousal before these persons are brought into varying states of immobilization and fight-or-flight behavior (van der Kolk, 1987).

Krystal (1988) suggested that dissociative states are adapted to evolutionary functions consisting of a complex pattern of survival strategies that are necessary throughout the animal world. All mammals respond to the feeling of a lack of control and helplessness with aggression, anxiety, depression, passivity, and suppression. Among other things, dissociative states protect the person against unbearable emotional and physical pain through affective paralysis and a numbing of the nervous system. When all other coping strategies are exhausted, the person will withdraw, which leads to disengagement or avoidance of engagement. Initially, a child will use the self-protection mechanisms that are available on her current level of mental organization. If this proves inadequate, the nervous system regresses to a previous protection strategy, and if that too proves ineffective the organism will engage in more profound dissociation. Dissociation on the level of the brain stem is a mental flight state when physical flight or escape is impossible. Dissociation in the autoregulating autonomic nervous system is the ultimate defense strategy, and the freeze response occurs in situations that offer no other means of escape. A child who engages in prolonged dissociation in autoregulating states will miss the vitally crucial space of development for engaging in interactive regulation and affective attunement (Schore, 2003b).

Dissociation at the Limbic Level

Anita is a 15-year-old girl who lacks confidence. She is good at making and having friends; she can be moody but is often caring, considerate, and fun-loving and keen to make others happy. She often describes a feeling of emptiness where she feels abandoned. When she does poorly psychologically, she somatizes; for example, she may go to school with big scarves wrapped around her neck. She has problems with affect regulation and with delaying gratification. Her reality-testing is poor, and she has difficulty controlling her temper and has many impulsive outbursts.

Early traumatic events or regulation disorders cause dissociation in structures between the diencephalon and the limbic system (e.g., between the hypothalamus and the amygdala), between structures in the limbic system (e.g., between the amygdala and the hippocampus), and between the limbic and prefrontal regions (e.g., between the amygdala and the orbitofrontal cortex).

The amygdala has many connections both to the hippocampus and the orbitofrontal cortex, and dissociation in the connection between the amygdala and the hippocampus means that emotional perceptions cannot integrate with explicit (conscious) memory, and that it is difficult to place emotional experiences in a context of time and place. Dissociation between the amygdala and the orbitofrontal cortex prevents basic intuitive emotional perceptions from connecting with the mentalizing and self-reflecting functions, which leads to a feeling of inner emptiness. "Not knowing oneself is part of being traumatized and means that the sense of self has been lost" (van der Kolk, 2000, quoted from personal notes). It is the mentalization capacity that lets us distinguish our mental state from external reality. For example, a person who is caught up in a panic attack cannot tell whether the fear is mental, triggered by anxious memories, or whether the situation is real. The self-regulation strategies associated with activity in the prefrontal cortex, for example, self-regulation through internal speech, impulse inhibition, and reality-testing, break down when limbic and prefrontal structures dissociate (Kaplan-Solms & Solms, 2002).

Dissociation Between the Right and Left Hemispheres

Mark is 11 years old and cries easily but is unable to explain what it is that upsets him or how it feels. When he talks about difficult incidents he hides under his jacket until the topic changes to something more neutral. He may appear deeply shamed one moment and then switch instantly to something else, telling fantastical, constructed tales. He seems to bounce from one mental state to the next.

Internal representations are neurally connected through horizontal and cross-modal circuit connections. The left and right hemispheres may dissociate in a way that makes it difficult for children to understand their own actions and motivations. The right hemisphere enables us to perceive bodily sensations, affects, and intuitions, because this hemisphere is dominant in relation to perceptual bodily representations and the monitoring of somatic and bodily states. The left hemisphere enables us to handle the world in abstract verbal terms, independent of the emotional context, because the left hemisphere constructs our social self and interprets right-hemisphere information (Hart, 2008). Teicher (2002) found that children who had suffered severe neglect or abuse had reduced blood flow in the corpus callosum, which forms the link between the two hemispheres. Older children and adults with heightened activity in the right hemisphere are more negative and have lower self-esteem. Most emotional experiences are stored in the right hemisphere, and disociations between the right and left hemispheres will cause these experiences to be unknown to the left hemisphere (Joseph, 1982). A lack f integration of the two hemispheres means that a child with left-hemisphere dominance deals with "as if" feelings based on adaptation to social norms, idealization, and a denial of actual conditions, for example, in relation to severe disability or disease; in the case of right-hemisphere dominance, the child will be characterized by concrete thinking, egocentricity, and emotional instability (Kaplan-Solm & Solms, 2002).

Dissociation Between Implicit and Explicit Memory

Karina is 17 years old. Two years ago she was the victim of a dramatic rape, which she recalls only like a blurry film. Every time she looks up at the Big Dipper in the sky, she feels a sense of panic in which her throat contracts, she is unable to utter a sound, and she begins to shake and cry.

When the nervous system is exposed to experiences that it is unable to handle, the implicit (unconscious) memory system will dissociate from explicit memory (daytime consciousness). In severely traumatizing experiences, explicit attention will focus on something other than the abuse itself, for example, the starry sky. The explicit memory can only be encoded through focusing, unlike the implicit memory, which requires no focus to encode. Traumatic memories are preserved in implicit memory, and when implicit memory is activated through the amygdala, the child will be unable to associate the emotional response with a cognitive or narrative explanation. The implicit memory and the emotions associated with the trauma return as intrusive emotional states such as anxiety, panic, emptiness, delusions, depersonalizaton, and impulse breakthroughs. This form of dissociation may allow the child to function relatively normally while the traumatic event is unfolding, and much of the personality will remain unaffected by the trauma. The dissociation may be lifelong without psychopathological consequences (Siegel, 2004; van der Kolk, 1987, 1994).

In the following, I offer a systematic review of familiar psychological disorders based on a model that associates various forms of dissociation with a nuanced understanding of the disorders on the three levels: autonomic, limbic, and prefrontal. Thus, in this understanding, psychological disorders all represent under- or overactive neural circuits that have dissociated vertically or horizontally on many different levels within the nervous system.

Anxiety and Anxiety Management

The typical distinction between fear and anxiety is that fear has a visible trigger factor, while anxiety states have no external trigger factor. For example, a person may be afraid of spiders (fear) but feel apprehensive without knowing why (anxiety). Fear is the response to anything dangerous and life-threatening. Fear tells the organism to be ready to act, and in its adaptive form it makes us behave cautiously and hesitantly. Energy is mobilized through sympathetic arousal in the form of increased muscle tone and heart rate and through the release of adrenaline and noradrenaline. The neural circuits involved in fear and anxiety involve both hemispheres on every level of the nervous system, and they enable a capacity for increased attention to anything from a door slamming to an existential crisis. Some forms of fear seem to be innate and specific to all primates and are associated with present and earlier survival needs.

Fear is part of the human condition, and just as pain is the organismic response to physical damage, our ability to feel both fear and anxiety is an important source of protection that is crucial to survival. Anxiety is not in itself psychopathological, but when anxiety feels overwhelming, is chronic, or is aroused without any outside stimuli it is a symptom of a profound psychological problem. Mild degrees of anxiety or apprehension do not inhibit a person's functioning; for example, some degree of anticipatory apprehension may stimulate an enhanced performance.

Developmental or identity anxiety is a common feature of normal childhood development. Development consists of constant movement between the organization, disorganization, and reorganization of the nervous system; the constant pressures on the nervous system during childhood give the child a sense of discontinuity and disruption, which may in time develop into existential anxiety. Anxiety is part and parcel of being in constant development and living with the contradictions that emerge in the process. Anxiety may stem from a fear of annihilation and dissolution; it may be associated with suppressed and unresolved grief or anger, with kindling of the amygdala; or it may be triggered by conscience anxiety when the child violates the caregivers' rules. The different forms of anxiety organize on different levels in the hierarchical brain.

Unlike other mammals, humans are able to feel anxiety in relation to potential future events and situations that do not exist; this is due to our expanded prefrontal cortex and the resulting higher mentalization capacity. Anxiety may be associated with all sorts of signals from the environment and may be triggered by internal sensations, feelings, and thoughts that lie outside our explicit attention. The left hemisphere interprets the situation and offers rational support for achieving a cognitive understanding of the anxiety that does not always match the signal that triggers the nervous system. When physiological and emotional reactions are triggered without the presence of any real danger, the result is a panic attack.

In the following, I address how anxiety can be triggered by various states and on various levels in the hierarchical nervous system: the autonomic, limbic, and prefrontal levels.

Autonomic Anxiety

Sean, age 8, is controlled by immediate impulses. He sometimes runs away for no reason. He feels insecure very easily, and anything out of the ordinary will make him anxious. When his anxiety is triggered it is impossible to get through to him, and he seems to drift off in daydreams and internal associations. He has no personal boundaries, and in conversations he keeps his anxiety at bay by daydreaming and expressing fantasies of an extremely violent character, which vitalize him and elevate his mood.

When the immature nervous system disorganizes into autoregulating structures, the experience is one of primitive and indefinable pain. Disintegration in the autonomic structures is perceived as a form of dissolution of the core self. If the experience of internal psychological coherence is threatened, it may lead to an anxiety of fragmentation, and when children experience not being in command of their own emotions, they lose their sense of agency or volition. In a sense, the anxiety does not exist as a phenomenon on an autonomic level, but threatening experiences are associated with a sense of discomfort, which the nervous system will do anything in its power to escape.

Limbic Anxiety

Rita is 17-year-old girl who suffers from recurring panic attacks. She manages to go to school but has many sick days because she is worried about suddenly having an attack and not being able to breathe, and she is afraid of dying. She has had multiple examinations for heart disease, but there does not seem to be any physiological basis for her problems. In talking about her father she comes across as a devoted daughter, but at the same time she says that he used to terrorize her when she was younger. When she speaks about him, her mouth gets dry, she is unable to breathe, and her heart races. The anxiety can become so powerful that she considers suicide.

The amygdala is involved in most forms of anxiety; for example, researchers distinguish between amygdala-based fear-anxiety and cingulate gyrus-based panic-anxiety, where the latter is associated with separation anxiety (Sørensen, 2006). The hippocampus, the amygdala, and the cingulate gyrus are closely connected, and while the amygdala plays a key role for the emotional and somatic organization of experiences, the hippocampus is a key structure in relation to conscious, logical, and social functions. The frontal part of the cingulate gyrus is involved in counteracting previously acquired impulses, and the back part enables us to form lasting and profound emotional attachments and to feel grief. The amygdala is involved in generalization, while the hippocampus is involved in discrimination. For example, the amygdala will trigger fear at the sight of a snake, while the hippocampus enables the person to remember that the snake is neither poisonous nor dangerous, so there is no cause for alarm, and the front part of the cingulate gyrus and the orbitofrontal cortex lets us counteract the impulse coming from the amygdala. The hippocampus has a regulatory function, and through the discrimination function it is able to regulate the arousal system. When the amygdala dissociates from the above-mentioned structures, it will be difficult to associate the anxiety experience with a specific event, and when the fear system is not subject to cortical control, there is no way to inhibit the primitive impulses. Many emotional responses are able to form without any explicit (conscious) or cognitive involvement.

The amygdala normally receives fear information before it reaches the prefrontal areas and reacts to crude templates of the environment.

Slightly later, the amygdala receives information from the prefrontal cortex where it has been subjected to advanced processing. If the circuit connections to the hippocampus and the prefrontal cortex are weak, the amygdala will activate a response that has not been balanced by the prefrontal regions. High and prolonged levels of cortisol may reduce hippocampal function, which leads to a vulnerability to stress and may explain why some people respond much more strongly than others to the same trauma. We do not yet know whether a reduced hippocampus volume makes the individual more vulnerable to developing anxiety and PTSD, or whether the hippocampus may actually shrink as a result of a chronically raised cortisol level—or whether both effects are in play (LeDoux, 1989, 1994, 1998; van der Kolk, 1996a).

Once a fear response has been conditioned by sounds or light, for example, it may be difficult to extinguish. Even if the stimuli that are associated with the danger no longer exist, the amygdala may still trigger a fear response unless areas in the prefrontal cortex are able to inhibit the activation. Fear learning occurs when a thought, emotion, act, or sensation is associated with an unpleasant stimulus such as pain, shock, shame, and so on. The amygdala is able to recognize previous experiences, and throughout life it may link a fear stimulus with an anxiety or fear that is not accessible to conscious processing. When the hippocampus is unable to maintain its integrative function, sensations and memory are shattered into fragments or isolated images, bodily sensations, smells, and sounds that seem alien and separate from other life experiences. The fragmented experiences seem ego-alien and timeless.

When a child encounters a stressor that reminds him of an event where the nervous system was previously disintegrated, the amygdala will activate the fear system. Over time, small specific reminders will be generalized, and, for example, simply hearing a recognizable sound may trigger the response. A child whose amygdala has been kindled lives in a chronic stress state, and over time such a child will display motor hyperactivity, anxiety, impulsivity, sleep problems, and muscle tension. The child will have difficulty managing his or affect regulation, and mild forms of insecurity may serve to hyperactivate the amygdala and instantly thrust the child into a panicky state of anxiety. This limbic sensitivity means that minor everyday discomfort may escalate and reach painful levels, and when the connections to the orbitofrontal prefrontal cortex are inadequately developed, the startle response is easily triggered, and the child has difficulty calming down (Lewis et al., 2001; Perry, 1994; van der Kolk, 1996a).

Conditioned fear is stored in the implicit (unconscious) systems, and fear conditioning is extremely difficult to extinguish. Once the amygdala is kindled, a basic and unsymbolized form of generalized anxiety is triggered that eludes interpretation by the limbic-prefrontal circuit (van der Kolk, 1996a). Inadequate inhibition of amygdaloid arousal can cause the nervous system to lose its flexibility and be kept on a limbic level, which will inhibit the capacity for mentalization and self-reflection. Negative expectations are associated with anxiety, which triggers either panic attacks or counterphobic behavior in the form of a search for thrills and excitement as a counterresponse to the anxiety, which in turn triggers a simultaneous activation of dopamine and opioids. To overcome the anxiety the child may release a cascade of noradrenaline, adrenaline, and dopamine, which triggers a fight-or-flight state that eliminates the anxiety. Subsequently, there is a phase of release with a high level of noradrenaline-based activation, dopamine release, and the release of endogenous opioids that produce pleasure, well-being, and alertness and dissolve the sense of time and place.

Anxiety reactions may be triggered by an activation of autonomic structures, including sympathetic activation with the release of noradrenaline, or by a hyperactivation of the amygdala. Prolonged activation of the noradrenaline-based system results in increased hyperarousal, tension, and an unmodulated startle response, which produces a feeling that the world is a dangerous place that requires constant vigilance. Anxiety on a limbic level is unsymbolized and nonverbal and may therefore take on monstrous forms, for example, suicidal behavior, fear of dying, inability to breathe, and so on. Because the anxiety is locked into the limbic system there is no mentalizing capacity to balance it, and it may overwhelm the person emotionally.

Prefrontal Anxiety

Sandra was 7 years old when her mother died after having been ill for just a few weeks. She felt that it was her fault because in the time leading up to the disease she had been angry with her mother. She did not want to talk about the mother's death, and the people around her respected this wish. She began to be afraid of the dark, and she believed that she saw the mother's unhappy figure at night. Her anxi-

*ety grew until she was eventually afraid to go out and began to have
difficulty going to school.*

Around the age of 3–4 years, the prefrontal structures are so well developed that they are normally capable of inhibiting impulses from the
subcortical structures. At this time, the child is able to tell what the caregivers perceive as appropriate behavior and is able to inhibit impulses
that are not deemed acceptable. For example, if a child perceives that
displaying her full vitality or anger is not acceptable, she will be able to
inhibit the emotion. The child suppresses the forbidden feelings, since
the repression mechanism is effective on this level. The forbidden feelings are kept away from the daytime consciousness through structures
in the prefrontal cortex, and the child has no opportunity to mentalize or
reflect on them. These feelings remain unsymbolized and may be lived
out either somatically or behaviorally, for example, through anxiety.
Structures in the prefrontal cortex ward off the feelings associated with
the forbidden area or the pain associated with a traumatic event. The
subcortical structures are activated through reminders about the event,
and structures in the prefrontal cortex inhibit the impulses and keep
them from reaching the daytime consciousness. Structures in the prefrontal cortex that are in charge of volitional control attempt to achieve
control over external events as well as internal processes, and anxiety
arises when the feelings manifest on a limbic level because they are outside the control of volitional mechanisms.

The processing that takes place on the subcortical level differs from
the perceptual processing that takes place on a prefrontal level. A dissociation of circuit connections between the limbic system and the prefrontal cortex leads to a weak grasp of the emotions related to the
traumatic event. Since on a prefrontal level emotions can be actively repressed, sublimated, displaced, and so on, once the prefrontal cortex
deactivates the inhibition mechanism, it is possible to grasp the emotional content and bring it into contact with the mentalizing capacity.

Aggression and Aggression Management

Mammalian aggression circuits may activate for any number of reasons:
fear, maternal instincts, irritation, sexual feelings, territorial instincts,
hunting instincts, and so on. The aggression circuit runs from the

midregions of the amygdala through the hypothalamus and into the brain stem. The aggression and fear circuits overlap in several places, including the hypothalamus. Affect rage is triggered in the hypothalamus; this activates the sympathetic nervous system, which in turn increases the anxiety response and suppresses parasympathetic activity. As mentioned earlier, so-called cold-blooded and hot-blooded aggression probably involve different circuit connections. Hot-blooded aggression is triggered by an activation of the amygdala and the hypothalamus, while cold-blooded aggression only involves the hypothalamus (Hart, 2008; Panksepp, 1998; Schore 2001b).

In the amygdala, fear and rage are clearly separate but intimately related systems. Due to the close connections between fear and rage within the amygdala, fits of rage, fear, and anxiety can intermingle. One function of the amygdala is to initiate fight-or-flight actions or the freeze response; all of these are response systems that involve the activation of defensive rage or fear. Both the fight system and the flight system trigger sympathetic activation, but while anxiety is associated with a sense of panic, aggressive responses trigger intense rage. While anxiety triggers the flight and freeze systems, aggression triggers the fight system (Schore, 2003a, 2003b). The human brain seems to be evolutionarily prepared to blame others for emotions that are evoked, and structures in the prefrontal cortex enable us to refine our aggression. Damage to the orbitofrontal cortex causes a lack of inhibition of impulses from the subcortical regions and leads to aggressive behavior. The orbitofrontal cortex exercises an inhibiting control over the areas in the hypothalamus that trigger aggression and fear. PET studies have revealed that both predatory and affective murderers show reduced prefrontal and increased subcortical activity (Schore, 1994, 2003a).

Autonomic Aggression

Frank, age 8, is very confrontational. He seems incoherent and spiteful. He speaks badly of everybody, except his mother. He often loses his temper and shows no inhibition, and when he is in affect he loses his sense of pain. He lacks empathy and is cruel to animals. When he feels discomfort he notes it but is unable to talk about it. On the other hand, he makes very offensive comments with no apparent sense of his own behavior. He is absorbed by thoughts about extremely violent situations with no form of empathy.

Arousal is important for all mental functions; without arousal the child will not engage in explorative behavior or pay attention to the environment. In a hyperarousal state the child becomes tense, restless, and unproductive. If the amygdala has been overstimulated throughout early childhood, for example, through prolonged traumatic stress, the development of circuit connections to the orbitofrontal cortex is impaired; this in turn leaves affect regulation up to the amygdala. In an unstable nervous system, even minor disturbances risk being amplified into an intense negative state. Schore (2003a) suggested that early and severe abuse or neglect, where the child is chronically exposed to prolonged chaotic and traumatic regulation, leads to widespread pruning of limbic and autonomic connections. Pruning of the circuit connections between the amygdala and the hypothalamus, for example, will deactivate the amygdaloid response to fear stimuli. As a result, a child will appear fearless because he does not sense the fear signals that are normally initiated by the amygdala. However, the child still responds with the fear system that is activated in the hypothalamus, which seems far more instinctive and cold-blooded.

When the amygdala disengages there is a reduction in heart rate and cortisol level. The child enters a low-arousal state, and the autonomic system will seek stimulation to increase arousal. Aggressive behavior on the hypothalamic level can be considered a form of stimulation-seeking behavior, and the child's aggression and fight behavior can be stimulating. In a sense, the slightly older child's nervous system acts reptilian, that is, without compassion but with the capacity for cognitive planning that characterizes the neocortical brain. There is no inhibition, for example, in relation to beating someone up, even in response to minor frustrations, partly because compassion has not been established. Children who have failed to establish a bond of trust with their caregivers in infancy often misinterpret other people's intentions and social signals. For example, eye contact may be perceived as a threat, and a friendly touch may be perceived as a precursor of something unpleasant (Lewis et al., 2001; Perry, 1999).

As mentioned earlier, the anger and anxiety circuits are closely related, and when the amygdala is not activated, it is hunting aggression, not the fight-or-flight system, that is activated. Dopamine and noradrenaline levels are activated, and in an anxious and fragile nervous system fear stimuli will trigger hunting aggression and activate the dopamine and opioid systems. On a background of even minimal fear stimuli, an unregulated nervous system will respond with increasing levels of activation, and the hunting behavior is intensified.

Limbic Aggression

Twelve-year-old Nicholas has difficulty being together with peers. He is bossy and gets angry and upset if things do not go his way when they play. He is irritable and gets worked up and eventually attacks. He is self-righteous and consequently often winds up in power struggles with adults if he cannot have his way. He is extremely irritable and never seems calm and relaxed. In conversations he says that everybody is out to get him, but he is sorry about his angry outbursts.

Normally, the amygdala is associated with anxiety activation, but a hyperactive amygdala can lead to aggression. Hot-blooded aggression is associated with a hot temper and agitation that is triggered by contact. As long as the orbitofrontal cortex and the corpus callosum have not yet matured sufficiently, a child cannot perceive his own and other people's emotional states, mentalization capacity is inadequate, and the child has difficulty associating emotions with symbolic and verbal representations. The impulse-inhibiting structures have not been established, and as a result the child can quickly be filled with narcissistic rage and unable to inhibit aggressive impulses. When observations of other people's actions cannot be mentalized, the child can only understand other people's behavior through concrete observable behavior without consideration of the underlying intent (Fonagy, 1999b).

Prefrontal Aggression Suppression

Karen is 16 years old and has been hospitalized repeatedly with severe stomach pains. She is unable to sit in a closed room without feeling that she is suffocating. She would like to move away from her mother, as she cannot stand hearing about the mother's problems any longer and taking responsibility for her drinking problem. She often cries and feels like a bad daughter and feels guilty when she rejects her mother. She would like take a break from her mother but feels bad about wanting to do that.

In Western European societies, aggression and outbursts of anger are often taboo, and many children are socialized into inhibiting their anger. They control and suppress the forbidden feelings, which are thus kept from additional processing by structures in the prefrontal cortex. The forbidden feelings remain unsymbolized, and when they cannot be integrated on a semantic and linguistic level, they will organize on a more primitive level, for example, through somatic reactions or acting out. When the aggression can be contained in daytime consciousness through structures in the prefrontal cortex, the child can process and analyze it in a controlled fashion and convert it to more mature forms of anger. The subcortical structures are inhibited and controlled by the prefrontal cortex, and the prefrontal cortex converts the aggression to more acceptable external behavior. If the inhibition is so strong that the impulses cannot be processed on a prefrontal level, there is a high internal cost to pay. Impulse inhibition creates a field of tension that can take on many different representation forms on a limbic level, such as depression, somatization, eating disorders, encopresis, and so on. Neurobiological studies have shown that the orbitofrontal cortex and the frontal part of the cingulate gyrus perform an inhibiting control over the amygdala and the hypothalamus and are thus involved in suppressing and regulating aggression.

Depression

Many different psychological theoretical explanations of depression have been developed. For example, Bowlby argued that depression arises when a child is kept in the phase of despair after the protest phase. His view was that depression is related to attachment behavior, and that prolonged separation can be a threat to the organism, both psychologically and physically. Freud considered depression a failed grieving process, and Stern suggested that depression develops when the child takes over the mother's depression in the early interaction as the child grieves over the mother's psychological absence and identifies with her in the hope of reaching her. Stern argued that the state is created through identification in an interpersonal interaction without an external and clearly identifiable loss. Schore argued that when a child is kept in the shame response, the child's self-esteem, energy, and vitality are reduced;

the child is unable to escape the low-arousal states and will be inhibited, shy, and timid and attempt to avoid attention. Fonagy (2005) pointed out that during depression one loses contact with the external world by barring others from entering a shared psychological reality. Deeply depressed people lose their curiosity and their motivation to engage in a joint attention focus with others.

Electric stimulation in a particular region of the brain stem activates a sense of hopelessness. The activation causes weeping, and the person has a sense of being depleted of energy, without hope, and exhausted. The experience can be characterized as a temporary feeling of overwhelming sadness. Both Freud and Bowlby emphasized the importance of distinguishing between grief and depression, where grief is a response to the absence of an important attachment figure, while depression is a cumulative state or a frozen version of one of the many stages of grief processing. Sadness can be triggered by thoughts, because neural networks are interconnected in the hierarchy of the brain. Unresolved loss in relation to a specific overwhelming event may be hidden from the daytime consciousness, leaving the child in a state of tension with a sense of incoherence. Depression can also result from a prolonged stress state due to a reduction of noradrenaline and serotonin levels and an increase in the corticotropin-releasing factor (CRF) level. Studies have shown that when rats are exposed to unpleasant situations that they cannot escape, their noradrenaline level drops. Nemeroff (1999) found that depressive individuals have a raised CRF level, and if CRF is injected directly into a mammal's central nervous system, the animal responds with depression-like symptoms including loss of appetite, altered activity in the autonomic nervous system, reduced pleasure, and sleep disorders. Depression may be associated with anxiety states and learned helplessness. In rats and mice, a chronic exposure to uncontrollable stressful stimuli lead to reductions in responsiveness, flight behavior, appetite response, sexual behavior, and body weight as well as sleep disorders—all symptoms that are also observed in depressed humans (Allen, 2002; Bradley, 2000).

Depression involves a wide range of symptoms and expressions and probably reflects a variety of disorders. From a neuroaffective point of view, depression can be explained as either a hyperactivation of the sympathetic nervous system or a fixation of the parasympathetic freeze system. In relation to depression that originates in the sympathetic nervous system, Gray has proposed three independent behavioral systems, all originating in the sympathetic nervous system: the fight-or-flight system, a reward system called the behavioral activation system (BAS), and a punishment system, the behavioral inhibition system (BIS). (These systems are also described in Chapter 3, the section on neuroaffective development, p. 98). In summary, BAS is a motivation system that handles approach behavior or active avoidance behavior, and which is sensitive to reward signals. BIS is activated in situations that involve novel and unfamiliar aspects, high-intensity stimulation, punishment, and evolutionarily prepared fear. It manages withdrawal behavior, controlled passive avoidance, and extinguishing (Beauchaine, 2001; Fonagy & Target, 2002). All three structures are probably mediated by the limbic system and may be a fundamental cause of very high or very low levels of nonvolitional control. Children who are securely attached to their caregivers and who are behaviorally inhibited have a heightened noradrenaline activity, which intensifies the BIS, a pattern that is seen in certain forms of depression (Kagan, Reznick, & Snidman, 1987). High cortisol levels are associated with BIS activity and hyperactivation of the right prefrontal cortex. The normal pattern in most people is an active left hemisphere, which is associated with positive emotions and a willingness to be accommodating, which in turn is associated with BAS activity and the activation of dopamine circuits. Depressive people often have lower left-hemisphere activity, and one of their characteristics during a depressive phase is a reduced blood flow through the left prefrontal cortex, which is associated with apathy and reduced speech output (Lichter & Cummings, 2001; Tomarken, Davidson, Wheeler, & Doss, 1992).

Depression may also be associated with a downregulation of the BAS, which is an innate seeking system that helps the organism satisfy needs. This system is associated with dopamine activation and originates in the brain stem (the ventral tegmental area and substantia nigra), continuing through the hypothalamus to the basal ganglia (nucleus accumbens), where most nerve pathways terminate. Like BIS it projects into the cingulate gyrus and prefrontal regions. Underactivation leads to inadequate arousal, psychomotor inhibitions, and a lack of interest and curiosity. There is reason to assume that underarousal, that is, inadequate amounts of dopamine, stems from a combination of an innate reduction in dopamine release and, even more importantly, the lack of satisfaction of relational needs in the close caregiver-child dyad (Sørensen, 2006). The connections between BAS and BIS and the frontal cingulate gyrus serve to moderate the effect of previously developed activation processes, and it becomes impossible to develop self-control. Disturbances in the cingulate gyrus may inhibit the ability to moderate BIS and BAS activity. Introverted children with a low degree of volitional control and a high degree of nonvolitional control (children who lack the spontaneity and control that may be a prerequisite of healthy adaptation) and acting-out children with a low degree of both volitional and nonvolitional control have neither executive nor motivational inhibitions to rely on for self-control (Fonagy & Target, 2002).

There may be a hereditary link between a short allele on the gene that codes for the serotonin transporter 5HTT and the development of depression. For example, a lack of serotonin regulation may hamper grief processing. Imbalances in the regulation of noradrenaline and dopamine make it difficult for a child to maintain attention and engage in reward-motivated behavior. The child becomes sensitive to misattunements in maternal behavior that make him engage in temporary dissociation (Fonagy et al., 2002).

Some types of depression are activated through learned helplessness, where the child is unable to find solutions or initiate action. In other forms of depression the child is kept in a narcissistic deflation affect (shame state), while yet other types of depression are characterized by the child seeking secondary rewards or responding with introverted aggression. In the following sections, various forms of depression are described in light of the three levels: autonomic, limbic, and prefrontal.

Anaclitic Depression

Jonah is 3 years old, and his mother has not been able to look after him properly. When he was an infant, she would fall asleep early in the evening and wake up late the next morning, while Jonah was still in his bed, staring into space. She could not remember when he had been fed last and became frustrated and angry when he showed signs of hunger. At the time he rejected contact and was patient, without making a sound. Today he is an apathetic and passive boy without facial mimicry. When he is handed his pacifier he shuts down, and one loses contact with him. He prefers lying in his bed and is able to stay there all day.

Spitz (1945, 1946) was one of the first to describe that institutionalized infants with little human contact had severely flawed development in spite of high hygienic and nutritional standards. Together with his assistant, Katherine Wolf, he studied 70 infants and found that 34 of them displayed symptoms resembling adult depression. When the infant had been separated from the mother for 1–2 weeks, the child would stop crying and become increasingly passive. When Spitz picked up the infant, the child resisted contact, and later would often refuse to eat. After some time the child would begin to engage in self-stimulating behavior, and after about 3 months, he became apathetic and failed to respond to external stimulation. Spitz found examples of 15-month-old infants who weighed the same as average 3-month-olds. In the most severe cases, the children's biological development was so affected that they died.

Spitz labeled this form of withdrawal anaclitic depression; a common term for the condition today is infant depression. On a neuroaffective level the infant probably enters a vegetative parasympathetic freeze state, which gives rise to an inner feeling of emptiness. When the infant is unable to achieve attuned contact with a primary caregiver, the child can only revert to the innate autoregulating state (Dubovski, 1997). The child is not "psychologically born," which is evident as emptiness and an extremely weak sense of identity. This form of depression is very different in nature from later developing forms.

Anaclitic depression is characterized by dysregulated parasympathetic hyperactivation, which reduces the heart rate and blood pressure, raises the cortisol level, and decreases the receptiveness of the cortisol receptors. This leads to progressively reduced sensitivity of the stress response system (HPA), which makes the child stop responding to environmental stimuli. When the child enters the vegetative parasympathetic state, in some cases opioids are released, which leads to an isolated sense of dysphoria with a simultaneous sense of paralysis and detachment. There is not sufficient energy within the nervous system to connect the neural structures, and the child loses the capacity for autoregulation and for intersubjective self-regulation. Sometimes there is an insufficient release of opioids, and the state is associated with discomfort. Some children turn to self-harming behavior, for example, by banging their head against the wall to reduce the sense of dysphoria and to self-stimulate and activate the opioid system. Self-harming behavior is rarely associated with any sensation of pain, probably because it activates the opioid system (Allen, 2002). The organism relies not only on dissociation as protection against pain but also on pain numbing, a response that corresponds to an 8-mg morphine injection (Schore, 2002a; Sørensen, 2005; van der Kolk, 1996c). In severe neglect or traumatic abuse the infant dissociates not only from the external world but also from the internal world, that is, the chaotic and painful stimuli that originate in the body itself.

Narcissistic Depression

Marlene, age 10, was raised by her mother, who was always a single parent. The mother suffered from severe depression, and during the first years of Marlene's life in particular, the mother was severely depressed and highly medicated. Marlene is a very quiet girl with little facial mimicry, who seems sad, joyless, and resigned. She seems avital, and even though she is physically larger than the other children in her class, she puts up with her classmates' vicious teasing without objections or resistance. In my conversation with her she lacks initiative but appeals to an extreme degree. While she seems defeated and inhibited she hungrily maintains contact, as if she simply cannot get enough.

Dennis is 17 years old and was raised in a strict Catholic home with many siblings. He is the oldest child and had a baby brother when he was about 1½ years old. When his younger brother was born the mother devoted all her love to him, and Dennis was often scolded and reprimanded. Dennis was always an introverted and somewhat timid child who did what the mother asked and clung to her. When he was 15 years old, he began to experiment with cannabis, which made him manic, a condition that subsequently developed into deep depression.

Narcissistic depression includes early- and late-developing forms. Marlene is an example of a pattern of communication between caregiver and child that has been established prior to the shame development phase, while Dennis is an example of a disturbance in narcissistic deflation. A cautious and hypersensitive child with an insecure attachment to the primary caregiver will be constantly worried about experiencing a loss of love and do anything to avoid losing the feeling of parental love. The child feels powerless to act and can become quiet or weepy and turn the anger on himself when facing conflicts. Some of these children reflect their parents' depression. Field et al. (1988) have documented how children of depressive mothers also show depressive behavior when they are with adults who are not depressive. When the child has been unable to arouse the parents' capacity to share engagement and joy in the interaction, the child's world collapses, and she retreats inside. The child learns that her actions have no communicative effect; she stops reaching out but still has an unmet need for contact. These children are often easy to socialize because they submit to avoid negative consequences or to gain some semblance of contact (Karr-Morse & Wiley, 1997). At this time, such a child is unable to differentiate between what belongs to others, and what belongs to herself. Due to the child's omnipotence she risks introjecting the parents' anger or rejection and feels rejected and unloved. People with severe depression do not allow anyone inside their subjective world and rely on two different mechanisms: One option is to build one's world inside the other person, attributing often aggressive intents to the other (projective identification); the other option is to withdraw, which leads to a sense of deadness (Fonagy, 2005).

One might imagine that these omnipotent, hypersensitive children would be easily influenced by narcissistic deflation, which they have difficulty regulating their way out of on their own. If the caregiver either maintains or fails to help the child escape the deflation, the child is kept in a toxic state of low arousal. The child loses the sense of being able to regulate internal states, and the nervous system is locked into deflation, which may later cause manic-depressive fluctuations. The manic phase corresponds to the mental organization that the child has achieved around the age of 12 months, where dopamine-based omnipotence is at its peak, just before the development of shame is initiated. In the manic-depressive state the nervous system switches between being locked in joy-filled omnipotence and in narcissistic deflation, both mechanisms that are regulated subcortically.

The striatum is a structure in the basal ganglia in the diencephalon that helps filter the thoughts, ideas, and notions that reach consciousness. When the dopamine circuits are underactive, thought activity is impaired. When the dopamine circuits are overactive, far too many impressions pass through, and the states of mind change in a manic or paranoid direction (Hansen, 2002). Severe depression often involves both a raised CRF level and an extremely elevated cortisol level along with abnormal levels of both noradrenaline and serotonin. The raised cortisol level reflects a raised stress level, which the hippocampus is unable to downregulate. There is a link between stress and depression. Stress factors commonly trigger the first depression, but subsequently depression is initiated without a trigger factor. Studies with rats, among other research, have shown that a rat that has learned helplessness requires increasing levels of activation to show joy (Sapolsky, 1998).

Secondary Depression (Neurotic Depression)

John is 18 years old and in high school. He has always done well in school and comes from a home where his mother has always backed him up and given him attention when he was sad or felt under the weather. At the same time, she never made any secret of the fact that she considered him the brains of the family and that she had high hopes for his career. In an exam he received a low grade, and afterward he felt so low that he was sick for a long time. He was passive, apathetic, and unable to handle anything, but at the same time he was very attention seeking and was keen to talk for hours about how poorly he was doing. He was extremely self-reproachful, and every time he tried to make excuses for himself in a sort of self-soothing attempt, there was another internal element that reproached him, which made him feel even more useless.

Secondary or neurotic forms of depressions are characterized by exaggerated feelings of guilt or introverted anger with the suppression of unpleasant feelings and some appeal for acceptance and understanding of the painful state from the outside world. Often, the person suffers from extreme self-hatred, and on a conscious level is in touch with various contradictory internal representations. One of these is likely to be a highly condemning internal representation that constantly demeans the person's self-values and attempts at liberating himself from the emotional inhibition. This form of depression seems to be controlled by dissociation between limbic and prefrontal structures. The prefrontal regions are well developed and capable of inhibiting and suppressing unacceptable emotions. The person is able to use a variety of contradictory internal representations, which often consist of a contrast between superego structures or idealized representations and the more identity-bearing ego structures, which leads to powerful internal states of tension. This form of dissociation requires a well-developed nervous system that is capable of mentalizing and symbolizing, and it is often possible to help the person differentiate and distinguish the various internal representations once attention is directed at them.

Hyperactive Children and Children With Attention Deficit Disorder

Children who are hyperactive or have attention deficit disorder are alert and restless and often experience intense negative emotions. There is considerable disagreement as to whether genes or environmental factors affect children with these disorders and, if so, to what degree. In psychiatry, these disorders are covered by the label of ADHD. Several studies have found a close link between nature and nurture in virtually all psychological disorders. For example, we have long known that animals with a hereditary disposition for a short allele on the 5HTT gene (which reduces the serotonin level) manage stress poorly (Hart, 2008; Suomi, 2000). Similarly, human studies (Caspi et al., 2003; Kendler, Kuhn, Vittum, Prescott, & Riley, 2005; Sørensen, 2005) have shown that individuals with a short allele on the 5HTT gene respond more strongly to negative experiences and crises; even more so if they have two short alleles. It appears that the same level of stress affects different people very differently, and that the likelihood of depression and acting out is far greater for individuals with short alleles on the 5HTT gene. For example, studies show that someone with a short allele is more than twice as likely to respond with depression or acting out than someone with two long alleles when exposed to the same stressful event. Another study shows that someone with two short variants of the serotonin transporter gene has upward of eight times the risk of developing depression when exposed to stressful life events. The studies also document that the short genetic variant is not in itself enough to trigger depression or acting out. A person with the short variant of the gene must be exposed to stressful events for the disorder to be expressed; thus, conversely, the risk remains low if an at-risk person leads a calm, stable, and secure life.

Already in the 1970s Michael Rutter pointed out the psychosocial risk of psychological disorders through childhood experiences in his study of children from the Isle of Wight and central London (Faraone & Biederman, 1998). Carlson, Jacobvitz, and Sroufe's (1995) and Jacobvitz and Sroufe's (1987) research shows that overstimulation, inadequate delimitation, and dysregulation from the caregiver are often early precursors of ADHD. A study by Fearon and Belsky (2002) found a clear link between ADHD and an insecure attachment pattern. This disorder may result from temperamental features such as excessive sensation seeking and externalizing behavior in combination with an inadequate care environment that either offers too much punishment or not enough regulation (Bradley, 2000).

Rutter et al. (1999) did an extensive study of the relationship between genetic and environmental factors in a number of disorders and concluded that the familial influence is not enough to activate the syndromes without a preexisting genetic vulnerability. Goldberg (2001) concluded that ADHD is not related to any one well-defined cause, and that the processes that produce the disorder do not normally follow man-made classification systems. Rutter et al. (Kreppner, O'Connor, & Rutter, 2001) did a large-scale study of institutionalized Romanian children seeking to uncover a link between ADHD and institutionalization. They concluded that the Romanian children's ADHD seems to be part of a deprivation syndrome that more likely represents a more general disorder of self-regulating behavior. The children who were studied at the age of 6 years, and who had been adopted after the age of 6 months, showed far higher average rates of ADHD than children adopted before age 6 months. The difference was most pronounced for the children who were not adopted until the age of 2 years. Rutter et al. pointed out that there are likely to be different causes for attention deficit and hyperkinetic disorders, and that no disorder should be considered in isolation from the child's context.

Children with attention deficit and hyperactivity are unable to fixate their attention and inhibit their impulses, and they have difficulty making plans. Several neuroaffective theories have been proposed concerning ADHD. The most widespread hypothesis is that the symptoms are due to a dysfunction in the circuit between the limbic system, the frontal part of the cingulate gyrus, and the prefrontal cortex. The motivational control by the cingulate gyrus and the inhibiting control by the prefrontal cortex are weak and unable to inhibit or control the limbic functions. Among other things, researchers suggest that it is a disturbance of the noradrenaline-and-dopamine-based circuit that renders the prefrontal cortex unable to activate the inhibiting structures enough to suppress impulses from the subcortical structures. It is a dysregulation (with excessive or inadequate levels) of noradrenaline that impairs the attention functions (Faraone & Biederman, 1998).

Impulse control consists of multiple functions, including the ability to inhibit the urge to act out an impulse, to stop an ongoing response, to assess whether a given behavior should continue, be altered, or end, and to persist with a task or a line of thought without being disturbed by irrelevant internal or external stimuli. The capacity for impulse inhibition lets a child assess the impulse before acting on it. A child who is governed by impulses reacts to the here-and-now situation without prior analysis or any conscious processing of the situation. Barkley (1997, 1998) described that attention deficit disorder marks a failure of the capacity for behavioral inhibition and a failure to use executive functions to plan and control behavior and actions.

The U.S. National Institute for Mental Health found that regions in the right prefrontal cortex, the basal ganglia in the diencephalon, and the cerebellar vermis are smaller in children who have been diagnosed with ADHD. The prefrontal cortex handles impulse inhibition and maintains attention over time. The basal ganglia control automatic responses and thoughts, filter out inappropriate actions and thoughts, and coordinate neurological input from the cortex. This structure is essential for the initiation of movements and more complex behavior. The vermis plays a key role for motivation regulation (Barkley, 1998). The amygdala has extensive connections to the basal ganglia, and under optimum conditions the orbitofrontal system will exercise control over the amygdala and the basal ganglia and thus expand the affect-regulating capacity. The expanded connections of the amygdala to the basal ganglia make it possible to perform nonvolitional acts on the basis of fear impulses. Disturbances in the basal ganglia are often associated with Tourette's syndrome, and the basal ganglia regulate the activating and rewarding neurotransmitter dopamine. Thus, there is reason to assume that there is a close link between ADHD, Tourette's syndrome, and various forms of anxiety. Together with the thalamus, the basal ganglia can be considered the evolutionary precursors of the neocortex. In the course of human evolution their natural role was taken over by the prefrontal cortex, which in higher mammals exercises an inhibiting influence over the basal ganglia (Goldberg, 2001).

Attention and concentration rely on the coordination of many different neural circuits. This coordination is subject to a wide range of potential disturbances, and even if the symptoms in children diagnosed with ADHD or ADD are relatively uniform in many respects, the disorder may stem from different causes and dysregulation on different hierarchical levels in the neural circuits that contribute to our attention capacity. For example, based on studies of the hierarchical brain, Mirsky and Duncan (2001) suggested that our capacity for attention control is the result of coordinated activity in several parts of the nervous system. Attention consists of several different functions. The ability to focus, directing our attention at objects of relevance, relies on structures in the reticular activation system in the brain stem. The ability to maintain focus is conditioned by arousal and the inhibition of irrelevant stimuli, which is controlled by structures in the reticular activation system in cooperation with the prefrontal cortex; and the ability to perform shifts in attention and the working memory is related to structures in the prefrontal cortex. Thus, attention functions can be related to a range of structures in the nervous system. Their common basis is the reticular activation system in the brain stem, which connects hierarchically to increasingly advanced levels and eventually to the dorsolateral prefrontal cortex, which is in charge of plans and goals. Thus, the energy to maintain attention is generated in the reticular activation system, while the control and regulation of attention is managed by the dorsolateral prefrontal cortex. The reticular activation system is able to selectively activate the cortex through bottom-up processes, but these processes are controlled and regulated by the prefrontal cortex through top-down processes. This means that attention can be described as a circular process that involves complex interactions between the prefrontal cortex, the reticular activation system, and other cortical regions (Goldberg, 2001). The capacity to receive stimuli, processing, affective coloring, and behavior are all essential aspects in relation to attention and psychomotor control. A lack of impulse inhibition, for example, will always disturb the executive functions and prevent effective cognitive or emotional processing.

Based on Mirsky and Duncan's (2001) and Goldberg's (2001) work, attention deficit disorder and hyperkinetic disorders can be viewed as a breakdown anywhere in the attention circuit: in the reticular activation system, the cingulate gyrus, the orbito- and dorsolateral prefrontal cortices, or in the transfer of information between the right and left hemispheres. Teicher (2002) pointed out that heightened activity in the right hemisphere can also be a source of attention deficit disorder. For example, internalization and externalization problems in children are evident as elevated activity in the right prefrontal cortex and reduced activity in the left prefrontal cortex, whether the arousal is positive or negative. Different anatomical patterns will disturb attention in different ways, and there are many different attention systems. It appears that the ability to focus and maintain arousal is established during the first years of life through the autonomic nervous system. When a child is about 2 years old, the orbitofrontal and the dorsolateral prefrontal cortices take over the impulse-inhibiting functions and control over the attention system and the volitional motor system.

The neurochemical basis of attention is probably a noradrenaline-based stimulation of the sensory cortex and a dopamine-based stimulation of the motor cortex. The noradrenaline-based system regulates which incoming stimuli are received by the organism, while the dopamine-based system regulates what the organism does with the incoming stimuli. These two systems must be mutually balanced, and both under- and overactivation can lead to attention deficit disorder. The systems are controlled by brain stem structures that coordinate with self-regulating structures in the limbic system and the prefrontal cortex (Schore, 2003a; Teicher, 2002). In connection with attention deficit disorder, the limbic system can be either under- or overactive, while the frontal part of the cingulate gyrus, the orbitofrontal cortex, and the dorsolateral prefrontal cortex are underactive. In connection with hyperactivity, the amphetamine-like drug Ritalin sometimes has a positive effect because it raises the level of activating neurotransmitters simultaneously in the brain stem structures, the limbic system, and the prefrontal cortex. Ritalin raises the level of arousal, thus focusing attention, which facilitates the impulse-inhibiting functions (Beauchaine, 2001; Smith, 2001).

Autonomic Attention Deficit Disorder

Janet is 5 years old; she is a confused little girl with extremely limited mimicry. She is attentive and sensitive, constantly scanning everything. She is always going full speed ahead; she is unable to concentrate on anything and her attention is easily captured by arbitrary stimuli. She is physically restless, and the only thing that can hold her attention for a short while is children's songs. She is always happy and cheerful, but when things do not go her way she will hit and kick. She has no sense of time, no empathy, and cannot resist tormenting animals, although she is not aggressive.

From birth, some children are difficult to regulate and have hypersensitive sensory systems, and it can be difficult to help them thrive. Their sensitivity to stress may persist, and some children react psychosomatically, for example, with diarrhea. These children are often restless and weepy; it is difficult to achieve physiobiological regulation, for example, to establish a stable circadian pattern. This inhibits their psychobiological regulation, and it can be difficult to establish eye contact. Due to their innate sensitivity they have trouble developing a self-regulating capacity, vitality, and endurance, and their curiosity and explorative behavior are often impaired. They are quick to cry and become restless, they are hard to comfort, and even the slightest disturbance in the environment can cause hyperactivity or immobilization and sleep and eating disorders.

As mentioned several times, early attunement is about helping the child maintain a focus of attention. During this period the nervous system practices handling increasing levels of arousal without disorganizing. In abuse or neglect the child has not received the necessary support to maintain attention through regulation, dyadic transactions, and arousal training, which facilitates the development of the nervous system. The child is unable to maintain attention on specific pleasant or unpleasant perceptions and develops no sense of "figure versus ground." One given stimulus is no more pertinent than any other, and thus, the child is unable to distinguish essential from inessential. Dopamine-based activation is crucial in the early caregiver-infant contact. During this period, the caregiver establishes a joy-filled vital contact with the child, which raises the level of dopamine. Thus, an inadequate childhood environment can be a contributing factor in an underactivation of the dopamine circuit.

Attention requires three elements: activation, orientation, and focus. When the nervous system is incapable of maintaining focus and regulating through an attuned contact, modulating capacity is impaired in the brain stem and the limbic regions, among other places. This leads to insufficient stimulation of the prefrontal cortex. The vermis coordinates motor, emotional, and cognitive aspects of various stimuli and is involved in balancing the release of dopamine, among other functions. MRI scans of more than 200 children have shown that the main difference between children diagnosed with ADHD and typical children is a reduced cerebellum volume in children with ADHD (Diamond, 2000). Because the neural systems in the cerebellum are involved in cognitive, emotional, and motor coordination, even small differences in size and differentiation can have major consequences. The vermis develops during the period when the caregiver rocks and cradles the infant, and if the infant does not receive adequate care at this early stage, the result may be various forms of attention deficit and hyperkinetic disorders.

Studies have found that a dysfunctional amygdala also inhibits essential aspects of the attention function. Normally, attention means focusing on one stimulus while ignoring others. Selective attention allows the nervous system to focus on one task at the time, and if another stimulus is affectively important it may interfere with the selection process; this sort of selection does not occur when the amygdala is damaged (LeDoux, 2001).

Limbic Attention Disorder

Five-year-old Jonah is a charming, happy, and active boy, who smiles easily and has good gaze contact. He quickly becomes inattentive and absorbed by what goes on around him, picking up on even the slightest sound. In tasks that require attention he soon becomes impatient and restless and loses concentration; he is difficult to motivate and has difficulty being absorbed by an activity. When he meets demands, at first he tries distraction by changing the subject, then he says that he does not remember, and if he is still kept to the task he becomes restless and slips down onto the floor and under the table like a much younger child. He is keen to help out with chores but is easily distracted and loses interest. He pays attention to facial expressions, seems constantly alert, and continuously scans his environment without being able to relax.

Trauma research shows that traumatized children and adults have an impaired capacity for information processing; they are easily distracted and have difficulty concentrating. The nervous system is in a constant state of high arousal, which makes it hypersensitive and highly reactive. A child whose nervous system is in a constant fear state will have problems with attention and concentration (Scaer, 2001). A child who has suffered abuse or has been raised in an unpredictable environment will have a constantly activated amygdala. The child has been forced to be sensitive to external stimuli all the time, ready to respond with fight-or-flight behavior or freezing. When the environment changes, this survival strategy is rendered inappropriate. The child's attention deficit and hyperkinetic disorder is the result of a "use-dependent" neural organization of the brain. The child spends so much time in a fear state that he is constantly focused on features in the environment that are potentially harmful, which impairs the acquisition of advanced cognitive skills (Nemeroff, 1999; Perry, 1997, 2002).

If the brain receives stimuli that are perceived as threatening, adrenaline and noradrenaline will be released. The reticular activation system in the brain stem scans the environment for stimuli, and any fear stimuli are recorded by the amygdala, which initiates the fight-or-flight response, and all other activity ceases. If too much energy goes into activating this system, the child will have difficulty maintaining attention on anything else. The chronic activation of the sympathetic nervous system means that the child will have difficulty maintaining attention control and self-control. Attention deficit disorder generally involves difficulties with excluding irrelevant information, which ultimately impairs flexibility and cognitive processing (Bradley, 2000; Gunnar & Barr, 1998; Jacobvitz & Sroufe, 1987). Barkley (1998) has suggested that disorders of attention without hyperactivity (ADD) may be associated with a dysfunction of the hippocampus due to a chronically elevated cortisol level.

Prefrontal Attention Deficit Disorder

Mike is 15 years old; his parents were recently divorced. He complains about not being able to concentrate; he considers this is a big problem, because he wants to do well in his final exams. His thoughts revolve around his parents, and every time he tries to concentrate on his studies, eventually he has to close the book, because he is unable to recall what he has read. He describes this experience as a "thought grinder" that he is unable to control.

Through the circuitry that connects the limbic system to the prefrontal areas, powerful emotional signals are able to generate neural background noise and thus sabotage the ability of the prefrontal regions to maintain working memory. Persistent emotional concerns impair the child's intellectual abilities and paralyze the child's ability to learn. Maintaining attention requires a number of functions. Selective attention through the dorsolateral prefrontal cortex enables us to select an activity and thus inhibit the execution of other activities based on an analysis of the situation. This requires an inhibiting mechanism that is capable, among other things, of balancing the concentration of noradrenaline and dopamine, which increases the child's ability to target attention for a prolonged period. This inhibiting mechanism is disturbed when the person is under emotional pressure.

Eating Disorders

Eating disorders are usually divided into anorexia, bulimia, and psychogenic obesity (comfort eating), and many attribute the different symptoms to different etiologies (Joseph, 1993; Lier, Isager, Jørgensen, Larsen, & Aarkrog, 1999). In the following sections, based on the triune model of the brain, I categorize eating disorders in relation to different hierarchical structures: an autonomic eating disorder that stems from the child's lack of a sense of hunger or satiety; a limbic disorder that develops as a sort of self-soothing in relation to emotional discomfort; and a prefrontal disorder that stems from a tension-filled control of contradictory and suppressed emotions (anorexia and bulimia).

Autonomic Eating Disorder

Amanda is 6 months old and severely undernourished. She already seems old and harrowed. The mother comes from Iran, and she has only been in the country for a very short time. She seems depressive and has a hard time adjusting to Danish conditions. She is suspicious and rejects interference. Her relationship with Amanda seems joyless and based on obligation. Amanda refuses to eat, and every time the mother tries to nurse her, she resists and screams. She prefers to be left alone, and there is concern for Amanda's life.

Eating disorders in infants are often related to severe regulation disorders or deprivation. When the infant is unable to achieve balance in the autonomic functions between sympathetic and parasympathetic activation, the child is uncomfortable and has trouble managing the feeding and digestive process, which rely on autonomic functions. In severe cases the infant enters anaclitic depression, sensing no signs of discomfort or hunger. Children who have been severely deprived or abused in infancy seem to have difficulty sensing basic sensations, including hunger and satiety. In some children the eating disorder may also be expressed as overeating. Some children stuff themselves with food to the point of vomiting. This is probably because certain regions in the insula, deep inside the hemispheres, have not matured sufficiently. The insula records changes in the autonomic nervous system, which is typically perceived as distress or bodily discomfort. It is also in this area that pain impulses from the inner organs are recorded, and the organism becomes aware of the pain. Damage to the right-hemisphere insula in particular destroys the awareness of bodily states (Damasio, 2003; Hart, 2008).

Limbic Eating Disorder

Katherine is 17 years old; she is 5 feet 2 inches and weighs 325 pounds. Her father recently passed away of obesity-related conditions, and Katherine does not understand why she is not more grief-stricken than she is. When she is confronted with situations that have been difficult for her, she develops a sudden, massive headache, gets nauseous, and has to lie down. She says that her father was a bully, and her mother always defended him and was subject to his whims. She often felt alone with her father's bullying; he used her as his "butler" and never allowed her to have a life of her own together with her peers.

Psychogenic obesity alleviates an inner sense of emptiness, creates psychological boundaries, and protects the organism against psychological pain. When emotional discomfort cannot integrate with the mentalizing functions in the prefrontal cortex, it will be expressed on a limbic level, for example, through somatization. This dissociation creates an inner sense of emptiness as the child replaces a diffuse emotionality with something else, for example, food. This is often referred to as an oral need, because the child regresses to a state where her physiological and psychological needs were met unconditionally, filling the "hole inside" with food. The limbic system feels satisfied, regardless what it is that meets the need; the original need is temporarily stilled, although it is never actually satisfied. Eating can soothe loneliness because it produces a feeling of pleasure that activates the same structures as those related to the need for social contact (Joseph, 1993). Sugar stimulates the release of opioids, which in turn reduce both physical and emotional pain. Experimental studies have shown that mice that are separated from their mothers make fewer separation calls if they are fed sugar water (Blass, Fitzgerald, & Kehoe, 1986).

Obesity also offers protection against internal psychological pain because it reduces sensitivity to tactile sensations. Even though body weight goes up, the number of touch-sensitive cells remains the same. Thus, these cells are farther apart, which offers protection from overwhelming sensory stimulation that might otherwise trigger painful memories. Obesity also generates a psychological "membrane" between the child and any abusive boundary transgressions from the parents.

The hypothalamus regulates the release of hormones that control bodily processes and thus plays a role in relation to the metabolism. The metabolic balance is determined by hereditary factors that remain unknown, and the explanation models for obesity involve multiple factors. The hypothalamus plays a key role in appetite regulation, because an area in the hypothalamus records drops in glucose levels and signals hunger, while a different area responds to increases in glucose levels, signaling satiety. Damage to the hypothalamus is relatively rare, and thus it seems likely that most dysfunctions in the hypothalamus are due to a disturbance in the neurotransmitters that transfer messages to and from the hypothalamus. Serotonin, for example, reduces activity in the distal part of the hypothalamus, and thus a high serotonin level would probably reduce appetite, while a low level would increase it (Carter, 1998).

Prefrontal Eating Disorder

Camilla, age 16, has just started high school. For years, she has had an eating disorder and has engaged in self-harming behavior. She has considerable artistic talent, which she uses to draw sketches of death and destruction. Camilla says that she cannot stand her mother's tears, and that she does not want to be around her parents. When she is confronted with the fact that she seems angry with her

mother, she denies it. Camilla spends most of the time in her room,
but when she is with her parents she is nice and does not appear to
have any problems.

Anorexia and bulimia can be considered disorders that develop on the
basis of an extreme need for control and massive introverted aggression.
The disorders can be characterized as an inhibition of forbidden impulses that are suppressed by the prefrontal cortex and the left hemisphere,
such as anger. However, in severe cases the disorder may also be associated with internal tension that has more to do with limbic disorders, such
as borderline states.

Anorexia and bulimia, like all other psychological disorders, have
a multifactor background, which may be expressed through self-
destructive behavior, a fixation on food, and an obsession with dieting.
The disorder often develops in prepubescent girls and is characterized
by ambivalence. On the one hand, the sufferers reject care, while on the
other hand they display dependency. The ambivalence is evident as
powerful passive aggression, which often persists even after the eating
disorder has gone away (Karen, 1998). Prefrontal eating disorders are
associated with affect inhibition and rigid behavioral control and commonly represent repressed aggression toward the parents. An angry person with anorexia can attract attention and control the family's activities
through the eating disorder and thus express rejection of the parents'
love. Crittenden (1995) pointed out that when the young person, in addition to the eating disorder, distorts and twists the parents' statements
and behavior and sees them as hostile, this should be attributed to a
compulsive personality pattern that is part of a more profound relational
disorder corresponding to borderline states (see Chapter 6, the section
on psychological disorders on the limbic level, pp. 273–276).

Anorexia and bulimia often appear in combination with self-harming
behavior. Severe anorexia and self-harming behavior can be characterized as intense internal tension that the child or young person dramatically attempts to regulate his way out of through self-harming behavior.
Severe hunger and self-harming acts raise opioid activity, which soothes
both physical and psychological pain. The opioid system reduces noradrenaline activity and calms the nervous system down. In women with
severe anorexia, this pain-relieving function represents an obstacle to
treatment. The psychodynamic character of the state is gradually re-

placed by a form of biologically conditioned self-medication, where the person has a need to starve and engage in additional self-harming behavior to achieve calm and relief.

In the previous sections, the specific psychological disorders have been categorized in accordance with the triune hierarchy to demonstrate that a more specific characterization can be a meaningful aid to understanding the underlying psychodynamics of various psychological disorders. In the following sections, various forms of personality disorders are categorized according to the same model to enable a more nuanced understanding of the possible causal backgrounds of these disorders.

Schizoid, Antisocial, Borderline, and Neurotic Personality Disorders

In this section, a number of psychological disorders are categorized according to their symptom presentation on an autonomic level as antisocial and schizoid disorders, on a limbic level as borderline and psychopathic disorders, and on a prefrontal level as neurotic disorders. The psychological disorders are described within the framework of the triune brain and viewed from a neuroaffective perspective. Fonagy (2003) suggested, for example, that a failure of empathy may stem from one of three levels: the amygdala, the orbitofrontal cortex, or a combination of areas deep inside the prefrontal cortex (the cingulate gyrus and orbitofrontal and dorsolateral areas). Individuals with reduced amygdala response will have failed to develop an intuitive and embodied sense of their own emotions, while individuals with an intact amygdala function but reduced orbitofrontal activation will have failed to develop a sense of empathy. The disruption of links between structures deep inside the prefrontal cortex may cause the individual to experience affects in relation to other people's unhappiness or distress, but their experience of the affect will be incorrectly or inadequately associated with perceptions and intentions.

Here, it should be reiterated that psychological disorders must be understood in a multifactor perspective, and that innate components play an important role for the development of personality disorders. Psychological symptoms may be either introverted or extroverted, and the individual's way of handling difficulties may present as different symptoms that are possibly related to the same underlying neural structure and attachment pattern. Similarly, overregulation, underregulation, or disorganized regulation can carry different consequences for a child; thus, even a disorder concerning one particular neural structure, such as the limbic system, may present a variety of different symptoms.

Psychological Disorders on the Brain Stem Level

On the brain stem level there are two different types of disorders. One is early emotional frustration or antisocial disorder, and the other is the schizoid disorder. In the following passage both will be described.

Early Emotional Frustration (Antisocial Disorder)

Matthew is a smart 8-year-old boy with no capacity for deep concentration; he is indiscriminate in his approach to others and has no positive expectations. In supermarkets he walks up to strangers with no reservations. He is uninhibited and does not know how to handle himself. He is negative, hits others, speaks rudely, and is violent and destructive in his behavior toward other children. He does not respond to verbal or physical punishment and is often accused of lying. He has no sense of danger, stuffs himself with food without inhibition, never feels full, and does not notice when he is too cold or too warm. He is introverted and has a serious look on his face, and he seems neither happy nor sad. He never seeks physical contact, and when an adult holds him his body goes rigid. When met with demands, he turns and walks away. He can be helpful to younger children, but at the slightest frustration he becomes aggressive, kicks whatever is around, or becomes very self-destructive. He is afraid of anything novel and has difficulty being on his own. He has no empathy or compassion with others; he laughs if others get hurt and is cruel to animals. He lacks confidence but has fantasies of omnipotence and idealizes his mother.

Children with early emotional damage, who as adults are often characterized as sociopaths or antisocial, have a limited capacity for attachment behavior and emotional processing. They are insensitive, feel no remorse, and have limited behavioral control. Their insensitivity includes characteristics such as an absence of shame, guilt, morals, and empathy, and their body sense is poor. Perry (1997) pointed out that just as a child with mental retardation lacks the capacity to grasp abstract cognitive concepts, a child who has suffered early emotional damage lacks the capacity to feel connected to others in an appropriate way. Remorse, empathy, sympathy, and so on are all experience-dependent capacities. A child who has suffered early emotional damage is unable to perceive bodily sensations and to distinguish between his own needs and those of others.

Often, these children have been exposed to chaotic, disorganized regulation with no fundamental sense of order or consistency. They have an attachment figure, but the attachment is characterized by early imprinting without object permanence. They have no understanding of other people's feelings and are often characterized by negative emotions. They often experience an inner sense of emptiness, which is probably a consequence of a lack of bodily sensations in combination with a lack of mental representations, which leads to a profound sense of isolation and lack of meaning (Fonagy, 1999b; Fonagy et al., 1997; Schore, 2001b, 2003a).

Emotional states that are not anchored in the body will be highly fleeting. Damasio (1994) pointed out that social behavior develops through emotional learning, which is based on somatic reactions, which in turn link behavior with pleasant and unpleasant experiences. The amygdala is believed to be responsible for immediate perception and for linking a stimulus with an emotional somatic state. Damasio (1994) explained how amygdala disorders mean that the person cannot be guided by emotions, and no decision feels more right than any other. There is no intuitive sense to guide behavior, which makes it difficult to prioritize. The orbitofrontal cortex triggers an emotional response based on internal perceptions. The infant relies on a well-functioning amygdala to associate the observation of other people's fear, distress, or anger with a somatic state. This learning is a prerequisite for the development of the orbitofrontal cortex to enable the child to form internal perceptions of bodily sensations and emotions. The organic development of the orbitofrontal cortex depends on the amygdala. When the circuit connections between the amygdala and the orbitofrontal cortex are fully matured, the orbitofrontal cortex appears to be able to function relatively independently of the amygdala and interact with the hypothalamus and other structures. The ability to imagine the consequences of punishment and reward and the capacity for remorse require the hypothalamus, the amygdala, and the orbitofrontal cortex to work together. This circuitry is crucial for the capacity of internal perceptions to activate somatic sensations (Bechara, Damasio, & Damasio, 2003).

Children who have suffered early emotional frustration probably have an undeveloped mammalian vagal system, which places them in a chronically dissociated sympathetic fight-or-flight system with a simultaneously activated vegetative parasympathetic freeze system. Hare and Jutai (1983) pointed out that individuals with extreme psychopathic features have a low degree of responsiveness in their autonomic nervous system. As mentioned earlier, Schore (2003b), Panksepp (1998), and others referred to two different types of aggression: hot-blooded and cold-blooded. Hot-blooded aggression is activated through a highly active amygdala and is expressed as irritable, emotionally charged aggression, while cold-blooded aggression is controlled by the hypothalamus, which is associated with low arousal and a low heart rate and is expressed as aggression that is seeking, controlled, targeted, and emotionally cold. The amygdala is active from birth, and damage to the amygdala can lead to a distorted perception of one's own and other people's emotional responses and later a lack of empathy. There is evidence that deprivation or chaotic and disorganized care can cause damage to the amygdala (Pollak, Cichetti, Horming, & Reed, 2000).

Damasio (2003) pointed out that young children with damage to the orbitofrontal cortex, for example, as a result of a car crash, fail to develop feelings of shame and guilt later in life and seem to have a poor sense of identity. Children with early damage to the orbitofrontal cortex often display antisocial behavior and are unable to adhere to rules. Children with antisocial behavior who have suffered massive early emotional neglect or abuse appear to have damage related to both the amygdala and the orbitofrontal cortex.

As mentioned earlier, children who have suffered early emotional damage have low serotonin and cortisol levels and thus a slower resting pulse. It appears that the child's parasympathetic and sympathetic nervous systems function independently of one another, which leads to an underactivation of behavioral inhibition; this facilitates impulsive behavior, because the behavior-seeking activity functions relatively unrestrained (Beauchaine, 2001). Reduced responsiveness of the stress response system reflects a high risk of antisocial and aggressive behavior and a disturbance of fear conditioning and the startle response. A child with an impaired stress response system will fail to respond to punishment stimuli, feel fear, and associate actions with previous punishment. The child does not learn from making mistakes, even in tasks where the child is rewarded for making the right choice, which suggests damage to the orbitofrontal cortex. Children with early emotional damage show fear to innate fear stimuli, such as bared teeth, but not to acquired fear stimuli, which rely on visual perceptions (Blair et al., 1999; Blair & Frith, 2000; Spear, 2000). In a study of antisocial boys, McBurnett, Lahey, Rathouz, and Loeber (2000) found that the earlier the antisocial behavior develops, and the more emotionally flat the child seems, the more likely it is that the behavior is associated with a reduced cortisol level.

Biologically, aggressive facial expressions represent danger, while sad facial expressions are a sign of submission. Most social mammals have an innate mechanism that inhibits violence, and certain features of submission typically put a stop to an attack; for example, an aggressive dog stops attacking when the other dog bares its neck. In humans, a sad facial expression probably signals submission, and the violence-inhibiting mechanism is typically activated when the other party shows a sad or anxious face. Encountering such an expression normally results in increased mammalian parasympathetic activity, which reduces the sympathetic fight activation. However, this fails to occur in children with early damage (Blair, Colledge, Murray, & Mitchell, 2001), and these children have difficulty identifying sad facial expressions. Children who have suffered physical abuse respond strongly to faces expressing anger but not sadness.

Damage to the amygdala means that the child has difficulty processing fear. In studies of the galvanic skin response to sad facial expressions, adults with an antisocial disorder showed a diminished skin response, which reflects a lack of sympathetic activation. The same was not the case for angry faces. These adults are able to identify sad facial expressions, but they have no autonomic response. Blair et al. (2001; Blair, Jones, Clark, & Smith, 1997) pointed out that children with sociopathic tendencies show selective disturbances in the processing of sad and fearful faces but not in the processing of faces that are angry or happy; this suggests a disturbance of amygdala functioning. Innate emotional reactions to fear or sadness form the basis of the development of empathy and morals. These children are insensitive to immoral acts and incapable of distinguishing between minor and major transgressions, since such a distinction relies on responses to discomfort.

Children with autism do have a physiological response and thus a perceptual understanding of other people's feelings, but they lack the ability to attune emotionally with others and form internal representations of other people's internal state. Children with early damage have no physiological response to other people's suffering because they are incapable of empathizing emotionally with others. Unlike children with autism, these children are able to understand other people's feelings on a behavioral level, even if their assessments are often distorted. Children with early emotionally damage and sociopaths have a dysfunctional emotional perception but are able to attune with other people's external behavior (Blair 1999; Blair et al., 1996).

Schizoid Disorder

Toby, age 13, has had severe social problems ever since first grade. He is mostly nice and polite but seems overadjusted and without emotional involvement. His mimicry is difficult to read, and he often makes strange noises. He does not respond emotionally, although he is always on his toes and notices a lot of things. In a drawing of his family he depicts a close and idyllic family without including himself; he explains that his place is in heaven. In personality-related tasks, Toby notices many small details, quickly begins to form associations, and blurs fantasy and reality; he does not appear to know when he crosses the line. He has violent and aggressive fantasies and uses a world of primary process thinking to remove the dangerous and aggressive content from his consciousness, using associations, denial, and idealization. He often seems to be overwhelmed with doubt and pessimism without expecting anything from the future, and he often feels that he is being attacked and pursued by evil, imaginary figures. His anxiety is easily aroused, and he begins to fantasize incoherently, imagining demon exorcism, and so on.

Risk studies of preschizophrenic children generally describe that these children have extensive social difficulties and limited communication skills and that they are withdrawn and suspicious and have low self-esteem. They seem vulnerable in social situations, and they are often insensitive and awkward with others. In connection with conflict and criticism they often feel overwhelmed, lack strategies for conflict resolution, and retreat to a world of their own. When their arousal level increases it is difficult for them to maintain a perspective that allows them to distinguish between their internal world and the external world. Their inability to manage anger and frustration makes them fearful, and when their anxiety is aroused reality gets twisted, and they hallucinate. Some of these children have behavioral problems, while others are isolated, withdrawn, and invisible (Mirsky, Ingraham, & Kugelmass, 1995; Mirsky, Kugelmass, Ingraham, Frenkel, & Nathan, 1995).

Stern argued that the schizoid personality structure stems from dysregulation on the level of the core self. The schizoid personality structure uses basic self-protection strategies that are characterized by identity confusion and inadequate reality testing. The extremely weak sense of identity leads to a feeling of depersonalization, which stems from the lack of a sense of internal coherence and a fusion of self and other (Mortensen, 2001).

We are still far from a full understanding of the neuroanatomy of schizoid dysfunction, and the models at this point remain speculative and in mutual disagreement. However, there does seem to be a strong link between dissociative detachment on a parasympathetic freeze level and psychotic symptoms. The parasympathetic freeze state means that the individual's hold on the external world is weak, which disrupts reality testing and drives the individual into an internal world that may resemble a nightmare. The dissociative freeze response not only deprives people of a connection to the external world; they also lose the sense of being connected to their body, which in turn weakens the sense of self and of their own actions. Dissociative detachment can lead to feelings of severe alienation, an experience described by many patients with psychosis. Thus, dissociative detachment not only leads to alienation from relations in the external world; it also leads to alienation from oneself (Allen, 2002).

MRI scans have documented neural changes; for example, in addition to being associated with dissociative detachment, reality distortion and the sense of alienation also appear to be associated with reduced activity in the parietal lobes, the hippocampus, the orbitofrontal cortex, and the dorsolateral prefrontal cortex in combination with elevated activity in the right hemisphere. The greater the imbalance, the more severe the psychotic symptoms. The psychotic symptoms appear to break through when the prefrontal cortex is unable to inhibit the impulses from the subcortical regions. One theory suggests that increased dopamine activity lets thought processes that are normally filtered by the basal ganglia and inhibited by the left hemisphere break through, which causes hallucinations and paranoia. In psychotic states primary process thinking intrudes into the normal states, disrupting reality testing and causing distorted thinking; this experience is often described as a dreamlike state (Cozolino, 2000). Another theory points to a difference between the dopamine circuits, which all originate in two structures in the brain stem: the ventral tegmental region and the substantia nigra. The dopamine paths that originate in the substantia nigra project to the basal ganglia and play an important role in regulating movements, while the dopamine paths that originate in the ventral tegmental region branch out into two areas: the limbic system and the frontal lobes. The modern view of schizophrenia focuses on disorders in the latter circuit, which may lead to abnormal cognitive development, among other consequences (Goldberg, 2001). Subtle changes have also been identified in the frontal part of the cingulate gyrus, which is part of a circuit with the amygdala and the hippocampus, changes that cause attention deficit disorder and an inability to counteract impulses from the limbic system (Kandel, 2005).

Many of the negative symptoms in schizophrenia, such as the lack of initiative, the flat emotions, and the impaired working memory, mental flexibility, and executive functions, resemble the problems seen in association with damage to the dorsolateral prefrontal cortex. Normal problem solving involves an activation of prefrontal regions and a reduction in temporal lobe activity, as the prefrontal cortex inhibits impulses from the limbic system, among other structures. In psychosis, however, there is no synchronicity between prefrontal activation and temporal deactivation. The positive symptoms of schizophrenia such as paranoia, hallucinations, and reality distortions stem from an overactivation of the dopamine circuit (Hansen, 2002). Children who are in a high-risk group for developing schizophrenia show neurointegrative shortcomings and dopamine-based hyperactivation at an early stage in their lives. People with schizophrenia have a tendency toward perseveration, which is a frontal lobe syndrome, and the first obvious manifestations of schizophrenia typically appear around the age of 16–18 years, which is the age when the frontal lobes become functionally mature.

Psychological Disorders on the Limbic Level

Borderline Personality Disorder

Sandra is 14 years old, and toward people she does not know she is a nice, helpful, and charming girl. She is good at making friends, but they are often replaced. She is impulsive and can tell made-up stories so convincingly that, for example, she once bluffed the police for 3 hours concerning her identity. She has no respect for her teachers; she resists demands and often makes offensive remarks. When it was her mother's birthday, she stole a bag that one of her classmates had made and gave it to her mother as a birthday present. She enjoys close contact; for example, she enjoys sitting on her mother's lap like a much younger child.

Conflicts at home culminated with Sandra pushing her grandfather down the stairs and kicking him while he was down. On another occasion she attempted to strangle her younger sister, leaving black marks on the little girl's neck. When she is confronted with what she has done, she cries; however, she does not seem remorseful but laughs with contempt. Her father's current wife is the only person capable of occasionally "softening" her enough to describe in words what she is feeling; usually this happens after a prolonged conflict when Sandra breaks down crying, and then she remains nice and easy to deal with for a few days.

In 1938, Adolph Stern introduced the term borderline about patients who did not fit the definitions in the diagnostic system that was in use at the time, but the beginnings of a diagnosis that lies between psychosis and neurosis date back to the early 1900s (Gammelgaard, 2004). As Sørensen (1996, 2005) has explained, it is feasible and appropriate to view the personality structure in borderline personality disorder as a borderline mode, which means a characteristic organization of the personality structure. With gradual transitions, this mode may exist both as a personality feature and as a personality disorder. Kernberg (Sørensen 2006) distinguished between early and late-developing borderline personality organization; Schore (1994) also mentioned that the neurobiology differs in early and late-developing borderline states. In my opinion, the distinction between early and late borderline disorders hinges on the presence or absence of feelings of shame or embarrassment. Kernberg argued that the borderline state is not an isolated personality disorder but in fact encompasses many different personality disorders with the common feature of being organized on a borderline level (Gammelgaard, 2004). There is a distinction between the extrovert variant, which is characterized by emotional instability and a lack of impulse control, and the introvert variant, which is characterized by insecure self-perception, discontent, intense and unstable relationships with others, and a tendency toward self-destructive behavior. A person with an extrovert borderline personality disorder lives out her narcissistic rage and often relates dramatic experiences involving herself without any emotional content. A person with an introvert variant reacts with passive anger, for example, through self-destructive behavior, which facilitates the release of endogenous opioids, as mentioned earlier (Perry, 1997).

Borderline personality disorder is characterized by a pattern of unstable relations and a disturbed and insecure self-image. There are severe disturbances of secondary process thinking and frequently problems with affect regulation, reality testing, and impulse control; for example, the mood is unstable and capricious. The difficulties with affect regulation lead to a high degree of reactivity in relation to slight triggers, as the person responds with inappropriate aggressive outbursts or severe anxiety. The tolerance of emotional discomfort and pain is low, which results in destructive behavior to self and others, for example, in the form of substance abuse, prostitution, self-harming behavior, and aggressive outbursts. Severe pressure may lead to psychotic episodes, as regression to primary process thinking occurs in unstructured situations or in situations involving strong emotional pressure (Gammelgaard 2004; Herman & van der Kolk, 1987).

The borderline state is characterized by self-protection strategies such as splitting and projective identification, a feeling of inner emptiness, and thoughts of suicide. Under stress the autonomic regulatory functions are activated and lead to freezing or hyperactivity. The splitting keeps powerful and contradictory emotions apart, and what feels evil and unbearable is dissociated and lives its own separate life. Other people are perceived as fully good or fully evil, and the borderline individual either does not worry about these contradictions or uses denial. The person's self-perceptions shift between omnipotence and impotence (Schore, 1994). Winnicott argued that the transitional object has a comforting function, and others have argued that this is a prerequisite for repression to begin to replace the more primitive splitting mechanism.

The infant needs the caregiver's support to develop more mature self-protection strategies. If the child has been exposed to extensive dysregulation, where for example, ambivalence or hostility has prevented the child from having his basic needs for loving care met, the limbic regions do not develop adequate connections to the frontal section of the cingulate gyrus and the orbitofrontal cortex, among other structures (Juengling et al., 2003; Schore, 2003a). Hence, the borderline states are probably characterized more as a disintegrated than a regressive disorder, although most people under heavy psychological pressure may regress to borderline states. Inadequate development of the orbitofrontal structures does not necessarily mean that the person lacks artistic creativity but rather the form of creativity that unfolds in mentalizing interactions with others. The development of the prefrontal cortex lets us separate past, present, and future. Part of the difficulty is that grieving cannot take place, just as imagination and thinking turn into concrete references—this implies that thinking is the same as action or realization. Internal representations have no symbolic character; instead, fantasy becomes compulsive activities that must be lived out. Unlike symbolized representations, the fantasies are not subject to sublimation, repression, and so on. Being stuck on a level of limbic organization means being stuck in the present, seeking immediate gratification. "Living in the moment may seem existentially enriching. Being trapped in the time perspective of the moment may in fact be quite the opposite" (Gammelgaard, 2004, p. 110; translated for this edition).

Children and adults with a borderline personality often have a dramatic attitude; they shun intimacy, and like the ambivalent child they may be demanding or possessive. They do possess empathy but are unable to distinguish between their own needs and those of others, and often they are only briefly able to reflect on their own and other people's feelings. The frequent shifts in dissociated mental states often lead to a chaotic and unspoken fear, which they attempt to escape. Stressful social events often trigger a sympathetic state in the form of rage or a parasympathetic state of despair in the form of freezing, which creates a sense of not being in charge of one's own impulses or of disappearing into nothing (Karen, 1998; Schore, 1994). A desperate longing for symbiotic intimacy results in brief periods of intense attachment, where the other is idealized, but this quickly turns to rage and painful withdrawal when the person's unmet need for care is frustrated. Thus, attachment relationships are often brief, ambivalent, and chaotic but extremely intense. There is often an appeal for contact, but as soon as the contact is established, ambivalence and the limited mentalization capacity that characterize the borderline personality organization lead to frightening emotional confusion and an inner chaos that renders the relationship problematic and destructive. A person with a borderline personality disorder is unable to differentiate clearly between his internal representations and those of others or between internal representations and external reality. As the feeling of attachment grows, so does the feeling of being excluded, which leads to a state of extreme internal tension from which the person has to flee. The person is frightened by his own aggressive impulses and fantasies about the other, and very soon the person will either reject or arrange to be rejected by the other. As Gammelgaard (2004) put it, persons with a borderline personality disorder are always moving toward something as well as moving away. They fear intimacy as desperately as they yearn for it.

Omnipotence and Psychopathy

Kasper is a charming 8-year-old boy, who in his parents' eyes has always been a particularly wonderful and special child. As an infant he slept little; he was a demanding baby who was breast-fed about 10 times a day. He has never been able to delay the gratification of his needs. When he was young he wanted to be carried all the time, and if he was left to himself he would scream. He has always been precocious, demands a great deal of attention, and is very physically active with no ability to concentrate. He has no situational awareness, and he is argumentative. He enjoys being the center of attention and wants to be the best at everything he does. He is able to play on his own for hours on end, but it is difficult for him to spend time with children his own age because he is bossy and likes to change the rules when it suits him.

Omnipotence is a narcissistic disorder that is characterized by the child's need to be the center of everyone's admiration. Criticism or opposition is met with anger; the child considers himself the natural center of attention and has difficulty empathizing. The child feels grandiose, but behind this feeling is often a profound sense of insecurity. Omnipotent children have often been raised by parents who were full of admiration and who accepted the child's omnipotent sides without intervening with shame regulation and helping the child progress from need-based behavior to the reality principle. The child has been neither confronted nor disciplined, and the parents have found it difficult to tolerate the child's distress. Shame is associated with the expectation of painful disorganization, and the child will do anything to avoid this state (Schore, 1994).

The child remains in the intense positive affect that feeds the grandiose state; unlike children with a borderline structure, children with a narcissistic disorder are often securely attached to their parents. The parents have been good caregivers for their child but have failed to act as adequate socialization agents. The inhibition of infantile grandiosity and omnipotence does not take place, and feelings of shame are routinely avoided. The noradrenaline-based system fails to develop properly and is not balanced by the dopamine-based circuit, which prevents the impulse-inhibiting structures in the orbitofrontal cortex from reaching full maturity. The maturation of emotional control through inhibition is the prerequisite for developing affect-regulating structures in the orbitofrontal cortex (Schore, 1994). Apparently, other medial parts of the prefrontal cortex do mature, enabling the child to predict and perceive other people's emotions through cognitive representations of other minds. However, the child is unable to connect these representations with the emotional control centers in the orbitofrontal cortex. At a later time, the child learns to inhibit impulses with the objective of enhancing the feeling of grandiosity and furthering his own needs. The omnipotent child distinguishes between his own and others' needs but is so preoccupied with having his own needs met that other people's needs are ignored. In some adults, this state is characterized as psychopathy.

Psychological Disorders on the Prefrontal Level

Disorders that develop after the circuit connections to the orbitofrontal and dorsolateral prefrontal cortex have been established can be categorized as impulse inhibition disorders. Impulses from emotionally related structures such as the basal ganglia and the amygdala are prevented from being expressed in a symbolized form due to exaggerated impulse inhibition, among other factors. Psychological disorders on this level of mental organization are characterized by a normal development of limbic functions and the ability to engage in close and deep relationships. The child is able to tolerate anxiety and capable of impulse control, and is capable of targeted and creative behavior and of inhibiting, repressing, and sublimating desires and impulses. Often, the child's difficulties consist of feelings of guilt or of a desire to be able to control himself as well as the environment.

Hysteriform Disorders

Seven-year-old Matthew is only barely able to sit and incapable of standing or walking. A somatic examination revealed no physical reasons for these difficulties. He seems older than his years and is keen to express himself verbally to adults; he is chatty, laughs, and moves about, but when he is with his parents he is weepy and says that he is in pain. He does not seem to notice this contrast in behavior. He is one of the best in his class but does not think of himself as a high achiever. He finds school difficult to handle because it is so noisy. He seems competent but vulnerable and almost unrealistically anxious about his achievements.

Hysterical reactions mean that the child is unable to feel or sense certain parts of his body. The amygdala is connected to the extrapyramidal (nonvolitional) motor system in the basal ganglia and the parietal lobes, which control body sensations. Emotional activity in the limbic system connects to the motor and body-sensing systems that control the body senses and muscles. Impulses from the limbic system that are inhibited by the prefrontal cortex cannot be expressed on a higher mental or symbolized level. When emotional impulses cannot be expressed, they organize on a lower hierarchical level, partly through somatization. Inhibiting neurotransmitters probably deactivate sensory and motor functions in certain body parts. For example, dissociated anger that is not expressed verbally may find a somatic expression through hysterical symptoms. Recent neuroimaging methods have documented that wriggling one's fingers will make the motor cortex (which is responsible for sending out orders about the proper motor sequence) and the premotor cortex (which prepares the finger movements) light up. A brain scan of a hysterically paralyzed patient showed that when the patient attempted to move his leg, the motor cortex did not light up the way it should, even though the patient claimed that he was trying to move his leg. The reason was that the frontal parts of the cingulate gyrus and the orbitofrontal cortex were activated instead, apparently inhibiting the patient's attempts at moving the leg. The frontal parts of the cingulate gyrus and the orbitofrontal cortex are intimately connected with the limbic system, and hysteria is an emotional disorder, which in this case prevents the person from moving his "paralyzed" leg. We still know very little about the underlying neurobiology of hysteriform disorders (Damasio, 2003; Ramachandran, 2003; Schore, 2003b).

Obsessive-Compulsive Disorders

Niles, age 16, was raised in a nuclear family by parents who were both academics. When Niles was 9 years old his mother died of cancer after being ill for just a few weeks. Niles says that from that time on he began to pray. He prayed for longer and longer periods, and eventually it became an obsession that might last several hours. He began to clean the house, until it was spick-and-span. He washed his hands constantly, and he would vacuum for 4 hours a day. When he came close to breaking down, his symptoms increased in strength. He felt that a disaster would ensue if he did break down. He was trapped in rituals and even ritualized his rituals until he felt that he was caught in a web that he could not escape. He is ambitious and would like to study, but his many rituals keep him from pursuing this dream. Lately he has felt depressed and has considered suicide because of his obsessive-compulsive symptoms.

Obsessive-compulsive disorder (OCD) consists of obsessive-compulsive thoughts (e.g., "Did I turn off the stove?" "Did I lock the door?"), acts (such as excessive hand washing out of an anxiety about germs), and rituals (often associated with superstition or religiosity). The thoughts and acts seem meaningless or exaggerated, but the child cannot escape them, often out of fear of what might happen or because resisting the compulsion makes the child uncomfortable. The child has to be perfect and often has to repeat the acts over and over again to live up to self-imposed standards. Obsessive-compulsive thoughts do not occur until the child is 9–13 years old and are most common in boys (Thomsen, 1996).

OCD is probably caused by intrusive reactivated emotional impulses from the limbic system that the child is unable to process. Structures in the prefrontal cortex inhibit the intrusive and dangerous emotional impulses by causing stereotypical and repetitive behavior. It appears that OCD is a form of displacement activity that the person relies on when a particular pain seems unbearable or unmanageable.

The subcortical neural circuits that are activated by the reminder of anxious stimuli initiate a cycle where the prefrontal cortex is hyperacti-vated to ward off the anxious stimuli. Meanwhile, the subcortical im-pulses intensify in strength. The symptoms present on a subcortical level, which gives the child a sense of being controlled by this internal state. The original event that triggered the circuit gradually loses impor-tance, as the neural circuits come to be triggered by stimuli that are merely derived from the original cause (Bradley, 2000; Panksepp, 1998).

The person shuts out forbidden emotional impulses through repres-sion. To control the impulses and keep them from reaching daytime consciousness, the feelings are controlled and inhibited through obses-sive-compulsive acts, thoughts, and ritualized behavior. The nervous system is in a state of constant sympathetic activation with a downregu-lation of the serotonin level and an overactivation of noradrenaline but not of cortisol. This activation reflects the attempt of the nervous system to manage the state, even if the coping strategies are counterproductive (Sapolsky, 1998).

Neurobiologically, OCD is associated with excessive frontal lobe activ-ity, which results in the inhibition of impulses and movements that are under frontal lobe control. OCD is also associated with excessive activity in the basal ganglia (caudate nucleus), which handle certain aspects of automatic thinking; the frontal part of the cingulate gyrus, which is in charge of motivation, is also highly activated. Damage to the frontal part of the cingulate gyrus improves the OCD state, among other things by reducing neurotic behavior. In OCD, cognitive and motor acts are acti-vated in an attempt to cope with the threat (Carter, 1998; Juengling et al., 2003; Tucker & Derryberry, 1992), but for OCD too, we have yet to fully crack the neurobiological code, and the chain of causal factors out-lined above remains speculative.

Summary

A child's innate capacities and the environment that the child interacts with combine to determine personality development. How much stress a child can handle depends on the innate constitution of the nervous sys-tem. Vulnerability depends on the interaction of nature and nurture and is not explained by either genes or experiences alone. Certain syndromes only develop in some parts of the world and not in others, which must mean that the expression of mental disorders is partially shaped by our environment.

No hereditary disposition for mental illness is so massive that the environment cannot mitigate, stop, or prevent its outbreak. A sufficiently malign environment can generate mental illness, regardless of disposition. One key aspect of our human biology is that we can only fully develop our humanity with the help of other loving human beings (Sørensen, 1996, p. 298).

Our neuroaffective knowledge is still insufficient to allow us to link psychological disorders with neural circuit disorders. But as this knowledge grows, it will hopefully have a greater impact on the psychological and psychiatric assessment and treatment of psychological disorders. As Sørensen (2005) pointed out, imprecise diagnoses carry an overwhelming risk of imprecise treatment that does more harm than good. Greater knowledge in this field would allow us to offer more precise and targeted treatment by enabling us to target our interventions toward specific neural networks.

In Part III I discuss how intervention and treatment can be targeted from a neuroaffective and developmental point of view. Chapter 7 reviews the aspects that are crucial for the establishment of a psychotherapeutic working alliance. Chapter 8 describes how interventions take place through bottom-up and top-down processes and take aim at specific structures in the hierarchical brain, and Chapter 9 discusses aspects of psychotherapeutic intervention in a family dynamics perspective.

PART THREE

—⧓—

Intervention
and Neuroaffective
Developmental
Psychology

CHAPTER SEVEN

Limbic Exchange:
Treatment Effect Across
Therapeutic Approaches

*Within the effulgence of their new brain, mammals developed a
capacity we call limbic resonance—a symphony of mutual exchange and internal adaptation whereby two mammals become
attuned to each other's internal states. . . . Limbic resonance sup-
plies the wordless harmony we see everywhere but take for granted. . . . [T]he limbic activity of those around us draws our emotions into almost immediate congruence.*

Thomas Lewis et al. (2001, pp. 63–64)

Effect studies (Lambert, 1992; Roth & Fonagy, 1996; Weinberger, 1993)
of therapy have found that a successful therapeutic process relies much
more on the therapeutic alliance than on the particular approach and
theory. Orlinsky and Howard (1986) found that clients who trusted their
therapist were far more cooperative and achieved better attunement.
Although the various forms of therapy like to promote their differences,
the therapeutic relationship appears to be the most powerful healing
factor, and there are far more similarities than differences in the therapist's interactions with clients in successful therapeutic processes. Psychotherapy and environmental treatment (an intervention form where
the physical and social environment is used as the arena for psychotherapy) essentially address a basic human need to feel seen and understood
by others, a need that evolved from mammals' needs to feel socially related to others (Cozolino, 2000; Schore, 2003b). The current use of the
term relational disorders is, as Sørensen (2005) pointed out, indicative
of the source and appropriate treatment of personality disorders. There
is a wide range of psychoactive drugs targeting psychological symptoms,

but they only treat the symptoms; a cure requires a relationship that in many ways resembles the healthy caregiver-infant relationship. It is the mutual emotional attunement between client and therapist that constitutes the treatment, not intellectual or emotional insight or emotional release. The only thing capable of curing an attachment disorder is the establishment of an attachment based on appropriate emotional attunement, which is why psychotherapy can be effective.

As mentioned earlier, Daniel Stern has described how self-perception relies on other people's presence and actions, and how the child's development is facilitated by a caregiver who engages in interactions with the child, as if the infant's mastery goes slightly beyond what maturity level would predict (Stern, 1995, p. 51). Lev Vygotsky (1978) argued that the basic mechanisms for internalizing higher psychological functions arise within interactions, which only later develop into intrapsychic mechanisms. The internalization process takes place within what Vygotsky calls the zone of proximal development, which he defined as those functions that have not yet developed but which are emerging. What the child is currently only able to do with help from the caregiver, he will master independently in the future (cf. Chapter 1). Thus, all higher personality functions develop as the result of social interaction. In asymmetric relationships, such as teacher-student, therapist-client, and so on, there is a responsibility to protect and support the child or client through the zone that lies beyond their current coping capacity. The qualities that are found in the healthy caregiver-child relationship are replicated in the healthy therapist-client interaction. Forming an alliance with the client and possessing qualities such as warmth, understanding, and a focus on therapeutic goals are the underlying factors that determine the therapeutic outcome. Indeed, more recently developed therapeutic approaches do seem to put far greater emphasis on the therapist's supportive empathic qualities and the authenticity of the connection to ensure that clients feels safe to express emotions and to risk addressing emotionally painful aspects of their life. Although this chapter explores the relational aspect of the therapeutic process, the importance of theories, concepts, and systematic knowledge about therapeutic intervention should not be underestimated.

This chapter addresses the understanding of the asymmetric therapeutic alliance in the perspective of so-called dynamic systemic theory, which views the brain as a nonlinear self-organizing system that develops through interactions with another nonlinear self-organizing system.

As stated earlier, the asymmetric alliance has similarities with the attunement that takes place in the healthy caregiver-child relationship, and the present chapter illustrates how this attunement can be transferred to the therapeutic relationship. The following section outlines the philosophical basis for nonlinear systems, while the section after that relates this perspective to the nervous system.

Dynamic Systemic Theory as an Explanation Model for the Therapeutic Process of Change

Brain systems organize in hierarchical patterns that are interconnected in complex circuits. This principle of neural development applies to all successive learning, and according to systemic theory it also applies to all forms of development based on self-organization. In nonlinear systems, various movement patterns are present simultaneously, and even small initial variations can alter the course. Everything is interconnected, whether neurons, human beings, or planets (Strogatz, 2003). Nonlinear systems are characterized by the fact that the whole is different from the sum of the parts. Life depends on nonlinear systems, and biology relies on them everywhere.

According to systemic theory, new adaptive forms of self-organization develop on the basis of underlying components to form a complex hierarchical structure. As new competencies develop, the underlying components stabilize (Thelen, 1989). The neural patterns form out of the many components, and thus the self-organizing system becomes more interconnected and organized. The nervous system is stabilized by the many neural connections and combinations and becomes increasingly able to maintain constancy in the face of environmental variation. The nervous system is sensitive to even minor changes that can be used to stabilize and direct the nervous system toward a desired state. Even minor changes may initially destabilize the nervous system, but this process helps to enhance flexibility to generate a wide repertoire of adaptation strategies (Thelen, 1995). As the nervous system develops, it prefers a certain organization and a certain environmental context, and it seeks out previously established patterns. The stability of the system depends on its capacity for switching between states. The nervous system develops through a process of self-organization where levels of mental organization are established, one on top of the other. Each level of mental organization builds on the preceding level, and all the mental organization patterns are represented in the hierarchical development. The maturation of the nervous system during childhood is characterized by varying stages of rapid and slow development and stabilization on different levels (Sander, 1977, 1983, 1988).

The nervous system is a complex organization, which changes in a process that develops new forms of adaptation while preserving overall continuity. Changes occur in a nonlinear fashion, and no one can predict when a given change will occur, or which specific form the development will assume. Development represents a new element that is generated through the self-organization of the nervous system, and which may push the nervous system into a new state. In a nonlinear system, many different patterns and movements may change simultaneously, which may alter the course of the system. These changes may cause turbulence; sometimes they confer a developmental advantage, while at other times they thrust the system into chaos. Systemic theory predicts that even minor changes in self-organization can lead to major changes in behavior, which is what makes psychotherapy possible (Schore, 2003b; Siegel, 1999). From the very beginning, caregiver and infant are mutually related, and normally they will coordinate their activity with each other. Their way of engaging in an attuned dyadic process is extremely flexible and has room for wide variation in a process that is crucial for the integration and differentiation of the nervous system (Thelen & Smith, 1994).

The Self-Organizing Brain

In any dyad, whether it is the caregiver-child or the therapist-client relationship, the nervous system acts as a self-organizing system that generates its own states of brain organization. This organization can be expanded to more coherent and complex states by interacting with another self-organizing system. The motivation to establish emotional bonding is an innate capacity. When two persons fail to attune homeostatically or emotionally, there can be no development.

Due to the nonlinear character of the nervous system, it is not only the specifically activated brain structure that changes in the dyadic process. For example, when a rabbit is presented with various olfactory impressions, a specific electric pattern is activated in the rabbit's brain.

When the rabbit is presented with a new smell, not only does the brain develop a new pattern for this particular olfactory impression, but when a previously encountered olfactory impression is presented again, this pattern has also changed. The new olfactory impression not only generates a new pattern, it also results in the reorganization of existing patterns. Existing neural circuits are altered by what happens in the present, and thus, what happens in the present has the power to alter the past. A successful therapeutic process should reorganize and integrate the neural circuits that were formed through inappropriate regulation strategies in the past (Freeman, 1994; Morgan, 1998).

The changes in the therapeutic relationship take place through microscopic moments of meeting (see Chapter 1, the section on the interactive dance and present moments, pp. 26–27) that cause microscopic changes in the neural circuits. Rigid and inflexible patterns may be resistant to change, and certain neural patterns that have emerged through severely traumatic events may be immune to what happens in the present. Past events have a radical influence on the present, and at times it takes a long, hard effort to alter previously established neural circuits, despite the general principle that the present constantly rewrites the past. Some neurophysiological changes may be irreversibly established at an early stage in development through critical periods and severe trauma and conflict. The consequences of massive early emotional deprivation are an example of neural circuits that are so entrenched that we have yet to find interventions capable of changing them (Gunnar, 2001; Stern, 2004).

Today, the brain is considered a self-organizing system, but it is nevertheless a permeable system that relies on external stimulation for its development. In personality development, stimulation occurs through the child's interactions with the primary caregivers and later with other key individuals, including peers. The following sections describe how the dyadic process unfolds through psychobiological regulation and limbic resonance, among other avenues.

Psychobiological Regulation

As discussed in Chapter 1, physiobiological and psychobiological regulation begins from the moment the child is born. The main focus of the first 2 months is on the regulation of physical needs; later, psychological states are regulated as well. In this process the caregiver provides psychological coherence, and regulation is modified from moment to moment. In the early regulation, vocalization soon becomes important, and rhythm and vocal tonality have a direct effect on psychobiological motivation. In the therapeutic process, the therapist also strives to provide a caring context that can facilitate growth and development. Through the therapeutic alliance and the empathic attunement with the client, the therapist attempts to activate attachment processes, modulate anxiety and stress levels, and create an optimum biochemical environment that can promote neural plasticity. When internal or external factors prevent the person from approaching challenging, stressful situations, the neural system tends to remain underdeveloped and unintegrated. The ability to self-organize is biological, and receiving support in challenging this capacity facilitates development and vitality.

Mutually synchronized attunement generates autonomic and limbic attunement, which in addition to developing the affective areas also fine-tunes the heart rate, blood pressure, body temperature, immune functions, oxygen metabolism, glucose levels, hormones, and so on. In the psychotherapeutic relationship the therapist seeks to alter the micro-anatomy of the client's brain. When an autonomic or limbic connection has been established as a neural pattern, it takes an autonomic or limbic connection to change it. The integration and reintegration of neural circuits require the nervous system to connect and engage in a field of resonance with another nervous system. Successful limbic attunement enables the nervous system to develop flexibility and integrate neural patterns that spread hierarchically throughout the brain. Dyadic communication makes it possible to create resonance and coherence within the nervous system.

Development and integration emerge in a balance of care and optimum levels of stress. Moderate arousal or optimum levels of stress integrate and consolidate neural circuits, provided the stress level does not exceed the capacity of the nervous system. Activation of the nervous system past this threshold leads to substantial sympathetic activation, which inhibits cortical processing and disrupts the integrative functions. Moderate sympathetic arousal intensifies the ability of the network to process and integrate information. The therapeutic process consists of emotionally calm and agitated moments and thus reflects the underlying neural rhythm for growth and change. Optimum levels of arousal and stress result in an increase in neurotransmitters and neural growth hormones, which enhances learning and cortical reorganization. A successful therapeutic process develops the brain circuitry, and much of the neural integration and reorganization takes place in the associative regions in the frontal, temporal, and parietal lobes; brain regions that coordinate, regulate, and direct large numbers of neural circuits (Cozolino, 2000).

Limbic Resonance

As mentioned earlier, as humans we have an innate potential for engaging in attuned and synchronized interactions with our environment, and the stability of the interaction depends on early synchronization with a caregiver. Limbic circuits develop through stimulation, and the child can only achieve full limbic potential when engaging in affectively attuned contact with the caregiver. The child responds emotionally to others as if they represented important characters from the past, and the meaning of past events can distort new attunements. As humans, we include each other in our emotional reality through limbic attunement and trigger implicit memories and emotional states both in ourselves and in others. When we interact, we are attracted by each other's emotional worlds; we attune emotionally and thus affect each other. Our understanding of others is reflected back to us and may influence others' self-perception and neural circuitry. Our limbic resonance enables us to understand our own and other people's internal worlds. Limbic resonance is comparable to primary intersubjectivity, which is described in Chapter 1. Affective attunement and affirmation are aspects of being seen and acknowledged, and it is this relational process that develops our personality. Through limbically attuned contact, information is transmitted about the other person's inner world, and when two people allow the field of resonance to be accessed, we are able to develop a sense of what it is like to be inside the other person's emotional universe. Feeling that one is being seen or "limbically known" by someone is the first step in an emotional healing process and in changing one's experiential world (Lewis et al., 2001; Schibbye, 2005).

Resonance Phenomena

Resonance occurs when vibrations or oscillations in one system set off oscillations in another system, which amplifies the oscillations in both involved systems. Resonance plays a key role in brain organization and in the regulatory processes of the central nervous system. The switch between attunement and misattunement occurs through rapid organizational shifts in the nervous system. Sander (1977) has argued that infants begin life with an endogenous rhythmic activity that has to be coordinated with a partner, and that the nervous system has a biological motivational capacity for arranging information, discovering regularities, and acting on expectations. The internal process is organized by the nervous system through mutual regulation with another nervous system, and these common experiences gradually generate intimacy, attachment, mutual attunement, self-regulation, and self-reflection. Through cross-modal transfer the behavior one observes in a partner, such as a facial expression, is associated with one's own internal emotional state and perception (Beebe & Lachmann, 2002).

The human nervous system seeks to discover other people's experiences by engaging in fields of resonance with them. As humans we are born interactive, and most of the time the boundaries between ourselves and others are apparent but permeable. Individuals with a well-integrated nervous system engage in fields of resonance with each other's intentions, emotions, and thoughts, which are constantly modified or generated in dialogues with other people's perceived intentions. Thoughts originate in dialogues, even when these dialogues are intrapsychic. By observing another person's facial expression, posture, and movements, we are able to have feelings that are fairly close to that person's feelings. The nervous system is constructed to enable us to experience someone else's nervous system from within by generating a field of resonance with it and thus partaking of the other person's perceptions. Apparently, the nervous system is emotionally affected by the other person's behavior, and this phenomenon forms the very basis of empathy (Stern, 2004).

In the therapeutic process, the therapist must be able to achieve a vitalizing positive attunement with the client. The core of empathy is the ability to match the other person's affect and respond in resonance. The positive attunement builds trust and acts as the driving force in the establishment of attachment bonds. Through resonance and synchronicity, the therapist forms attachment bonds with the client and thus promotes the client's implicit (unconscious) awareness of previous relational strategies that have hampered psychological development. The therapeutic process is implicit, and the therapist has to notice the mood, the feeling behind the words, as well as the turning point when a state is beginning to change. The key is to "listen to the music behind the words." When the therapist is empathically attuned with the client's internal state, the contact is amplified and vitalized (Hammer, 1990; Schore, 2003b; Stern, 1984; Trevarthen, 1979).

Right and Left Hemisphere

Schore (2003b) noted that the right hemisphere is mostly involved in implicit (unconscious) activity and spontaneous expressions. The right hemisphere enables a dialogue between two or more persons' limbic systems, and this is where the therapeutic alliance emerges. The key is to communicate in resonance and to sense intuitively when a state is changing. The left hemisphere is also important and active in the verbal exchange and logical reflections on the client's life as well as in the processing of the emotions that are brought out in therapy. Left-to-left hemispheric resonance unfolds as verbal communication, which is linear and logical. Right-to-right hemispheric resonance involves nonverbal components such as intonation, gestures, and facial expressions (Siegel, 1999).

The Improvisational Process

Primary intersubjective relating or limbic resonance unfolds through microinteractions that cannot be improved upon, as they are an improvisational process that caregiver and child create together in the present moment (Stern, 1998a, 1998b, 2004). This process can be transferred to the therapeutic process.

In the caregiver-child interaction many activities come to represent schemas for ways of being with others. Stern (1998b) pointed out that infants need a special form of care that adults have to provide. The mother has to fall in love with her child, and the child has to fall in love with the mother; this rarely occurs right away but develops gradually through an improvisational process. A mother has to trust her innate maternal behavior, and to keep her infant interested and aroused she has to improvise and vary her behavior. This is the process that should be duplicated in the therapy room.

Psychotherapy, which is based on limbic resonance, follows this process through improvisational interaction. Most of the time this is simply a back-and-forth exchange, and then suddenly there is an intense shift. This is a movement between two people that requires an authentic presence in the intersubjective space, where the implicit knowledge between therapist and client is allowed to merge. Both the therapist and the client must be able to move freely in this process, and there has to be time for fun if the process is to be productive. "You have to improvise, ad hoc, and let things happen as they will. The therapist and the client don't know what's going to happen the next moment. Good therapy follows the process, not the theory. What is said is created the moment it happens" (Stern, 2001, quoted from my personal notes).

To move forward in the therapeutic space is a spontaneous and unpredictable process, and seen from the outside it may be difficult to discern any sense of direction. Connecting in the intersubjective space requires many different spontaneous exchanges, many misunderstandings, misattunements, and so on. Even the best interactions include many misattunements, but most of them are quickly repaired by both parties. The misattunements are valuable because they lead to negotiations around the reparation of misattunements, and these little mistakes are essential for getting to know one another. The unpredictable process is only potentially creative when it unfolds in a well-established setting, for example, the client-therapist relationship. It is essential that the therapist work within a particular technique and theory where he or she feels comfortable. Stern (2004) noted the importance of having a clear theoretical framework for the unfolding events in order for them to make any sense. Bowlby described how the best therapy takes place with a therapist who is naturally intuitive, that is, who can use subjective implicit experience, and who is guided by a well-chosen theory (Schore, 2003b).

Therapy as a Momentary Process

> There is never anything but the present, and if one cannot live there, one cannot live anywhere. (Watts 1957, p. 124)

The past affects the perceptions and experiences that are formed in the present. In therapy the objective is to change the internal representations of the past in order to be able to choose other elements that might influence the future. We live in the present, and this is where the experiences from our past unfold. Thus, the present is the moment when past and present come together. The part of the past that affects the present can be reorganized in the intersubjective meeting, which consists of a series of present moments (Stern, 2004). In the present moments the child "becomes aware that another is aware of what the child is aware within" (Sander, 1995, p. 590). Present moments like this facilitate identity development; they are healing and capable of changing the organization of the brain. They help create neural coherence and develop self-regulating strategies. Psychotherapeutic healing takes place in the meeting with the other rather than through insight. Through the mutual affirmation of the other's gaze, one becomes present in one's own right. This is the essence of identity development, and if one is not met with this form of affirmation, there is no space within which the identity can unfold.

The connection between two nervous systems involves a dyadic form of resonance, where energy and information can flow freely. When the connection is fully synchronized it feels like an overwhelming sense of closeness, clarity, and authenticity. These high-energy moments are what Sander calls "moments of meeting," where the client really feels met, and where a transformation from one developmental level to the next is possible. This high-energy moment is created by the two together and requires authenticity from both the client and the therapist. This is the event that transforms the intersubjective field between therapist and client and thus also the client's implicit knowledge about being with a significant other. For these meetings to occur, there must be a mutual recognition of the other's subjective reality, and each person must understand and affirm a common version of what is going on between them. The present moment provides a sense of openness and bonding that activates the hippocampus, the frontal part of the cingulate gyrus, and the orbitofrontal cortex and enables an integration process (Lyons-Ruth, 1998; Sander, 1992; Siegel, 2004).

Present Moments

Present moments are steps in a process of moving along. A present moment is typically brief and consists of the time it takes to develop a sense of what is happening right now. In the parent-child interaction the repetition of activities is like a movement that generates a repertoire of present moments. The repetitions are familiar catalogs of the expected shape of life moments with a specific other person as the two move along together (Stern, 1998a). When present moments are linked together, they form a process of moving along (see Fig. 7.1) that is an improvisation, where something begins to move toward a target. Each step in this process of moving along is a present moment, where one unit of subjective time plays out a motif in order to microregulate the content and goal of psychotherapy and adjust the intersubjectivity. The therapeutic process is often made up of countless undramatic moments of meeting and maybe a few dramatic ones, which generate change when they are linked together. Often, it is the small changes that bring about the large changes (Morgan, 1998). Sometimes, a present moment takes affective significance for the therapeutic process. These moments are called now moments. A now moment is a special form of present moment that pulls the participants more actively into the present. In a now moment something important happens between two people that affects the future. Now moments are characterized by something new coming up in a complex dynamic system. When a now moment is seized and acknowledged by both parties, that is, when both parties provide an authentic, personal

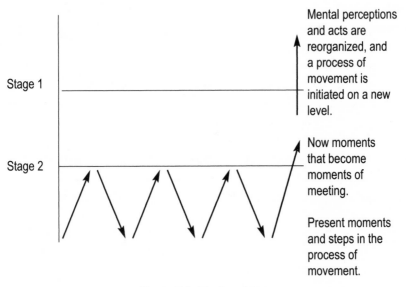

Figure 7.1. Moving along

response, the moment becomes a moment of meeting, which occurs when both parties share the same experience, and there is a mutual experience of sharing a mental landscape. A moment of meeting occurs as a sudden, unexpected qualitative and distinct leap that is affectively charged, and which pulls the participants into the present. It is a nonlinear leap that may surprise both the therapist and the client. Stern (1998a, 1998b) used an example from the caregiver-child interaction to explain a moment of meeting: Suddenly a funny expression or an unexpected outburst may cause a synchronization that makes them both laugh at the same time. The interaction is pushed to a higher level of activation, and the infant experiences a joy that he had not previously achieved, and which had not previously been shared by the two. The altered state enables new mental perceptions and acts, and previous events can be reorganized (Stern et al., 1998).

In therapy, present moments repeat variations on routine features in a relationship, that is, the unique character of the movement within any therapeutic dyad. Present moments are limited by the character of the therapeutic technique, the participants' personalities, and the psychological disorder in question. In everyday communication and thus also in the therapeutic space, it is a common occurrence that one party is not present in the moment because he is preoccupied with the past, the future. or other aspects of the present. To push development to a new level requires the courage to meet these moments with an authentic response that is spontaneous and therefore has to carry the therapist's personal signature. In now moments the therapy shifts to a new improvisational process but in an expanded intersubjective field that is open to new possibilities. It is the affective state that signals whether one has reached a juncture where the therapeutic process might move to a new level (Stern, 1998b, 2001; Stern et al., 1998). Through the activation of her intuitive limbic system the therapist senses when a change occurs that might generate a moment of meeting. It is the relationship that does the work, and in therapy the key is to create a safe environment with room to unfold private and internal perceptions. The affective attunement or limbic resonance enables joint regulation in the dyadic system. The improvisational process consists of moving along, now moments, which are the precursors of moments of meeting, and it is during this phase that client and therapist begin to reach each other through affective attunement. Both client and therapist usually have a goal in sight, which they begin to move toward in the improvisational phase.

The neural circuits that are activated in the present moment determine which parts of the past are activated, and how past components are combined to meet the present situation. The present moment alters the functional past, not the historical past. Recognition memories occur in relation to perceptions emerging in the present. This may involve the recognition of a smell, a sound, a melody, a word, and so on that integrates with the given moment. In every moment of recognition the experience is slightly different, because we select different fragments in relation to what is happening in the present (Stern, 2004). Internal representations are put together, taken apart, and put back together in relation to the moment when the action unfolds (Beebe & Lachman, 2002). Certain dissociated traumatic memories can suddenly come to light in the therapeutic process, and when the nervous system allows the implicit memories to become explicit, the present moment arises as the past is rewritten. A present moment may be interpreted by the left hemisphere and turned into explicit knowledge, which may be useful in some situations. An interpretation that is attuned in relation to a present moment may take on particular gravity and value if it is well-timed. In the next section I look at the unfolding of the developmental dialogue in the intersubjective space.

Intersubjectivity and the Developmental Dialogue

Optimum social communication and development occur in a balanced regulation of the interaction with sufficient flexibility to move back and forth. Even though the therapeutic process between adults or older children and their therapist involves a relationship between nervous systems with a more complex degree of integration, much of the process resembles the early caregiver-child relationship. Securely attached 1-year-olds have a balanced interpersonal communication with their mothers based on a regulation of, for example, vocal rhythms that is flexible and not stuck in either over- or underregulation. An internal process is regulated both through self-regulation and interpersonal regulation. Both processes are always present and mutually influence each other, and no process is more important than the other. In the therapist-client contact, the therapist must observe both his own process and the inter-personal regulation and communication (Beebe & Lachmann, 2002).

The desire to enter an intersubjective field with another person is es-sential for the formation of a relationship and in driving the psychothera-peutic process forward. We need someone else's eyes to shape and keep ourselves together, and without them our human identity dissolves. The intersubjective field can only be created in the present, and when it is successfully established there are moving moments when resources are developed, and the person shows enhanced flexibility and mental health. Our psychological states are reflected through one another's behavior, and when both parties meet in this shared moment, both have an en-hanced experience (Stern, 2004).

Virtually everybody possesses the potential for forming emotional connections. But emotional modulation and affective attunement are not acquired in the same way as cognitive skills. Emotional skills stem from living life in the present through dyadic interactions that are learned im-plicitly. Stern (1998b) has explained how a pattern is repeated through-out therapy, and how what happens during the first 30 seconds is likely to keep repeating itself in the affective pattern. In a healthy relationship the pattern is often more varied and constantly changing. The more pathological a relationship is, the more repetitive the pattern is.

Secondary Intersubjectivity

Stern (1995) compared what happens in the therapeutic process to the early caregiver-infant relationship. He argues that the big leap in re-lation to the uniquely human quality of emotional relations occurs around the age of 7–9 months when the infant discovers that he is separate from the caregiver, has his own thoughts and feelings, and develops skills that support secondary subjectivity. This allows us to shift our external acts and reactions to internal subjective states that underlie our external be-havior. At this time, the infant begins to master psychological intimacy and become willing to open up. As mentioned in Chapter 1, Stern de-scribed three mental states that are crucial for early intersubjective rela-tions. One is the ability to enter into a field of joint attention; the second is the experience of having joint intentions; and the third is the ability to share someone else's affective states, all of which are also qualities that lay the foundation for a therapeutic process.

Psychotherapy is based on an experience of understanding and responding physically and mentally to the client's state by perceiving the client through gaze contact, body, prosody, and so on. The expanded intersubjective space that emerges in the typically developing 7–9-month-old infant provides new possibilities and other ways of being with others. The experience is shared as it arises, and the way of being together unfolds in the present, before the experience has been transferred or rephrased verbally. Change is based on perceived experience. The nervous system develops through the subjective experience as it takes place, not when it is later reproduced. Interpretations and narratives may facilitate change but only once they are associated with the moment in which the contact unfolds. An event must be lived with emotions and actions in the present, in real life, with real people (Stern, 2004).

The process of change in psychotherapy and in everyday life occurs when two people create an intersubjective contact through a present moment, which involves a feeling that "I know that you know that I know" or "I feel that you feel that I feel" (Stern, 2004, p. 75), that is, the ability to empathize with the other's emotions. Intersubjective meetings can be brief and span one or more present moments. The absence of intersubjective connectedness often leads to anxiety, which mobilizes defensive strategies. In psychotherapy the key is not to satisfy the client's needs but to understand them and acknowledge them. The needs should be offered a space outside the person, so that the perception of the needs can be observed.

Curiosity and Fascination

It is the meeting and acceptance, free of judgment or condemnation, in the intersubjective field that affirms the client's perception of the world. This form of acknowledgment involves an immediate emotional presence, accessibility, and self-boundaries. The moment is always new, yet relational behavior patterns repeat themselves, albeit not in exactly the same form. In the here-and-now situation something is happening that has not happened in exactly the same way before, and every moment is an opportunity for embracing the new, even if it carries some of the old within. The dialogue that unfolds in the improvisational process unfolds in the moment but contains both participants' previous internal representations. For example, the client may try to maintain an image of herself as sweet and nice, which perpetuates an element from the past that acts as a defense against an anxiety related to anger. The intersubjective field expands the range of possible perceptions when the perceptions are given a space and made accessible. The two attune with each other's affects, sharing them when possible, and connecting by meeting on the same level of intensity and with matching emotions.

In the developmental dyadic process, the therapist must maintain a stance of curiosity toward the client's world and share it mentally, and this sets off reflective processes. Through the therapist's curiosity and attunement, the client's internal representations enter into an intersubjective space with the therapist that is different from the intersubjective field where the internal representations were originally created. It is in this intersubjective field that the transformation of the client's perceptual world is achieved, and it is this process that enables the client to reflect on internal perceptions. It is the space of perceptual possibility that contains the transformation potential.

Holding and Containing

The intersubjective dialogue includes both the client's and the therapist's implicit knowledge. This dialogue is preverbal and wordless and represents a complicated human choreography. Affective attunement requires that two people share the same focus. In therapy, the therapist is interested in knowing what the client's world is about, and the therapist aims to create positive moments. Good therapy is supportive, regardless of the form of therapy. In this context, Stern employs Winnicott's concept of holding or Bion's concept of a containing function in relation to the supportive aspect, which must be established both within and outside the therapeutic space if any psychological development is to ensue. It is necessary to be able to support and contain the client before engaging in a process of reflection, and it is often necessary to remain in this supportive position for a long time before the client is able to engage in a reflecting process concerning potential trauma. Holding or containing is a key aspect of the therapeutic process, because the caregiver has not been sufficiently able to contain the painful feelings that the client had in childhood; hence, these experiences were not attuned with the child in a way that facilitated integration.

The clients bring whatever personality patterns into therapy that they happen to have, and what some might consider an attack might simply reflect the client's personality organization. It is the entire personality structure that is reproduced in the therapeutic setting (Gammelgaard, 2004). Winnicott (1971b) noted that the therapist must have an intuitive understanding of the client's emotional history and developmental level, but at the same time the therapist should also have a theory about emotional childhood development and an understanding of the relationship between child and environment. A child or an adult who was raised in an environment with uncaring or chaotic caregivers will often develop a lack of trust and confidence in the environment. The client's lack of positive experiences throughout life may lead to a basic suspicion toward the therapist. Only when clients dare believe in a positive relationship with the therapist will they be able to engage in a therapeutic process. Thus, much of the therapeutic process is about establishing a secure attachment. A predictable emotional environment where the client develops a trusting relationship with the therapist through containment can be a crucial element in the therapeutic process.

Attachment, Separateness, and Disengagement

In the therapeutic process the therapist takes a curious stance toward the client's perceptions of the world, and the client knows that this world is shared with the therapist. To share an experience with the client, the therapist must be authentic; that is, there must be consistency in body language, emotional expressions, verbal expressions, and internal experience. Consistency between internal experience and external expression is a crucial aspect of authenticity. As Schibbye (2005) mentioned, attachment must be experienced in separateness, and separateness must be experienced in bonding. The client must be able to approach without anxiety about being invaded and swallowed up and without feeling separate and abandoned. In therapy it is important to establish patterns for interactions but also for sharing differences. Therapy is about modifying the client's personality patterns—reorganizing the framework. Improvisation in therapy renders the process unpredictable, and change is achieved by modifying the framework as much as the client can handle. When the framework is reorganized, the client undergoes stressful moments in a process that could be described as a series of minor crises.

Sander (1988), who was inspired by Winnicott, emphasized that the caregiver-child dyad needs moments where the two disengage from contact, giving them both a break and a chance to assimilate. Sander observed that in the dyadic process between caregiver and child a present moment is followed immediately by an open space where caregiver and child disengage from contact. Stern observed that the same occurs in psychotherapy with adults, who also seem to need a moment of disengagement and assimilation to find a new balance in the altered intersubjective state (Stern, 1998a). The therapeutic process requires finding the balance between attachment and autonomy and between mutual regulation and self-regulation. Clients who were raised with insecure attachment patterns have often retreated to their own internal world, as they seek isolation as a means of self-protection. When the therapist respects this need for psychological or physical disengagement, the client feels understood. Disengagement is used to organize, reorganize, and manage the arousal level to achieve emotional balance and to organize cognitively—all functions that we categorize as self-regulation. This facilitates the development of coping strategies and represents a psychobiological need. For example, infants disengage by avoiding gaze contact, covering their ears, and closing their eyes (Allen, 2002).

Misattunements

As mentioned earlier, Tronick and Cohn (1989) found that when caregiver and child engage in unattuned contact, it takes approximately 2 seconds before some 70% of misattunements are turned into attunement. This powerful tendency to reestablish the interaction with more coordinated states is also seen in the therapeutic contact. Like the caregiver-child relationship, the therapeutic process also includes misattunements, where the two parties fail to attune. Misattunements within a certain manageable spectrum are facilitating, stressful experiences that are necessary in any process of change. By contrast, chronic misattunement and misattunements that go beyond the child's or client's zone of development are severe, because they make the child or the client feel emotionally abandoned and, in some situations, humiliated and helpless. The therapeutic process will probably always include moments of meeting that are missed due to misattunement (countertransference). If this happens frequently, and the moments are not reestablished, it can have serious consequences for the therapeutic contact. The therapist fails to understand the client if the therapist does not feel included in a relationship with the client.

Chronic misattunement in the therapeutic process can provoke a form of retraumatization, since this pain probably resembles the pain in the client's past (Siegel, 1999). The therapeutic process involves a release of emotions that are associated with painful memories, and in the client's contact with the therapist an emotional depth is generated that helps break down counterproductive defenses, something that is always associated with insecurity and stress. The client's ability to experience, manage, and learn through misattunements or internal pain is an important component of the therapeutic process and should be facilitated by the therapist in the current context.

The Current Context and Memory

Nothing in the brain can change without being activated. Brain structures change through lived experiences, as information is internalized and stored based on lived experiences, and the stored information is recognized when the person is faced with experiences that resemble past events. The relationship that is established between therapist and client probably differs from the client's previous relationships, and hence the hope is that something else will happen in this new context. Memory researchers Edelmann and Bartlett pointed out that the experience of remembering takes place in the present, not in the past, and that it is the current context that determines what comes up in memory, and how memory fragments are combined. In therapy it is essential to create a memory context that elicits recognition in order to generate reflections that can facilitate a transformation of internal representations.

In the therapeutic process, the client's biography is reshaped, but aspects of the original story are part of the present. The therapist is attributed qualities in the current situation that the client has experienced with others in childhood. The client will misinterpret current relational experiences based on past experiences (Schibbye, 2005). In describing his psychoanalytical technique, Freud stated that the clients often relived certain aspects of their childhood through their relationship with the therapist and reacted to him as if he were their parent. This form of transference is not only a feature of the analytical relationship but of all relationships that involve a significant other in an asymmetrical relationship, such as the teacher-student relationship. Freud said, "The transfer arises spontaneously in all human relations and in the relations of the patient to the physician" (Freud, 1919/1986, p. 43). This transference may be positive or negative, and it is subject to change. The internal representations are played out in relation to the therapist, and in this process it is essential for the therapist to take a stance that does not complete the client's attempts at staging previous, counterproductive relationships. A therapist who fails to become a part of the client's or child's fixed expectations becomes a secure person who opens a possibility for the client or child to begin to change interactions and self-regulating processes that have proved counterproductive.

The amygdala, the hippocampus, the orbitofrontal cortex, and the dorsolateral prefrontal cortex contribute to the distinction between past and present. The amygdala and other deep subcortical structures respond to and process immediate changes in the current context, such as rapid changes in the other's facial mimicry—a process that lies far from our daytime consciousness. The hippocampus places the experiences in a context of time and place and balances impulses from the amygdala. The orbitofrontal cortex refines and processes the impulses on a preconscious level, and only when the experiences are recorded in the dorsolateral prefrontal cortex can they be processed explicitly. In a sense, our implicit and explicit knowledge is potentially dissociated; at least, we cannot assume that the associative connections between implicit and explicit knowledge are always made. Affective attunement is a process that occurs on a subcortical level and represents implicit knowledge. The limbic structures contain early acquired relational knowledge and control the way in which a communication proceeds from moment to moment, for example, in relation to the regulation of gaze contact and vocal rhythms.

Activation of Internal Representations and Narratives

An important part of our personality lies hidden in our implicit memory schemas or representations of interactions that have been generalized, which connect to our procedural memory (Hart, 2008; Stern, 1985). This knowledge is not immediately accessible to the cortical regions and can only be made accessible when the regions in charge of autobiographic memory, including the hippocampus, are activated. Self-reflection, which requires the activation of the orbitofrontal and dorsolateral prefrontal cortices, is only possible when we engage in situations where the knowledge that is locked inside our autobiographical memory is recognized. Through the improvisational process and present moments a new context emerges, where hopefully it will be possible to include new information about the client's relational patterns. When the therapist's and client's nervous systems create a field of resonance, implicit relational knowledge is generated that can be explored. When the client has the courage to examine his relational strategies in the interaction with the therapist along with the vulnerability and pain that may be associated with recalling traumatic experiences, an opportunity arises for engaging in a new form of relationship. The therapist's empathic attunement and the safe and structuring context of the therapy process enable the client to tolerate increasing levels of anxiety and pain, which may gradually make room for more memories and thoughts. It is the awareness of the life circumstances that created the difficulties that eventually enables the integration. Thus, integration requires an activation of the mentalizing structures in the orbitofrontal and dorsolateral prefrontal cortices. The integration of implicit and explicit knowledge often occurs through narratives and helps facilitate psychological development and an expansion of identity. Our self-image changes in relation to the many people around us, and past encounters can take on many different forms when viewed retrospectively. One of the crucial human resources is our intellectual capacity to imagine alternatives and other ways of being, acting, and so on.

The processing of narratives and interpretations can present an obstacle to a psychological development process unless limbic attunement is in place and the right present moment emerges. Clients often look for explanations driven by the need of the left hemisphere for consistency and meaning. Offering explanations to satisfy the need for meaning and consistency on a cortical level may lead to a superficial therapeutic process that fails to facilitate change in the implicit subcortical structures. "Patients are often hungry for explanations, because they are used to thinking that neocortical contraptions like explication will help them" (Lewis et al., 2001, p. 177).

Winnicott wrote that he dreaded to think about how many profound changes he had prevented or delayed in his patients in a certain classification category due to his personal urge to interpret. He emphasized that the client himself would reach understanding, and that it was the client, and only the client, who held the answers. Thus, interpretation should not take place before the alliance and trust have been established, and the therapist should always be willing to admit a mistake if the client feels that the interpretation does not fit (Winnicott 1971a; Schibbye, 2005).

The neocortical brain masters abstractions and cannot achieve changes in the neural systems without activating other structures. Language lets us form an autobiographical story about our internal representations, which eventually becomes the narrative or life story that the client presents to the psychotherapist. These narratives represent the left-hemispheric understanding of personality structures that were created preverbally, but this understanding is rarely coherent or consistent. Children and adults who have been exposed to inappropriate relational patterns and who therefore have not been able to develop adequate integration between the right and left hemispheres tend to create a set of narratives around their life story that seem dissociated or detached from their implicit knowledge. It is not the reconstruction and cognitive understanding of the client's history that facilitate personality development but rather the present moments that arise in the relationship between therapist and client as the client's implicit history is made explicit. The words must be associated with the experience, or they will remain detached from the implicit relational knowledge (Schibbye, 2005).

The Role of the Asymmetrical Relationship for Affective Attunement

In the caregiver-child relationship it is the caregiver who helps the child engage in a social context that offers learning opportunities. The child expresses a need, and the caregiver responds and assumes responsibility. In the caregiver-child relationship, the child borrows the mother's more advanced consciousness and uses it as scaffolding (Bruner, 1985). In any asymmetrical relationship, such as mother-child, teacher-student, or therapist-client, there is an asymmetrical distribution of responsibility. Like the caregiver, the psychotherapist must assume responsibility for his objectives and pay attention to the asymmetrical nature of the relationship. The therapist should make room for the client's self-organization and make sure to meet the client within his zone of proximal development (Øvreeide, 2001a).

No one can understand another person's feelings unless they share the bond that is created through the improvisational process and the present moments. Healthy caregiver-child interactions stimulate the release of oxytocin, opioids, and dopamine, among other substances, all of which promote positive and rewarding feelings and facilitate the development of neural circuits. Even minor nonverbal attitudes, like the way the therapist looks at the client, can elicit positive relational experiences, and the therapeutic process makes it possible to establish a relationship that is different from a potentially insecure attachment that the client carries from previous relationships. The development of affective and mentalizing capacity can only be achieved in close relations with a significant other (Fonagy, 1999a).

Bowlby (1988) argued that the therapist should offer the client a secure base from which to explore the painful aspects of her life. Thus, the therapist should be able to offer support, encouragement, and sympathy. Bowlby emphasized the importance of empathy, arguing that the therapist should be compassionate, dedicated, and appreciative to understand and help create coherence in the client's experiences. As Kathrin Asper (1987) has pointed out, the development of a strong sense of self-worth requires being mirrored in a good mother's loving gaze. The fundamental ability to engage in emotional attunement is present from birth, and it is this competence that the therapeutic process seeks to engage.

A secure and empathic relationship establishes an emotional and neurobiological context that promotes the process of neural reorganization; an environment is created where the client feels safe enough to handle optimum levels of stress. The working alliance or the feeling of attachment reduces anxiety and offers emotional protection in stressful situations, and both children and adults seek protection from stress and anxiety in close, intimate relationships. The therapist must dare to be present with her personality, since this is a condition for offering an authentic presence. Present moments cannot be achieved without this presence, and in providing it the therapist mimics the positive mirroring that parents would give their children under normal circumstances.

The Concept of Neutrality

In Freud's conception of neutrality, the therapist should abstain from judging or assessing the client's experience (Schibbye, 2005). Like the good mother, the therapist should be able to contain the client's disorganized and frustrated state and address it neutrally. The client should have an experience of being able to lean on the therapist without getting involved in the therapist's unresolved conflicts. Neutrality does not imply disengaging emotionally from the contact or being uninvolved. Neutrality means engaging in an interaction in a caring, sensitive, and loving way, without condemnation and without getting emotionally carried away. Only through this neutral stance can the therapist achieve an improvisational process that is capable of giving rise to present moments.

Like the affectively attuned mother, the therapist is the initiator of the self-regulating and identity-forming process. When the present moments arise, they trigger an emotional vulnerability that can give the person a sense of being exposed. In these situations, therapists have to be secure in their own personality foundations; good therapists do not get frightened or disengage but remain emotionally present and available to the client when affective insecurity and pain are at their highest. This emotional availability has a calming effect, among other things by activating the parasympathetic nervous system. In the asymmetrical relationship, therapists must remain aware which affects are the client's and which are their own. Even if therapists attune with the client's sad feelings, they must avoid sinking into the client's sense of despair. As in the caregiver-child dyad, the therapist must maintain reliable self-boundaries and attune with the client's distress by adjusting to the client's arousal level and containing the client's feelings without being wrapped up in them (Morgan, 1998; Schibbye, 2005).

The concept of neutrality is essential in all therapeutic work and involves the therapist's ability to balance between maintaining his own emotionality and engaging in affective attunement with the client. In all therapeutic work it is important to position oneself in relation to the child's or client's communicative repertoire and offer a different statement than the client is used to, assuming responsibility for what happens in their mutual relationship. It is not helpful, for a child or an adult, to stick to a communicative repertoire that is counterproductive but familiar. It is through warmth, acceptance, authenticity, spontaneous encouragement, nonpossessive love, and unconditional acceptance that the client or child develops, although there should be room for establishing boundaries and for misattunement. Between the client and the therapist there should be a match that is achieved through affective attunement.

The Potential of the Psychotherapeutic Process

[Emotional expression] has the advantages of being instantly decoded and so of making immediate impact. Here again the concern of a psychoanalyst is . . . whether he knows what his feelings are and what has aroused them. These are issues of intrapsychic communication . . . the constant interaction of, on the one hand, the patterns of communication, verbal and non-verbal, that are operating within an individual's mind and, on the other hand, the patterns of communication that obtain between him and those whom he feels he can trust. . . . The more complete the information that a person is able to communicate to someone he trusts the more he himself becomes able to dwell on it, to understand it and to see its implications—a process well illustrated by the adage, "How can I know what I think until I hear what I say?" Conversely, the more adequately a person can process information on his own the more capable will he be to communicate it to some other person. A key word here is trust. (Bowlby, 1993, p. 294)

In the therapeutic process there is a learning of new experiences that do not repair the past but which generate new experiences that can be integrated in the nervous system. Changes in the neural circuitry make it possible to establish a new context, where something new can emerge. The process has to be repeated over and over again to strengthen the neural circuits. In a sense, the past is reshaped or recast by being put back together in a new way. New experiences have the power to rewire the neural circuits that contained previous memories. The therapeutic process with its many present moments helps rewrite history and old narratives (Stern, 2004).

Sander (Schore, 2003b) has pointed out that it is not the past one looks for in one's clients but rather the logic of the client's strategies with regard to the regulation of mental states. Affect regulation is part of the implicit memory system, and regulation mechanisms are activated when a situation matches a prototype of a previous experience where this behavior was useful. When the nervous system encounters stress states that it is unable to manage via the prefrontal cortex, these regulating functions will be deactivated. The therapist must try to capture the client's self-regulating capacity though the present moments and attune with the client's nervous system to calm it.

Therapy can provide a new model of the nature of close relationships and ultimately help the client reflect on events, feelings, behavior patterns, and so on. The client becomes able to address all of her ages, which interact in the mental organization, and develop a more caring relationship with the child she once was than the caregivers were able to establish at the time. This also offers a chance to mourn losses or develop an understanding of one's own behavior that might alleviate any self-reproach. Therapy can open a space for shame and other unpleasant feelings that the client has not previously been able to share with someone else in confidence, and which she has therefore been fleeing from. Childhood experiences can carry feelings of being wrong that are so powerful that they are denied or split off.

Summary

The core of the therapeutic process in a relational perspective is finding a way for the therapist to activate the client's implicit knowledge through present moments and recognition. A successful therapeutic process generates memories that enable self-reflection and facilitate changes in internal representations. There is a constant dynamic and reciprocity between many elements in both the intrapsychic and the interpersonal field. On an intrapsychic level, the activation of implicit knowledge, recognition, and self-reflection expand the neural circuits in an integrative process that may continue to unfold throughout the life span. The most ambitious goal of psychotherapy is to integrate and reintegrate the neural circuits that control our emotions. Most of what goes on in the therapeutic relationship takes place outside the field of theory.

The human nervous system consists of innate structures that determine the interactions we invite and engage in. In turn, the responses we receive from the environment affect and alter these structures. Thus, there is no inside and outside the nervous system. In the next chapter I examine the connections between psychotherapy and neuroaffective developmental psychology.

CHAPTER EIGHT

Intervention and Neuroaffective Developmental Psychology

Therapy is not just the rewriting of a client's story; it is the teaching of a method, a process of integration, an assessment and recalibration of perception, and a set of principles for future organization. In this way, therapy is both a form of reparenting and the learning of a strategy for reediting the self.

Louis Cozolino (2000, p. 170)

More than a hundred years ago, Freud argued that the brain develops through experience, and that it may change as a result of psychotherapy; ever since, various approaches to psychotherapy have competed, each laying claim to being the most effective. It would, however, be more productive to develop multimodal intervention forms based on principles that incorporate neurobiological growth, regulation, and integration. There are still considerable gaps in our knowledge about the brain and its complexity, and as the picture is filled in bit by bit, hopefully we shall be able to integrate it in the diversity of psychotherapeutic intervention forms. As yet, as described in Chapter 7, no single form of psychotherapy has proved superior to all others in relation to all psychological disorders.

The psychotherapeutic connection aims to provide a series of key relational experiences that allow the client to unfold a greater potential than was possible prior to the therapeutic intervention (Bentzen & Hart, 2005). Psychotherapy or environmental treatment is not just about calming the client's or child's nervous system but also about expanding the capacity for self-development and adaptive adjustment. Affective disorders are an essential element of all psychological disorders, and all psychological treatment approaches aim to find methods that enable the nervous system to achieve affect regulation. The various psychological treatment approaches focus on different areas of the brain's hierarchical structure such as cognition, emotions, behavior, or sensations, and all therapy forms seek to reintegrate and balance processes in the neural networks (Bradley, 2000; Cozolino, 2000; Schore, 2003b).

Although a variety of psychological treatment approaches may foster psychological development, it is important to carry out a thorough assessment of the client's or child's psychological disorder. For example, it is essential to know whether the affective disorder is due to a dysregulation of the autonomic, the limbic, or the prefrontal system, and whether the disorder is related to innate aspects such as autism or whether it arose in a relational context—or both.

This chapter outlines considerations concerning intervention strategies based on the neuroaffective developmental understanding that has been established throughout the previous chapters of the book. In this chapter, psychological disorders are assessed based on a model inspired by the theory of the triune and lateralized brain with the purpose of describing the differences between various forms of intervention and their approach to initiating a psychological development process.

Intervention Strategy and Developmental Disorder

A mature personality structure is reflected in a flexible nervous system that has highly integrated neural networks and mature self-protection strategies that only rarely manifest themselves because the nervous system is flexible, and the person is able to apply self-reflecting skills. The more primitive and immature the self-protection strategies are, the more the personality is locked into a rigid state that is easily overwhelmed by chaos with a risk of disintegration. Thus, the choice of intervention strategy should be determined by the client's developmental disorder. For example, one cannot rely on the same therapeutic approach for an emotionally empty, violent child as for a child with anorexia. Effective treatment and prevention strategies require an effective assessment of the child's emotional behavior and cognitive social functioning.

As mentioned earlier, our self-protection strategies reflect how neural networks have organized through the course of development we faced difficulties that either stayed within or exceeded the zone of proximal development. Therapeutic intervention is focused on recognizing sensations, emotions, and thoughts that have never been adequately regulated within the relationship. The self-protection strategies are implicit and rarely integrated with explicit awareness.

Evoking emotions that are associated with explicit awareness helps organize neural growth, and when the prefrontal cortex and the explicit memory system have the capacity to link up with implicit memory fragments capable of regulating the anxiety behind the self-protection strategy, symptom reduction normally ensues. The ability to tolerate and regulate affect enables continued brain development. Affect tolerance and affect regulation may be the most important outcome of the psychotherapeutic process, as this process enables the nervous system to contain and regulate more arousal, which in turn promotes psychological development.

It is important to know a client's history and psychological development to determine an appropriate intervention approach. Securely attached children and adults with a good mentalizing capacity have probably developed such a high degree of self-constancy that they will be able to engage in dynamic and interpretative forms of treatment. Others who do not have sufficiently formed identity and impulse inhibition will not be able to benefit from this psychological approach, and one should instead turn to methods that are more directed at attunement in deeper subcortical structures. As Roth and Fonagy (1996) noted, the question is not which therapeutic intervention facilitates development but rather which intervention form can facilitate development for whom.

Mentalizing Capacity

Adults and older children with a mentalizing capacity are able to symbolize and have fantasies, desires, and so on that help organize self-regulation patterns and the interaction with the therapist. The emotional maturation consists of elevating primitive presymbolic sensorimotor affects to mature symbolic representations. This involves increasing flexibility and developing self-regulating skills (Beebe & Lachmann, 2002). In working with clients who lack a reflective capacity, the therapist must be able to receive and contain the client's projections over a prolonged period. For example, a person with a borderline structure will have to undergo a lengthy therapeutic process aimed at affect regulation and the activation of subcortical structures. This person will only slowly develop a mentalizing capacity, unlike a client with a neurotic disorder with a mentalizing capacity, who will soon be able to benefit from insights and act on them. Interpretation, symbolization, and insight-building intervention forms will be contraindicated for borderline disorders but not for neurotic disorders. It is essential to assess the client's mentalizing capacity to avoid applying a therapeutic method that relies on a level of mental organization that is still immature or not yet sufficiently "online" in the client. For example, one should be wary of expecting children with behavioral disorders and dysfunctions in the frontal part of the cingulate gyrus and orbitofrontal cortex to profit from therapy that relies on symbolism and verbal processing. Fonagy (2005) noted that certain interventions are indeed harmful, because they evoke capacities that the client has not developed. That makes clients feel that they cannot keep up, which makes them feel even more useless or incapacitated.

Erik H. Erikson was one of the first to mention the long-term effect of basic trust and mistrust. He defined basic trust as the capacity to receive and accept what is given. He associated trust with identity formation and described identity fusion as a state that reflects difficulties with the sense of self. Erikson said that mistrust can disrupt the therapeutic process, because mistrust implies that the client has no faith in the world or in himself (Fonagy, 2001). Severely traumatized children are hypersensitive to other people's mental states; they are vigilant and constantly try to guess what others are thinking and feeling to avoid additional traumatization. They are constantly scanning their environment for threats and are unable to reflect on any deeper meaning. These children develop a psychological understanding of others at the cost of knowledge about their own internal states and fail to develop self-reflective skills or mentalization. A child who has suffered early emotional frustration, who is without empathy, whose nervous system is highly sensitive and constantly at risk of disintegrating, and who has difficulty forming internal perceptions will not be able to benefit from a therapy form that intervenes on a cognitive, verbal, or symbolic level. It takes a long time before a child who has constant expectations of frustration is able to enter into a working alliance and establish limbic resonance.

A client with a borderline structure, who is sensitive to rejection and betrayal and who constantly seeks an intimacy that he is nevertheless afraid to accept, will have difficulty achieving personality development, among other things because the client's emotions cannot integrate with his mentalizing and symbolizing skills. The client's relationship with others unfolds in a fractured, black-and-white world, which makes attachment with others (including the therapist) vulnerable and ambivalent. Individuals who lack the ability to put their emotions into words (alexithymia) will have difficulty benefiting from conversation therapy, as they are unable to express themselves emotionally or use ideas to expand their self-perception. We have not yet discovered the neurological basis for alexithymia, but one possible explanation might be dissociation between the right and left hemispheres, so that emotional and somatic information in the right hemisphere cannot connect with the verbal system in the left hemisphere (Cozolino, 2000; Schore, 2003b).

Flexibility and Integration: The Potential for Change in the Nervous System

Attachment relationships are formative because they promote the development of the self-regulating mechanisms in the brain, and if the individual strengthens self-regulating skills through interactions with others, the self-organizing potential will unfold. Through hierarchical integration, each mental organization is coordinated with previous levels of organization, and reorganization occurs when development progresses (Cicchetti & Tucker, 1994; Fonagy, 1998b).

From Self-Regulation to Self-Organization

The difference between self-regulation and self-organization is that self-regulation is a process of adaptation that alters the surface structure, while self-organization is evident as spontaneously developing, profoundly structural changes in the nervous system (Carroll, 2004). Network integration requires a simultaneous and repetitive activation of neurons. Neural circuits that are activated simultaneously form and amplify connections (cf. Hebb's axiom: "Neurons that fire together wire together"). Simultaneous activation of neural circuits allows the nervous system to form connections in the association areas that coordinate and integrate a variety of functions. Affective systems are coordinated through learning, and the more the child can experience without the nervous system disintegrating, the more capable the child will be at managing arousal levels and emotions in a flexible manner. Learning peaks when the nervous system reaches its maximum level of arousal without disintegrating, and this point marks the best opportunity for the brain to coordinate learning across brain systems.

Neural circuits connect through synapses, and synaptic changes in one area will change synapses in other areas. LeDoux (2001) concluded that since traumatic experiences can make the personality disintegrate, the personality will also be able to integrate through experiences that establish, alter, and renew the connections. Both the hippocampus and the orbitofrontal cortex are superconvergence zones where input from anatomically separate areas comes together. These areas coordinate social cognition, episodic, autobiographical, and autonoetic (self-understanding) memory, sensations, perceptions, and so on. When the person is overwhelmed emotionally, these functions shut down. In therapy, the key is to strive both for an expansion of the optimum arousal level of the nervous system and for the development of coping strategies to regulate the overwhelming state. The convergence zones are important for the therapeutic process. The therapeutic process aims to engage areas that are already activated in an attempt to nudge areas that are fixed or inactive.

Any new neural wave of organization dissolves the former organization, and thus there are periods of transition when the client's previous mode of functioning is no longer adequate, and new modes of functioning have yet to fully establish themselves; these transitional periods will be characterized by doubt, confusion, and frustration. Psychotherapy causes pain, anxiety, and confusion in the client because it intensifies the conflict between established structures, which are being broken down, and newly emerging processes that still seem alien. When the client is able to integrate the anxiety and the pain, the experience changes, and the personality is reorganized. Emotional intensity, emotional shifts, and the identification of alien emotions are all involved in developing and changing the nervous system through its capability for self-organization (Bentzen & Hart, 2005; Carroll, 2004; Schibbye, 2005).

Self-Organizing Changes

Throughout life, the human mind carries all its mental organizations with it, and more immature and early developing organizations continue to exist on deeper psychological levels. The internal representations are embedded on every level of mental organization, and conflicts can play out intrapsychically on all hierarchical levels. More developed structures reflect and recapture the organization in less developed structures, and a dysfunction on a lower level will become evident on a higher level. Thus, a psychological conflict will often be represented on many levels within the nervous system, and often it will not be possible to resolve it on the level where the symptom appears most prominently but only on deeper levels in the nervous system.

Structures in both neocortical and subcortical structures must be activated for self-organizing changes to take place. While the neocortex has the capacity to process new stimuli, it is in the lower structures, which are not under volitional control, that the behavior is maintained and consolidated. Studies have shown that when we try to control a particular behavior or deliberately evoke a chain of thoughts, the brain activity that is a sign of spontaneous reorganization (alpha waves) will fail to appear (Robbins, 1980). The prerequisite for the entire nervous system to change is the development of the capacity of the autonomic nervous system to tolerate high levels of arousal, the capacity of the limbic system to tolerate anxiety, and the capacity of the prefrontal cortex for grasping understanding and for assuming a more accepting, nondefensive attitude.

The psychotherapeutic space aims to intensify neuronal growth and integrate neural networks. This growth and integration are intensified through the client's and the therapist's working alliance, which causes the simultaneous activation of neural networks that are disturbed, disintegrated, or dissociated. The therapeutic environment must be safe enough that the arousal intensity stays on a level that the nervous system can handle. This process lets the nervous system progress to a higher level of functioning. If the arousal intensity reaches a level that exceeds the capacity of the nervous system, it will regress to a lower level of functioning (Bentzen, 2010). Psychological development is about expanding the arousal capacity of the nervous system and activating complex and abstract levels of higher neocortical activity, ultimately enabling the client to self-reflect and manage impulse control. A process of change can only occur once the nervous system is calm and has a balanced arousal level. Neocortical processing can lead to rapid changes, while the limbic brain requires a great deal of repetition. The higher up in the hierarchical brain system the processing occurs, the greater is the plasticity of the brain, and the more rapidly changes can occur.

Psychological maturation normally takes place in small steps, and it must be assumed that the integration of neural connections is strengthened through countless learning waves. Occasionally, there will be quantum leaps, while at other times development proceeds at a slow and imperceptible pace. Development normally strives for external adaptation and internal satisfaction. Development only occurs through the activation of neurons and can only take place on the current level of mental organization. The nervous system seeks to connect active neurons on all hierarchical levels. As mentioned above, neural circuits connect synaptically in a self-organizing process, and integration, particularly in the association cortex and convergence zones of the nervous system, helps drive changes in personality.

Psychotherapy and the Hierarchical Brain

Internal representations are complex, often conflicting, and exist on many different levels, implicit as well as explicit. Processes in the nervous system are holistic in nature, and the internal representations influence many neural systems and bodily functions, producing sensations, perceptual images, fantasies, emotions, and thoughts. Self-representations do not consist of one single brain structure but are the result of many different but interrelated brain structures, from the brain stem to the neocortex (Carroll, 2004). As mentioned in Chapter 6, dissociation and thus integration can occur on many hierarchical levels, vertically as well as horizontally. Failure to achieve resolution on one level of mental organization may result in developmental delays or stagnation in the nervous system (Cicchetti & Tucker, 1994). Vertical integration connects functions in the brain stem and limbic regions to higher processing functions in the frontal lobes. Horizontal integration coordinates same-level functions between the two hemispheres, such as the left and right hemispheres in the prefrontal cortex, as well as same-level structures placed front and back, for example, between the prefrontal cortex and the parietal lobes in the same hemisphere, that is, between input and output functions of the nervous system. The regulation and representation of bodily functions, which is mediated by the autonomic system, are controlled on a general level by the orbitofrontal cortex, and vertical integration means that the orbitofrontal cortex assumes control of lower functions. Both the dorsolateral prefrontal cortex and the orbitofrontal cortex are closely connected to the basal ganglia, which makes it possible to inhibit maladaptive motor programs. The integration of these neural circuits is crucial for the development of new behavioral responses (Siegel, 1999).

Since the brain is a self-organizing system, the integration is immediate, unpredictable, and complex. Processes unfold on multiple levels at the same time, and changes can occur in unexpected ways. It is the goal of any form of therapy to achieve integration between brain regions. The various forms of therapy rest on various locations in the hierarchical structure of the brain. For example, some forms of therapy address integration with an emphasis on the autonomic nervous system, others work through the limbic system, while yet others operate through functions in the prefrontal cortex.

In the following three sections I review each of the three vertical and hierarchical levels of mentalization and discuss which structures are activated on each level, and how the therapist might connect and attune with them. The case stories in these sections involve adult clients to illustrate how the various structures remain active in the fully developed brain.

Intervention on the Level of the Autonomic Nervous System

As mentioned in Chapter 3, Paul MacLean referred to the brain stem and the autonomic nervous system as the level of protomentation. This part of the brain is related to somatic sensations and being; it operates instinctively and prepares basic motor planning. Among other things, it controls primitive emotions such as seeking, certain aspects of anxiety behavior, aggression, and sexuality. This is also the area that regulates our breathing, heart rate, the metabolism of various organs, and the production of many neurochemicals. On this level there is a constant regulation of the essential being state, which is inescapable, and which cannot be grasped through cognitive processes. The processes on this level include vitality affects, categorical affects, and sensations. They are unsymbolized, wordless, and often implicit, although some of them may be made accessible to explicit sensation if they are verbalized and reflected cognitively (Bentzen & Hart, 2005).

Emotions rely on the communication between the autonomic nervous system and the central nervous system. Without the autonomic nervous system we would not be able to sense emotions, since emotions and assessments are anchored in somatic sensations. Feelings of pleasure and displeasure are perceived through the autonomic nervous system and the insula and form the basis of perceptions and assessments that later guide our thoughts and behavior. The autonomic nervous system provides the physiological basis for our ability to sense anything at all and constitutes the root of our emotions. Structures in the brain stem are crucial for our spontaneous involvement in the world, and it is on this very fundamental level that the basic circuits for attention control and

Potentials on the thinking level of mentalization:
Structuring, organizing, and handling long-term planning. Expanding an emotion with thoughts about that emotion. Preserving and manipulating mental images. Delaying gratification and selecting one strategy over another, thus making it possible to inhibit or control emotions and act differently. Controlling primitive behavior and basic emotions.

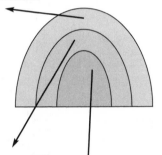

Potentials on the emotional level of mentalization:
Refining social interactions through emotions such as playfulness, exuberance, and sadness. Development of categorical emotions. Enabling fine-tuning of responses. Handling additional processing and refinement of affects and connecting perceptual and cognitive processes. Filtering and assessing what happens internally and externally.

Potentials on the level of protomentation:
Somatic sensations and being. Developing basic motor plans and controlling primitive emotions. Regulating breathing, heart rate, the metabolism of various organs, and the production of neurochemical substances. Sensing the state of being through vitality affects.

Figure 8.1. Potentials on the different levels of mentalization

awareness are found (Bentzen & Hart, 2005; Damasio, 1998; Lewis et al., 2001).

The consciousness processes of the brain stem unfold outside our volition and essentially beyond the influence of our daytime consciousness. Affects are a body-based psychobiological phenomenon that communicates through the autonomic nervous system, including the vagal nerve, which mediates information from the stomach, intestines, heart, lungs, and so on. The sympathetic nervous system mobilizes, and the parasympathetic system calms down. The autonomic nervous system is crucial for our ability to regulate stress situations, normally through the mammalian vagal system. If the nervous system is overburdened, it regresses into an autonomic regulation of fight-or-flight or immobilization behavior (freeze). In the case below, Britt describes how she experiences the state of immobilization. Other clients describe the same state as unpleasant because they lose touch with the world and feel fixated.

Intervention Form

Britt is 48 years old; she is seeking therapy because there have been a number of sudden deaths in her close family, and suddenly she feels overwhelmed. For many years, Britt has suffered from fibromyalgia, and her state has recently deteriorated considerably. She remembers as a child being afraid of her father, who periodically had a severe alcohol problem. When she was younger she stayed with her grandmother for long periods of time because the parents could not handle having her around due to their marital problems. She has experienced many deaths: Her best friend died in a traffic accident when she was 8 years old; her first child died at the age of 1 year; and later in life she lost many close family members and friends. She says that when she thinks of the many losses, she is seized by a feeling of unreality and numbness. In a therapy session she remembers an incident when her father frightened her, and at the same time she describes how her body feels frozen and numb, and how she feels as if she is being sucked through a long tunnel. She feels that she is inside a bell jar, and the world is so far away that no one can reach her where she is sitting. She feels lonely, but that does not matter, because she feels comfortable. In therapy, a prolonged period is devoted to helping Britt avoid the freeze state through a number of somatic coping strategies (e.g., breathing, relaxation, distance/closeness, basic trust). Gradually she is able to approach certain experiences, including situations when her father scared her, without disintegrating, and she is able to respond emotionally to some of the many losses. Only after a prolonged therapeutic process is she able to form internal representations of good and bad experiences concerning childhood memories and present experiences and to mentalize in relation to the events.

On the autonomic level the therapist enters into a field of resonance with the client's autonomic nervous system through body communication. The therapist notes and responds to the client's minimal bodily changes, for example, with regard to breathing, skin color, and posture. The therapist notices some of these changes through her own implicit somatic sensations, which resonate with the client's autonomic nervous system. The interaction between the body and the situation that the body is in provides an implicit somatic sensation that is often undifferentiated and wordless. The therapist attunes with the client's autonomic nervous system through gaze contact, among other things, which offers a direct pathway to the autonomic nervous system through the subcortical levels of the occipital lobes. In this context, it should be noted that gaze contact has a strong effect on the autonomic nervous system, and in anything but the most intimate relations gaze contact activates the sympathetic nervous system, thus intensifying traumatic or dissociated states.

The activation of the sympathetic nervous system creates a reflexive attention focus with deep sensations and a deep action response, and the activation of the calming system creates a relaxed and vegetative state. The fluctuation between the two polarities enhances the individual's responsive capacity, regeneration capacity, and stress management (Bentzen & Hart, 2005). On this level, the therapist and the client organize through bodily or nonverbal activities, where the client feels his presence in the room in a field that is larger than his own field; there is no sense of relating, only being.

In the therapeutic process the therapist first helps clients get to know their own autonomic rhythm of mobilization (challenge) and calming. When this self-strengthening fluctuation between polarities begins to stabilize, it acts as an integrating tool in relation to passive or hyperactivated states and somatic functions. The flexibility of the autonomic processes is mainly facilitated through the exploration of small somatic changes and motor impulses. A characteristic feature of this process is that neither the therapist nor the client can know what is going to unfold until the process is underway. Thus, this approach requires that both parties are able and willing to be openly present in processes that do not "make sense" (autonomic or limbic) and to support meaning and understanding (prefrontal) that organize and contain the somatic and emotional experiences (Bentzen & Hart, 2005). On the autonomic level there is an inherent, instinctive ability to dissolve trauma that may be blocked by anxiety, such as the anxiety associated with reliving an intense feeling of helplessness. In some cases, touch can reduce anxiety and lower cortisol levels; in clients who do not associate touch with anxiety, calm touching can trigger the release of oxytocin and reduce anxiety levels. Between mammals, touch has a calming function as well as the function of strengthening the bonds between members of the same group or between parents and offspring (Joseph, 1993; Uvnäs-Moberg, 1998).

The goal of the therapy is to discover resources through the autonomic nervous system, among other things by bodily anchoring sensory experiences and somatic sensations. Establishing a somatic and emotional sensation can give the organism a sense of what feels right. "A normal and well-functioning sense of identity is somatically founded. . . . [O]n a thought level anything can be right, since it is possible to imagine anything" (Sørensen, 1996, p. 75). Wilhelm Reich's vegetotherapy was partially based on functions in the autonomic nervous system. Reich viewed the autonomic nervous system as a structure involved in emotional self-regulation. He worked with respiratory functions to release chronic tensions in the tissue, which he believed disrupted self-regulation. Reich saw the self as a structure that was deeply rooted in innate self-regulating skills that can be utilized in psychotherapy (Carroll, 2004).

Intervention on the Level of the Limbic System

As mentioned in Chapter 3, MacLean called the limbic system the level of emotomentation. The development of the older mammalian brain added more sophisticated emotions such as joy and grief to the basic reptilian emotions. The limbic system enabled the development and refinement of social interactions and thus also of social emotions, including playfulness, exuberance, or sadness, and made it possible to fine-tune responses. The limbic system serves to further process affects, adding nuance, and connects perceptual and cognitive processes. It is able to adapt to a rapidly changing environment and to organize new learning. The function of the limbic system is to filter and assess what goes on both internally and externally. Like the brain stem level, this level lacks the capacity for verbal communication (Bentzen & Hart, 2005; Hart, 2008; Lewis et al., 2001).

One of the goals of psychotherapy on the limbic level is to regulate the immediately felt state in the intersubjective field (Stern, 1995, 2004). The limbic system records shifts in mood through internal and external sensory impressions and initiates powerful emotions. This is where the raw feelings of joy, anger, grief, anxiety, security, pleasure, and so forth are perceived. This system has the recognition function but not the re-call function, which is developed on the neocortical level. The limbic system activates neural circuit connections between the amygdala and the hippocampus. In the case below, the client's self-perception is very different from her sensory and emotional reactions. On a limbic level, negative feelings (sadness and anger) are expressed that cannot associate with her mentalizing functions. Thus, the client is unable to consider her own needs since she cannot associate these emotions with her mentalizing capacity.

Intervention Form

Kirsty, age 58, is seeking therapy because at times she feels that everything is crashing down around her. Then she shuts herself off, and during these periods she drinks heavily. She has trouble understanding what is happening to her, as she thinks that she has a good life with a nice husband and wonderful children and grandchildren. Kirsty says that her mother was always emotionally distant and cool, always busy, and Kirsty remembers that she and her sister had to look after themselves. Kirsty was closest to her dad, who had a moderate alcohol problem, and who cheated on her mother. Kirsty found out about the father's extramarital affair and had to cover for him. She was always shown off as the happy, cheerful child who always did well, and she has always been there for her parents when they needed a helping hand. In therapy, the effort is focused on Kirsty's internal sensations of herself and the perceptual images she forms in this regard. It is a slow endeavor that requires a deep limbic attunement process. Kirsty gets in touch with both anger and grief, feelings that have been dissociated, and which it takes her a long time to come to terms with. Then she embarks on a slow processing effort where she learns to be more aware of her own needs.

Limbic emotional processes are essential in almost all psychotherapeutic processes, and they are inseparable from somatic states and sensations. As discussed in Chapter 7, psychotherapeutic trust and a working alliance are achieved through limbic attunement. The therapeutic process is about capturing the client's self-regulating capacity and attuning with her nervous system, so that it can be calmed and then activated in a productive manner. Thus, it is always important to be curious and listening in the limbic attunement process, since this is the only potential source of information about which mental level is active (Bentzen & Hart, 2005).

Timing is essential in the therapeutic process, and it is important to remain in the field of resonance that activates the autonomic and limbic structures as long as it takes to activate the structures sufficiently without being prematurely captured by sense-making insights. If the therapist introduces interpretation and insights prematurely, the consciousness is drawn out of limbic resonance and onto the next level of mental organization, which is the area of ratiomention (see the next section). Through the implicit experience that emerges through the limbic resonance, an emotional immersion takes place that would not occur if the focus was only on making sense of the client's responses. In therapy that is aimed at limbic resonance there is often no reason to verbalize the implicit content, and even if the experience requires verbalization, it is only a small part of the implicit knowledge that can be articulated verbally.

Two limbic systems engage in a mutual field of resonance through facial expressions, gaze contact, prosody, and body movements. In children, new synapses form in the limbic structures, the cingulate gyrus, and the orbitofrontal cortex, among other places, when the child engages in affective attunement through play and contact. Limbic attunement leads to a vitalizing buildup of energy that initiates neural growth. This attunement with the environment enhances the resilience and flexibility of the nervous system to stressors. The capacity to engage in affective attunement forms the basis for subsequent emotional self-regulation. Through the limbic system there is an automatic, rapidly responding regulation of emotional states between client and therapist. Freud touched on this aspect when he wrote that psychotherapy always involves affects, and that the therapist must direct his unconscious at the client's unconscious to reconstruct the client's unconscious (Schore, 2003b).

The limbic system exchanges emotional information and does not deal with causal connections. On this level, the therapy aims to establish or reactivate limbic attunement to facilitate self-regulation processes and neural integration as in the primary relations. As mentioned earlier, therapeutic intervention on this level is a laborious effort, since this system requires a high degree of repetition to develop. As Bentzen (2010) pointed out, nature established limbic attunement with a view to long-term relations, not processes of 10–12 sessions.

Intervention on the Level of the Prefrontal Cortex

MacLean called the third layer ratiomentation, and this area consists mainly of the neocortex, especially the prefrontal cortex, which makes it possible to structure, organize, and carry out long-term planning. The neomammalian brain is often associated with the thinking brain that expands a feeling with the thoughts that are thought about it. This is where mental imagery can be preserved and manipulated, and plans and perceptual images are created. This area makes it possible to delay gratification, to select one strategy over another, and to suppress or control emotions or act differently in order to manage a situation better.

The prefrontal cortex is situated close to all the main subcortical structures both in the brain stem and in the limbic system, and it is in charge of ultimate affect regulation. The area is crucial for the formation of object permanence and plays a key role in the maintenance of emotional stability. The many connections between the prefrontal cortex and the rest of the neocortex give humans a more powerful imagination than any other species and the ability to form complex ideas (Bentzen & Hart, 2005; Hart, 2008). The orbitofrontal cortex has a large number of functions. For example, an intact orbitofrontal function makes it possible to distinguish mental states from physical reality, and, as mentioned above, the function enables object permanence and impulse inhibition. An example is described in the case story below, where Jon draws on his prefrontal regions to suppress and inhibit impulses from the subcortical regions but also manages to dissolve this inhibition through the prefrontal regions.

Intervention Form

Jon, age 28, is seeking therapy because he has suffered from depression for 3 years and has been taking antidepressants. He would like to phase out the medicine, but he is worried that the depression might return. Jon explains that his parents were always very appropriate and correct, and he thinks that he had to suppress many sides of himself as a child to earn his parents' love. He has always felt a high level of inner energy and vitality that could not be expressed, and, for example, when he told his parents that he had been out partying, singing, and playing in a band, or driving race cars, they responded with tacit disapproval. Jon speaks in a soft voice and thinks twice before he says anything. He says that there is a thought grinder inside him that never stops, and he always makes sure to think before he speaks. The therapeutic process is brief, as Jon quickly becomes aware how he suppresses his emotions to adjust to others' needs. He quickly agrees with himself that he is going to live out his potential more and express his emotions and his thoughts. He begins to speak louder, go to rock concerts, take part in car races, and so on. He knows that he is making both his parents and his girlfriend worried, but he is now able to have a reasonable dialogue with them about it.

The vast majority of psychological therapy forms involve the orbitofrontal cortex. It is in this region that somatic sensations, feelings, and self-reflection reach awareness. The therapeutic process here aims primarily at making the client aware of the perceptual images, words, and narratives that summarize the totality of the individual's perceptions of himself and his relations in life. Next, these internal representations can be examined and adjusted in relation to the individual's actual life and possibilities. The activation of structures in the orbitofrontal cortex leads to a higher degree of flexibility in the nervous system, as the orbitofrontal cortex is a superconvergence zone that receives input from all sensory and emotional circuits and sends information back to the sensory and affective regions. The association areas in the orbitofrontal cortex establish the sensorimotor integration of the self in time and place and enable us to plan future events. An appropriate activation of the orbitofrontal cortex makes it possible to sense emotional continuity, regardless of the current mood state here and now. This enhances the stabilization of the sense of identity and makes it possible to relate to the past, be in the present, and make plans for an imagined future (Schore, 1994, 2003b).

Intervention Aimed at Overactivated or Underactivated Prefrontal Structures

As mentioned in the introduction to this chapter, one should distinguish between psychological disorders anchored in limbic dysfunction, for example borderline issues (as in the case of Anna below), and disorders that are anchored in prefrontal, inhibiting disturbances, such as traditional neurotic states (as in the case of Jon). Borderline personality disorders consist of unstable and overactivated representations that require interventions that last long enough to coordinate the limbic interaction processes with prefrontal images and conclusions. Neurotic states consist of excessive inhibition in the prefrontal cortex, which prevents the subcortical functions from being expressed in an appropriate manner. On this level, short-term intervention is often an option (Bentzen & Hart, 2005).

In disorders where the prefrontal cortex is underactivated, as in borderline disorders and PTSD, the main issue is often that the client does not want to let go of an ambivalent and defensive way of relating to others, or that there is an ongoing retraumatization of the original events. The lack of mentalizing capacity and the retraumatization probably occur because the prefrontal and verbal structures are not activated. In PTSD, the client seeks protection from anxiety, and when the anxiety is triggered, she feels in instant danger. In this situation, the client must first be supported in remembering the traumatic event rather than reliving it. By mentalizing the incident, the client can turn it into a memory. A memory is a mental state that elicits thoughts, feelings, and images, where the client is able to distinguish internal life from physical reality. Not only the internal representation needs to be changed but also the capacity for mentalization as a reflective function.

Anna is 52 years old and seeks therapy because she sometimes feels depressive and lonely. Since she was 30, she has been a successful career woman. She was divorced 10 years ago but still sees her ex-husband on weekends, when she invites him to her home. She has an adult daughter with whom she has had a problematic relationship ever since the girl reached puberty. Currently, there are long periods of time when Anna does not want to have any contact with her. Anna was raised in the country as the third of four siblings. Her father died early, and her mother continued to run the family farm. Anna describes that she was always in poor health and was considered stupid. When she was about 10 years old she was sexually abused on several occasions by one of the farmhands. She was close to her younger brother, who died at age 15. As an adult she felt a need to prove herself to her mother, so she moved to the city and bought a retail business. When Anna talks about her life she complains and feels that she is being treated unfairly, especially by her closest family and friends. She is unable to reflect on her own share in the altercations. She complains about an array of somatic problems and about the doctors not taking her seriously. Every time the therapist disagrees with her or asks her to focus on her own feelings, she gets hostile and feels misunderstood. She refers to statements by the therapist that she felt were hurtful and offensive, but the therapist has trouble recognizing these statements. The therapeutic process goes on for years with one session per week, and for a long time it is hard to discern any progress. The therapist makes herself available in a limbically attuned and neutral field, accepting Anna's ambivalence and abuse. She does not confront Anna but contains and supports her. After a few years, Anna angrily asks the therapist what she thinks Anna is getting out of the therapy. It is only when the therapist laughs and replies that they both appear to be surviving that there is a moment of meeting that shifts the therapeutic process to a new level where it is possible to begin working with internal sensations, perceptual images, and mentalization processes.

The mentalizing capacity develops in a secure relationship, and as already described, children who have been exposed to abusive and insecure attachment relationships often find it hard to mentalize. In the therapeutic process the goal at this level of mentalization is to activate the neural circuits in the orbitofrontal cortex and the medial part of the prefrontal cortex. This enables the client to reflect and to link emotions and reflections, which changes the client's way of relating to others. Personality development is not achieved by developing new cognitive skills, having new insights, or dissolving repressions. The point is to develop an openness to new possibilities, to feel and think in new ways (Allen, 2002; Fonagy, 1999a).

Integrating Insight

Winnicott (1971a) has suggested that psychotherapy takes place in the overlap of the patient's and the therapist's areas of playing. If the patient is unable to play, the first step must be to enable him to play. The prefrontal regions have a high degree of plasticity throughout life, and the therapeutic process utilizes this experience-dependent maturation by creating flexibility in the frontal lobe system. The use of metaphors, for example, is particularly integrative as it activates structures in exactly this region, which is connected to a large number of subcortical structures. The development of self-awareness makes it possible for the client to reflect. Insight develops an explicit and more volitional potential for behavioral changes. The mentalizing part of the emotional brain integrates emotional and motivational aspects in relation to cognitive impressions, which makes it possible to process affect-related meaning (Schore, 2003b).

The dorsolateral prefrontal cortex, which contains the executive functions (among other functions), combines sensory, motor, and emotional information and shapes it into plans, actions, thoughts, and ideas. The dorsolateral prefrontal cortex is at the top of the hierarchy and is in charge of the ultimate integration of neural circuits. The executive functions contribute to a reorganization of neural circuits and connect and integrate input that makes it possible to devise goal-oriented plans and implement them within a planned temporal structure. This region connects imaginative and creative capacities, involving, among others, the parietal lobes and limbic regions. An integration of the dorsolateral prefrontal cortex with the limbic and autonomic nervous systems means that the planning and execution of plans will be "in the service of the self." On this level of mental organization, learning takes place through focused attention, and ego organization is unhindered. Psychoanalytic, cognitive, and narrative therapy forms are aimed at structures in this part of the nervous system, and personal development is only fully integrated when a reflective mentalization of emotions and sensations has taken place on this level through prefrontal self-reflection, among other processes (Bentzen & Hart, 2005).

We have now looked at the vertical or hierarchical organization of the brain and at the way in which the therapeutic process connects and attunes with the various levels of mental organization. As mentioned earlier, a thorough evaluation of the client's issues and level of mental organization is crucial for assessing which therapeutic method is capable of effecting a neural process of change. Dysfunctions that are anchored in the autonomic nervous system will probably benefit from interventions aimed initially at functions related to sensory integration and attunement within a physiobiological field. Dysfunctions that are anchored in the limbic system will probably benefit from interventions aimed initially at psychobiological limbic attunement in the intersubjective field, while prefrontal impulse-inhibiting disorders will probably benefit from intervention strategies aimed at perceptions, thought content, and cognition. In the next section we will look at the horizontal or lateralized organization of the brain and at the way in which the therapeutic process pursues integration across the two hemispheres.

Intervention in the Lateralized Brain

Before the acquisition of language, the infant may experience an immediate, holistic, and continuous sense of being. The development of language introduces a split between symbols and firsthand experience. Language is only partially able to grasp experiences. In healthy development, language functions in the left hemisphere integrate with unsymbolized being in the right hemisphere. When language fails to connect with the unsymbolized representations, words may actually distance the person from the experience. The left hemisphere enables us to reason and interpret abstract content, while the right hemisphere carries the implicit knowledge about emotional states that is associated with the events that the client has lived through. This might also be referred to as the refinement of raw emotions into symbols. Normally, the internal representations are associated with interpretations through a process of symbolization and reasoning. If the right-hemispheric representations cannot connect with the left hemisphere, the left hemisphere will rely on acquired rules and logic.

The transfer of information from the right to the left hemisphere enables the development of linguistic symbols capable of representing the meaning of an experience, while the emotion that the experience generates is perceived and felt. Neural circuits that connect language to regions throughout the rest of the frontal lobes enable both spoken and internal language to guide behavior and regulate affect. Creating and recalling stories requires connections between multisensory, emotional, temporal, and memory capacities. Only once these connections have formed is language able to organize the brain and play a role in psychotherapy (Schore, 2003b, 2001c; Siegel, 1999).

When a client embarks on a therapy process, the left hemisphere acts as the interpreter that tells the story about the client, but the story is rarely enough. In many cases, the narratives that organize the explicit identity are not enough to describe the implicit identity. The right hemisphere presents itself through bodily expressions, body language, emotions, and attitudes. The therapist has to note both representations and any discrepancies between them. An important aspect of the therapeutic process on this level is to make room for experiences to be verbalized and included in a narrative, intersubjective community. The therapist helps the client search for meaningful content to facilitate the reconstruction of a psychodynamic understanding. In this process, the therapist has to take the client's experiences seriously, feel them within, and share them with the client. The integrative process has a direct influence on the capacity of the right hemisphere to regulate basic emotional states.

On this level, interpretations are important, but they require timing and readiness and must be incorporated in the development of present moments and limbic attunement. The implicit and explicit systems and the right and left hemispheres are profoundly interconnected. When the interpretation is presented at an appropriate moment the client will have a strong emotional reaction, as limbic and autonomic regions integrate with the prefrontal cortex across the hemispheres, and the client will begin to sense the feelings that she was defending against. Subsequently, the client will often be able to express herself in a more self-reflecting way. Interpretations should be addressed and repeated in many different situations to build new memory networks. This helps expand and stabilize new associative areas in the brain and build new narratives. These narratives may contain altered aspects of self-identity, which were not previously integrated in the autobiographical memory.

Episodic and autobiographical memory and the ability to form narratives are specifically human qualities, and no therapeutic process can cause profound changes unless the bodily and emotional components are integrated with the autobiographical memory and narratives, a topic that I revisit in the following section.

The Integration of Memory Networks and the Narrative Construction

Episodic and autobiographical memory is stored symbolically as language or mental images in the explicit memory system. Edelman and Tononi said, "Memory is more like the melting and refreezing of a glacier than it is like an inscription on a rock" (2000, p. 93). In a sense, memory is part of a perception or fantasy, and we all carry false memories in the sense that we combine memory fragments, remember erroneous details, and fill in the gaps with qualified guesswork. Implicit knowledge is not always stored as episodic and autobiographical memory, and hence it cannot be recalled as such. Episodic memory relies on the hippocampus, and while the implicit memory system is functioning from birth, the explicit memory system does not develop until the age of 3–5 years. After this age, implicit and explicit knowledge is increasingly integrated through intersubjective events, and thus, more of the client's world is made explicit and verbally comprehensible. The client begins to be able to define and redefine herself through the reflections that she exchanges with the therapist. Reflecting on one's emotions and thoughts helps develop the internal representations and make them an integrated part of a more individualized self-perception. Much of our identity is developed and consolidated in this process. When it becomes possible to symbolize emotions, the self is integrated on a higher level, which develops a new self-perception (Schore, 1994; Stern, 2004).

Through language, experiences can be converted to narratives and stories. Language seems to be a key integrative mechanism, and halfway through the second year of life, a sensitive period for the language regions, language functions in the left hemisphere integrate with communicative and prosodic elements that have already developed in the right hemisphere (see Chapter 3, the section on neuroaffective development, pp. 93–94). Language combines actions with emotional sensations, and through the narratives sensations, emotions, thoughts, and actions are interlinked in ways that organize both an internal and an external reality.

The language that is used for mentalization and self-reflection reflects a level of integration that is situated in the prefrontal cortex, and through verbal self-reflection, cognition mixes with affects and sensations, which makes it possible for us to have thoughts about emotions. Through self-reflection, emotions connect with an explicit understanding that is capable of editing our own narratives about who we are.

Many forms of human interaction involve a common construction of narratives. Narratives are an important joint construction between the client and the therapist, and the story that is constructed has a greater impact on the client's current psychological life than the historical facts. Narratives are reorganized in a way that enables clients to tell their stories about their feelings at a given moment, and together, clients and therapists search for meaning through the narratives. All verbal content and narratives, including questions about what is felt within the body here and now, spring from implicit nonverbal information that is reshaped to explicit content through verbalization (Siegel, 1999; Stern, 1995, 2004).

Most of the time, language is used to share nonessential information, and most of the time verbalization is predictable and repetitive, replete with phrases that serve to fill out moments of silence, and so on. Left-hemispheric language is often fantastical and idealizing; this is the public language that is used without necessarily being connected to self-reflection, and which integrates the left and right hemispheres. Through the narrative process the client attempts to make the world make sense and get a grip on his or her own states, and occasionally the narratives are used for cognitive self-reflection. Narratives are a valuable tool in the organization and integration of neural networks, and self-reflection helps modify autobiographical memory. As humans, we have the capacity to reorganize our life story and thus find new ways of perceiving and experiencing it. The exchange of narratives helps strengthen and develop the cingulate gyrus and the orbitofrontal cortex, and it is through the narrative organization that the raw emotions are converted to symbols. Senses and emotions are regulated in the orbitofrontal cortex once this structure is mature, and these right-hemispheric experiences are communicated to the left hemisphere for further processing, which enables an integration of nonverbal implicit experiences with explicit verbal regions that can then be conveyed to others. Verbal symbols attribute meaning to the experience of feeling of perceiving.

The Integration of Narratives and Autobiographical Memory

Through autobiographical and autonoetic (self-perceiving) memory, narratives are created that connect processes from various neural networks to a coherent and integrated story about the self, which supports affect regulation. However, the narratives may be dissociated from episodic and autobiographical memory. Clients' ability to have autobiographical memories that support their narrative generalizations reflects the degree of integration of their nervous system. The therapist must be aware of the relationship between narrative generalizations and episodic and autobiographical memories. A lack of balance between generalizations and specific memories reflects that the internal representations are not integrated in the various structures in the nervous system. One often gets the impression, for example in the adult attachment interview, that clients protect themselves from dealing with unpleasant childhood experiences with caregivers. They use self-protection strategies to maintain the attachment, even if the strategy causes a fragmentation of emotions and experiences (Fonagy, 2001).

The narrative constructions that children originally form in collaboration with the caregivers reflect the implicit values and problem-solving strategies and the parents' worldview, which child use at an early stage to define themselves and discover a complex world. The social language in the left hemisphere serves to create a logical, coherent, and positive presentation of the social world and also contains an internal language that enables us to have private thoughts and plans and prepare behavior. There is also an implicit aspect to the internal language, as there may be critical voices, for example, in reflection of early shame experiences. The mentalizing self-reflection process requires higher levels of affect regulation and cognitive processing.

Bottom-Up and Top-Down Intervention

The limbic system balances impulses between the autonomic arousal states and the prefrontal cortex, and this system relies on both bottom-up and top-down control (see Fig. 8.2). Both therapies that operate through top-down and bottom-up integration connect the levels in the triune brain and merge body, emotions, and conscious awareness. This

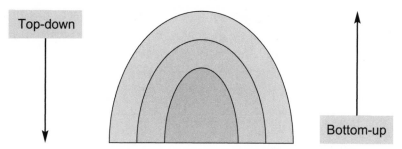

Figure 8.2. Top-down and bottom-up processes in the triune brain

integration includes a balancing of the arousal systems in the sympathetic and parasympathetic nervous systems, the regulation of raw emotions, and a development of the capacity for processing, inhibiting, and organizing impulses and emotions in the prefrontal cortex. Sensations, affects, and cognition are all necessary aspects of the therapeutic process to achieve integration of dissociated neural circuits.

Most forms of therapy work with integration. In body psychotherapy the client's bodily expressions are interpreted and made available for conscious reflection. Tense muscles form body armors, while muscles that lack tone make the body collapse. The body shapes itself in response to the attunement processes and the misattunements or trauma that emerge in contact with the caregivers. Body armors and low muscle tone develop on all levels in the nervous system and are reflected throughout the individual's existence. A verbalization of somatic experiences normally allows the client to integrate intense sensory and emotional states in the explicit field of awareness. For example, Gestalt therapy works directly with emotional aspects and facial expressions, gestures, movements, and so on that are brought into the field of awareness and exaggerated and eventually externalized and understood through verbalization.

Psychoanalytic and narrative therapy forms interpret and analyze the sensory and emotional states and thus integrate implicit consciousness with explicit consciousness through metaphors and symbols. Cognitive therapy focuses on clients' distorted and dysfunctional thoughts, assessments, and belief systems, which determine their emotions and actions and which generate and exacerbate psychological disorders. By activating cortical processing through the deliberate control of thoughts and emotions, these therapy forms facilitate more positive assessments and promote an understanding of emotional reactions that affect feelings and behavior. Among other things, these intervention forms aim at processing internal representations on a cognitive level, that is, in the medial part of the prefrontal and dorsolateral prefrontal cortex. The purpose of this intervention is to give the client an experience of being able to understand and manage symptoms by activating circuits in the prefrontal cortex, so that they can connect with and possibly inhibit impulses from the subcortical levels.

The key is to combine intervention methods that can maximize the integration process, that is, which can initiate top-down processes through the cortical control of limbic structures through narratives, externalization, symbolic processing, and interpretation as well as bottom-up processes through a regulation of limbic and autonomic circuits. The more neural structures are activated, the greater is the possibility of neural integration. Sensations, motor functions, emotions, actions, and mental phenomena must be considered and combined. It is the dialectic between the various methods of intervention that are ultimately of most interest in relation to the integration of hierarchical brain structures. As Sørensen (2005) pointed out, it is not always relevant whether the pendulum swing begins in one position or another—whether it is the body that is incapable of containing the thoughts or whether it is the emotions that disrupt logical thinking. Integration can take its point of departure in the intellectual understanding or in bodily meaning. As much as therapy is about establishing attachment and relationships, it is about the reorganization of brain structures, including the promotion of mentalization. One of the goals of therapy is to shake up fixated patterns and create an integration process through top-down as well as bottom-up intervention.

Summary

The integration and reintegration of neural circuits requires the nervous system to connect with another nervous system and enter into a field of resonance with it. Biologically, psychological healing and development are about expanding the arousal capacity of the nervous system, expanding neural connectedness in the hierarchical structures of the brain, and activating complex and abstract levels of higher neocortical activity that are connected with the more primitive levels of mental organization. A successful therapeutic process will activate all levels of consciousness. The key is to integrate bodily sensory, perceptual, motor, emotional, associative, and rational functions and bring them into a mutual dialogue (Bentzen & Hart, 2005).

A child's personality structure is created through an integration of innate structures and the child's interactions with primary caregivers and, later, significant others. In previous chapters I have discussed how an insecure attachment pattern can lead to later problems with affect and arousal regulation, mentalization, and ways of relating to others. Thus, when we consider psychological forms of intervention in connection with children, it is important to include the family and environmental perspective. In particular, systemic and structural theory have emphasized the child's role as the symptom bearer for family issues, and in this regard, a number of intervention methods have been developed. In Chapter 9, I discuss the need to provide consistent and well-considered interventions to offer children with psychological difficulties the best possible support.

CHAPTER NINE

Intervention Within a Dynamic System: Family and Environmental Therapy

[T]here were essential similarities in information processing across cells, organs, organisms, humans, groups, and social organizations. Each level has its own unique characteristics, but all are living systems open to energy and information. They maintain themselves in a changing environment by regulating inputs and outputs of matter, energy, or information and by preserving internal steady states of critical variables through governance of subsystems. These living systems also share similarities in the way they respond to overload or "underload" of information, both of which can lead to pathology of the system.

Beatrice Beebe and Frank Lachmann (2002, p. 24)

Winnicott pointed out that no child exists without a mother, and that it is an abstraction to fail to consider this relationship. In treating children with psychological and behavioral difficulties, it is crucial to include the child's parents and other family members as well as the network that makes up the child's everyday environment. Our culture is changing all the time, and Bowlby (1988) noted that in previous generations, mothers were surrounded by their own mothers, teenage sisters, cousins, and others, all of whom were involved in raising the children. These helpers not only enabled the mother to take breaks from her role as caregiver, they also provided friendship, advice, and support. The child had access to alternative attachment figures, and the parent-child relationship and attachment formation were under less pressure. With the current situation, the family system is more vulnerable, and the parents' potential inadequacies as caregivers may lead to severe damage in the parent-child relationship, as there is no extended family network to take over periodically when the parents are overburdened.

This chapter addresses a variety of views on child therapy that go well beyond the mental organization of the intrapsychic construction. As Eia Asen (2005), among others, pointed out, there are many levels in the child's life that have to be integrated if one hopes to change the child's psyche and behavior, ranging from the child's functioning level, the parents' way of relating to the child, the family constellation, the social context that the family finds itself in, and the professional support provided to the family. This chapter addresses some of these levels, including the structuring and handling of a holistic treatment approach, relational therapy, psychotherapy with children, and environmental therapy.

The systemic and structural understanding of the child as the symptom bearer for the family's challenges and issues is essential, and many theoreticians have emphasized the importance of the way in which the psychopathology reflects the interpersonal or family dynamic relationships. First, I offer a brief description of dynamic systemic theory.

Dynamic Systemic Theory

Throughout most of the 20th century there was an interest in the inner workings of systems, and since the 1950s so-called dynamic systems theories that focus on the relational aspect have developed. These theories operate with a circular concept of causal relations: No event has one single causal explanation, and the focus is on reciprocity and on the movement between separate phenomena (Isager, 1999).

A system is an organized pattern or network of elements that are coordinated in mutual dependency and operate as a whole. The whole cannot be broken down to its parts without something essential being lost, and the parts cannot be understood without being seen in relation to the whole, which is different from the sum of its parts. Everything is part of a system, and an observer will have to choose a point of view. Biological and social entities are open systems that rely on boundaries with a certain degree of permeability.

A system can be divided into an infinite number of subsystems, from microsystems to macrosystems (see Fig. 9.1). For example, the child's close environment (e.g., family, friends, school) constitutes one level,

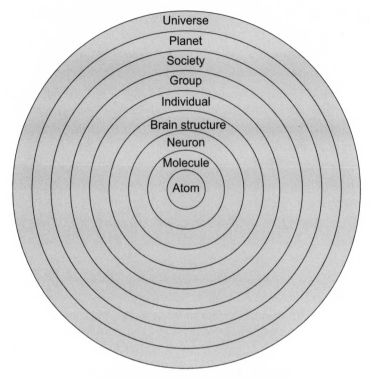

Figure 9.1. A system with subsystems: atom, molecule, neuron, brain structure, individual, group, society, planet, universe.

while the relationship between home and school constitutes another. A third level includes other aspects that affect the child's life, such as the social services department. In addition, there are overall structures within the surrounding culture including economic, social, and political systems, which all the aforementioned subsystems depend on.

Macrosystems regulate social standards for behavior in the subculture, while microsystems regulate daily activities and reflect the recurring patterns and demands that exist in any family. The macrosystems that make up the cultural and societal level structure the child's social environment and consist of a set of control and support systems that are based on norms and cultural codes for interactions. The macrosystem regulates the relationship between individuals on a general level and becomes embedded in societal myths that help regulate the family codes. Any family member is involved in the family's interactions, and the parental figures contain individualized interpretations of the cultural and

familial codes. The parents' interpretations
their previous interactions with significan'
formed their own internal representations

The self and others are interconnecte
velopmental process requires both dif
many levels simultaneously, e.g. in the
namics. Many elements in the system ..
namic interdependency, and any change in in u..
will lead to change in the intrapsychic context. Thus, cha..
of the system leads to system-wide change. Self processes and rela..
processes are interconnected. Change is evident in the present, even
though it is colored by previous events. What appears in the present is a
concretization of previously formed patterns, which manifests itself
within a particular environment (Stern, 2004).

The child's psychological difficulties rarely exist in the child alone but
virtually always in the relationship between a unique child and an environment that fails to facilitate the necessary experiences required for
the child to self-regulate and for the development of more advanced
levels of mental organization. No sophisticated social mammal can be
understood independent of its relationships (Sameroff, 1989). The caregiver has a crucial impact on the child's personality development, as do
other family members, including grandparents, uncles and aunts. When
the child enters daycare or school, it is also important how the child is
perceived and encountered by teachers, peers and others. Other people's perception of the child is of crucial importance for the child's sense
of self and coping strategies, as is other people's perception of the parents and the family in general. Children with psychological and behavioral difficulties often have a large network around them consisting of
social workers and (mental) health professionals, and the family often
receives support on many levels. In this context, it is essential how the
various agencies manage to coordinate their efforts, both with regard to
their perceptions of the child and the family, intervention strategies, a
topic that I review in the next section.

Finding Coherence in an Incoherent Environment

*Shirley and Fred are brother and sister, aged 12 and 10 years, re-
spectively. They both attend a mainstream school, but due to their*

*...hey receive special needs services. Fred is enrolled in in-
...sychotherapy in a child psychiatric ward because he is an
...ly timid and vulnerable boy, who mostly lives inside his own
...y world. Shirley has recently completed a prolonged stay in a
...th psychiatric ward after several attempts at suicide. She is cur-
...ently enrolled in an outpatient therapy group at a youth psychiatric
ward. Their mother has been diagnosed with borderline personality
disorder; she feels extremely guilty about the children's problems, because she feels that they stem from her emotional instability. The
father supports the mother as much as he can; he has a hard time
managing and coping with the family's emotional difficulties. Both
parents receive psychological counseling from a private psychologist
concerning how they should deal with their children's difficulties and
their own relationship. The mother receives counseling from a community psychiatric clinic, where her medication is regulated; in addition she is in frequent contact with her general practitioner. There
is no cooperation between the children's school and the many different treatment professionals.*

To consider the child's psychological difficulties as part of a family system, one has to coordinate and achieve consistency within and among the
family's and the child's treatment and support systems. The view of the
child's difficulties in the professional network is crucial for determining
which interventions are implemented, and an inadequate coordination of
treatment interventions can make the effort inconsistent and ineffectual.
Carr (1999) mentioned that a lack of coordination may perpetuate the
difficulties and maintain an unnecessary degree of fragmentation. In
some areas this fragmentation or lack of coherence in the macrosystem
resembles dissociation in the microsystem of neural circuits.

A family is a dynamic system. To achieve coherence and integration,
the various agencies must have compatible perceptions of the difficulties
of the family system, explicitly pursue a common goal, and each be aware
which level their intervention addresses. When a family enters a treatment system whose efforts are uncoordinated and unintegrated, there is
a real risk that fields of tension emerge between the various agencies or
entities. The individual family members do not receive the support they
need to address their relational patterns and the reflections that the interventions give rise to. The family's difficulties are fragmented, and the

individual members may expose different sides of themselves in different contexts. This hampers development and may lead the individual treatment professionals to develop widely different perceptions of the individual family members and hence pursue different goals.

Fields of tension often develop due to a lack of agreement between the various systems. Children generally have a hard time dealing with fields of tension, especially between their primary caregivers and another important entity. Children are loyal to their caregivers, and if the child has a good relationship, for example, with the school, an environmental therapy setting, a foster family, and so on, the child faces a conflict and potentially stress-related dissociation if the parents express resistance to the interventions that are being implemented. Therapeutic interventions aimed at the child that leave the caregivers feeling excluded or circumvented, and which meet with resistance from the caregivers, are usually contraindicated, as fields of tension will tend to perpetuate the child's psychological difficulties.

Nicholas is 12 years old, and for the past 3 years he has attended a school for children with socioemotional difficulties. The teachers explain that he is maladaptive, lacks empathy, and frequently winds up in conflicts with the other children. His mother says that she has always had an extremely close bond with Nicholas, and she characterizes their relationship as symbiotic. When Nicholas was younger, his father worked abroad and spent very little time at home. Today the parents are divorced, and there are big differences between them and in their way of dealing with Nicholas's problems. While the mother is nervous and worried about letting Nicholas out of her sight, the father thinks that Nicholas is generally capable of handling himself. A year after Nicholas began first grade, he underwent psychological assessment due to learning problems. The assessment concluded that the problems were due to a relational disorder and proposed family therapy. The social worker assigned to the case established a family therapy intervention, and the family attended some seven sessions before the process was interrupted for some reason. The school stated that they could no longer handle Nicholas, and Nicholas switched to the school he is currently attending. The present school states that Nicholas has developed during his 3 years of environmental therapy, but also states that it is doubtful whether he will ever be ready to switch to a mainstream school. The parents have not been offered any support since the original family therapy attempt.

Even though children in our culture are influenced by the relational experiences they have elsewhere, for example day care, school, and peer groups, the caregiver-child relationship and the family unit are still the main locus of children's attachment and their primary source of care. In any treatment context it is essential to support the caregivers in their responsibility and enable them to be active and responsible participants in the efforts to help their child. If this is not possible, the parents should be shown respect based on their capabilities, and the treatment professionals should attempt to attune with them on their level of mental organization.

The Family System

As early as 1946, when Bowlby joined the Tavistock Clinic in London, he did therapy with parents and children where he saw the whole family together. Although it was not until the 1960s that family therapy was widely acknowledged as a therapeutic approach, its basis had already arisen in the United States in the 1920s when psychiatrist Harry Stack Sullivan described mental illness as an interpersonal disorder. In particular, anthropologist Gregory Bateson was known for laying the philosophical foundation for the systemic thinking and therapeutic method that were developed in the 1950s and the 1960s. In the 1970s structural and systemic family therapy was introduced.

The underlying premise of systemic family therapy is that the child's internal representations emerge through relationships, and that every member of the family system reflects the whole. The internal representations are shaped in a network of relationships that are passed on to other relationships and generations through the internal representations. The parents' internal representations, which were shaped by their childhood history, are bearers of the dyadic relationship that they create with their own children. The dyadic relationship is supported by the general system of family relations, which is part of a larger system that has considerable influence on the individual family members' adaptation.

Implicit processes are transferred to ways of being together and the family members' perceptions of each other. For example, a child knows when he is not supposed to say anything negative about the mother, although it is acceptable to speak badly of the father but only to the mother, and so on, or that it is not acceptable to be angry or to mention or feel sadness. The individual family members perceive the others in accordance with their own internal representations and try to affect the others through unconscious staging efforts. The child may be cast as the brains of the family, the straggler, the wild one, and so on, which affects the way in which the parents approach and relate to the child. In this context, internal representations are often viewed as family myths, a system of opinions or common convictions that the individual family members hold about themselves or others, their views of the environment, and their strategies for handling the environment. In some cases, a family member may become a scapegoat, often one or more of the children; in that case, the parents project feelings onto the child to avoid confronting their own pain or anger (Schibbye, 2005).

Salvador Minuchin, who was involved in developing structural family therapy, emphasized the importance of a clear generational hierarchy to the health of the family. Destructive intergenerational alliances lead to dysfunctions. Systemic family therapy, which is often called the Milan approach, states that what impairs a family's current function is a lack of clarity concerning the family members' mutual relations and the rules governing their interactions. The systemic approach to family therapy tries to eliminate the strict boundary between individual and environment without losing sight of the individual. Instead of viewing the individual as the bearer of the pathology, the pathology is treated as a part of the family system, and the child should be viewed as the symptom bearer for unfortunate family interaction patterns (Isager, 1999; Marner, 1999).

The family can be viewed in the framework of linear or nonlinear models. The linear model focuses on the individual family member with somatic, psychodynamic, and behavioral difficulties, while the nonlinear model (the systemic approach) views the child as embedded in a context. Dysfunctional family patterns halt personal growth, and the family stabilizes through coping strategies, attempting to preserve some form of homeostasis and to reduce the anxiety level. The caregivers' dysregulated nervous systems create imbalances in the family system. Over time the neural dysfunction becomes part of the child's neural architecture.

For example, a family system with a weak generational hierarchy does not give the individual family member opportunities to develop a separate sense of self (Sroufe, 1989b).

Minuchin et al. (1978) identified a variety of characteristics that contributed to maintaining a dysregulated family pattern. At one end of the spectrum, he identified an enmeshed and overprotective family pattern, and at the other end, a disengaged and unprotected family pattern. In an enmeshed family system, the family members are overly involved in each other; there are many alliances, and the boundaries are vague and easily violated. Individual features are lost, and the boundaries that define individual autonomy are so vague that differentiated functioning is almost impossible. Overprotection is evident through high levels of concern for each other's well-being, and the family members are hypersensitive to tension or conflict. The parents' overprotection impairs the child's ability to develop autonomy, competence, and interests, and the child often feels a big responsibility for protecting the family. At the other end of the spectrum are the disengaged families that have communication difficulties, and where the family members are unable to protect each other. The parents do not respond, even when a response is called for. In the disengaged family structure the parents do not show relevant concern for their children and may, for example, fail to respond to a child's criminal behavior.

Often, the parents are themselves from enmeshed or disengaged homes that have lacked differentiation, and if the parents have not previously established a generational hierarchy for themselves and their family, anxiety or tension can make the parent turn to the child for needs satisfaction. The parents' own unresolved needs are projected onto the child, and the child comes to fill this role not only because of his vulnerability but also because he senses that it makes the parents less tense and more predictable. All children, even those who have been abused, are loyal and attached to their parents. Children may be sad, may feel that they are treated unjustly, and may be trapped in destructive mood swings that deprive them of the possibility of receiving the love that they yearn for, but nevertheless they remain attached to the parents, although the attachment pattern is insecure. Even children who deny the attachment often yearn to express their love and receive love in return. As mentioned in previous chapters, the child's life is initially organized through the relationship with the caregiver, but over time the child becomes a more active agent, and eventually the child will behave in ways that preserve the pattern.

Often, what distinguishes parents who are able to establish secure attachment with their children from parents who have established an avoidant, ambivalent, or disorganized attachment is the capacity for mentalization and self-reflection in relation to internal states and other people's behavior. The parents' own disorder means that their internal representations and behavior remain unconscious and can be difficult to change, especially if they are not motivated for change or do not think that their children's difficulties constitute a problem. All parents love their children and want to do what is best for them. However, a parent's personality can be so severely affected by his or her own history that the ability to parent is compromised. Thus, prior to setting up a family therapy intervention it is important to assess parenting competence and the family system, which is the topic of the next section.

Assessing the Family System

When a child shows signs of a behavioral disorder or psychological problems, the first assessment must be based on the biological or environmentally reactive foundation of the disorder and on the interaction of environmental and biological factors. In relational disorders the main focus should be on the child's relationship with the attachment figure rather than on the child's behavior or psychological disorder. However, the quality of the interactions that make up a relationship is one of the hardest aspects to evaluate. What matters in the caregiver-child relationship is not only what the persons do together but also how they do it. For example, if the mother responds with sensitivity to the child's needs and expresses that she enjoys contact with the child, this marks a very different relationship than one where the mother is insensitive, dutiful, and distant. The quality must also be assessed on the basis of a description of the interaction pattern, including timing, sequence, affective tone, vitality, and so on. For example, it makes a big difference when the caregiver comforts the child, whether she does so in response to the child's expressions, and whether the infant falls into the caregiver's embrace or is tense. It is important to assess the level of hostility, admiration, and joy and the degree of affective attunement and misattunement, mutual emotional support, and the establishment of a joint field of attention. Another important dimension is the caregiver's flexibility and tolerance toward conflict and conflict resolution. For example, is the relationship easily threatened by conflict, or is there a tolerance of ambiguity and difference? Relational disorders consist of recurring inappropriate interaction patterns over time. A study of families with children with aggressive difficulties found that in problem families the child's aggression was five times more likely to elicit a hostile response from the parents compared with families that were not defined as problem families (Hinde & Stevenson-Hinde, 1986; Sameroff, 1989; Sroufe, 1979, 1989b).

It is necessary to combine the history of family dynamics with direct observations of the child and the caregiver. There is often a dynamic link between the child's way of relating to the caregiver from early childhood and their later mutual relationship and bond (Zeanah et al., 1993). Internal representations remain fairly stable over time and give rise to a particular social behavior. By assessing the dyadic and triadic relationships in a family, it is possible to put together a mosaic of the family's combined internal representations. The stability of the internal representations exists not only on an individual level but also in the family's collective way of coordinating their mutual behavior (Reiss, 1989).

Assessments have to consider the fact that the child relates differently to different caregivers; hence, it is necessary to assess the child's relationship with different family members. In family therapy, the therapist is able to observe the interactions of the various family members, while individual therapy has to rely on what the client says about her perceptions of present and former interactions with significant individuals. To be able to observe the intersubjectivity or family dynamics in the context where it unfolds on a daily basis offers a unique set of therapeutic possibilities, which I address in the following sections.

Intervention in the Family System

Mona, age 14, was referred to the local family therapy center because she refused to go to school. Despite her parents' efforts and an arrangement where the school picked her up from home, the problem persisted, and Mona repeatedly ran away when she was being picked up. She insisted on being home schooled. She was described as a sweet and clever girl who had become increasingly isolated. She seemed depressive and talked about not wanting to live. The parents were caring and very concerned for Mona. She did not wish to go into counseling with her parents, and therefore she was initially offered individual counseling with the family center therapist. It took the therapist a long time to establish a trusting relationship with her, but when this was accomplished, Mona told the therapist that she was raped. She never dared tell anyone else about it until then. At the same time, the parents were in counseling with another therapist at the family therapy center. Eventually, joint therapy sessions were arranged for the parents and Mona, but she did not want to tell her parents about the rape. At one point the mother requested individual sessions with her therapist, and after an intensive psychotherapeutic process she said that she was sexually abused by her own father. She spoke of severe anxiety and sexual difficulties. Eventually, the mother agreed to tell her husband about her experiences. Through this process the family developed a closer bond, and Mona eventually felt secure enough to tell her parents what happened to her. Mona opened up more, her mood lifted, and she was able to go back to school.

In a systemic therapy situation, the therapist must be able to decode the family dynamics and create a context where psychotherapeutic intervention is possible. Before the therapeutic context is established, the family therapist has to consider which family member to focus on first, how frequent the intervention should be, how long the individual sessions should be, and where the therapy should take place, for example, whether it should be in the family's home or in the therapist's office. The family therapist must consider an activity to do with the family to create a context that can also be addressed therapeutically. Finally, it is also necessary to consider which family therapy method to apply, whether psychodynamic, systemic, or something else (Asen, 2005), knowing full well that the fundamental therapeutic stance and general relational processes (reviewed in Chapter 7) remain the same whether the therapy involves individuals, couples, or family groups.

Whether the therapist chooses to begin the intervention in the family system through sessions with the entire family, with the parents alone, or with the child alone, the focus must involve the entire family system, and the parents must always be included in the therapeutic context. For example, one may direct an intervention at the parents by addressing their internal representations and parenting behavior, and one may assist the child in perceiving the attachment figures more accurately and attuning emotionally with them to give the child an alternative and positive set of relational options. The younger the child is, the more the intervention has to be directed at the caregivers. It is important to remember that the intervention should not prevent the development of contact between the child and the parents by having the therapist take over the care functions. The parents are irreplaceable, and if they are unable to meet crucial caring needs, this must be clarified with them in an attempt to make them accept that the child has a need that should be met by someone else.

If the child actively opposes the parents' requests, the parents' task is more complicated. The parents of a child who is filled with anger and resistance often have problems acting openly and lovingly. It may be hard for them to handle the child's destructive and aggressive behavior in an emotionally neutral manner that does not make the child feel rejected, especially if the parents already have emotional difficulties of their own. In many cases the child only needs support when the caregiver fails to contain or manage his difficulties within a contact that facilitates development. The family therapist's dialogue with the parents aims to help them understand their child and use their intentions constructively. When the child begins to experience receiving increasing support from the parents, the child will also be more secure in interactions with them (Øvreeide, 2001a).

In therapy, a relational problem is often resolved on the age level that the child is on, but the parents may return with a new problem associated with the same relational disorder but presented in a different way when the child is older. Stern (1995) pointed out that this does not necessarily mean that the therapy was unsuccessful in changing an inappropriate interaction pattern. Occasionally, brief but recurring interventions may be appropriate. Often, an intensive process will have enabled the parents to change counterproductive interaction patterns, but when the child's development challenges the parents' competence on a new level, they become insecure and need temporary support.

There are many approaches to and variants of family therapy. Here, the term family therapy is used broadly, as it often consists of a combination of family observation, family sessions, and sessions with the parents and child alone. For example, sessions with the parents may be necessary if a marital conflict impairs the child's development, or if there is a highly charged field of tension between them. Sessions with the parents alone may also address their internal representations and any stress factors that do not concern the child directly. The child may need some time to discuss difficulties with a neutral person, because he is worried about the parents' response. Systems-oriented forms of family therapy emphasize that the child should not be perceived as a patient or a scapegoat; instead, the child's responses should be understood in the context of a dysfunctional family system.

Family Therapy for Parents and Infants

Fred was 18 months old when he was referred to a child psychiatric ward due to his failure to thrive. He eats little; ever since birth he has had serious screaming fits, and his parents are exhausted by lack of sleep. According to the parents' description, when Fred started day care, he ate well in the day care facility and much less at home. He is better at eating with his father than with his mother. Similarly, the father has an easier time putting him to bed at night, and the mother describes that the son is bossy toward her. The parents are receiving family therapy, which examines and discusses the interactions between them and Fred. At the 6-month evaluation the parents say that they are ready to end the therapy, even if the counterproductive interaction patterns continue to occur, especially when they feel tired or under pressure. They feel that they are now able to handle the difficulties on their own.

Even though the same relational disorders can underlie an infant's eating problems at the age of 2 months and interaction problems at the age of 10 years, the child's age is crucial for family therapy. In intervention methods aimed at the early caregiver-infant interaction, the main emphasis is on the parents' internal representations, their sensitive empathy with the infant, and their emotional openness and accessibility. Family therapy with infants and their parents often takes place on a concrete behavioral level. The therapeutic focus on the interactions between the parents and the infant, interpretations of the interactions, and discussions with the parents about their possibilities in the interaction can change the parents' internal representations of the child.

When the mother interacts with her infant, her internal representations of being with her infant are constantly activated. The activated representations attribute meaning and emotional quality to the concrete interaction and moment. Parents who interact with their child are in a meaningful current context, where the child's nervous system is affected and matured through the many microinteractions. It is the recurring everyday events that have the greatest impact on the child's development. Family therapy focuses on microinteractions, and the key element is the caregiver's and child's way of engaging in attunement, misattunement, reparation of misattunements, and so on, which constantly play out in the unfolding interaction. Typically, parents tend to attribute positive qualities to their child, and an absence of this feature is a serious prognostic indicator (Møller & Hart, 2001; Stern, 1995).

It is important to make the caregiver see herself through the child's eyes. An essential aspect of parenting competence is the parents' ability to change, and it is important to encourage the caregiver to mentalize based on concrete reality and to process it metaphorically, hypothetically, and reflectively, for example, by asking the caregiver to assume different roles in a sort of pretend play. In a relational therapeutic context this can be pursued through enactment, which means using the therapeutic situation to give the caregiver and the child an experience they have never previously had, for example, by creating a situation where the child voluntarily sits in the mother's lap. On the brain stem level, the therapist should observe and decode the participants' body language and distance or closeness. The therapist achieves limbic resonance by attuning with both the child and the caregiver to create a secure context. On a prefrontal level, the internal representations and perceptions are clarified together with the caregiver. Like individual therapy, interaction therapy is about integrating the various levels of mental organization by associating body language with emotions, symbols, reflections, and verbalizations.

Family therapists are not authorities with an answer to the parents' problems, but in a shared effort the parents' interactions with the child can be explored in an inquisitive and curious approach to uncover new possibilities of being together in more satisfying ways. The precondition for a successful therapy outcome is offering the parents the necessary help to discover their own potential, believe in their own parenting behavior, and approach themselves and the child with curiosity. It is crucial for the outcome not to offer the parents ultimate interpretations of their interaction behavior but hypotheses that give them an opportunity to discuss what makes sense from their perspective. It is important to appeal to the parents' curiosity and to make them authorities on their own life with the child. An important part of the process is to promote the parents' ability to mentalize about their interactions with the child. Through family therapy the parents can be made aware of aspects and expressions in their child that they had not previously noticed. It is important to try to promote more vital and reality-adjusted representations of the child; one means of doing this is to confront the caregiver with the real child as the family therapists see him.

Family Therapy for Parents and Schoolchildren or Teenagers

Suzanna, age 16, has been referred to counseling because of behavioral problems, self-destructive behavior, and severe mood swings that prevent her from handling her schoolwork, although she is a very gifted girl. In a preliminary session with Suzanna and her mother, it becomes clear that the two are unable to engage in emotionally attuned contact with one another. Suzanna is unable to articulate her view of her own problems and seems disinterested. Her mother speaks about Suzanna as if she were not present, describing her temper tantrums, her inappropriate peer relationships, and how she has always been different and malcontent. Suzanna responds by turning her back to her mother and says that she cannot handle her mother's worrying, and that she thinks that her mother is selfish. Suzanna does not wish to participate in a therapy session while her mother is present. Suzanna and her mother are offered separate counseling sessions with different therapists, with one joint session for her mother and Suzanna and both therapists approximately once every 3 months. The mother discovers how difficult it is for her to distinguish between her own internal preoccupation and insecurity, which has nothing to do with Suzanna, and actual concerns, and she is able to process her own life story. In a process parallel to the family therapy process, the class teacher receives supervision in maintaining requirements for Suzanna. The cooperation between school and home is expanded with a monthly meeting between the mother and Suzanna's class teacher.

Relational disorders that have developed while the child was younger are incorporated into the child's patterns of communication and present themselves in contexts where the child interacts with others. Often, the difficulties do not become problematic until the child gets older, and the parents or others in the child's network are no longer able to meet all the child's needs. The older child demands other things from the parents than the baby does. Symptoms such as hyperactivity, impulsivity, and attention deficit disorder are often due to a combination of the child's sensitive and extroverted temperament and a relational disorder where the child was not met with sufficiently clear boundaries and on an appropriately matching energy level. School-age problems often occur in children whose parents complain, nag, criticize, and yell at the child—or who fail to enforce their authority in the face of inappropriate behavior. The parents' inadequate conflict resolution strategies in crisis situations often lead to tension rather than problem solving. The parents may have a hard time balancing care and demands, and they do not manage to meet the child with clear and unambiguous authority that is also associated with love, care, perceptiveness, and receptiveness to the child's needs.

When children reach adolescence, the experiences and internal representations that they formed through their close relations become part of a more integrated personality. They are capable of containing varying internal representations, which may be contradictory and difficult to integrate, and there may be a big difference between the actual self and the ideal self, which poses problems for them. In adolescence the nervous system undergoes rapid development; the capacities for mentalization and abstraction develop, which may pose difficulties for children with relational disorders, for example, when they have to struggle with contradictory internal representations. At the same time, this development enables children to engage in more reflecting and narrative processing than before. In adolescence, children are becoming more independent of the parents but remain closely attached to them and dependent on them. The teenage years are often an emotionally turbulent period, where it is essential to have stable relationships that can contain young people's frustration, and if teenagers fail to find this with their parents, they will often go to others in their social or family network. The difficulty of family therapy with teenagers is to balance the parents' responsibility for restructuring the relationship with the need to make the teenager coresponsible for the change process.

In some cases it is not constructive or even possible to establish a family therapeutic context, for example, if the caregivers are not deemed to have the necessary potential for change, or if they are deemed incapable of containing the child's emotional difficulties. In these cases, other treatment options should be offered instead to support the child's development. In the following three sections I discuss, first, the possible forms of family support in cases where there is no expectation that the parents can develop parenting skills, and where the child's difficulties are assessed as manageable enough that it is possible to offer support without actual treatment. In the second section I examine various aspects of child therapy, where the child needs therapy to facilitate development for a while, perhaps because the caregivers are not able to provide the intersubjective framework that is required to help the child develop. In the third section I look at environmental therapy as an intervention form where the child's psychological development is supported in an everyday context where the child has to relate to other children and adults.

Maintenance Treatment

Stella is 13 years old and lives with her mother, who is periodically severely psychotic and has been diagnosed with schizophrenia. Stella's family network is limited, but she does have an older sister who has left home, whom she visits occasionally. Stella does well in school, is mature for her age, and does her homework. It took a long time before Social Services became aware of the family's problems, because Stella solved them on her own. For example, she had her mother committed for psychiatric treatment on several occasions without Social Services catching on to the fact that Stella was now living on her own. Stella's class teacher became aware of the family's problems, and Stella and her mother were each assigned a contact person, who keep each other up to date about the mother's state and Stella's reactions.

Studies have shown that children who have a relatively stable nervous system are able to compensate for neglect or abuse by engaging in supportive interaction relationships with persons outside the family, even if they live with very low-functioning parents (Schore, 2003a; Verney,

2002). At the same time, experience shows that the child may benefit from the parents being in touch with a stable person who can help them develop more realistic perceptions of themselves and the child.

Maintenance treatment is not an actual therapy form, as the support is aimed at families where the child does not seem traumatized or is only moderately affected by the situation, and where the parents are not deemed to have a potential for change. The child seems well-adapted, while the parents are either mentally ill or of very low intelligence. Maintenance treatment aims to establish long-term contact with the parents and the child by assigning them separate contact persons. The task of the parents' contact person is to let them create an intersubjective space with another person, where they feel respected, even if there may be conflicts of interest between the child's and the parents' needs. Similarly, the child should also have a contact person to share experiences and thoughts with, a person who can help maintain the child's perspective and ensure that the child's basic needs are met. The two contact persons must cooperate closely, and the child and the parents should be kept up to date about each other's conversations. The main task in maintenance treatment is an interdisciplinary collaboration with a clear distribution of roles and tasks (Hylander, Krabbe, & Schwartz, 2005).

Psychotherapy With Children

Sinead is 11 years old; she lives with a foster family and attends a school for children with emotional difficulties. She previously spent some time in a child psychiatric ward where she was under observation for severely maladaptive behavior. She has a brother, 2 years older, who several years ago reported his father to the police for sexual abuse and stated that Sinead had suffered the same abuse as he did, which Sinead denied. Sinead was very close to her mother, but her mother was not able to establish demands and boundaries: She either involved the girl in her own problems as a peer or treated her as a much younger girl. Sinead was placed in a foster family and immediately began psychotherapy. In the first session she talked about sexual abuse during visits in the father's home. When Sinead talked about these experiences, she dissociated into a freeze state and seemed unaffected. At this point Sinead had not seen her father for 6 years,

but she said that she was so afraid that her father would come to see
her that she always kept a knife handy. During the therapy process
Sinead became aware that in addition to being angry with her father
she also missed him, as he had both a bad side and a good side, and
Sinead missed the good side. Together with Sinead the psychologist
met with the foster family and the mother. The mother and the foster
family were informed about the therapy process and they likewise
informed Sinead and the therapist about their perceptions of Sinead.
Sinead wanted to meet her father. In collaboration with her mother it
was arranged that Sinead and the psychologist would meet her father,
initially only to talk about the good experiences. Sinead also wanted
to talk about her experiences with her brother, but he declined.

Theories about individual therapy with children did not begin to take shape until after World War II, based on psychoanalytic theories. Today there are two main trends in child therapy: one that emphasizes content, and one that emphasizes relations. Content-oriented therapy emphasizes interpretation and giving children insight into their own problems. Relational therapy emphasizes attunement and the creation of an inter-subjective field with the child on the his own terms to enable him to attune with a neutral adult and express himself (Theophilakis, 1999). The current trend in child therapy is toward the relational perspective.

Crittenden (1992a) pointed out that the main objective of the intervention is to help children perceive and respond to their actual environment rather than expending their energy on mental processing. She drew parallels between explicit memory and attachment patterns. For example, an insecurely attached child often has internal representations that twist and distort the establishment of future relationships. Through limbically attuned contact with the child, the therapist should modify the child's relational patterns through the supportive relationship and thus develop more adaptive relational strategies. Crittenden suggested intervening on particular levels in the child's memory system to match intervention strategies that are aimed at the sensing, feeling, and thinking aspects of the nervous system. As in the caregiver-child relationship, the therapist should establish the contact process and let the child get to know her. The child should have an opportunity to develop his competencies and feel acknowledged by being allowed to be an active participant in the contact. As in adult therapy, limbic exchange and nonverbal dialogue are a creative process, where the child's ability to take part in the dialogue is developed, and where the child expresses the patterns of communication that have been incorporated through the child's past.

By the age of 2 years language already plays a key role in a child's ability to communicate experiences. Although children also rely on play and other behavior to express emotions and bodily impulses, they use language to build dialogues. The better children are at communicating experiences through language, the better is their ability to share experiences in a nuanced way and be met with understanding. On every level of mental organization a child has experiences that have not yet been verbalized. The integration of levels of mental organization is essential, and if this integration cannot be achieved in the relationship between caregiver and child, a therapeutic process with a person who is able to contain the child's perceptions and history is crucial. Many children who have suffered abuse or neglect have difficulty expressing themselves, especially with regard to emotions. Children need to feel seen with their experiences and share these experiences through narratives that are created within an intersubjective field.

A child must be met in his zone of proximal development, and a child who is on an immature organization level, where the cingulate gyrus and the orbitofrontal cortex are not sufficiently developed to support a play capacity, will not be able to engage in play therapy aimed at externalizing internal conflicts. An attempt to apply play therapy would run the risk of further disorganizing the child's fragile nervous system. The intervention must be directed at areas where the child has developed sufficient competence, and it must match the child's level of mental organization (cf. Chapter 8). Thus, in therapeutic work with children who have severe relational disorders it may be necessary to apply a bottom-up intervention in the form of autonomic and limbic attunement before it is possible to introduce methods aimed at higher levels of functioning.

The Dyadic and Asymmetrical Process With Triadic Consequences

Psychotherapy with children is a compensatory solution when the caregivers are unable to provide sufficient support for the child. Communication and relations between parents and children are an important topic for the therapist's work, regardless whether the parents take part in the sessions. When the therapist sees a child, the child is already in an established relationship with the caregivers. If at all possible, the most productive approach is to help the primary caregivers engage in attuned contact and create a developing dialogue with the child. An individual therapeutic intervention should only be applied if the assessment is that there is insufficient capacity in the child's network to facilitate the child's development. The therapist compensates for the caregiver's shortcomings by acting as a neutral person in a confidential space where the child is able to share his thoughts and ideas. Supportive sessions may be indicated when the child needs to sort out relationships that may seem chaotic to him. For example, if the child is caught in a conflict of loyalty between the parents or between the parents and the foster family, the child may need to discuss the situation with a neutral person who is able to attune with the child and his difficulties.

Øvreeide (2001a, 2001b, 2002) has pointed out that the dialogue between a therapist and a child is dyadic in process but triadic in consequence. By this he means that engaging in a therapeutic process with a child offers the child an opportunity to be seen and contained with his difficulties, while also offering the parents an opportunity to see the child in a new light. Thus, Øvreeide always lets the parents participate in the therapeutic sessions with the child. The purpose of the sessions with the child is to bring parents and child closer together. The therapist attempts to engage in the form of attunement and dialogue with the child that the parents have failed to engage in, as the child's difficulties often spring from the parents' inability to attune with the child's needs and problems. The inability to attune with the caregivers in relation to specific experiences or ideas renders the child isolated and in need of support to verbalize his experiences and be seen by someone else to facilitate identity development. The adult's acknowledgment and guidance are necessary for the child to develop appropriate relational strategies and social skills. The interaction between an adult and a child, whether the adult is a parent or a therapist, must be based on a mutual relationship but characterized by asymmetrical responsibility. From the beginning of the conversation, the therapist should take charge of breaking up the child's inappropriate relational pattern. As Schwartz and Hansen (2005) pointed out, individual therapy with children is a tricky balancing act within a complicated organization. The therapist's contact with the child requires confidentiality and exclusivity, but on the other hand the therapeutic space should not become isolated; it is essential to coordinate and build permeable boundaries between the therapeutic space and the network that surrounds the child.

Environmental Therapy

Stella is 10 years old, and since she was 1 year old she has lived with her father. Before then, Stella was in an institution for infants because her mother was not able to care for her properly. Her father has been involved in crime, and during the times when he was in prison, Stella stayed with her paternal grandmother. The grandmother has substantial influence on the father's and Stella's life. Due to maladaptive behavior Stella is not able to attend a mainstream school, and she is therefore enrolled in a special needs school, where she is receiving therapy to address her relationships with peers, among other issues. Stella is an anxious and stress-sensitive girl, and when she feels troubled she hides under the table. She needs to feel secure to trust that nothing bad is going to happen. The environmental therapists spend a great deal of time calming her and attuning with her. Stella has learning difficulties because her anxiety is triggered so easily. She receives considerable support to learn to understand social signals and attune with them. The family rejects family therapy or other supportive measures.

Environmental therapy emerged as a specific intervention form in the 1950s. Instead of simply viewing the child's everyday environment as an appropriate place for the child to be looked after until an individual treatment option was available, professionals planned everyday activities to accommodate the individual child's unique needs through daily interactions. The deliberate planning of the physical setting, daily interactions, routines, and organization of an institution to accommodate therapeutic purposes is what is currently referred to as environmental therapy.

Children's pattern of communication is a key aspect of their social skills in maintaining social interactions, and counterproductive patterns tend to repeat and become self-affirming. Children will seek to enter into concrete interactions in a way that affirms their internal representations, as this is the source of their relative sense of security. Sroufe and Fleeson

(1986) have documented how early attachment patterns are reproduced in the school-age child's relations with peers and teachers (cf. Chapter 4). Thus, the relationship is not only internalized in the child but recreated in new relationships outside the caregiver-child relationship.

The goal of environmental therapy is to enable the child to develop relational competencies in a social context where the child's difficulties are met with understanding. Environmental therapy can take place either on an outpatient or an inpatient basis. It is often used with children with behavioral difficulties who lack the capacity for self-regulation, and who are unable to reflect on their own behavior. In environmental therapy the interaction between the child and the adult forms the key therapeutic instrument, and the therapeutic setting is activated through concrete daily activities. Children who are aggressive or easily feel offended react instantly when they feel they are being teased, and they often reject demands and requirements. Environmental therapy aims at making the child learn to pause to reflect on the situation. On a neuroaffective level this corresponds to activating the frontal lobe system. The left frontal lobe in particular helps calm distressing emotions through the verbalization process. The activation of the language areas and the integration of language and emotional aspects help the child understand and manage emotions.

Environmental therapy balances between care/support and demands/challenges. Many children who need environmental therapy have suffered childhood neglect or abuse, which has made them view the world as threatening and incoherent, or they have innate dysfunctions such as pervasive developmental disorders. Often, their nervous system is fragile and disintegrates frequently into regressive autonomic states of fight-or-flight or freeze behavior. These children have had difficulty establishing adequate self-regulation and an identity, and they are consequently not able to protect themselves against stressful experiences.

Environmental therapy is not a clearly defined intervention form, and it is often made up of a variety of therapeutic approaches. Regardless how the therapy is structured, it is important to know which groups of children can benefit from being together. For example, it is usually counterproductive to place children with relational disorders together with children who have severe neurological disorders or autism. There is a difference between solely attempting to make the child's world predictable and secure through clear boundaries, as is required, for example, for children with autism, and aiming at the same time to promote development, as is appropriate for children with relational disorders. An attempt to promote development in children who do not have a capacity for it will have the effect of further disintegrating their nervous system.

Children with relational disorders, autism, and severe neurological disorders often have dysfunctions on an autonomic and limbic level. In particular, children with severe relational disorders will often stage situations that provoke what they fear the most, partly because it involves some degree of recognizability, and partly because it offers a sense of being able to control one's environment and not being the victim of a capricious universe. These children are often in a state of chaos and are at the mercy of the autoregulating states. The slightest frustration or restriction will trigger a panic response and thrust the child into a state where he is constantly bombarded with subcortical stimuli that he is unable to regulate. One moment the child may appear accommodating and friendly, only to be virtually consumed with infantile rage the next. Psychological breakdowns often occur for no external reason, and the child is unable to control his impulses through external emotional social demands and expectations.

Both children with autism and those who have suffered early dysregulation and varying and unpredictable contact have an insecure self-image and a fragile and tender nervous system that is at risk of disintegrating. In environmental therapy it is essential to establish a framework that is well structured, clear, unambiguous, and predictable; in other words, it is necessary to give the child a "frontal lobe corset" (see Fig. 9.2) that prepares him for future events. This corset consists of the following elements: structure/framework, rhythms, predictability, preparation, and emotional neutrality. A fragile nervous system that is prone to disintegration is best able to use its potential when the environmental therapist uses a firm framework, structure, and predictability to create a secure context that makes it possible to contain the child's insecurity and create an atmosphere that places relevant demands and requirements on the child.

To calm the child's nervous system, the environmental therapist will have to remain emotionally neutral and avoid becoming part of the child's emotions when he goes into affect. In this context, emotional neutrality means that the therapist is able to interact with the child in a caring, loving, and nonjudgmental way without getting caught up in her own emo-

The frontal lobe corset consists of:
1) Structure/framework
2) Rhythms
3) Predictability
4) Preparation
5) Emotional neurality:
   Personally anchored
   Caring/loving
   Neither judgmental nor condemning

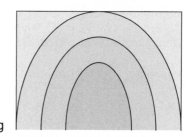

Frontal lobe corset

Figure 9.2. Frontal lobe corset

tions. Emotional neutrality involves the therapist's ability to contain and maintain her own emotions while engaging in affective attunement with the child. A child who becomes chaotic and lacks impulse control needs help to structure himself and requires an adult who is clear, unambiguous, directing, and instructional. The child experiences arousal but does not know where it is headed, and the adult must help the child control or inhibit this arousal. The child needs to feel that the external environment offers something to hold onto when affective breakthroughs occur, and the task of the adult is to remain calm regardless how emotionally affected the child is to prevent the child's nervous system from disorganizing further. In unfamiliar situations, children with relational disorders or autism will need adults to take active and concrete measures to structure the situation. The child's maladaptive behavior reflects insecurity, and in this situation, the child needs structuring and attunement.

Children need predictability and therefore seek confirmation of their internal representations. The plasticity of the brain enables neural patterns to change when children are introduced to variation and change in other people's expected interaction patterns. The relationally developing effort consists of finding ways to communicate that are capable of altering a child's internal representations and offer the necessary developmental support. A child with a relational disorder interacts on the basis of early interaction patterns, and teachers will often engage in unfortunate patterns of communication because they are seduced into taking part in the child's dance. In their input to the dialogue, these adults risk contributing, for example, to a controlling and angry interaction or to excessive protection (Sroufe, 1989b).

Attunement on the prefrontal level:
Experiences are verbalized with the
adult. The child receives support and
affirmation through verbal dialogue.

Attunement on the limbic level:
The child achieves emotional contact
with the adult through limbic attunement.

Attunement on the autonomic level:
The child is supported through grounding,
controlled breathing, and relaxation,
perhaps by being held and contained
within a field.

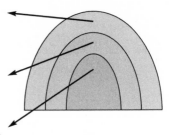

Figure 9.3. Attunement in the triune brain

Children should receive support that matches their personality development level, that is, support in the areas where they seek competence and coping skills, and should be offered the opportunity to display independence in the areas where they have developed competence. An adult must attune with a child on all levels of mental organization (see Fig. 9.2).

Working With Parents

In environmental therapy, it is important to include the child's parents. The child is still a member of a family, and changes in his patterns of communication activate emotions and altered thought patterns in the child which are then brought into the family. In environmental therapy it is similarly crucial to view the child's difficulties as part of a family pattern. The parents must be included as partners in the therapy by offering extensive knowledge about the child's everyday life in the therapeutic setting, and they should be respected for their knowledge of the child and their points of view. When differences of opinion emerge between the professionals and the parents, the collaboration should be expanded to examine any possible ways of reaching an agreement. Measures that are part of the therapy must be coordinated with measures in the home.

For example, it is important that the parents avoid undermining the work that goes on in the therapeutic setting or act negatively, since this would risks imposing a conflict of loyalty on the child. It is hard for a child to alter his pattern of communication unless the parents alter their relationship with him. In therapy, the professionals should assess whether the child is able to manage the daily switch between home and therapeutic setting. The effect of environmental therapy often depends on the parents' motivation and capacity for involvement.

We have now looked at various treatment options where the child continues to live with the parents. Sometimes, it is necessary to place children in a foster family or in an institution if the parents are unable to engage in a relationship with their child that promotes development to a sufficient degree. This may be due to inadequate parenting skills, or it may be necessary if the child's difficulties are so severe that development is not possible in the home environment.

The Impact of Primary Attachment and the Transfer of Care

Meg is 13 years old, and at age 6 she was removed from her home together with her sister, who is 2 years younger, due to the mother's mental illness and both parents' alcohol abuse. For a number of years prior to this, the children had suffered severe neglect, and Meg often took on a protective adult role in relation to her younger sister. She was born with fetal alcohol syndrome and is an extremely fragile girl who responds to high levels of arousal by vomiting. Both in her infancy and when she and her younger sister were visiting the parents she had severely traumatic experiences, as the parents often fought physically, threatened to kill each other, and even engaged in knife fights. The younger sister was the parents' favorite child, and she was often openly favored at Christmas and birthdays. Meg is a sad child, who is afraid of setting off her father's violent temper, and in her relationship with the foster parents she is a well-adjusted child who is older than her years. She has asked the foster parents whether they will adopt her, and she has often faked illness to avoid the obligatory visits with her biological parents. The younger sister, on the other hand, still has a strong desire to remain closely attached to her mother and is unable to let go of her emotionally.

When children are placed in foster families or institutions, others take over the role of the parents, either for certain periods of the child's life or throughout the rest of childhood. In these situations it is important to understand the importance of primary attachment: The child is loyal and often idealizing, regardless how neglecting or abusive the parents have been. Family therapy is only appropriate in relation to families where the parents are motivated and have a relevant concern about their child and a meaningful degree of mentalizing capacity, and it must be meaningful to work with the dysfunctional interaction. When removing a child from the context that led to an attachment disorder or a relational disorder, one must note and respect the child's attachment to the parents, even if the child might say otherwise. Even if the child is relocated to a different environment, he still has the same internal representations and communicates on the basis of the same capacity. The case described above illustrates both an example of a child who has trouble mentally moving in with the foster family and a child who turns her back on her parents and wants the foster parents to take over. In either case it is essential to address the child's relationship with the parents and achieve a balanced relationship with the foster parents. In these situations, conversations with a neutral person can often be helpful.

Established relational patterns are difficult to change, and, as mentioned earlier, the child often reproduces the relationship in a new context. Relational patterns are acquired in relationships and can only be changed gradually based on understanding of and respect for the child's patterns of communication. When familiar relational patterns are evoked, the child is acting on previously acquired strategies. As mentioned in the section on emotional neutrality, it can be exceedingly difficult to avoid confirming the child's maladaptive patterns of communication, especially in an ordinary family context. If the child's internal representations developed in relation to hostile and punishing relationships with adults, positive responses will appear incomprehensible and make the child feel insecure. If the child is met with punishing behavior, the relational pattern is confirmed, and the child finds himself in a familiar, secure, and painful situation. The balance between security and development is a major challenge in working with children who have suffered abuse or neglect (Sroufe & Fleeson, 1986).

Balancing the Caregiver Function and the Role of Therapist in the Foster Family Setting

Camilla, who is 8 years old, was raised by a mentally ill mother. At the age of 5 years she was put into foster care, and the foster parents say that at the time she was a quiet, observing girl. Today her thinking is extremely concrete, her attention is fleeting, and she is always in the same mood. She walks up to strangers indiscriminately and has never been able to participate in role-playing games or close relationships. She needs to be reminded to eat and has difficulty sitting still at the dinner table. The foster parents have a feeling that if she left them she would forget about them instantly.

A child with a vulnerable personality who is placed in a foster family needs clear boundaries to be able to navigate and maintain a realistic image of her environment. At the same time, the foster parents should meet the child with care but downregulate their arousal level lest the child disintegrate. The foster parents should challenge the child in all the areas where she has a developmental capacity, but they should also avoid asking more of the child than she is able to handle. The child does not change simply as a result of moving to a normal environment. A child with a severe relational disorder needs an environment that is structured to accommodate her difficulties. Children who have suffered early and severe neglect or abuse often have neuroaffective dysfunctions on deep subcortical levels that affect their basic personality structure. For example, the zone of proximal development for a child who has suffered early emotional frustration is physiobiological and psychobiological attunement, and she will need to develop competencies that a typically developing child establishes during the first 8 months of life. The child needs to enter into an intersubjective field that is mirroring and is characterized by imitation, protoconversations, and clear and precise affective attunement. On this level, the nervous system organizes sensory meaning and coherence, and it is the foster parents' task to hold, comfort, calm, create rhythms, and so on. The child will not receive adequate developmental support if the foster parents lack sufficient insight into the child's severe emotional difficulties and fail to acknowledge the role of developmentally supportive regulation on this level. This may be the case, either because they view the child like any other child who should be allowed to live out her impulse breakthroughs, or because they see the foster child as a poorly disciplined child who struggles for dominance and needs to be kept in check (Schwartz & Hansen, 2005).

Among other sources, the Canadian studies of institutionalized Romanian children (cf. Chapter 4) have found that the age of the child at adoption makes a difference. A follow-up study of children who were adopted from Romanian orphanages found that those who were adopted between the ages of 4 and 24 months continued to have severe adaptation problems at the age of 6 years, in contrast to children who were adopted before the age of 4–6 months (Chisholm, 1998; Gunnar, 2001). It appears that children who have suffered long-term and massive abuse or neglect from birth will fail to overcome emotional difficulties if they are adopted too late. The same must be assumed to apply to children who are placed in foster families or institutions. It makes a big difference for the child's emotional development that the intervention is implemented in a timely fashion. It appears that there is a developmental window of opportunity for establishing attachment relationships, which closes at an early age. However, additional research will show whether intensive and long-term interventions aimed at autonomic and limbic structures might be able to affect the deep subcortical structures.

Foster Parents' Collaboration With the Biological Parents and the Rest of the Network

Annette is now 6 years old; at age 5 she was placed in a foster family on short notice due to her mother's psychotic state. At the time, Annette was insecure and afraid of being with her psychotic mother. The foster mother gave Annette lots of care. When her mother had recovered from her psychosis, she wanted increased visitations with Annette without the foster mother's presence. The foster mother was uncomfortable about this idea because Annette said that she did not want to be with her biological mother. The foster mother clearly had reservations about the biological mother. Annette spent a great deal of energy on defensive strategies and on adjusting. She idealized her foster family and denied her attachment and her strong ambivalent emotions toward the mother.

The vast majority of children who are removed from their biological families in Denmark live in foster families. A foster family is often part of a larger organization that includes, in addition to the foster family itself, the child's biological family, Social Services, the child's school, and so on. As Schwartz and Hansen (2005) pointed out, there are many stakeholders, and there is a real risk of an unclear distribution of roles. If the foster parents assume a greater responsibility than their role implies, for example, if they take over control of the child's visitation arrangements with the parents, or if they believe that they should single-handedly rescue the child, the result may be severe tensions between the biological parents and the rest of the professional network. For a number of reasons it can be difficult for the foster parents to allow the child to grieve over or have ambivalent feelings toward the biological parents. It takes a strong personal foundation for the foster parents to neither identify with the child's negative feelings toward the biological parents nor feel disqualified by the child's longing for the parents.

A child who moves in with a foster family is still related to the biological parents, unless the shift happens at birth or very soon after. The role of the foster parents is not only to take care of the child; they also need to cooperate with the biological parents according to the instructions from Social Services. It can be difficult for the foster parents to establish a positive relationship with biological parents who are angry and do not understand why the child was removed. If this positive relationship is not established, the child is trapped in a field of tension and a conflict of loyalty between the biological parents and the foster parents. Being involved in a conflict between adults that they love can have far-reaching consequences for children. Foster children who have frequently been exposed to severe neglect or abuse and who were psychologically fragile prior to the move are faced with an impossible paradox in this case that may undermine their developmental possibilities.

When a child is removed from the home, it is important to consider whether there should be a permanent transfer of care, or whether the measure is a temporary arrangement until the parents are once again able to assume their role as parents. If the placement is intended to last throughout the rest of childhood, it is necessary to make arrangements to maintain contact with the biological parents to enable the child to preserve a realistic image of them, although of course the child should be protected from any traumatic experiences. An idealized image of the parents will make it impossible for the child to assess the parents realistically, while a negative image of the parents might give the child a negative self-image, as the parents are part of the child's identity. If the placement is temporary, it is necessary to establish a developmentally supportive contact between the parents and the child, possibly through family therapy.

Studies by SFI, the Danish National Centre for Social Research, of children who have been removed from their family found that the likelihood of a positive outcome is highest when the parents support the decision and tell the child that staying with the foster parents is the best option (Nissen, 1999). The parents' understanding is not a given, as they often have many thoughts, considerations, feelings of guilt, and so on related to the decision. Therefore, one should make sure to support the parents after the child is removed. They need support from someone who is not part of the field of tension.

When the child is with the biological parents, earlier relational patterns will often be activated. Even if the foster parents have been supporting the child, so that the child is at ease and therefore rarely disintegrates, the child's neural scaffolding will remain fragile for a very long time and will be at risk of disintegration, for example, when the child is confronted with emotionally charged situations. Seeing the child's maladaptive reaction patterns reappear often makes the foster parents worried, especially in the case of younger children. Often, the foster parents interpret the child's reaction negatively, and they conclude that the child cannot handle seeing the biological parents. The foster parents' worries about visitation can contribute to keeping the child in a maladaptive behavior pattern before and after visits with the parents.

Children who have been placed in foster care have often experienced severe neglect or abuse, and, as mentioned earlier, some of these children appear to have a hard time overcoming environmentally reactive emotional damage at a later age. Even if the child's developmental potential in the emotional area is limited, the child should be supported in developing other skills to compensate for the dysfunctional development.

Compensatory Strategies

Children are often resilient to individual traumatic experiences; typically, it is prolonged, ongoing neglect or abuse that has a negative long-term effect on personality development. The cumulative effect of negative experiences for a child is bigger than the sum of the individual events. The main reason that cumulative negative experiences often have such a radical impact on the present is that the past has created entrenched neural circuits in the nervous system. That impairs the ability of the nervous system to develop through new experiences. Neurophysiological changes that have become irreversibly fixed at an early stage in development during sensitive or critical periods due to trauma and conflict can confer a lifelong emotional impairment on the child. Early and severe affective deprivation has severe developmental consequences for the child's ability to relate to others, and few of these children are able to fully redress the damage.

Experience shows that in treating children with early trauma who have suffered early and severe neglect or abuse, treatment professionals should proceed with cautious optimism. They must meet the child on his level of mental organization without making demands that exceed his capability. A child with severe and irreversible emotional damage needs compensatory strategies to manage his emotional impairment, and the child has to learn to navigate and get by in the world despite lacking essential functions, such as attachment capacity and empathy.

At this point, there is relatively little empirical data concerning effective treatment methods for children who have suffered early emotional frustration, and it remains uncertain whether these children will be able to benefit from interventions on an autonomic or limbic level. The plasticity of the brain also applies to the subcortical levels, and the future will show whether it is possible to support and help children who have suffered early and severe neglect or abuse. We know that neurotransmitters such as serotonin, dopamine, and noradrenaline are involved in regulating the nervous system, and that it is possible to stimulate the activation of these substances through positive experiences and social interactions. Whether a targeted therapeutic intervention directed at deep subcortical regions might trigger neural integration and balance the nervous system remains uncertain at this time.

Summary

In principle, personality changes are possible at any age. The child's way of perceiving and interpreting the environment is harder to modify the older the child is, and with age the child's willingness to embrace new behavior patterns is gradually reduced. It is crucial to offer early preventive interventions that cover all the aspects of the child's environment. The child learns about the nature and workings of the environment at a very young age and applies a variety of communication strategies in an attempt at mastering this environment. Children's relationships with primary caregivers affect their capacity for self-regulation and mentalization and their perception of others and events. Early intervention aimed at maladaptive parent-child interactions is associated with very good chances of success, even with interventions on a limited scale (Karen, 1998; Tetzchner, 2002).

> The memory of trauma is carried not only throughout the lives of individuals through their neurobiology, but also in the lives of families by family myths, childrearing practices and belief systems. Major traumatic events in the history of a people or culture are memorialized as well and carried forward across generations in the literature, laws and social structures. (Perry, 1999a, p. 32)

EPILOGUE

It is through our close interpersonal relationships that we are able to fulfill our needs for safety, comforting, and understanding, and to develop our ability to work through the loss of love. With few exceptions, the potential for an integrated personality structure is embedded in all individuals, but a healthy personality development is not to be taken for granted (Lewis et al., 2001). The human brain is use dependent, and its development relies on adaptive patterns that develop during infancy and childhood. The brain's developmental capacity depends on its environment, and children reflect the immediate environment where they were raised.

Throughout evolution, humans have developed not in isolation but through relationships with others, and our nervous system has evolved to mature on the basis of experience. Early trauma, abuse, or neglect causes molecular and neurobiological changes; these in turn cause the nervous system to adjust and prepare the adult brain to survive and reproduce itself in a dangerous world. In the course of evolution, the environment of the first 2 years of life was probably the same as the environment of adulthood and old age. Since the environment did not change much, there was no need for deep-lying subcortical structures to be plastic. For example, early stressful experiences make the brain develop anxious or antisocial behavior through environmental adaptation. Through a chain of events, anxiety, violence, and abuse are passed on from generation to generation.

In seeking to limit this generational transfer, how we view and treat our most at-risk children is crucial. It is essential to offer early intervention for at-risk families, as the chances of successful intervention aimed at later developing psychological disorders are greatest in the early years of life. Without early intervention, many of these children will develop personality disorders, an insufficient self-regulation capacity, and inadequate abilities for self-reflection. The children with the most severe disorders develop antisocial personality disorders; some develop psychiatric disorders associated with extreme psychological pain; and others live a life of crime, prostitution, and substance abuse. When these children reach adulthood and have children of their own, the social and personal legacy is passed on. Thus, the goal of early intervention is clear: No child should lack the opportunity to develop mentalizing functions due to inadequate support in the earliest relationships. Early intervention will have a long-term effect on appropriate adaptation strategies that support lifelong development.

Bruce Perry, who has studied childhood traumas for years, said, "A society functions as a reflection of its childrearing practices. If children are ignored, poorly educated and not protected from violence they will grow into adults that create a reactive, non-creative and violent society. . . . All societies reap what they have sown" (2001, p. 16).

As Mary Ainsworth pointed out, approximately a third of all children are believed to have a deficient attachment pattern. Of these, about 3% have a relational disorder that is serious enough to qualify as severe psychopathology. In the Western world, there is a great deal of doubt about the appropriate course of action, and resources are limited. On this basis, it would be advisable and humane to allocate resources to identify the most effective forms of assessment and intervention. We have to consider just how many children and adults with psychological difficulties society is able to handle. Society is a self-organizing, living organism, which, like the nervous system, must be able to integrate its outcast or dissociated parts. An intrinsic aspect of the human biological potential is the need to enter into a community with other humans, and attachment is paramount for the very process of becoming human.

> The mother is far enough ahead of the child so that she cannot actually support the child, but she holds out her arms. She imitates the child's movements. If it totters she swiftly bends as if she would seize it—so the child believes that it is not walking alone. The most loving mother can do no more, if it be truly intended that the child shall walk alone. And yet she does more; for her face, her face, yes, it is beckon-

ing like the reward of the Good and like the encouragement of Eternal Blessedness. So the child walks alone, with eyes fixed upon the mother's face, not on the difficulties of the way; supporting himself on the arms that do not hold on to him, striving after refuge in the mother's embrace, hardly suspecting that in the same moment he is proving that he can do without her, for now the child is walking alone.

Kierkegaard, 1847/2008, p. 38

REFERENCES

Ainsworth, M. D. P. (1972). Attachment and dependency: A comparison. In J. L. Fewirtz (Ed.), *Attachment and dependency* (pp. 97–137). Washington, DC: Winston.

Ainsworth, M. D. P. (1993). Attachments and other affectional bonds across the life cycle. In C. M. Parkes, J. Stevenson-Hinde, & P. Marris (Ed.), *Attachment across the life cycle* (pp. 32–51). New York: Routledge.

Ainsworth, M. D. S., Bell, S. M. V., & Stayton, D. J. (1971). Individual differences in strange situation behaviour of one-year-olds. In H. R. Schaffer (Ed.), *The origins of human social relations* (pp. 17–52). New York: Academic Press.

Ainsworth, M. D. S., Blehar, M. C., Waters, E., & Wall, P. (1978). *Patterns of attachment: A psychological study of the strange situation.* Hillsdale, NJ: Lawrence Erlbaum.

Aitken, K. J., & Trevarthen, C. (1997). Self-other organization in human psychological development. *Development and Psychopathology, 9,* 653–678.

Allen, J. G. (2002). *Traumatic relationships and serious mental disorders.* New York: Wiley.

Anders, T. F. (1989). Clinical syndromes, relationship disturbances, and their assessment. In J. Sameroff & R. N. Emde (Eds.), *Relationship disturbances in early childhood: A developmental approach* (pp. 125–144). New York: Basic Books.

Anders, T. F., & Zeanah, C. H. (1984). Early infant development from a biological point of view. In J. D. Call, E. Galenson, & R. L. Tyson (Ed.), *Frontiers of infant psychiatry* (vol. 2, pp. 55–69). New York: Basic Books.

Asen, E. (2005). *Connecting systems and psyche.* Paper presented at conference, Psyche and Systems: The Inner World—the Outer World. LO-skolen, Elsinore, March 9.

Asper, K. (1987). *Verlassenheit und Selbstverfremdung: Neue Zugänge zum therapuetischen Verständniss.* Olten, Germany: Walter-Verlag.

Austin, J. H. (1998). *Zen and the brain.* Cambridge, MA: MIT Press.

Barkley, R. A. (1997). *ADHD and the nature of self-control.* New York: Guilford.

Barkley, R. A. (1998). *Attention-deficit hyperactivity disorder: A handbook for diagnosis and treatment.* New York: Guilford.

Baron-Cohen, P. (1995). *Mindblindness.* Cambridge, MA: MIT Press.

Bartels, A., & Zeki, P. (2004). The neural correlates of maternal and romantic love. *NeuroImage, 21,* 1155–1166.

Basch, M. F. (1985). Interpretation: Toward a developmental model. In A. Goldberg (Ed.), *Progress in self psychology* (pp. 33–42). New York: Guilford.

Beauchaine, T. (2001). Vagal tone, development, and Gray's motivational theory: Toward an integrated model of autonomic nervous system functioning in psychopathology. *Development and Psychopathology, 13,* 183–214.

Bechara, A., Damasio, H., & Damasio, A. R. (2003). Role of the amygdala in decision-making. *Annals of the New York Academy of Science, 985,* 356–369.

Beebe, B. (1998). A procedural theory of therapeutic action: Commentary on the symposium, "Interventions That Effect Change in Psychotherapy." *Infant Mental Health Journal, 19*(3), 333–340.

Beebe, B., & Lachmann, F. M. (1988). Mother-infant mutual influence and precursors of psychic structure. In A. Goldberg (Ed.), *Frontiers in self psychology* (vol. 3, pp. 3–27). Hillsdale, NJ: Analytic Press.

Beebe, B., & Lachmann, F. M. (2002). *Infant research and adult treatment: Co-constructing interactions.* Hillsdale, NJ: Analytic Press.

Beebe, B., & Stern, D. (1977). Engagement-disengagement and early object experiences. In N. Freedman & S. Grand (Eds.), *Communicative structures and psychic structures* (pp. 35–55). New York: Plenum.

Belsky, J. (1996). Parent, infant, and social-contextual determinants of attachment security. *Developmental Psychology, 32,* 905–914.

Belsky, J., Rosenberger, K., & Crnic, K. (1995). The origins of attachment security: Classical and contextual determinants. In P. Goldberg, R. Muir, & J. Kerr (Eds.), *Attachment theory: Social developmental, and clinical perspectives* (pp. 153–183). Hillsdale, NJ: Analytic Press.

Belsky, J., Rovine, M., & Taylor, D. G. (1984). The Pennsylvania infant and family development project, III: The origins of individual differences in infant-mother attachment: Maternal and infant contributions. *Child Development, 55,* 718–728.

Benjamin, L. P. (1996). An interpersonal theory of personality disorders. In J. F. Clarkin & M. F. Lenzenweger (Eds.), *Major theories of personality disorder* (pp. 141–220). New York: Guilford.

Bentzen, M. (2010). Shapes of experience-neuroscience, development psychology and somatic character formation. In G. Marlock & H.Weiss (Eds.), *The handbook of bodypsychotherapy.* Manuscript in preparation.

Bentzen, M., & Hart, P. (2005). Neuroaffektiv udvikling og det terapeutiske rum. *Psykolog Nyt, 2,* 16–22.

Bertelsen, P. (1994). Kernen i det menneskelige tilværelsesprojekt er rettethed mod rettetheden. In A. Neumann (Ed.), *Det særligt menneskelige. Udvikling-spsykologiske billeder.* Copenhagen: Hans Reitzels Forlag.

Bion, W. R. (1962). *Learning from experience.* New York: Basic Books.

Bion, W. R. (1967). *Second thoughts.* New York: Jason Aronson.

Blair, R. J. R. (1999). Psychophysiological responsiveness to the distress of others in children with autism. *Personality and Individual Differences, 26,* 477–485.

Blair, R. J. R., Colledge, E., Murray, L., & Mitchell, D. G. V. (2001). A selective impairment in the processing of sad and fearful expressions in children with psychopathic tendencies. *Journal of Abnormal Child Psychology, 29*(6), 491–498.

Blair, R. J. R., & Frith, U. (2000). Neurocognitive explanations of the antisocial personality disorders. *Criminal Behaviour and Mental Health, 10,* 66–81.

Blair, R. J. R., Jones, L., Clark, F., & Smith, M. (1997). The psychopathic individual: A lack of responsiveness of distress cues? *Psychophysiology, 34*(2), 192–198.

Blair, R. J. R., Morris, J. S., Frith, C. D., Perrett, D. I., & Dolan, R. J. (1999). Dissociable neural responses to facial expressions of sadness and anger. *Brain, 122,* 883–893.

Blair, R. J. R., Sellars, C., Strickland, I., Clark, F., Williams, A., Smith, M., et al. (1996). Theory of mind in the psychopath. *Journal of Forensic Psychiatry, 7*(1), 15–25.

Blass, E., Fitzgerald, E., & Kehoe, P. (1986). Interactions between sucrose, pain, and isolations distress. *Pharmacology, Biochemistry and Behaviour, 26,* 483–489.

Bower, T. G. R. (1977). *Barnets tidlige udvikling.* Copenhagen: Nyt Nordisk Forlag.

Bowlby, J. (1969). *Attachment and loss. Vol. 1: Attachment.* London: Random House.

Bowlby, J. (1973). *Attachment and loss. Vol. 2: Separation.* New York: Basic Books.

Bowlby, J. (1978). Attachment theory and its therapeutic implications. In S. C. Feinstein & P. L. Giovacchini (Eds.), *Adolescent psychiatry: Developmental and clinical studies* (vol. 6, pp. 5–33. Chicago: University of Chicago Press.

Bowlby, J. (1979). *The making and breaking of affectional bonds.* New York: Routledge.

Bowlby, J. (1988). *A secure base: Clinical applications of attachment theory.* London: Routledge.

Bowlby, J. (1993). Postscript. In C. M. Parkes, J. Stevenson-Hinde, & P. Marris (Eds.), *Attachment across the life cycle* (pp. 293–297). New York. Routledge.

Bradley, P. (2000). *Affect regulation and the development of psychopathology.* New York: Guilford.

Bråten, P. (1993). The virtual other in infants' minds and social feelings. In A. H.

Wold (Ed.), *The dialogical alternative* (pp. 77–97). Oslo: Scandinavian University Press.

Bråten, P. (1998). *Kommunikasjon og samspill fra fødsel til alderdom.* Oslo: Scandinavian University Press.

Bråten, P. (2006). Andencentreret deltagelse—fra vuggen til klasseværelset. Om en basal relationskompetence i læring og samvær. In R. Kristensen (Ed.), *Fantastiske forbindelser—relationer i undervisning og læringssamvær* (pp. 12–24). Frederikshavn: Dafolo.

Brazelton, T. B. (1984). Why early intervention? In J. D. Call, E. Galensch, & R. L. Tyson (Eds.), *Frontiers of infant psychiatry* (vol. 2, pp. 267–275). New York: Basic Books.

Brazelton, T. B., & Cramer, B. G. (1990). *The earliest relationship.* Reading, MA: Addison-Wesley.

Brazelton, T. B., Koslowski, B., & Main, M. (1974). The origins of reciprocity. In M. Lewis & L. Rosenblum (Eds.), *The effects of the infant on its caregiver* (pp. 49–70). New York: Wiley.

Bretherton, I. (1980). Young children in stressful situations: The supporting role of attachment figures and unfamiliar caregivers. In G. V. Coehlo & P. I. Ahmed (Eds.), *Uprooting and development* (pp. 179–210). New York: Plenum.

Bretherton, I., Bates, E., Benigni, L., Camaioni, L., & Volterra, V. (1979). Relationship between cognition, communication, and quality of attachment. In E. Bates, L. Benigni, I. Bretherton, L. Camaioni, & V. Volterra (Ed.), *The emergence of symbols* (pp. 223–269). New York: Academic Press.

Bretherton, I., Golby, B., & Cho, E. (1997). Attachment and the transmission of values. In J. Grusec & L. Kuczynski (Eds.), *Parenting and children's internalization of values: A handbook of contemporary theory* (pp. 103–134). New York: Wiley.

Brodén, M. B. (1991). *Mor og barn i ingenmandsland.* Copenhagen: Hans Reitzels Forlag.

Bruer, J. T. (1999). *The myth of the first three years: A new understanding of early brain development and lifelong learning.* New York: Free Press.

Bruner, J. P. (1985). Vygotsky: A historical and conceptual perspective. In J. Wertsch (Ed.), *Culture, communication and cognition: Vygotskian perspectives* (pp. 21–34). Cambridge: Cambridge University Press.

Bruner, J. P. (1986). *Actual minds, possible worlds.* Cambridge, MA: Harvard University Press.

Bruner, J. P. (1990). *Acts of meaning.* Cambridge, MA: Harvard University Press.

Carlson, E. A., Jacobvitz, D., & Sroufe, L. A. (1995). A developmental investigation of inattentiveness and hyperactivity. *Child Development, 66,* 37–54.

Carr, A. (1999). *The handbook of child and adolescent clinical psychology: A contextual approach.* London: Routledge.

Carroll, R. (2004). At the border between chaos and order: What psychotherapy and neuroscience have in common. In J. Corrigall & H. Wilkinson (Eds.), *Revo-*

lutionary connections: Psychotherapy and neuroscience (pp. 191–211). New York: Karnac.

Carter, R. (1998). *Mapping the mind.* London: Weidenfeld & Nicolson.

Caspi, A., Sugden, K., Moffitt, T. E., Taylor, A., Craig, I. W., Harrington, H.,et al. (2003). Influence of life stress on depression: Moderation by a polymorphism. *5-HTT Genetic Science, 301,* 386–389.

Cassidy, J. (1999). The nature of the child's ties. In J. Cassidy & P. R. Shaver (Eds.), *Handbook of attachment: Theory, research and clinical applications* (pp. 3–20). New York: Guilford.

Chess, P., & Thomas, A. (1982). Infant bonding: Mystique and reality. *American Journal of Orthopsychiatry, 52,* 213–222.

Chess, S., Thomas, A., & Birch, H. G. (1965). *Your child is a person.* New York: Viking Press.

Chisholm, K. (1998). A three year follow-up of attachment and indiscriminate friendliness in children adopted from Romanian orphanages. *Child Development, 69*(4), 1092–1106.

Chisholm, K., Carter, M., Ames, E., & Morison, P. (1995). Attachment security and indiscriminately friendly behaviour in children adopted from Romanian orphanages. *Development and Psychopathology, 7,* 283–294.

Chugani, H. T. (1997). Neuroimaging of development nonlinearity and developmental pathologies. In R. Thatcher, G. Lyon, J. Rumsey, & N. Krasnegor (Eds.), *Developmental neuroimaging: Mapping the development of the brain and behaviour* (pp. 187–195). San Diego: Academic Press.

Chugani, H. T. (1999). Metabolic imaging: A window on brain development and plasticity. *Neuroscientist, 5*(1), 29–40.

Chugani, H. T., Behen, M., Muzik, O., Juhász, C., Nagy, F., & Chugani, D. (2001). Local brain functional activity following early deprivation: A study of postinstitutionalized Romanian orphans. *Neuro Image, 14,* 1290–1301.

Chugani, H. T., Phelps, M. E., & Mazziotta, J. C. (1987). Position emission tomography. Study of human brain functional development. *Annals of Neurology, 22,* 487–497.

Cicchetti, D. (1991). Fractures in the crystal: Developmental psychopathology and the emergence of self. *Development Review, 11,* 271–287.

Cicchetti, D., Toth, P., & Lynch, M. (1995). Bowlby's dream comes full circle: The application of attachment theory to risk and psychopathology. In T. H. Ollendick & R. J. Prinz (Eds.), *Advances in clinical child psychology* (pp. 1–75). New York: Plenum.

Cicchetti, D., & Tucker, D. M. (1994). Development and self-regulation structures of the mind. *Development and Psychopathology, 6,* 533–549.

Clarke, A. S., Hedeker, D. R., Ebert, M. H., Schmidt, D. E., McKinney, W. T., & Kraemer, G. W. (1996). Rearing experiences and biogenic amine activity in infant rhesus monkeys. *Biological Psychiatry, 40,* 338–352.

Cohn, J., Campbell, P., & Ross, P. (1991). Infant response in the still-face paradigm at 6 months predicts avoidant and secure attachments at 12 months. *Development and Psychopathology, 3*, 367–376.

Colin, V. L. (1996). *Human attachment.* New York: McGraw-Hill.

Cozolino, L. J. (2000). *The neuroscience of psychotherapy: Building and rebuilding the human brain.* New York: Norton.

Crittenden, P. M. (1983). The effect of mandatory protective daycare on mutual attachment in maltreating mother-infant dyads. *Child Abuse and Neglect, 7*, 297–300.

Crittenden, P. M. (1988). Relationships at risk. In J. Belsky & T. Nezworski (Eds.), *Clinical implications of attachment* (pp. 136–177). Hillsdale, NJ: Lawrence Erlbaum.

Crittenden, P. M. (1992a). Quality of attachment in the preschool years. *Development and Psychopathology, 4*, 209–241.

Crittenden, P. M. (1992b). Treatment of anxious attachment in infancy and early childhood. *Development and Psychopathology, 4*(4), 575–602.

Crittenden, P. M. (1994). Peering into the black box: An exploratory treatise on the development of self in young children. In D. Cicchetti & S. L. Toth (Eds.), *Disorders and dysfunctions of the self. Rochester symposium on developmental psychopathology* (pp. 79–148). Rochester, NY: University of Rochester Press.

Crittenden, P. M. (1995). Attachment and psychopathology. In P. Goldberg, R. Muir, & J. Kerr (Eds.), *Attachment theory: Social, developmental, and clinical perspectives* (pp. 367–406). Hillsdale, NJ: Analytic Press.

Crittenden, P. M. (2000). A dynamic maturational approach to continuity and change in pattern of attachment. In P. M. Crittenden & A. H. Claussen (Eds.), *The organization of attachment relationships: Maturation, culture, and context* (pp. 343–357). New York: Cambridge University Press.

Damasio, A. R. (1994). *Descartes' error: Emotion, reason and the human brain.* New York: Putnam/Grosset.

Damasio, A. R. (1998). *The feeling of what happens.* New York: Harcourt Brace.

Damasio. A. R. (2003). *Looking for Spinoza: Joy, sorrow, and the feeling brain.* London: Harcourt.

Davidson, R. J. (1994a). Asymmetric brain function, affective style, and psychopathology: The role of early experience and plasticity. *Development and Psychopathology, 6*, 741–758.

Davidson, R. J. (1994b). Temperament, affective style, and frontal lobe asymmetry. In G. Dawson & K. Fischer (Eds.), *Human behavior and the developing brain.* New York: Guilford.

Davidson, R. J., & Fox, N. A. (1982). Asymmetrical brain activity discriminates between positive versus negative affective stimuli in human infants. *Science, 218*, 1235–1237.

Davidson, R. J., & Fox, N. A. (1988). Cerebral asymmetry and emotion: Development and individual differences. In P. Segalowitz & D. Molfese (Eds.), *Develop-*

mental implications of brain lateralization (pp. 191–206). New York: Guilford.

Davidson, R. J., & Fox, N. A. (1989). Frontal brain asymmetry predicts infant's response to maternal separation. *Journal of Abnormal Psychology, 98*(2), 127–131.

Davidson, R. J., Putnam, K. M., & Larson, C. L. (2000). Dysfunction in the neural circuitry of emotion regulation. A possible prelude to violence. *Science, 289*, 591–594.

Dawson, G. (1994). Development of emotional expression and emotion regulation in infancy: Contributions of the frontal lobe. In G. Dawson & K. W. Fischer (Ed.), *Human behavior and the developing brain* (pp. 346–379). New York: Guilford.

Dawson, G., & Fischer, K. W. (1994). Preface. In G. Dawson & K. W. Fischer (Ed.), *Human behavior and the developing brain* (pp. 346–379). New York: Guilford.

Dawson, G., Frey, K., Panagiotides, H., Osterling, J., & Hessl, D. (1997). Infants of depressed mothers exhibit atypical frontal brain activity: A replication and extension of previous findings. *Journal of Child Psychology and Psychiatry, 38*, 179–186.

Dawson, G., Frey, K., Self, J., Panagiotides, H., Hessl, D., Yamada, E., et al. (1999). Frontal brain electrical activity in infants of depressed and nondepressed mothers: Relation to variations in infant behavior. *Development and Psychopathology, 11*, 589–605.

Depue, R., Luciana, M., Arbisi, P., Collins, P., & Leon, A. (1994). Dopamine and the structure of personality: Relation of agonist-induced dopamine activity to positive emotionality. *Journal of Personality and Social Psychology, 67*, 485–498.

Diamond, A. (2000). Close interrelation of motor development and cognitive development and of the cerebellum and prefrontal cortex. *Child Development, 71*(1), 44–56.

Ditlevsen, T. (1942) Lille verden. In *Digte*. Copenhagen: Athenaeum.

Donaldson, M. (1987). The origins of inference. In J. Bruner & H. Haste (Eds.), *Making sense: The child's construction of the world* (pp. 97–108). New York: Methuen.

Donovan, W., & Leavitt, L. (1985). Physiologic assessment of mother-infant attachment. *Journal of the American Academy of Child Psychiatry, 24*, 65–70.

Dubovski, S. L. (1997). *Mind-body deceptions: The psychosomatics of everyday life.* New York: Norton.

Dunn, J. (1987). Understanding feelings: The early stages. In J. Bruner & H. Haste (Eds.), *Making sense: The child's construction of the world* (pp. 26–41). New York: Methuen.

Dunn, J. (1996). The Emanuel Miller Memorial Lecture 1995. Children's relationships: Bridging the divide between cognitive and social development. *Journal of Child Psychology and Psychiatry, 37*(5), 507–518.

Dunn, J., Slomkowski, C. M., Donelan-McCall, N., & Herrera, C. (1995). Conflict understanding and relationships: Developments and differences in the preschool years. *Early Education and Development, 6*, 303–316.

Edelman, G. M., & Tononi, G. (2000). *A universe of consciousness: How matter becomes imagination.* New York: Basic Books.

Emde, R. (1984). The affective self: Continuities and transformations from infancy. In J. D. Call, E. Galensch, & R. L. Tyson (Eds.), *Biological and developmental principles: Frontiers of infant psychiatry* (vol. 2, pp. 38–54). New York: Basic Books.

Emde, R. N. (1988). Development terminable and interminable: Innate and motivational factors from infancy. *International Journal of Psychoanalysis, 69*, 23–42.

Emde, R. N. (1989). The infant's relationship experience: Developmental and affective aspects. In J. Sameroff & R. N. Emde (Eds.), *Relationship disturbances in early childhood: A developmental approach* (pp. 33–51). New York: Basic Books.

Emde, R. N. (1992). Social referencing: Uncertainty, self and the search for meaning. In P. Feinman (Ed.), *Social referencing and the social construction of reality in infancy* (pp. 79–94). London: Plenum.

Emde, R., & Sameroff, A. (1989). Understanding early relationship disturbances. In J. Sameroff & R. N. Emde (Eds.), *Relationship disturbances in early childhood: A developmental approach* (pp. 3–14). New York: Basic Books.

Faraone, P., & Biederman, J. (1998). Neurobiology of attention-deficit hyperactivity disorder. *Biological Psychiatry, 44*, 951–958.

Fearon, R. M. P., & Belsky, J. (2002). Attachment and attention: Protection in relation to gender and cumulative social-contextual adversity. *Child Development, 75*(6), 1677–1693.

Field, T., & Fogel, A. (1982). *Emotion and early interaction.* Hillsdale, NJ: Lawrence Erlbaum.

Field, T., Healy, B., Goldstein, S., Perry, S., Benndall, D., Schanberg, S., et al. (1988). Infants of depressed mothers show "depressed" behavior even with nondepressed adults. *Child Development, 59*, 1569–1579.

Field, T., Schanberg, S., Scafidi, F., Bauer, C., Vega-Lahr, N., Garcia, R., et al. (1986). Tactile/kinesthetic stimulation effects on preterm neonates. *Pediatrics, 77*(5), 654–658.

Fischer, K. W., & Rose, S. P. (1994). Dynamic development of coordination of components in brain and behavior: Framework for theory and research. In G. Dawson & K. W. Fischer (Ed.), *Human behavior and the developing brain* (pp. 3–66). New York: Guilford.

Fogassi, L., Ferrari, P. F., Gesierich, B., Rozzi, S., Chersi, F., & Rizzolatti, G. (2005). Parietal lobe: From action organization to intention understanding. *Science, 308*, 662–667.

Fonagy, P. (1991). Thinking about thinking: Some clinical and theoretical considerations in the treatment of a borderline patient. *International Journal of Psychoanalysis, 72*, 1–18.

Fonagy, P. (1998a). An attachment theory approach to treatment of the difficult patient. *Bulletin of the Meninger Clinic, 62*(2), 147–169.

Fonagy, P. (1998b). Moments of change in psychoanalytic theory: Discussion of a new theory of psychic change. *Infant Mental Health Journal, 19*(3), 346–353.

Fonagy, P. (1999a). Memory and therapeutic action. *International Journal of Psycho-Analysis, 80*, 215–223.

Fonagy, P. (1999b). *Pathological attachments and therapeutic action.* Paper presented to the Developmental and Psychoanalytic Discussion Group, American Psychoanalytic Association Meeting, Washington, DC, May 13. Available at http://www.dspp.com/papers/fonagy3.htm.

Fonagy, P. (1999c). *Transgenerational consistencies of attachment: A new theory.* Paper presented to the Developmental and Psychoanalytic Discussion Group, American Psychoanalytic Association Meeting, Washington, DC, May 13. Available at http://www.dspp.com/papers/fonagy2.htm.

Fonagy, P. (2001). *Attachment theory and psychoanalysis.* New York: Other Press.

Fonagy, P. (2003). The development of psychopathology from infancy to adulthood: The mysterious unfolding of disturbance in time. *Infant Mental Health Journal, 24*(3), 212–239.

Fonagy, P. (2005). Connecting the intrapsychic and the interpersonal. Paper presented at conference, Psyche and Systems: The Inner World—the Outer World. LO-skolen. Elsinore, March 9.

Fonagy, P., Gergely, G., Jurist, E. L., & Target, M. (2002). *Affect regulation, mentalization and the development of the self.* New York: Other Press.

Fonagy, P., Steele, M., Steele, H., Leigh, T., Kennedy, R., Mattoon, G., et al. (1995). Attachment, the reflective self, and borderline states: The predictive specificity of the adult attachment interview and pathological emotional development. In P. Goldberg, R. Muir, & J. Kerr (Eds.), *Attachment theory, social, developmental, and clinical perspectives* (pp. 233–278). Hillsdale, NJ: Analytic Press.

Fonagy, P., & Target, M. (1996). Playing with reality: I. Theory of mind and the normal development of psychic reality. *International Journal of Psychoanalysis, 72*, 217–233.

Fonagy, P., & Target, M. (1997). Attachment and reflective function: Their role in self-organization. *Development and Psychopathology, 9*, 679–700.

Fonagy, P., & Target, M. (2002). Early intervention and the development of self-regulation. *Psychoanalytic Inquiry, 22*, 307–335.

Fonagy, P., & Target, M. (2003). *Psychoanalytic theories: Perspectives from developmental psychopathology.* London: Whurr.

Fonagy, P., Target, M., & Gergely, G. (2000). Attachment and borderline personality disorder: A theory and some evidence. *Psychiatric Clinics of North America, 23*, 103–122.

Fonagy, P., Target, M., Steele, M., Steele, H., Leigh, T., Levinson, A., et al. (1997). Morality, disruptive behavior, borderline personality disorder, crime, and their relationships to security of attachment. In L. Atkinson & K. J. Zucker (Eds.), *Attachment and psychopathology* (pp. 223–274). New York: Guilford.

Fox, N. A., Schmidt, L. A., Cathins, S. D., Rubin, K. H., & Coplan, R. J. (1996). The role of frontal activation in the regulation and dysregulation of social behaviour during the preschool years. *Development and Psychopathology, 8*, 89–102.

Freeman, W. (1994). *Societies of brains.* Hillsdale, NJ: Lawrence Erlbaum.

Freud, S. (1986). *Five lectures on psycho-analysis.* Standard Edition. Vol. X. London: Hogarth Press. (Original work published 1919)

Frønes, I. (1994). *De ligeværdige. Om socialisering og de jævnaldrendes betydning.* Copenhagen: Forlaget Børn & Unge.

Gallese, V. (2001). The "shared manifold" hypothesis: From mirror neurons to empathy. *Journal of Consciousness Studies, 8*(5–7), 33–50.

Gammelgaard, J. (2004). *Mellemværende. En diskussion af begrebet borderline.* Copenhagen: Akademisk Forlag.

Gergely, G., & Watson, J. (1996). The social biofeedback theory of parental affect-mirroring: The development of emotional self-awareness and self-control in infancy. *International Journal of Psychoanalysis, 77*, 1181–1212.

Gergely, G., & Watson, J. P. (1999). Early social-emotional development: Contingency perception and the social biofeedback model. In P. Rochat (Ed.), *Early social cognition: Understanding others in the first months of life* (pp. 101–137). Hillsdale, NJ: Lawrence Erlbaum.

Gerhardt, P. (2004). *Why love matters: How affection shapes a baby's brain.* New York: Brunner-Routledge.

Giedd, J. (2002). Inside the teenage brain [interview]. *Frontline.* Retrieved from www.pbs.org/wgbh/pages/frontline/shows/teenbrain/interviews/giedd.html

Giedd, J., Blumenthal, J., Jeffries, N. O., Castallanos, F. X., Liv, H., Zijdenbos, A., et al. (1999). Brain development during childhood and adolescence: A longitudinal MRI study. *Nature Neuroscience, 2*(10), 861–863.

Glaser, D. (2004). Early experience, attachment and the brain. In J. Corrigall & H. Wilkinson (Eds.), *Revolutionary connections: Psychotherapy and neuroscience.* London: Karnac.

Goldberg, E. (2001). *The executive brain: Frontal lobes and the civilized mind.* New York: Oxford University Press.

Goldman-Rakic, P. P. (1987). Circuitry of the primate prefontal cortex and regulation of behavior by representational memory. In F. Plum & V. Mountcastle (Eds.), *Handbook of physiology* (vol. 5, pp. 373–418). Bethesda, MD: American Physiological Society.

Goldman-Rakic, P. P. (1994). Foreword. In G. Dawson & K. W. Fischer (Ed.), *Human behavior and the developing brain* (pp. ix–xi). New York: Guilford.

Goldman-Rakic, P. P., & Brown, R. M. (1982). Postnatal development of monoamine content and synthesis in cerebral cortex of rhesus monkeys. *Developmental Brain Research, 4*, 339–349.

Goleman, D. (2003). *Destructive emotions. How can we overcome them? A scientific dialogue with the Dalai Lama.* New York: Bantam Books.

Gopnik, A., Meltzoff, A. N., & Kuhl, P. K. (1999). *The scientist in the crib: What early learning tells us about the mind.* New York: William Morris.

Grossmann, K. E., & Grossmann, K. (1990). The wider concept of attachment in cross-cultural research. *Human Development, 33*, 31–47.

Grossmann, K. E., & Grossmann, K. (1993). Attachment quality as an organizer of emotional and behavioral responses in a longitudinal perspective. In:C. M. Parkes, J. Stevenson-Hinde, & P. Marris (Eds.), *Attachment across the life cycle* (pp. 93–107). New York: Routledge.

Gunnar, M. R. (2001). Effects of early deprivation: Findings from orphanage-reared infants and children. In C. Nelson & M. Luciana (Ed.), *Handbook of developmental cognitive neuroscience* (pp. 617–629). Cambridge, MA: MIT Press.

Gunnar, M. R., & Barr, R. G. (1998). Stress, early brain development and behavoir. *Infants and Young Children, 11*, 1–14.

Gunnar, M. R., & Donzella, B. (2002). Social regulation of the cortisol levels in early human development. *Psychoneuroendocrinology, 27*, 199–220.

Gunnar, M. R., Mangelsdorf, S., Larson, M., & Hertsgaard, L. (1989). Attachment, temperament, and adrenocortical activity in infancy: A study of psychoendocrine regulation. *Developmental Psychology, 25*, 355–363.

Gunnar, M. R., Morison, S., Chisholm, K., & Schuder, M. (2001). Salivary cortisol levels in children adopted from Romanian orphanages. *Development and Psychopathology, 13*(3), 611–628.

Gunnar, M. R., & Vazquez, D. (2001).. Low cortisol and a flattening of expected daytime rhythm: Potential indices of risk in human development. *Development and Psychopathology, 13*(3), 515–538.

Hammer, E. (1990). *Reaching the affect: Style in the psychodynamic therapies.* Northvale, NJ: Jason Aronson.

Hansen, P. (2002). *Fra neuron til neurose.* Copenhagen: Gads Forlag.

Hare, R. D., & Jutai, J. W. (1983). Psychopathy and electrocortical indices of perceptual processing during selective attention. *Psychophysiology, 20*, 146–151.

Harlow, H. F. (1958). The nature of love. *American Psychiatry, 13*, 673–685.

Harlow, H. F. (1959). Love in infant monkeys. *Scientific American, 200*(6), 68–74.

Harlow, H. F., & Harlow, M. K. (1966). Learning to love. *American Scientist, 54*, 244–272.

Harris, P. L. (1994). Understanding pretense. In C. Lewis & P. Mitchell (Eds.), *Children's early understanding of mind* (pp. 235–260). Hillsdale, NJ: Lawrence Erlbaum.

Hart, P. (2006). Læring og hjerneprocesser i et relationelt perspektiv. In R. Kristensen (Ed.), *Fantastiske forbindelser—relationer i undervisning og læringssamvær.* Frederikshavn: Dafolo.

Hart, P. (2008). *Brain, attachment, personality: An introduction to neuroaffective development.* London: Karnac.

Hart, J., Gunnar, M., & Cicchetti, D. (1995). Salivary cortisol in maltreated chil-

dren: Evidence of relations between neuroendocrine activity and social competence. *Development and Psychopathology, 7*, 11–26.

Hebb, D.O. (1949). *The organization of Behavior.* New York: Wiley.

Herman, J. L., & van der Kolk, B. A. (1987). Traumatic antecedents of borderline
personality disorder. In B. A. van der Kolk (Ed.), *Psychological trauma* (pp.
111–126). Washington, DC: American Psychiatric Press.

Hinde, R. A., & Stevenson-Hinde, J. (1986). Relating childhood relationships to
individual characteristics. In W. W. Hartup & Z. Rubin (Eds.), *Relationships
and development* (pp. 27–50). Hillsdale, NJ: Lawrence Erlbaum.

Hinde, R. A., Titmus, G., Easton, D., & Tamplin, A. (1985). Incidence of "friendship" and behaviour toward strong associates versus nonassociates in preschool-
ers. *Child Development, 56*, 234–245.

Hobson, R. P. (1993). The emotional origins of social understanding. *Philosophical Psychology, 6*(3), 227–249.

Hodges, J. (1996). The natural history of early non-attachment. In B. Bernstein &
J. Brannon (Eds.), *Children: Research and policy.* London: Taylor & Francis.

Hofer, M. A. (1975). Studies on how early maternal separation produces behavioral change in young rats. *Psychosomatic Medicine, 37*(3), 245–264.

Hofer, M. A. (1983). On the relationship between attachment and separation processes in infancy. In R. Plutchik & H. Kellerman (Eds.), *Emotion: Theory, research and experience* (vol. 2, pp. 199–219). New York: Academic Press.

Hofer, M. A. (1984a). Relationships as regulators: A psychobiologic perspective on
bereavement. *Psychosomatic Medicine, 46*, 183–197.

Hofer, M. A. (1984b). Early stages in the organization of cardiovascular control.
Proceedings of the Society for Experimental and Biological Medicine, 175,
147–157.

Hofer, M. A. (1987). Early social relationships: A psychobiologist's view. *Child Development, 58*(3), 633–647.

Hofer, M. A. (1990). Early symbiotic processes: Hard evidence from a soft place. In
R. A. Glick & P. Bone (Ed.), *Pleasure beyond the pleasure principle* (pp. 55–
78). New Haven, CT: Yale University Press.

Hofer, M. A. (1995). Hidden regulators: Implications for a new understanding of
attachment, separation, and loss. In P. Goldberg, R. Muir, & J. Kerr (Eds.), *Attachment theory, social developmental, and clinical perspectives* (pp. 203–
230). Hillsdale, NJ: Analytic Press.

Hofer, M. A., & Sullivan, R. (2001). Toward a neurobiology of attachment. In C.
Nelson & M. Luciana (Ed.), *Handbook of developmental cognitive neuroscience* (pp. 599–616). Cambridge, MA: MIT Press.

Huttenlocher, P. R. (1984). Synapse elimination and plasticity in developing human cerebral cortex. *American Journal of Mental Deficiency, 88*, 488–496.

Hylander, L., Krabbe, E., & Schwartz, R. (2005). Metoder og dilemmaer i lang-
varige behandlingsforløb for børnefamilier med psykisk syge forældre. *Psykologisk Pædagogisk Rådgivning, 42*, 177–204.

Isabella, R., & Belsky, J. (1991). Interactional synchrony and the origins of infant-mother attachment: A replication study. *Child Development, 62*, 373–384.

Isager, T. (1999). Familie- og systemteori. In L. Lier, T. Isager, O. P. Jørgensen, F. W. Larsen, & T. Aarkrog (Eds.), *Børne- og ungdomspsykiatri* (pp. 69–81). Copenhagen: Hans Reitzels Forlag.

Izard, C. E. (1971). *The face of emotion.* New York: Appleton-Century-Crofts.

Izard, C. E. (1991). *The psychology of emotions.* New York: Plenum.

Jacobs, W. J., & Nadel, L. (1985). Stress-induced recovery of fears and phobias. *Psychological Review, 92*, 512–531.

Jacobvitz, D., & Sroufe, L. A. (1987). The early caregiver-child relationship and attention-deficit disorder with hyperactivity in kindergarten: A prospective study. *Child Development, 58*, 1496–1504.

Joseph, R. (1982). The neuropsychology of development: Hemispheric laterality, limbic language, and the origin of thought. *Journal of Clinical Psychology, 38*, 4–33.

Joseph, R. (1993). *The naked neuron: Evolution and the languages of the body and brain.* New York: Plenum.

Juengling, F. D., Schmahl, C., Hesslinger, B., Ebert, D., Bremner, J. D., Gostomzyk, J., et al. (2003). Positron emission tomography in female patients with border-line personality disorder. *Journal of Psychiatric Research, 37*(2), 109–115.

Kagan, J., Reznick, J. P., & Snidman, N. (1987). The physiology and psychology of behavioural inhibition in children. *Child Development, 58*, 1459–1473.

Kalin, N. H. (1993). The neurobiology of fear. *Scientific American, 268*(5), 94–101.

Kandel, E. R. (2005). A new intellectual framework for psychiatry. In E. R. Kandel (Ed.), *Psychiatry, psychoanalysis, and the new biology of mind* (pp. 27–59). Washington, DC: American Psychiatric Publishing.

Kaplan-Solms, K., & Solms, M. (2002). *Clinical studies in neuro-psychoanalysis: Introduction to a depth neuropsychology.* New York: Karnac.

Karen, R. (1998). *Becoming attached.* New York: Oxford University Press.

Karr-Morse, R., & Wiley, M. (1997). *Ghosts from the nursery: Tracing the roots of violence.* New York: Atlantic Monthly Press.

Katzenelson, B. (1994). Mennesketilblivelsens koreografi og kundskabens grund-lag. In A. Neumann (Ed.), *Det særligt menneskelige. Udviklingspsykologiske billeder* (pp. 59–105). Copenhagen: Hans Reitzels Forlag.

Kendler, K. S., Kuhn, J. W., Vittum, J., Prescott, C. A., & Riley, B. (2005). The interaction of stressful life events and a serotonin transporter polymorphism in the prediction of episodes in major depression. *Archives of General Psychiatry, 62*, 529–535.

Kierkegaard, P. (2008). *Purity of heart is to will one thing.* Wilder Publications. (Original work published 1847)

Kohut, H. (1984). *How does analysis cure?* Chicago: University of Chicago Press.

Kraemer, G. W. (1992). A psychobiological theory of attachment. *Behavioral and Brain Sciences, 15*, 493–541.

Kreppner, J. M., O'Connor, T. G., & Rutter, M. (2001). Can inattention/overactivity be an institutional deprivation syndrome? *Journal of Abnormal Child Psychology, 29*(6), 513–528.

Kristensen, R. (2006). Et fantastisk nuværende øjeblik—et interview med Daniel Stern. In R. Kristensen (Ed.), *Fantastiske forbindelser—relationer i undervisning og læringssamvær* (pp. 2–11). Frederikshavn: Dafolo.

Krystal, H. (1988). *Integration and self-healing: Affect-trauma-alexithymia.* Hillsdale, NJ: Analytic Press.

Lambert, M. J. (1992). Psychotherapy outcome research: Implications for integrative and eclectic therapists. In J. C. Norcross & M. R. Goldfried (Ed.), *Handbook of psychotherapy integration* (pp. 94–129). New York: Basic Books.

LeDoux, J. E. (1989). Indelibility of subcortical emotional memories. *Journal of Cognitive Neuroscience, 1*, 238–243.

LeDoux, J. E. (1994). Emotion, memory and the brain. *Scientific American, 270*, 32–39.

LeDoux, J. E. (1998). *The emotional brain: The mysterious underpinnings of emotional life.* London: Weidenfeld & Nicolson.

LeDoux, J. E. (2001). *Synaptic self: How our brains become who we are.* New York: Viking.

Lester, B. M., Hoffman, J., & Brazelton, T. B. (1985). The rhythmic structure of mother-infant interaction in term and preterm infants. *Child Development, 56*, 15–27.

Lewis, H. B. (1979). Shame in depression and hysteria. In C. E. Izard (Ed.), *Emotion in personality and psychopathology* (pp. 399–414). New York: Plenum.

Lewis, M. H., Gluck, J. P., Beauchamp, A. J., Keresztury, M. F., & Mailman, R. B. (1990). Long term effects of early social isolation in Macaca mulatta: Changes in dopamine receptor function following apomorphine challenge. *Brain Research, 513*, 67–73.

Lewis, M., & Ramsay, D. (1995). Stability and change in cortisol and behavioural response to stress during the first 18 months of life. *Developmental Psychobiology, 28*, 419–428.

Lewis, T., Amini, F., & Lannon, R. (2001). *A general theory of love.* New York: Vintage.

Lichter, F., & Cummings, J. (Ed.). (2001). *Frontal-subcortical circuits in psychiatric and neurological disorders.* New York: Guilford.

Lier, L., Isager, T., Jørgensen, O. S., Larsen, F. W., & Aarkrog, T. (Eds.). (1999). *Børne- og ungdomspsykiatri.* Copenhagen: Hans Reitzels Forlag.

Lowen, A. (1976). *Bioenergetics.* New York: Viking Penguin.

Luu, P., & Tucker, D. M. (1996). Self-regulation and cortical development: Implications for functional studies of the brain. In R. W. Thatcher, G. R. Lyon, J. Rumsey, & N. Krasnegor (Eds.), *Developmental neuroimaging: Mapping the de-*

velopment of brain and behaviour (pp. 297–305). San Diego: Academic Press.

Lyons-Ruth, K. (1998). Implicit relational knowing: Its role in development and psychoanalytic treatment. *Infant Mental Health Journal, 19*(3), 282–289.

MacLean, P. D. (1967). The brain in relation to empathy and medical education. *Journal of Nervous and Mental Disease, 144*, 374–382.

MacLean, P. D. (1970). The triune brain, emotion, and scientific bias. In F. O. Schmitt (Ed.), *The neurosciences second study program* (pp. 336–349). New York: Rockefeller University Press.

MacLean, P. D. (1973). A triune concept of the brain and behavior: Lecture I. Man's reptilian and limbic inheritance; Lecture II. Man's limbic brain and the psychoses; Lecture III. New trends in man's evolution. In T. Boag & D. Campbell (Eds.), *The Hincks Memorial Lectures* (pp. 6–66). Toronto: University of Toronto Press.

MacLean, P. D. (1990). *The triune brain in evolution: Role in paleocerebral functions.* New York: Plenum.

Madsen, S. Å. (1996). *Bånd der brister—bånd der knyttes.* Copenhagen: Hans Reitzels Forlag.

Main, M. (1990). Parental aversion to infant-initiated contact is correlated with the parent's own rejection during childhood. In K. Barnard & T. B. Brazelton (Eds.), *Touch: The foundation of experience: Full revised and expanded proceedings of Johnson & Johnson Pediatric Round Table X. Clinical infant reports* (pp. 461–495). Madison, CT: International University Press.

Main, M. (1993). Metacognitive knowledge, metacognitive monitoring, and singular (coherent) vs. multiple (incoherent) model of attachment: Findings and directions for future research. In C. M. Parkers, J. Stevenson-Hinde, & P. Marris (Eds.), *Attachment across the life cycle* (pp. 127–159). London: Tavistock/ Routledge.

Main, M., & Cassidy, J. (1988). Categories of response to reunion with the parent at age 6: Predictable from infant attachment classification and stable over a 1-month period. *Developmental Psychology, 24*, 415–426.

Main, M., & Hesse, E. (1990). Parents' unresolved traumatic experiences are related to infant disorganized attachment status: Is frightened and/or frightening parental behavior the linking mechanism? In M. T. Greenberg, D. Cicchetti, & E. M. Cummings (Eds.), *Attachment in the preschool years: Theory, research, and intervention.* Chicago: University of Chicago Press.

Main, M., Kaplan, N., & Cassidy, J. (1985). Security in infancy, childhood and adulthood: A move to the level of representation. In I. Bretherton & E. Waters (Eds.), *Growing points in attachment theory and research. Monographs of the Society for Research in Child Development, 50*(209), 66–104.

Main, M., & Solomon, J. (1986). Discovery of an insecure-disorganized/disoriented attachment pattern. In T. B. Brazelton & M. W. Yogman (Eds.), *Affective development in infancy.* Norwood, NJ: Ablex.

Marcovitch, S., Goldberg, S., Gold, A., Washington, J., Wasson, C., Krekewich, K., et al. (1997). Determinants of behavioural problems in Romanian children adopted in Ontario. *International Journal of Behavioral Development, 20*(1), 17–31.

Marner, T. (1999). Familieterapi. In L. Lier, T. Isager, O. P. Jørgensen, F. W. Larsen, & T. Aarkrog (Eds.), *Børne- og ungdomspsykiatri* (pp. 411–425). Copenhagen: Hans Reitzels Forlag.

Martin, P. (1997). *The sickening mind.* London: Harper Collins.

Mathiesen, B. B. (2004). Psyken i hjernen? In P. Køppe (Ed.), *Kroppen i psyken* (pp. 49–84). Copenhagen: Hans Reitzels Forlag.

McBurnett, K., Lahey, B., Rathouz, P., & Loeber, R. (2000). Low salivary cortisol and persistent aggression in boys referred for disruptive behaviour. *Archives of General Psychiatry, 57*(1), 38–43.

Mead, G. H. (1934). *Mind, self, and society.* Chicago: Chicago University Press.

Meltzoff, A. N. (1993). The centrality of motor coordination and proprioception in social and cognitive development: From shared actions to shared minds. In: G. J. P. Savelsbergh (Eds.), *The development of coordination in infancy* (pp. 463–496). Amsterdam: Elsevier.

Meltzoff, A. N., & Moore, M. K. (1977). Imitation of facial and manual gestures by human neonates. *Science, 198*, 75–78.

Minuchin, S., Rosman, B. L., & Baner, L. (1978). *Psychosomatic families.* Cambridge: Harvard University Press.

Mirsky, A. F., & Duncan, C. C. (2001). A nosology of disorders of attention. *Annals of the New York Academy of Sciences, 931*, 17–32.

Mirsky, A. F., Ingraham, L. J., & Kugelmass, P. (1995). Neuropsychological assessment of attention and its pathology in the Israeli Cohort. *Schizophrenia Bulletin, 21*, 193–204.

Mirsky, A. F., Kugelmass, S., Ingraham, L. J., Frenkel, E., & Nathan, M. (1995). Overview and summary: Twenty-five-year follow-up of high-risk children. *Schizophrenia Bulletin, 21*, 227–239.

Møller, I., & Hart, P. (2001). Børn, neuropsykologi og udvikling. *Kognition og Pædagogik, 39*, 22–43.

Morgan, A. (1998). Moving along to things left undone. *Infant Mental Health Journal, 19*(3), 324–332.

Mortensen, K. (2001). *Fra neuroser til relationsforstyrrelser: Psykoanalytiske udviklingsteorier og klassifikationer af psykopatologi.* Copenhagen: Gyldendal.

Neisser, U. (1993). The self perceived. In U. Neisser (Ed.), *The perceived self: Ecological and interpersonal sources of self knowledge* (pp. 3–21). New York: Cambridge University Press.

Nemeroff, C. B. (1999). The neurobiology of depression. In A. Damasio et al. (Eds.), *The Scientific American book of the brain* (pp. 263–277). New York: Lyons Press.

Neumann, A. (1994). Introduktion. In A. Neumann (Ed.), *Det særligt menneskelige. Udviklingspsykologiske billeder* (pp. 7–16). Copenhagen: Hans Reitzels Forlag.

Nissen, P. (1999). *Kvalitets- og metodeudvikling i børne- og ungesager*. Copenhagen: Pædagogisk Psykologisk Forlag.

O'Connor, T., Rutter, M., & the English and Romanian Adoptees Study Team. (2000). Attachment disorder behavior following early severe deprivation: Extension and longitudinal follow-up. *Journal of the American Academy of Child and Adolescent Psychiatry, 39*, 703–712.

Olson, G. M., & Strauss, M. P. (1984). The development of infant memory. In M. Moscovitch (Ed.), *Infant memory: Its relation to normal and pathological memory in humans and other animals* (pp. 145–172). New York: Plenum.

Orlinsky, D. E., & Howard, K. I. (1986). Process and outcome in psychotherapy. In S. L. Garfield & A. E. Bergin (Ed.), *Handbook of psychotherapy and behaviour change* (pp. 311–381). New York: Wiley.

Øvreeide, H. (2001a). Barnet som familieterapeutisk bruker. *Fokus, 29*, 22–35.

Øvreeide, H. (2001b). Notes from course hosted by the Danish Psychological Association for Child and Family Therapy, November 20–21.

Øvreeide, H. (2002). *Samtaler med barn. Metodiske samtaler med barn i vanskelige livssituasjoner.* Høyskoleforlaget AS: Norwegian Academic Press.

Øvreeide, H., & Hafstad, R. (1996). *The Marte Meo method and developmental supportive dialogues.* Harderwijk, Netherlands: Aarts Productions.

Panksepp, J. (1998). *Affective neuroscience: The foundations of human and animal emotions.* New York: Oxford University Press.

Papousek, H., & Papousek, M. (1975). *Parent-infant interaction.* New York: Associated Science.

Papousek, H., & Papousek, M. (1981). Musical elements in the infant's vocalization: Their significance for communication, cognition and creativity. In L. P. Lippsitt (Ed.), *Advances in infant research.* Norwood, NJ: Ablex.

Perry, B. D. (1990). Adrenergic receptor regulation in posttraumatic stress disorder. In E. L. Giller (Ed.), *Advances in psychiatry: Biological assessment and treatment of post traumatic stress disorder* (pp. 87–115). Washington, DC: American Psychiatric Press.

Perry, B. D. (1994). Neurobiological sequelae of childhood trauma: Posttraumatic stress disorders in children. In M. Murburg (Ed.), *Catecholamine function in post traumatic stress disorder: Emerging concepts* (pp. 253–276). Washington, DC: American Psychiatric Press.

Perry, B. D. (1997). Incubated in terror: Neurodevelopmental factors in the "cycle of violence." Cybrary version. In J. Osofsky (Ed.), *Children, youth and violence: The search for solutions* (pp. 124–148). New York: Guilford.

Perry, B. D. (1999). Memories of fear: How the brain stores and retrieves physiologic states, feelings, behaviors and thoughts from traumatic events. Cybrary version. In J. Goodwin & R. Attias (Eds.), *Splintered reflections: Images of the body in trauma.* New York: Basic Books.

Perry, B. D. (2001). Violence and childhood: How persisting fear can alter the developing child's brain. Cybrary version from *The neurodevelopmental impact of violence in childhood.* In D. Schetky & E. Benedek (Eds.), *Textbook of child adolescent forensic psychiatry* (pp. 221–238). Washington, DC: American Psychiatric Press.

Perry, B. D. (2002). Childhood experience and the expression of genetical potential: What childhood neglect tells us about nature and nurture. *Brain and Mind, 3*, 79–100.

Perry, B. D., & Azad, I. (1999). Posttraumatic stress disorders in children and adolescents. *Current Opinions in Pediatrics, 11*(4), 310–316.

Perry, B. D., Pollard, R. A., Blakely, T. L., Baker, W. L., & Vigilante, D. (1995). Childhood trauma, the neurobiology of adoption, and "use-dependent" development of the brain: How "states" become "traits." *Infant Mental Health Journal, 16*, 271–291.

Piaget, J. (1973). The affective unconscious and the cognitive unconscious. *Journal of the American Psychoanalytic Association, 21*(2), 249–261.

Polan, H. J., & Hofer, M. (1999). Psychobiological origins of infant attachment and separation responses. In J. Cassidy & P. R. Shaver (Ed.), *Handbook of attachment: Theory, research and clinical applications* (pp. 162–180). New York: Guilford.

Pollak, S. D., Cichetti, D., Horming, K., & Reed, A. (2000). Recognizing emotion in faces: Developmental effects of child abuse and neglect. *Developmental Psychology, 36*, 679–688.

Porges, S. W. (1995). Orienting in a defensive world: Mammalian modifications of our evolutionary heritage. A polyvagal theory. *Psychophysiology, 32*, 301–318.

Porges, S. W. (1996). Physiological regulation in high-risk infants: A model for assessment and potential intervention. *Development and Psychopathology, 8*, 43–58.

Porges, S. W. (1997). Emotion: An evolutionary by-product of the neural regulation of the autonomic nervous system. .)*Annals of the New York Academy of Sciences, 807*, 62–77.

Porges, S. W. (2001). The polyvagal theory: Phylogenetic substrates of a social nervous system. *International Journal of Psychophysiology, 42*, 123–146.

Purves, D., Augustine, G. J., Fitzpatrick, D., Katz, L. C., LaMantia, A., McNamara, J. O., et al. (2001). *Neuroscience.* Sunderland, MA: Sinauer Associates.

Rakic, P., Bourgeois, J. P., & Goldman-Rakic, P. P. (1994). Synaptic development of the cerebral cortex: Implications for learning, memory, and mental illness. *Progress in Brain Research, 102*, 227–243.

Ramachandran, V. (2003). *The emerging mind.* London: Profile Books.

Reiss, D. (1989). The represented and practicing family. In J. Sameroff & R. N. Emde (Eds.), *Relationship disturbances in early childhood: A developmental approach* (pp. 191–221). New York: Basic Books.

Robbins, A. (1980). *Expressive therapy: A creative arts approach to depth-oriented treatment.* New York: Human Sciences.

Robertson, J., & Bowlby, J. (1952). Responses of young children to separation from their mothers. *Courrier Centre Internationale Enfance, 2*, 131–142.

Rosenblum, L., Coplan, J., Friedman, S., Bassoff, T., Gorman, J., & Andrews, M.

(1994). Adverse early experiences affect noradrenergic and seretonergic functioning in adult primates. *Biological Psychiatry, 35*(4), 221–227.

Roth, A., & Fonagy, P. (1996). *What works for whom? A critical review of psychotherapy research.* New York: Guilford.

Rothbart, M., Evans, D., & Ahadi, S. (2000). Temperament and personality: Origins and outcomes. *Journal of Personality and Social Psychology, 78*(1), 122–135.

Rutter, M. (1985). Resilience in the face of adversity: Protective factors and resistance to psychiatric disturbance. *British Journal of Psychiatry, 147,* 598–611.

Rutter, M., & Rutter, M. (1993). *Developing minds.* New York: Basic Books.

Rutter, M., Silberg, J., O'Connor, T., & Simonoff, E. (1999). Genetics and child psychiatry: II. Empirical research findings. *Journal of Psychological Psychiatry, 40*(1), 19–55.

Rye, H. (1997). *Tidlig hjælp til bedre samspil.* Copenhagen: Munksgaard.

Sameroff, A. (1989). Principles of development and psychopathology. In J. Sameroff & R. N. Emde (Eds.), *Relationship disturbances in early childhood: A developmental approach* (pp. 17–32). New York: Basic Books.

Sander, L. (1969). Regulation and organization in the early infant-caretaker system. In R. J. Robinson (Ed.), *Brain and early behaviour* (pp. 311–333). London: Academic Press.

Sander, L. (1977). The regulation of exchange in the infant-character system and some aspects of the context-content relationship. In M. Lewis & L. Rosenblum (Eds.), *Interaction, conversation, and the development of language* (pp. 133–156). New York: Wiley.

Sander, L. (1983). Polarity, paradox, and the organizing process in development. In J. D. Call, E. Galenson, & R. L. Tyson (Eds.), *Frontiers of infant psychiatry* (vol. I, pp. 333–347). New York: Basic Books.

Sander, L. (1985). Toward a logical organization in psycho-biological development. In K. Klar & L. Siever (Eds.), *Biologic response styles: Clinical implications* (pp. 20–36). Washington, DC: Monograph Series, American Psychiatric Press.

Sander, L. (1988). The event structure of regulation in the neonate-caregiver system as a biological background for early organization of psychic structure. In A. Goldberg (Ed.), *Frontiers in self psychology* (pp. 3–27). Hillsdale, NJ: Analytic Press.

Sander, L. (1992). Letter to the editor. *International Journal of Psycho-Analysis, 73,* 582–584.

Sander, L. (1995). Identity and the experience of specificity in a process of recognition. *Psychoanalytic Dialogues, 5,* 579–593.

Santostefano, P. (1978). *A biodevelopmental approach to clinical child psychology.* New York: Wiley.

Sapolsky, R. (1998). *Why zebras don't get ulcers: An updated guide to stress, stress-related diseases, and coping.* New York: W.H. Freeman.

Scaer, R. C. (2001). *The body bears the burden: Trauma, dissociation, and disease.* Binghamton, NY: Haworth.

Schacter, D. L. (1996). *Searching for memory.* New York: Basic Books.

Schacter, D. L., & Moscovitch, M. (1984). Infants, amnesics, and dissociable memory systems. In M. Moscovitch (Ed.), *Infant memory: Its relation to normal and pathological memory in humans and other animals. Advances in the Study of Communication and Affect* (vol. 9, pp. 173–209). New York: Plenum.

Schibbye, A. L. (2005). *Relationer: Et dialektisk perspektiv.* Copenhagen: Akademisk Forlag.

Schore, A. N. (1994). *Affect regulation and the origin of self.* Hillsdale, NJ: Lawrence Erlbaum.

Schore, A. N. (2000). Healthy childhood and the development of the human brain. Paper presented at conference, Healthy Children for the 21st Century. Healthy Children Foundation.

Schore, A. N. (2001a). The effects of a secure attachment relationship on right brain development, affect regulation, and infant mental health. *Infant Mental Health Journal, 22,* 7–66.

Schore, A. N. (2001b). The effects of early relational trauma on right brain development, affect regulation, and infant mental health. *Infant Mental Health Journal, 22,* 201–269.

Schore, A. N. (2001c). Minds in the making: Attachment, the self-organizing brain, and developmentally-oriented psychoanalytic psychotherapy. *British Journal of Psychotherapy, 17,* 299–328.

Schore, A. N. (2002a). Advances in neuropsychoanalysis, attachment theory, and trauma research: Implications for self psychology. *Psychoanalytic Inquiry, 22*(3), 433–485.

Schore, A. N. (2002b). Dysregulation of the right brain: A fundamental mechanism of traumatic attachment and the psychopathogenesis of posttraumatic stress disorder. *Australia and New Zealand Journal of Psychiatry, 36,* 9–30.

Schore, A. N. (2003a). *Affect dysregulation and disorders of the self.* New York: W.W. Norton.

Schore, A. N. (2003b). *Affect regulation and the repair of the self.* New York: W.W. Norton.

Schwartz, R., & Hansen, I. Ø. (2005). Behandling af børn anbragt i familiepleje. *Psykologisk Pædagogisk Rådgivning, 42*(3), 374–390.

Schwarz, E., & Perry, B. (1994). The post-traumatic response in children and adolescents. *Psychiatric Clinics of North America, 17*(2), 311–326.

Seligman, M., & Beagley, G. (1975). Learned helplessness in the rat. *Journal of Comparative and Physiological Psychology, 88,* 534–541.

Siegel, A. (2005). *The neurobiology of aggression and rage.* Boca Raton, FL: CRC Press.

Siegel, D. J. (1999). *The developing mind: Toward a neurobiology of interpersonal experience.* New York: Guilford.

Siegel, D. J. (2004). Seminar, EMDR Association, June 16, Copenhagen.

Smith, L. (2001). *Småbarnsalderens neuropsykologi*. Oslo: Gyldendal Akademisk.

Smith, L. (2003). *Tilknytning og børns udvikling*. Copenhagen: Akademisk Forlag.

Solms, M. (2005). A psychoanalytic contribution to affective neuroscience. In J. Maxine (Ed.), *Neuroscientific and psychoanalytic perspectives on emotion* (pp. 11–24). London: N-PSA.

Solms, M., & Turnbull, O. (2002). *The brain and the inner world*. New York: Other Press.

Sørensen, J. H. (2006). Introduktion. Affektregulering i udviklingspsykologi og psykoterapi. In J. H. Sørensen (Ed.), *Affektregulering i udvikling og psykoterapi* (pp. 9–130). Copenhagen: Hans Reitzels Forlag.

Sørensen, L. J. (1996). *Særpræg, særhed, sygdom*. Copenhagen: Hans Reitzels Forlag.

Sørensen, L. J. (2005). *Smertegrænsen. Traumer, tilknytning og psykisk sygdom*. Copenhagen: Dansk Psykologisk Forlag.

Sowell, E. R., & Jernigan, T. L. (1998). Further MRI evidence of late brain maturation: Limbic volume increases and changing asymmetries during childhood and adolescence. *Developmental Neuropsychology, 14*(4), 599–617.

Spangler, G., & Grossmann, K. E. (1993). Biobehavioral organization in securely and insecurely attached infants. *Child Development, 64*, 1439–1450.

Spangler, G., & Schieche, M. (1998). Emotional and adrenocortical responses of infants to the strange situation: The differential function of emotional expression. *International Journal of Behavioural Development, 22*(4), 681–706.

Spear, L. P. (2000). The adolescent brain and age-related behavioural manifestations. *Neuroscience and Biobehavioural Rewiews, 24*, 417–463.

Spitz, R. A. (1945). Hospitalism: An enquiry into the genesis of psychiatric conditions in early childhood. *Psycho-Analytic Study of the Child, 1*, 53–74.

Spitz, R. A. (1946). Hospitalism: A follow-up report on an investigation described in Volume 1, 1945. *Psycho-Analytic Study of the Child, 2*, 313–342.

Sroufe, L. A. (1979). Socioemotional development. In J. Osofsky (Ed.), *Handbook of infant development* (pp. 462–516). New York: Wiley.

Sroufe, L. A. (1989a). Relationships, self, and individual adaptation. In J. Sameroff & R. N. Emde (Eds.), *Relationship disturbances in early childhood: A developmental approach* (pp. 70–94). New York: Basic Books.

Sroufe, L. A. (1989b). Relationships and relationship disturbances. In J. Sameroff & R. N. Emde (Eds.), *Relationship disturbances in early childhood: A developmental approach* (pp. 97–124). New York: Basic Books.

Sroufe, L. A. (1996). *Emotional development: The organization of emotional life in the early years*. New York: Cambridge University Press.

Sroufe, L. A., Cooper, R. G., & Deltart, G. B. (1992). *Child development: Its nature and course*. New York: McGraw-Hill.

Sroufe, L. A., & Egeland, B. (1991). Illustrations of person-environment interaction from a longitudinal study. In T. D. Wachs & R. Plomin (Eds.), *Conceptualization and measurement of organism-environment interaction* (pp. 68–84). Washington, DC: American Psychological Association.

Sroufe, L. A., & Fleeson, J. (1986). Attachment and the construction of relationships. In W. W. Hartup & Z. Rubin (Eds.), *Relationships and development* (pp. 51–71). Hillsdale, NJ: Lawrence Erlbaum.

Sroufe, L. A., Fox, N. E., & Pancake, V. R. (1983). Attachment and dependency in developmental perspective. *Child Development, 54*, 1615–1627.

Sroufe, L. A., & Rutter, M. (1984). The domain of developmental psychopathology. *Child Development, 48*, 1148–1199.

Stein, J. (1987). *Internal medicine*. Boston: Little, Brown.

Stern, D. N. (1977). *The first relationship*. Cambridge, MA: Harvard University Press.

Stern, D. N. (1984). Affect attunement. In J. D. Call, E. Galensch, & R. L. Tyson (Eds.), *Frontiers of infant psychiatry* (vol. 2, pp. 3–13). New York: Basic Books.

Stern, D. N. (1985). *The interpersonal world of the infant*. New York: Basic Books.

Stern, D. N. (1989). The representation of relational patterns: Developmental considerations. In J. Sameroff & R. N. Emde (Eds.), *Relationship disturbances in early childhood: A developmental approach* (pp. 52–69). New York: Basic Books.

Stern, D. N. (1990). Joy and satisfaction in infancy. In R. A. Glick & P. Bone (Ed.), *Pleasure beyond the pleasure principle* (pp. 13–25). New Haven: Yale University Press.

Stern, D. N. (1993). The role of feelings for an interpersonal self. In U. Neisser (Ed.), *The perceived self: Ecological and interpersonal sources of self knowledge* (pp. 205–215). New York: Cambridge University Press.

Stern, D. N. (1995). *The motherhood constellation*. New York: Basic Books.

Stern, D. N. (1998a). The process of therapeutic change involving implicit knowledge: Some implications of developmental observations for adult psychotherapy. *Infant Mental Health Journal, 19*, 300–308.

Stern, D. N. (1998b). Seminar and workshop. DISPUK, Snekkersten, June 18–19.

Stern, D. N. (2001). Forelæsning: SICON-konferencen, November 9.

Stern, D. N. (2004). *The present moment in psychotherapy and everyday life*. New York: W.W. Norton.

Stern, D. N., Sander, L. W., Nahum, J. P., Harrison, A. M., Lyons-Routh, K., Morgan, A. C., et al. (1998). Non-interpretive mechanisms in psychoanalytic therapy: The "something more" than interpretation. *International Journal of Psychoanalysis, 79*(Pt 5), 903–921.

Strogatz, P. (2003). *Sync: The emerging science of spontaneous order*. New York: Theia.

Suomi, S. J. (1991). Up-tight and laidback monkeys: Individual differences in the response to social challenges. In P. Brauth, W. Hall, & R. Dooling (Eds.), *Plasticity of development* (pp. 27–56). Cambridge, MA: MIT Press.

Suomi, S. J. (1999). Developmental trajectories, early experiences and community consequences: Lessons from studies with rhesus monkeys. In D. P. Keating & C. Hertzman (Eds.), *Developmental health and the wealth of nations: Sociobiological, and educational dynamics* (pp. 185–200). New York: Guilford.

Suomi, S. J. (2000). A biobehavioral perspective on developmental psychopathology: Excessive aggression and serotonergic dysfunction in monkeys. In A. J. Sameroff, M. Lewis, & S. Miller (Eds.), *Handbook of developmental psychopathology* (pp. 237–256). New York: Plenum.

Suomi, S. J., Seaman, S. F., & Lewis, J. K. (1978). Effects of imipramine treatment of separation-induced social disorder in rhesus monkeys. *Archives of General Psychiatry, 35*, 321–325.

Target, M., & Fonagy, P. (1996). Playing with reality II: The development of psychic reality from a theoretical perspective. *International Journal of Psycho-Analysis, 77*, 459–479.

Teicher, M. H. (2002). Scars that won't heal: The neurobiology of child abuse. *Scientific American, 286*(3), 54–61.

Teicher, M. H., Ito, Y., & Glod, C. A. (1996). Neurophysiological mechanisms of stress response in children. In C. R. Pfeffer (Ed.), *Severe stress and mental disturbances in children* (pp. 59–84). Washington, DC: American Psychiatric Press.

Tetzchner, P. (2002). *Utviklingspsykologi, Barne- oq ungdomsalderen.* Oslo: Gyldendal Akademisk.

Thelen, E. (1989). Self-organization in developmental processes: Can systems approaches work? In M. Gunnar & E. Thelen (Eds.), *Systems and development: The Minnesota symposium in child psychology* (pp. 77–117). Hillsdale, NJ: Lawrence Erlbaum.

Thelen, E. (1995). Motor development: A new synthesis. *American Psychologist, 50*, 79–95.

Thelen, E., & Smith, L. (1994). *A dynamic systems approach to the development of cognition and action.* Cambridge, MA: MIT Press.

Theophilakis, M. (1999). Individuel psykoterapi. In L. Lier, T. Isager, O.S. Jørgensen, F. W. Larsen, & T. Aarkrog (Eds.), *Børne- og ungdomspsykiatri* (pp. 425–439). Copenhagen: Hans Reitzels Forlag.

Thomsen, P. H. (1996). *Når tanker bliver til tvang.* Copenhagen: Hans Reitzels Forlag.

Tizard, B. (1977). *Adoption: A second chance.* London: Open Books.

Tomarken, A., Davidson, R., Wheeler, R., & Doss, R. (1992). Individual differences in anterior brain asymmetry and fundamental dimensions of emotions. *Journal of Personality and Social Psychology, 62*, 676–687.

Trevarthen, C. (1979). Communication and cooperation in early infancy: A description of primary intersubjectivity. In M. Bullowa (Ed.), *Before speech: The beginning of interpersonal communication* (pp. 321–347). Cambridge: Cambridge University Press.

Trevarthen, C. (1989). Development of early social interactions and the affective regulation of brain growth. In C. Euler, H. Fossberg, & H. Lagercrantz (Eds.), *Neurobiology of early infant behavior* (55, pp. 191–215). Wenner-Gren International Symposium. New York: Stockton Press.

Trevarthen, C. (1990). Growth and education of the hemispheres. In C. Trevarthen (Ed.), *Brain circuits and functions of the mind* (pp. 334–363). Cambridge, UK: Cambridge University Press.

Trevarthen, C. (1993a). An infant's motives for speaking and thinking in the culture. In A. H. Wold (Ed.), *The dialogical alternative.* Oslo: Scandinavian University Press.

Trevarthen, C. (1993b). The self born in intersubjectivity: The psychology of an infant communicating. In U. Neisser (Ed.), *The perceived self: Ecological and interpersonal sources of self knowledge* (pp. 121–173). New York: Cambridge University Press.

Trevarthen, C. (1998). The concept and foundation of infant intersubjectivity. In I S. Bråten: *Intersubjective communication and emotion in early ontogeny* (pp. 15–47) Cambridge, UK: Cambridge University Press.

Tronick, E. Z. (1989). Emotions and emotional communication in infants. *American Psychologist, 44*, 112–119.

Tronick, E. Z. (1998). Dyadically expanded states of conciousness and the process of therapeutic change. *Infant Mental Health Journal, 19*(3), 290–299.

Tronick, E. Z., Als, H., Adamson, L., Wise, P., & Brazelton, T. B. (1978). The infant's response to intrapment between contradictory messages in face-to-face interaction. *Journal of Child Psychiatry, 17*, 1–13.

Tronick, E. Z., Brushweiler-Stern, N., Harrison, A. M., Lyons-Ruth, K., Morgan, A. C., Nahum, J. P., et al. (1998). Dyadically expanded states of consciousness and the process of therapeutic change. *Infant Mental Health Journal, 19* (3), 290–299.

Tronick, E. Z., & Cohn, J. F. (1989). Infant-mother face-to-face interaction: Age and gender differences in coordination and occurrence of miscoordination. *Child Development, 60*, 85–92.

Tronick, E. Z., & Gianino, A. (1986). Interactive mismatch and repair: Challenges to the coping infant. *Zero to three: Bulletin of the National Center Clinical Infant Program, 5*, 1–6.

Tronick, E. Z., Ricks, M., & Cohn, J. F. (1982). Maternal and infant affective exchange: Patterns of adaption. In T. Field & A. Fogel (Eds.), *Emotion and early interaction: Normal and high-risk infants* (pp. 83–100). Hillsdale, NJ: Lawrence Erlbaum.

Tronick, E. Z., & Weinberg, M. K. (1997). Depressed mothers and infants: Failure to form dyadic states of consciousness. In L. Murray & P. J. Cooper (Eds.), *Postpartum depression in child development* (pp. 54–81). New York: Guilford.

Tucker, D. M. (1992). Developing emotions and cortical networks. In M. R. Gunnar

& C. A. Nelson (Eds.), *Minnesota symposium on child psychology* (pp. 75–128). Hillsdale, NJ: Lawrence Erlbaum.

Tucker, D. M., & Derryberry, D. (1992). Motivated attention: Anxiety and the frontal executive functions. *Neuropsychiatry, Neuropsychology, and Behavioural Neurology, 5*(4), 233–252.

Tulkin, S. R., & Kagan, J. (1972). Mother-infant interaction in the first year of life. *Child Development, 43*, 31–42.

Turiel, E. (1998). The development of morality. In W. Damon & N. Eisenberg (Eds.), *Handbook of child psychology. Vol. 3. Social, emotional and personality development* (pp. 863–932). New York: John Wiley.

Uvnäs-Moberg, K. (1997). Oxytocin linked anti-stress effects—the relaxation and growth response. *Acta Psychological Scandinavia, 640*(Suppl.), 38–42.

Uvnäs-Moberg, K. (1998). Oxytocin may still mediate the benefits of positive social interaction and emotions. *Psychoneuroendocrinology, 23*, 819–835.

van der Kolk, B. A. (1987). *Psychological trauma*. Washington, DC: American Psychiatric Press.

van der Kolk, B. A. (1994). The body keeps the score: Memory and the evolving psychobiology of posttraumatic stress. *Harvard Review of Psychiatry, 1*, 253–265.

van der Kolk, B. A. (1996a). The body keeps the score: Approaches to the psychobiology of posttraumatic stress disorder. In B. A. van der Kolk, A. C. McFarlane, & L. Weisaeth (Eds.), *Traumatic stress: The effects of overwhelming experience on mind, body and society* (pp. 214–241). New York: Guilford.

van der Kolk, B. A. (1996b). Trauma and memory. In B. A. van der Kolk, A. C. McFarlane, & L. Weisaeth (Eds.), *Traumatic stress: The effects of overwhelming experience on mind, body, and society* (pp. 279–302). New York: Guilford.

van der Kolk, B. A. (1996c). The complexity of adaption to trauma: Self regulation, stimulus discrimination, and characterological development. In B. A. van der Kolk, A. C. McFarlane, & L. Weisaeth (Eds.), *Traumatic stress: The effects of overwhelming experience on mind, body, and society* (pp. 182–214). New York: Guilford.

van der Kolk, B. A. (2000). Seminar, County Hall, Sorø, July 3.

van der Kolk, B. A., & Fisler, R. E. (1994). Childhood abuse and neglect and loss of self-regulation. *Bulletin of the Menninger Clinic, 58*, 145–168.

van der Kolk, B. A., & McFarlane, A. C. (1996). The black hole of trauma. In B. A. van der Kolk, A. C. McFarlane, & L. Weisaeth (Eds.), *Traumatic stress: The effects of overwhelming experience on mind, body and society* (pp. 3–23). New York: Guilford.

Verney, T. R. (2002). *Tomorrow's baby*. New York: Simon & Schuster.

Vyas, A., Mitra, P., Shankaranarayana Rao, B. P., & Chattarji, P. (2002). Chronic stress inducing contrasting patterns of dendritic remodeling in hippocampal and amygdaloid neurons. *Journal of Neuroscience, 22*, 6810–6818.

Vygotsky, L. P. (1978). *Mind in society: The development of higher psychological processes*. Cambridge, MA: Harvard University Press.

Watson, J. P. (1994). Detection of self: The perfect algorithm. In S. T. Parker, R. W. Mitchell, & M. L. Boccia (Eds.), *Self-awareness in animals and humans* (pp. 131–148. Cambridge, UK: Cambridge University Press.

Watt, D. (2005). Concluding remarks. Neuroscientific and psychoanalytic perspectives on emotion. *International Neuro-Psychoanalysis Congress Proceedings, I*. London: N-PSA.

Watts, A. (1957). *The way to Zen.* New York: Random House.

Weinberger, J. (1993). Common factors in psychotherapy. In G. Stickler & J. R. Gold (Eds.), *Comprehensive handbook of psychotherapy integration* (pp. 43–56). New York: Plenum.

Winnicott, D. W. (1958). *Through paediatrics to psychoanalysis.* New York: Basic Books.

Winnicott, D. W. (1960). The theory of the parent-infant relationship. *Journal of Psychanalysis, 41*, 585–595.

Winnicott, D. W. (1962). Ego integration in child development. In *Maturational processes and the facilitating environment* (pp. 56–63). New York: International Universities Press.

Winnicott, D. W. (1970). The mother-infant experience of mutuality. In E. Anthony & T. Benedek (Eds.), *Parenthood: Its psychology and psychopathology* (pp. 245–256). Boston: Little, Brown.

Winnicott, D. W. (1971a). *Playing and reality.* London: Routledge.

Winnicott, D. W. (1971b). *Therapeutic consultations in child-psychiatry.* New York: Basic Books.

Winnicott, D. W. (1987). *Babies and their mothers.* Reading, MA: Addison-Wesley.

Yamada, H., Sadato, N., Konishi, Y., Kimura, K., Tanaka, M., Yonekura, Y., et al. (1997). A rapid brain metabolic change in infant detected by fMRI. *Neuro Report, 8*, 3775–3778.

Yamada, H., Sadato, N., Konishi, Y., Muramoto, S., Kimura, K., Tanaka, M., et al. (2000). A milestone for normal development of the infantile brain detected by functional MRI. *Neurology, 55*, 218–223.

Youniss, J. (1980). *Parents and peers in social development: A Sullivan-Piaget perspective.* Chicago: University of Chicago Press.

Yurgelun-Todd, D. (2002). *Inside the teenage brain.* Cybrary version of interview. PBS online and wgbh/frontline

Zeanah, C. H., Keener, M. A., Stewart, L., & Anders, T. F. (1985). Prenatal perception of infant personality: A preliminary investigation. *Journal of the American Academy of Child Psychiatry, 24*, 204–210.

Zeanah, C. H., Mammen, O. K., & Lieberman, A. F. (1993). Disorders of Attachment. In C. H. Zeanah (Ed.), *Handbook of infant mental health* (pp. 332–349). New York: Guilford.

INDEX

Page numbers in italic refer to illustrations.